# Graphical Thinking for Science and Technology Through Knowledge Visualization

Anna Ursyn
*University of Northern Colorado, USA*

A volume in the Advances in
Multimedia and Interactive
Technologies (AMIT) Book Series

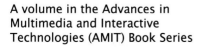

Published in the United States of America by
> IGI Global
> Information Science Reference (an imprint of IGI Global)
> 701 E. Chocolate Avenue
> Hershey PA, USA 17033
> Tel: 717-533-8845
> Fax: 717-533-8661
> E-mail: cust@igi-global.com
> Web site: http://www.igi-global.com

Library of Congress Cataloging-in-Publication Data

Names: Ursyn, Anna, 1955- author.
Title: Graphical thinking for science and technology through knowledge
> visualization / by Anna Ursyn.
Description: Hershey, PA : Information Science Reference, 2020. | Includes
> bibliographical references and index. | Summary: ""This book explores
> ways to integrate knowledge from various disciplines to think in a
> holistic way about data and information. It also examines how processes
> and products in nature allow us to think cross-disciplinary, use our
> abstract thinking skills, and re-examine our findings by graphical
> thinking through knowledge visualization"--Provided by publisher"--
> Provided by publisher.
Identifiers: LCCN 2019031663 (print) | LCCN 2019031664 (ebook) | ISBN
> 9781799816515 (h/c) | ISBN 9781799816522 (s/c) | ISBN 9781799816539
> (eISBN)
Subjects: LCSH: Information visualization.
Classification: LCC QA76.9.I52 U765 2020  (print) | LCC QA76.9.I52  (ebook)
> | DDC 001.4/226--dc23
LC record available at https://lccn.loc.gov/2019031663
LC ebook record available at https://lccn.loc.gov/2019031664

This book is published in the IGI Global book series Advances in Multimedia and Interactive Technologies (AMIT) (ISSN: 2327-929X; eISSN: 2327-9303)

British Cataloguing in Publication Data
A Cataloguing in Publication record for this book is available from the British Library.

For electronic access to this publication, please contact: eresources@igi-global.com.

# Advances in Multimedia and Interactive Technologies (AMIT) Book Series

Joel J.P.C. Rodrigues
Federal University of Piauí (UFPI), Teresina - Pi, Brazil; Instituto de Telecomunicações, Portugal

ISSN:2327-929X
EISSN:2327-9303

## MISSION

Traditional forms of media communications are continuously being challenged. The emergence of user-friendly web-based applications such as social media and Web 2.0 has expanded into everyday society, providing an interactive structure to media content such as images, audio, video, and text.

The **Advances in Multimedia and Interactive Technologies (AMIT) Book Series** investigates the relationship between multimedia technology and the usability of web applications. This series aims to highlight evolving research on interactive communication systems, tools, applications, and techniques to provide researchers, practitioners, and students of information technology, communication science, media studies, and many more with a comprehensive examination of these multimedia technology trends.

## COVERAGE

- Multimedia Services
- Web Technologies
- Digital Games
- Audio Signals
- Multimedia Streaming
- Internet Technologies
- Gaming Media
- Multimedia Technology
- Digital Watermarking
- Digital Technology

IGI Global is currently accepting manuscripts for publication within this series. To submit a proposal for a volume in this series, please contact our Acquisition Editors at Acquisitions@igi-global.com or visit: http://www.igi-global.com/publish/.

# Titles in this Series

*For a list of additional titles in this series, please visit:*
*https://www.igi-global.com/book-series/advances-multimedia-interactive-technologies/73683*

701 East Chocolate Avenue, Hershey, PA 17033, USA
Tel: 717-533-8845 x100 • Fax: 717-533-8661
E-Mail: cust@igi-global.com • www.igi-global.com

# Table of Contents

# Section 3
## Visual Projects Based on Bioinspired and Science-Based Solutions

**Chapter 6**

# Preface

## OVERVIEW

This book conveys some suggestions how we can integrate knowledge from various disciplines and think in a holistic way about data and information. It shows examples how examining processes and products in Nature allows us to think cross-disciplinary, use our abstract thinking skills, and re-examine our findings by graphical thinking through knowledge visualization. The framework of this book aims to create, interpret, and share visual information. Discussion is about how art and design support science understanding by visualizing concepts and processes. Art creation benefits from learning about scientific processes and concepts. Processes and products provide inspiration for creation of meaningful art, while art creation helps understand and memorize data framework and structure. The strength of this book is in emboldening science-oriented professionals and students to choose the artistic solutions for technical implementations. Keeping in mind that computers transform data into information and visualization converts information into a picture form, the readers of this book will explore ways of applying a visual language to present scientific information with images, symbols, and metaphors.

Knowledge Visualization is a growing discipline allowing the audience to analyze the facts and to look at the dynamic data from various perspectives. Technology allows us not only to change the point of view but also to find resources faster, and to discuss our findings with broader audience, often via collaboration. While researchers are acquiring particular skills and knowledge, cognitive approach adopted in this book allows us analyzing data and converting abstract concepts into projects depicting various scientific ideas. Examples of science-based art are provided.

The book is directed at professionals – from those in Academia to individuals doing self-motivational explorations, for Computer Graphics and Digital Media instructors – as a science-art connection type of research-based inspiration, and also students keen on comprehending and enhancing the role of images in computing, sciences, design, journalism, media communication, advertising, and marketing. Perusal of this book can become an important part of students' post-graduation job hunt, as it will provide experiences expanding their knowledge. The readers are encouraged to apply their visual literacy as an inspiration in their work, be it developing software, making visualizations, animations, designing posters or websites, and producing clipart or interactive components. Knowledge and skills in putting visuals to work will surely contribute to making their productions effective, in demand, and attractive for employers who are looking for people who are able to find their own solutions of problems and possess some artistic skills.

The sequence: technologies > knowledge > art has been accepted as a backbone of a narrative part of this book. We are constantly surprised when we learn about the developments in technology. New frames of reference result from recently acquired knowledge and provide favorable circumstances for a research-based creative inspiration. This book is addressed to those who like to read and learn in a self-motivated way, to seek their own way to grow, specialize in a chosen area, and discover ways to find collaboration with people from other disciplines. Reading about various fields of science may improve understanding of professional lingo, terminology, and thus make easier understanding other professionals and start collaboration. Understanding of some concepts about nature and current science seems important when they cross over several fields of knowledge and technologies. In this book a reader may find a selection of topics about nature and science that determine progress in knowledge, connect disciplines, and thus contribute for grasping general comprehension of present actuality.

## ART–SCIENCE CONNECTION

While describing an event in nature, we may focus on rules and tools related to our description. Mathematics may help in the rendering and interpretation of it, physics may allow understanding the rules, and chemistry may indicate tools enabling the description. For example, the eruption of a volcano can be described with the use of fractal geometry, obeys the rules of physics, while chemical reactions control the changes in matter activated by this event. When we examine the role of light in the life of plants, we may think about geometry of a prism and physical rules that cause refraction of light or breaking it up into spectral colors of the rainbow. We may also examine wavelengths that are crucial for plant's metabolism. With this respect, we can examine light-dependent photosynthesis in terms of chemical reactions.

Each concept discussed below could be seen differently through the eyes a specialist focused on a detailed field of knowledge: a physicist, chemist, physician, or a computing specialist. Even such familiar term as 'power' would have quite different meaning for an engineer, a general, a clergyman, a car driver, a politician, or a wealthy person. In this book, discussion of selected topics has a tendency to connect the ways of thinking in the context of tools, and developments in technology. One topic could have a specific meaning in a textbook written for a particular branch of study. At the same time, different approaches create a need for teamwork among specialists, which often results in an advance, even a breakthrough in their work. Thus, different ways of thinking may lead to collaboration and then new discoveries.

## FOCUSING ON VISUAL PRESENTATION

Tools and technologies typical of various disciplines provide an umbrella for common efforts. By making emphasis on visual presentation including visuals, computer graphics, and visualizations, we create another umbrella. Visual presentations are easier to absorb than the numerical, text based, or computational analyses. Projects offered to the readers are aimed at enhancing their digital visual literacy. In many walks of life the ability to create and to understand visual materials became crucial when one wants to come up with constructing new knowledge, creating media expressions, and communicating with others. As stated by Yildiz and Keengwe (2016), media literacy education in the digital age is crucial, especially in a globally connected world. However, current system of public education is not satisfactorily efficient in preparing visually literate graduates. Emanuel and Challons-Lipton (2013) performed "a survey which asked 358 college students to identify five photographs, five symbols, and five paintings that are generally recognized to be "famous." About 27% of all respondents claimed to recognize all the photographs, 23% recognized all the symbols, and 3% recognized all the paintings."

Computers help us in making observations, and then in conducting investigations aimed to answer research questions, and carrying out statistics, which are all necessary steps in conducting scientific inquiry. Computers also provide updates, networking, and sharing. The files, which are stored locally on individual computers, can be sent and data shared. Networks can be set up via cables, wireless networks, and fiber optic systems. The internet is the networking system of interconnected computers. The World Wide Web is the physical network of the internet made up of servers and computers. Internet protocol suite links devices worldwide, and a web search engine is a software system that search the World Wide Web for particular information specified in a web search query. Hypertext Transfer Protocol (HTTP) is the set of rules for transferring files (text, graphic images, sound, video, and other multimedia files) on the World Wide Web (Wikipedia.org, 2019). Web browsers that are used to navigate the web, such as Firefox, Safari, Opera Browser, Google Chrome, Microsoft Internet Explorer, Windows Internet Explorer, and many more, are programs with graphical user interface serving to display HTLM files. The Internet of Things (IoT) is a networking model working toward connecting a multitude of heterogeneous objects, devices, applications, industries, and academia. The 2019 IEEE International Conference on Internet of Things (iThings-2019) gathered people interested in theories, systems, infrastructure, tools, testbeds, technologies and applications for the IoT, as well as identifying emerging research topics and defining the future of everything interconnected via cyberspace.

Figure 1a and 1b presents a project of a folded brochure "How to Build a Computer" informing how to construct a computer from a scratch, designed by my Computer Graphics student from the University of Northern Colorado, Jeremy Rice.

No subject belongs just to one discipline, it is described with the use of its own system of names and terms, and so specialists cannot learn only within boundaries of one's own field. Growing lines of research interact, support each other, and overlap. This requires that to attain efficient collaboration and fast communication with people from other fields, we need to acquire skills and understand concepts belonging to these disciplines. For example, some say we know more about the cosmos than about what's deep under the ocean, while a need for energy sources results in intensive searches deep under ocean. We used to think within the terms of our senses; however, these investigations require learning about the ocean life: the way fish know about approaching danger, how deep-water creatures estimate the speed of other animals, and can record water vibrations resulting from distant earthquakes and tsunamis. By applying the bio-inspiration and bio-mimicry approaches, and incorporating biomaterials, engineers interested in underwater oil fields exploitation, use this knowledge in their interdisciplinary inquiries. Discussion of topics in this book emphasizes some general shifts in the developments in science and technology.

*Figure 1a. How to Build a Computer, part 1*
*(© 2018, J. Rice. Used with permission)*

*Figure 1b. How to Build a Computer, part 2*
*(© 2018, J. Rice. Used with permission)*

# INQUIRY INTO BIOPHOTONICS AND BIO-INSPIRED TECHNOLOGIES

One important trend is toward photonics – studies of the electromagnetic radiation of the visible and invisible light, its detection and generation. Advances in detection of various lengths in the light spectrum, apart from its visible segment, and analysis of the theories about light, mechanical and electromagnetic waves changed the way of describing everyday occurrences.

Another emphasis is put on advances in bio-inspired knowledge and technologies based on bio-mimicry and using existing biomaterial to create a hybrid with artificial material, where the source of inspiration and progress is drawn from observation of solutions present in nature by watching biological structures and behaviors. Studies about creatures, organisms, and their structures become even more important than before as they are crucial for a growing number of disciplines not only related to biology or medicine. Nanotechnology, swarm computing, genetic computing, and networking may serve as examples of biology inspired technologies.

Developments in photonics, physics examined at the micro- and nano-scale, and new technologies allow us doing research on those structures in a new way. For example, nanopositioning devices allow moving objects and applications in increments as small as one nanometer. Several types of motor-driven nanopositioning stages serve disciplines such as materials science, genomics, photonics, biophysics, defense, semiconductors, and more. A new line of thought about the origin of our universe resulted from the advances in quantum physics, which poses that particles can be in two states at the same time, and also from progress in measurement technologies such as spectrophotometry, which deals with visible light, near-ultraviolet, and near-infrared. That means discussion of following themes should include both micro and macro dimensions.

# DISCUSSION ABOUT LEARNING AND INSTRUCTION

This book examines various viewpoints about teaching and learning. It focuses on current ways of instruction with the use of social networking, and then concentrates on instruction in art based on science and technology in a multisensory and integrative way, and learning with the use of computer technologies. Further text offers curricular postulates about building this kind of teaching and learning philosophy, through engaging students in cognitive learning activities.

# WORKING ON DEPICTIONS OF CONCEPTS

This book comprises a collection of art works supported by writings that make an ambient background for the images. A reader will be invited to actively collaborate with the author in two ways. First, there will be a mental jogging – connecting data and information related to various ways of life, nature, and science with one's own visual presentations. Second, there will be visual tweets – an invitation to communicate with others through creating images and sketches about our own reaction to all the input caused by both the perceived artwork and the mental jogging.

This book is illustrated with works of students from the Computer Graphics > Digital Media area run by the author at the University of Northern Colorado, of the fellow artists, and of the author. Images serve as a visual counterpart for the texts.

# ORGANIZATION OF THIS BOOK

The first section of the book entitled 'Presenting Knowledge with Knowledge Visualization' examines the structure of our environment, including our bodies, within a wide spectrum of dimensions of objects.

## Chapter 1. Looking at Nature From the Perspective of Physical Sciences

Current inquiries on nature put emphasis on links between examining matter and investigating light. Also, our knowledge depends on understanding of events occurring in a micro and nano scale, so they came at the center of scientific interest. Many times, objects and events discussed in the following chapters are beyond the scope of our perception. In such cases knowledge visualization is helpful if not indispensable. The text contains projects and invites the reader to apply graphical thinking.

Chapter 1.1, 'Examining Nanostructures', tells how studying natural processes is unavoidably linked with applying knowledge and techniques that used to belong to other branches of science. Themes discussed this chapter include some general information about concepts of data, information, and knowledge; dimensions of objects and the ways to look on and interpret them; ways to watch events and how they depend on various factors, especially a nano-world. These issues are further examined with reference to our bodies and microbes that used to inhabit or attack us. The reader is invited to actively react to the related projects.

Chapter 1.2, titled 'In Nanosphere, Light and Organic Matter Connect', looks through a magnifying glass at matter and materials, and also examines how light and organic matter is interconnected. Themes involve materials such as soft matter, liquid crystals, and colloids, and then events occurring as waves in the quantum world, including the very beginnings of the Universe and processes going now in nature. Understanding of these issues results in developing new materials and technologies, which allows us to plan Mars colonization in the near future. The interdisciplinary field of materials science examines the relationship between the structure, properties, and performance of the natural and human-made materials at the macroscopic, molecular, atomic, and nano-scale levels. Materials science draws information from physical chemistry, chemistry, applied physics, electronics, engineering, and nanoscience. Developments in photonics shifted approaches toward studying matter in terms of light and wavelengths.

Chapter 1.3, 'Carbon as an Old and New Material', tells about carbon in its various forms, dimensions, reservoirs, and its role in living organisms.

## Chapter 2. How Do We Communicate?

Chapter 2 is inquiring 'How Do We Communicate'. In this part of the book the text examines our modes of imparting or exchanging facts and opinions. After discussion of the ways we, and other living beings, take it through the senses, further text is about communication between people, with computers, and with other living things.

Chapter 2.1 is entitled 'Modes of Gathering Information'. This text tells first about wavelengths as a medium for our perception and means of communication, and then describes senses, human and animal, as a source of gathering information. Some cognitive abilities for sensing numbers and language are also described, along with some technologies, which support our senses.

Chapter 2.2, 'How Do We Communicate With People?' discusses a notion of semantics as it tells about visual communication through images, art, and signs of different kinds. Description of basic art concepts, elements of design in art, and principles of design in art provides background information helpful in developing projects.

Chapter 2.3, 'Visualization of Nature and Knowledge as Communication', offers description of visualization, its techniques and domains, along with some other ways of sharing data and restrictions concerning these actions.

Chapter 2.4, 'How Do We Communicate With Computers?' examines, after short introduction to evolution of computers and programming languages, how computing and nano computing became inspired by our knowledge about solutions present in biological structures and organisms.

Chapter 2.5, entitled 'How Do We Communicate With Other Living Beings?' examines the ways animals convey messages about defending themselves, and charging their prey or predators. Animal communication often involves senses unavailable to humans. In Turn, knowledge about these actions enhances our communication, defense, and attack abilities related to many spheres of life.

## Chapter 3. Inquiries About Cognitive Thinking

Chapter 3, 'Inquiries About Cognitive Thinking', is about cognitive processes related to translating scientific concepts to the realm of mental imagery and visual thinking, to developing sensitivity inspired by nature and science based issues, and – on the other hand – supporting science- and technology related makers by enhancing their imagination and problem solving with graphical thinking and visual literacy.

## Chapter 4. Inquiries About Art and Graphics

Chapter 4 is titled 'Inquiries about Art and Graphics'. In this part of the book discussion pertains current background driven from the developments in computing, technology, and communication media, which inevitably has a strong effect on art creation and the ways of its installation. As a consequence, there is a need to update current formats of doctoral studies and doctoral degrees in art.

Chapter 4.1, 'Thinking in the Art Mode', discusses critical versus creative thinking, cognition in art, and abstract thinking in art and science.

Chapter 4.2, 'Graphical Thinking and Computer Graphics', comprises discussion about some tendencies in producing images in connection with technologies induced opportunities and requests. Further text tells about bout impact of technology and social networking on approaches to creating art graphics, along with programming and computing as tools for art generation and installation at digital art forums and exhibitions.

Chapter 4.3, 'The Growth of an Artist', discusses current formats of doctoral studies and doctoral degrees in art, and puts forward a proposition of developing a comprehensive curriculum for a doctoral program.

## Chapter 5. Bringing Learning and Teaching Up to Date

Section 2, entitled 'On Learning and Teaching', offers analysis and then propositions about instructional design, instructional technology, and the up-to-date learning and instruction.

Chapter 5.1, 'A Look Into Viewpoints About the Learning Process', tells about learning theories, which tell about the performance of learners who share the same purpose or intent and who are engaged in practice.

Chapter 5.2 is 'About Learning and Instruction'. Issues discussed in this part of the book pertain to discussion about transforming instructional design according to the developments in instructional technology. Background information is provided about viewpoints on the up-to-date learning and instruction, involving learning in a multisensory and integrative way and learning with the use of computer technologies.

Chapter 5.3 is 'The Tools for Teaching'. This chapter examines how visual and verbal forms of expression may interact, both in web delivery and in student's work. The further text tells about the learning with computing, and about storytelling as a teaching tool.

Chapter 5.4, 'Private and Social Networking in a Classroom and in an Online Setting', describes types of online instruction and then discusses application of storytelling as a teaching tool. Further propositions include instruction in art production based on science and technology, and several curricular postulates about the content and mechanics of teaching.

Chapter 5.5, 'Curricular Postulates', suggests inclusion into the school curricula several actions aimed at strengthening the curricular program: iterative and integrative learning; building mathematical foundation; supporting linguistic aptitudes; using visualization techniques; coding: introducing programming; and games that hone cognitive abilities.

## Chapter 6. Active Learning Aimed at Visual Development

Section 3, 'Visual Projects Based on Bioinspired and Science-Based Solutions', contains a set of projects offering a learning experience for the reader and possibly assisting a teacher in an integrative way of instruction.

Chapter 6, 'Engaging Students in Cognitive Learning Activities', provides possible ways to involve students' interest and engage them in active participation, and finding ways to secure that good grade means not only a good memorization for tests but also a good understanding of the course content.

## CONCLUSION

The goal of this book is to study and acknowledge the power existing beyond visual explanation and presentation of scientific and computational problems. Social networking and portable devises broke barriers for writing and sketching for people of any profession. One may say we are witnessing a shift toward computing-inspired study of nature through visuals: art and data graphics. For this reason, this book is about visual literacy, visual thinking, visual learning, and visual communication with the use of new media. It discusses with the readers the changing role of communication media and the role of visual presentation.

The book is aimed to impact the way we learn and teach and thus contribute to the task of updating education on the K–20 levels. An array of concepts, data, and information belonging to a number of disciplines has been discussed as possible resources useful for finding visual solutions of science and technology related concepts and the interdisciplinary approach to learning and teaching. Discussion of selected topics in the context of tools and developments in technology provides the readers with materials supporting learning and teaching in an integrated way. This approach builds a background for the curricular postulates, which suggest strengthening the curricular program by inclusion into the school curricula several science-based elements and teaching the basics of coding. Providing knowledge visualization early in the course of education may help to recognize and support the innate abilities of children and start an integrative training of their minds.

# REFERENCES

Emanuel, R., & Challons-Lipton, S. (2013). Visual literacy and the digital native: Another look. *Journal of Visual Literacy*, *32*(1), 7–26. doi:10.1080/23796529.2013.11674703

Yildiz, M. N., & Keengwe, J. (2016). *Handbook of Research on Media Literacy in the Digital Age*. IGI Global. doi:10.4018/978-1-4666-9667-9

# Acknowledgment

The author of this book wishes to thank many individuals for their input and help with this book.

First, I would like to thank the Members of the IGI-Global publishing team for their cheerful and personal assistance with this project.

I would like to thank my Students who contributed to this book by providing images and texts illustrating their projects.

Many thanks go to the Reviewers who diligently carried out a double blind review of this book, provided supportive suggestions and critiques, and thus helped to make each part of the book better.

I express my warmest thanks to my family, friends, and colleagues.

# Section 1
# Presenting Knowledge With Knowledge Visualization

Chapter 1

# Looking at Nature from the Perspective of Physical Sciences

## ABSTRACT

*This chapter of the book looks at the structure of our environment, including our bodies, by examining the wide spectrum of dimensions of objects. Themes discussed provide some general information about concepts of data, information, and knowledge; dimensions of objects and the ways to look on and interpret them; ways to watch events and how they depend on various factors, especially within a nano-world. These issues are further examined with reference to our bodies and microbes that used to inhabit or attack us. Discussion involves materials such as soft matter, liquid crystals, and colloids, and then events occurring as waves in the quantum world, including the very beginnings of the universe, processes going now in nature, and plans concerning Mars colonization in the near future. Further text tells about carbon in its various forms, dimensions, existing reservoirs, and its role in living organisms.*

## INTRODUCTION

Current inquiries on nature put emphasis on links between examining matter and investigating light. Also, our knowledge depends on understanding of events occurring in a micro and nano scale, so they came at the center of scientific interest. Many times, objects and events discussed below are beyond the scope of our perception. In such cases knowledge visualization is helpful if not indispensable.

DOI: 10.4018/978-1-7998-1651-5.ch001

First, the book looks at our environment by examining the wide spectrum of dimensions of objects. The text explores how studying natural processes is unavoidably linked with applying knowledge and techniques that used to belong to other branches of science. When we look at matter and materials through a magnifying glass, we can see how light and organic matter is interconnected. Materials such as soft matter, liquid crystals, and colloids, and events occurring as waves in the quantum world have been discussed as interconnected processes going now in nature and at the beginnings of the Universe. Understanding of these issues results in developing new materials and technologies, which allows us to plan Mars colonization in the near future.

The interdisciplinary field of materials science examines the relationship between the structure, properties, and performance of the natural and human-made materials at the macroscopic, molecular, atomic, and nano-scale levels. Materials science draws information from physical chemistry, chemistry, applied physics, electronics, engineering, and nanoscience. Developments in photonics shifted approaches toward studying matter in terms of light and wavelengths.

Further text tells about carbon in its various forms, dimensions, existing reservoirs, and its role in living organisms. We can consider carbon in its several aspects, as each one is crucial for our lives:

1. **Carbon as Mineral (Coal)**: Carbon in fossil fuels, sources of energy, mining and surface mining in the United States, the environmental cost of surface mining.
2. **Carbon as a Molecule**: The carbon cycle, issues related to carbon monoxide (CO).
3. **Carbon as Soft Matter**: Carbon in computers, biologically inspired models for computing.

The text contains projects and invites the reader to apply graphical thinking. The reader is invited to actively react to the related projects by creating their own solutions.

## 1.1. EXAMINING NANOSTRUCTURES

## Preliminary Remarks

Many processes happening in our surroundings are biological in their nature. However, we can understand them better by using concepts and tools typical of various kinds of science such as physics, chemistry, mathematics, or computing. Scientists look at events and processes in nature that occur at the intersection of physical and life sciences. They conduct collaborative, interdisciplinary research because new ideas happen often at the crossroads of fields of study. Also, product capability, quality, and global supply depend on savvy cooperation of people having experience that combines many fields and many technologies. According to the National Academies of Sciences, Engineering, and Medicine (2019), "Traditionally, the natural sciences have been divided into two branches: the biological sciences and the physical sciences. Today, an increasing number of scientists are addressing problems lying at the intersection of the two. For example, equilibrium, multi-stability, and stochastic behavior – concepts familiar to physicists and chemists – are now being used to tackle issues associated with living systems such as adaptation, feedback, and emergent behavior."

Sean Parker, the Napster cofounder stated, "You know, the advice I would give young people today is not to go into computer science; a much more exciting place to be is the world of biology. It's going through the same kind of transformation right now that occurred in information technology 20 years ago" (Parker & Marson, 2018).

## Project: Adding Scientific Background to Nature Observation

Choose a biological process such as a life cycle of a frog or a butterfly, growth of a plant (with stems and leaves going up while roots growing down), or seasonal changes in leaves' colors. Draw a sketch showing this process as a pretty picture. Then, add as many facts to your sketch as you can, which would be related to physics, geometry, geography, chemistry, or other fields of science. Present your connections with science as small drawings, infographics, arrows with short sentences or equations, or symbolic images. Finally, try to present your project in a style you choose, so it would be aesthetically satisfying.

## Data, Information, and Knowledge

**Data** means a collection of facts that by itself does not communicate anything. In computing, data can be stored, processed, or transmitted, but they still do not communicate by itself any message. **Information** is resulting from what has been intentionally done with the data using a cognitive and communicative activity. Information provides the data with a meaning, and it can be communicated to other people. In computing, information is gained when the data is processed, stored, or transmitted by a computer. We acquire **knowledge** through education and experience when we apply cognitive thought to make use of the data and information, thus gaining understanding, insight, and skills. Figure 1 shows a work by Anna Ursyn entitled "Signals and Data."

Communication as exchange of knowledge, insight, and information can be done both in verbal and non-verbal way. Many agree that a written text alone may not be the most effective way to communicate ideas and information, even if it goes in a language shared by both parts. Our communication with the world and people, conscious and unaware of, goes through many senses; for example, it is amazing how human back can sense the touch, hot, cold, soft, sharp, and pressure signals, using different kinds of receptors. Moreover, it is not decisive how we study sciences but how we think about them, connect data with facts, and then interpret them.

Communication often leads to cooperation, which involves different frames of reference, from physiological, physical, technical, to aesthetical. Visual way of presentation serves computer scientists and artists while working, for example with mathematicians, anthropologists, designers, and architects to

*Figure 1. Signals and Data*
*(© 2018, A. Ursyn. Used with permission)*

compute analysis of facades and architectural details. Specialists in fields of natural sciences, medicine, pharmacology, biology, geology, or chemistry examine and visualize symmetry and patterns in natural and human-made structures. Many artists have created masterpieces this way. On the other hand, skills in programming may lead to the negative use of computing, for example in oil or nuclear research, surveillance, and invasion of privacy. Such skill may also support hacking, spying, and altering data; hacking is becoming entangled with politics, voting, trading and selling customers' data to support advertisement, to the cases of identity theft and sneaking into bank accounts.

## Project: Weekday–Weekend

We plan our weekdays and weekends, and we visualize what we are hoping for, but it never turns out exactly the way we expect. Show visual grit of one selected month, with spaces for weekdays and weekends filled with visual representation of what you do expect. Add visual cues supporting your notion that it will turn out exactly the way you expect. You may be quite playful here. Feel free to develop own symbols or use photographic material. It is a very open-ended project, so feel free to go any direction that pleases you.

Figure 2 presents work by Anna Ursyn entitled "Weekday, Weekend."

*Figure 2. Weekday, Weekend*
*(© 2018, A. Ursyn. Used with permission)*

## Dimensions and Variables

The concept of a dimension is used in mathematics to measure a distance of a single point from the origin of an axis. Basic concepts employed in visualization involve such notions as a dimension and a variable. When visualizing higher dimensions the number of measurements that are needed to specify the position of a point depends on the number of dimensions (Cox, 2008). Thus, a line is one-dimensional because all is needed is one measurement of the distance between a point and the origin of an axis. In order to draw a two-dimensional plot on a plane, two measurements are needed to specify the distance of the point from the origin of the x and y-axes. To position the single point in three-dimensional space, three measurements are needed, along the x, y, and z-axes.

The notion of dimension is related to the number of represented variables. A variable is a measurable whole, which may assume a set of values. We use symbols of such wholes, for example in the expression $a^2 + b^2 = c^2$, a, b, and c are variables. In exploring high-dimensional space, measurements of more variables are needed. For example, a three-dimensional object may change its location in time, along with its other conditions, such as temperature, pressure, or density. Thus, in order to describe the speed and state of this object in space, seven variables are needed: x, y, z axes, time, temperature, pressure and density. A two-dimensional plot or graph can only show one relationship between variables. However, most of natural processes and events are complex and dynamic. Multidimensional visualization is required, to present the dynamics of variables under study. Superfast machines provide information in the form of billions of numbers.

## Project: Detecting Dimensions and Variables

Develop in the mind your own story about a nature-related event you have already encountered or learnt about, such as an avalanche, a flood, or an active volcano at work. First, describe it as a short essay, and then design a visualization project. How many dimensions would take the process you have described and how would you characterize the variables describing it? What kinds of relationships could you draw on simple graphs to show the development of the event?

## Looking at the Range of Sizes

In order to be able to look at the universe with perspective, the following text will discuss the way we measure and watch the tiny things.

Units of measurement of a diameter or length used in science are usually done in the decimal measuring system, known as the International System of Units, which is based on the meter. It uses prefixes such as deci-, centi-, and milli-, with a base unit of meter. In the following text we will find very small physical and biological structures measuring fractions of a meter: micrometer, nanometer, and picometer. Nanoscience explores structures between one and 100 nanometers. – A macroscale comprises visible objects with sizes of a millimeter or more (1 millimeter, 1 mm = 1/1,000 meter – $1 \times 10^{-3}$ m). For example, a human hair is about $10^{-4}$ m wide (about 100,000 nanometers wide).

- A microscale relates to objects with sizes about a micrometer to about 1/10 of a millimeter (1 micrometer, 1 μm = 1/1,000,000, one millionth of a meter – $1 \times 10^{-6}$ m). For instance, a single cell is about 1 micrometer, the length of bacteria is 1 to 10 micrometers, the width of a strand of spider web silk is between 3 and 8 micrometers, and the length of human chromosome is up to 10 micrometers. Red blood cells may have a size of several μm.
- A nanoscale encompasses a range of subjects from about a nanometer to about 1/10 of micrometer (1 nanometer, 1 nm = 1/1,000,000,000, one billionth of meter – $1 \times 10^{-9}$ m). For example, a DNA (deoxyribonucleic acid) molecule is between 2 and 12 nanometers wide, atoms are between 0.1 and 0.5 nanometers while ten hydrogen atoms (the smallest ones) would measure one nanometer. A virus is about 100 nanometers wide, while a human hair is about 60,000 nanometers in diameter. A diameter of a carbon nanotube is $10^{-8}$. Subatomic particles such as quarks and leptons, both natural and engineered are smaller than atoms: they range from one nanometer to tens of micrometers. When expressed in parts of a meter, a virus is about $10^{-7}$ m; a DNA is about $10^{-8}$ m; molecular structures are about $10^{-9}$ m.
- A picoscale is a size range of single atoms, both found in nature (and represented in the periodic table) and atoms man-made in accelerators for nuclear technology (1 ångström or angstrom (Å) = $1 \times 10^{-10}$ meters). The picometer ($1 \times 10^{-12}$ m) is one trillionth of a meter; thus, the picometer is one thousandth of a nanometer. Most atoms have diameter

between 62 and 520 picometers; for example, an estimated diameter of a helium atom is 62 picometers. The Laser Interferometer Space Antenna (LISA) probe, which is planned for launch in 2034, will detect and measure gravitational waves with a resolution of 20 picometers over a distance of 2.5 gigameters.

Looking in terms of relative sizes, we can tell that a human is about thousand times bigger than an ant (measuring a few millimeters), but an ant is roughly 1000 times bigger than an amoeba (about 1 micrometer).

Thus, although we cannot see many objects because they are too big or too small, we can present their sizes in mathematical notation. On a website entitled Molecular Expressions (Davidson, 2019) we can find an interactive visualization of successively smaller objects:

- The Milky Way galaxy ($10^{21}$ m).
- Our solar system ($10^{13}$ m).
- The Earth ($10^{18}$ m).
- A city ($10^4$ m).
- A tree ($10^1$ m).
- A leaf ($10^{-1}$ m).
- Cells ($10^{-5}$ m).
- Strands of DNA ($10^{-7}$ m).
- An atom ($10^{-10}$ m).
- Quarks ($10^{-16}$ m).

## Imaging Small Structures

The developments in nanoscale and molecular-scale technologies allow us to study the nanoscale objects: liquid crystals, soft matter, colloids, nanoshells, and carbon nanotubes. One nano is $10^{-9}$ meter; that means one-billionth of a meter. That means the size of a nanometer is to the size of a meter like a marble compared to the size of Earth. Many familiar objects are millions of nanometers big: a human nail on a little finger is about ten million nanometers across and a human hair is about 80,000 nanometers wide. A dollar bill is 100,000 nanometers thick. A small reptile gecko can cling upside down to the pane of glass because it has millions of microhairs on its toes; each hair is split into hundreds of tips 200 nanometers wide, which form nanohairs on its microhairs.

Advances in microscopy and spectroscopy (which records how matter interacts with or emits electromagnetic radiation) hasten discoveries in a nanoscale, which in turn cause that we see the world in a changed way. Atomic force microscopy provides resolution at the atomic level, so it is allowing surface measurement and inspection of semiconductors and piezo drives. The discipline of bioimaging explores biological structures and functions to create information visualizations in two, three, or four dimensions. Generally, bioimaging tools are based on electron beams; they produce images using electrons, inform about composition using x-ray photons, or they are the scanning probes. Bioimaging researchers gather and analyze information from sources such as light waves, nuclear magnetic resonance, x-rays, or ultrasounds. Bioimaging methods may include optical light microscopy, electron microscopy, x-ray tomography, and magnetic resonance imaging.

Several medical imaging techniques comprise magnetic resonance imaging (awarded the 2003 Nobel Prize. With the nuclear magnetic resonance spectroscopy, when external magnetic field is applied, atomic nuclei spinning about randomly oriented axes are aligned parallel (or antiparallel) to the external field. Hydrogen atoms excited by an oscillating magnetic field emit a radio frequency signal that is measured by the receiver. This method uses also contrast enhancement by hyperpolarized noble gas which enables pulmonary imaging for diagnosis and other applications), nuclear magnetic resonance imaging, magnetic resonance tomography, and functional magnetic resonance imaging (which allows monitoring in real time responses of the brain structures to external stimuli; it is possible to measure the hemodynamic response to changing neural activity in response to changes in the local blood oxygenation level: the ratio of oxyhemoglobin to deoxyhemoglobin). This type of imaging serves for diagnosis, estimation of the disease stages and tissue responses to ionizing radiation; it also serves in cardiovascular, musculoskeletal, gastrointestinal, and neuroimaging examinations (Irvin & Koenning, 2015).

Many other advanced approaches involving micro spectroscopy investigate structures at the scale of micrometers, for example Raman spectroscopy, photoacoustic imaging techniques, bioimaging with fluorescent, magnetic supernanoparticles, bioimaging with laser near-infrared fluorescence imaging with multifunctional nanostructures, among a number of other technologies. Raman spectroscopy allows choosing the laser wavelengths and software for coupling multivariate algorithms to 2D and 3D imaging. This allows applying tip-enhanced Raman spectroscopy for nanoscale resolution. It is now possible to identify in real time tumor margins during surgery. Raman measurements are done through an endoscope for studies of atherosclerosis, cancer, and bone diseases. It is possible to record and identify spectra of individual bacteria and then to differentiate them at the strain level (Sandros & Adar, 2015). Photoacoustics with ultrasound produces real-time images of blood vessels, organs, and body parts using a hand-held probe with a laser diode stack. It heats and expands the tissue but not damages it. Ultrasound detection can be synchronized with laser pulsing.

Optical microscopy, especially fluorescence microscopy is an essential tool. Imaging with optical microscopy requires choosing the right selection of a microscope depending on imaging depth needed (de Grand & Bonfig, 2015). This is important because features such as light scatter, absorption, background signals, achieving a sufficient collection of photons at the detector, and differences in refractive index become more challenging in the deeper specimens. Fluorescence microscopy with super resolution made possible to perform bioimaging within nanodimension; it won the 2014 Nobel Prize.

Researchers using fluorescence microscopy develop optical probes including upconversion nanoparticles. Nanoscale upconversion particles provide information about the temperature distribution in biological samples. The types of bioimaging probes include nontargeting fluorescent materials for direct imaging of cells and tissues; probes that bind to specific targets via chemical interactions, which allows combining imaging with therapy by adding targeted drug release; and probes that use fluorescence of the material as a sensor to measure the properties of a target such as its pH and temperature (Tesa, 2019).

In transmission electron microscopy or field emission transmission electron microscopy beams of electrons are transmitted through the specimen. Beams of electrons can also be bounced back (backscattered, as used in scanning electron microscopy, in quantum mechanical tunneling), or knocked back from an atom and come as the secondary electrons.

Scientists are working on imaging with the use of computed tomography such as soft x-ray tomography, and also cryogenic light microscopy in order to know how nanoparticles interact, undergo changes, and deliver drugs into the intended inside targets or only to a cell membrane. Tools enable obtaining atomic resolution images; they reveal atomic structure and speciation of elements. It is possible to count atoms, see lattices and clusters, to correlate particle size with atom count in various types of particle morphologies, and thus understand structural defects and disorders. Nanoscale-sized catalysts and catalytic technologies are important in refineries, automobile catalytic converters, and in developing catalytic fuel cells for powering laptops.

Superresolution microscopy involves techniques going beyond the diffraction limit characteristic of traditional microscopy. Superresolution microscopy enables the optical imaging of subcellular structures with nanoscale resolution. It is possible to probe transparent matter having a length of a tiny fraction of the wavelength of the imaging light. It is a new discipline, which makes possible the high spatial and temporal resolution, 3D imaging of very small objects, deep tissue and in vivo imaging, and more. These techniques provide information about cell membrane nanostructure. Neuroscience gains new insights about mechanisms of protein aggregation linked to the Alzheimer's and Huntington's diseases (Photonics Handbook, 2019a).

Figure 3 presents a work of Anna Ursyn entitled "Shrine of Knowledge," which combines wood and a three-dimensional print. Curiosity and a need for learning have been vehicles for discoveries leading to better description of the systems we obey. Mathematics helped philosophers understand and depict basic structures, processes, and products, and then develop tools for collecting facts and data, and thus improving our knowledge, which in turn served as a basis for further discoveries. In this work, Platonic forms and Platonic shapes are juxtaposed with a model of the Universe created by a mathematician, astronomer, and astrologer Johannes Kepler, who used it to depict his vision of how the Universe could look like. This composition underlies the basic forms seen as divine forms as described by Plato. We further use that knowledge to understand problems, issues, and ways to fix them.

*Figure 3. A shrine of knowledge*
*(© 2018, A. Ursyn. Used with permission)*

## Properties of Nanoparticles Depend on their Sizes

Materials at the nanoscale level display quantum mechanics effects, because their atomic structure is determined differently. When we look at the same materials we can determine they obey the laws of classical physics. At the nanoscale level only certain energy levels are allowed, and the levels allowed depend on the size of a particle; this creates difference in energy $\Delta E$ between a particle and its environment ($\Delta E$ becomes bigger when particles are smaller). As the size of a particle decides on the value of $\Delta E$, the same light wavelength would produce different colors of particles of silver and gold. Silver spheres of a size about 40 nm look blue; gold spheres ~80 nm look light green; gold spheres ~120 nm look yellow; gold spheres ~50 nm look deep green; gold spheres ~100 nm look orange; and silver spheres ~100 nm look green deep red.

In the natural settings, nanostructures at the butterfly wings scatter and diffract light giving us the perception of different colors. When seen at different magnifications, butterfly wing scales look different: a wing that is dark blue when looked at without magnification becomes yellow at 220x magnification, purple at 5000x magnification, and green at 20000x magnification (PennState modules, 2011).

Photonic crystals provide spectacular color displays of plants and animals. They interact with light and produce a structural color in a way different than dyes and pigments. Photonic crystals contain a repeating motif of alternating materials with high and low optical dielectric permitivities (value capacitance in an electric field in a particular medium). It happens in the range of the wavelength of visible light, which has a wavelength $\lambda$ between 400 and 750 nanometers. It happens in many species: in Pollia fruits, Begonia leaves, with the multicolored metallic iridescence of peacock tail feathers, in tropical butterflies, in the dynamic and adaptive color camouflage and displays of chameleons and squids, as well as in the blue skin of Mandrill monkeys (Corkery & Tyrode, 2017). Lycaenid butterflies have evolved biophotonic gyroid (infinitely connected triply periodic minimal surfaces) nanostructures within their wing scales. They have recently been replicated by nanoscale additive manufacturing (Corkery & Tyrode, 2017). When inserted into textiles, metal nanoparticles become easily ionized; they kill bacteria present there and thus make clothing odor-free and odor-resistant. When inside of a bacteria, silver ions prevent transport across the cell wall, metabolism, respiration, RNA replication, and thus reproduction of the bacteria. Soft materials are used in a number of applications (for example, in flat panel LCD TVs) because they have many chemical and mechanical characteristics that are useful in technology, including quantum size effects, responsiveness to small electrical fields and to chemical or thermal actions, and flexibility (PennState modules, 2011). Light interacts with nanostructures (scatters and diffracts) differently. These wave properties of the soft matter result from the size of nanostructures that is smaller than the wavelength $\lambda$ of visible light.

Airglow is a phenomenon causing that the night sky is not completely dark. Airglow is created by the light of atoms excited by the solar ultraviolet radiation occurring during a day. It produces mostly green light about 50 to 60 miles above the Earth's surface. Human eyes cannot discern its color because airglow intensity is below the threshold of our color perception. In contrast with airglow, aurora is chemical excitation produced by collisions of high-energy particles falling down from Earth's magnetosphere (Maine, 2019).

Nanoscale objects have a small size as compared to biological structures and macromolecules, and a large surface to volume ratio. Some properties for example, the melting temperature of gold depends on the surface to volume ratio. The smaller is a nanoparticle the lower is its melting temperature because there is higher percentage of the atoms on the surface that are not bound.

If we succeed to cut familiar materials and reduce them to a nanoscale size, they would develop odd properties. For example, aluminum foil, which would normally behave like aluminum, would explode when cut in strips 20 to 30 nanometers thick. Catalysis – the acceleration of chemical processes goes faster as the particles become smaller, the ratio of the surface area to the volume of the particles increases, and nanoparticle catalysts become more reactive. However, the smaller are nanoparticles the greater is their surface area to volume ratio, and the higher their chemical reactivity and biological activity. Hence there is growing concern about nanotoxicology and ecotoxicology, which determine a threat to the humans and environment.

Carbon nanotubes display several particular properties; they perform ballistic conduction – the flow of charged particles; they conduct phonons, which means quantum vibration; they absorb radiofrequency (which is promising in therapy); they also display surface plasmon (a quantum of plasma oscillation) resonance under an electrical field. Buckyballs – hollow spherical molecules composed of a large number of carbon atoms – are good electron acceptors from other materials. They are used to improve efficiency of solar cells that transform sunlight into electricity. Buckyballs can deliver drugs or radioactive particles to attack cancer cells. However, buckyballs may have different configurations; toxicologists from the Los Alamos National

Laboratory in New Mexico recommended the use of the non-toxic *hexa* configuration. Scientists also work on turning the *tris* buckyballs into a weapon for halting the spread of cancer cells or delaying the onset of Parkinson's or Alzheimer's disease in nerve cells. The cells exposed to the *tris* buckyballs enter the suspended animation state where they don't die, divide, or grow.

The mechanical tensile strength, high electrical and heat conductivity, and chemical inactivity of nanotubes make them useful in nanotechnology, electronics, optics, material and architectural science domains, and many other applications. They are applied for strengthening materials (e.g., carbon-fiber frames for bicycles), gluing, food processing, preservation with additives, packaging, coating transparent films, building artificial muscles, space elevators, a body armor, waterproof and tear-resistant textiles, non-cracking concrete, and a lot of other implementations. When exposed to red diode laser light, single-walled carbon nanotubes begin to fluoresce. They can be used as a smart film sprayed on a bridge, an aircraft, or a building to reveal the strain of the material. Smart photonics technology can modulate incoming radiation on smart windows coated with a smart film. Thermal image sensors based on photonic sensors can localize and count people in a smart building, and also regulate temperature, heating, ventilation, and air-conditioning.

Research teams focus on nanotechnology applications in countless areas of life. The precise delivery of drugs with the use of nanostructures (such as by the RNA strands 10 nano in diameter) may help avoid side effects. Nanotechnology applications serve in fighting cancer by attaching nanostructures and destroying cancer cells; in tissue engineering by building scaffolds for cell growth and differentiation; for clinical neuroscience to enhance neuronal signaling and survival potential by supplementing the nervous system with nanoparticles or nanomaterials; in surgery by welding tissues: building stem cell culture matrices as scaffolds for stem growth and tissue differentiation; and for diagnostics by utilizing contrast agents. Cantilevers are flexible beams built with the use of semiconductor lithographic techniques to provide rapid and sensitive detection of cancer-related molecules. Nanoscale cantilevers can provide rapid and selective detection of cancer-related molecules. Cancer specific molecules bind to molecules that act as sensors. DNA-coated gold nanoparticles form the basis of a system that also uses larger magnetic microparticles to detect serum proteins (Hassanzadeh, Fullwood, Sothi, & Aldulaimi, 2011).

## Early Nano Applications

In previous centuries the prehistoric, ancient, and medieval people were not fully aware of the omnipresence of nano structures. However, nano applications had preceded nano technologies. People were applying various techniques without knowing why their actions were effective. They applied molds on wounds without knowledge about the antibiotic properties of penicillin, and used cultured bacteria to produce cheese, bread, or soy sauce. About 13,000 B.C. the Upper Paleolithic inhabitants of the Altamira caves in Spain created cave drawings and polychrome rock paintings of wild mammals and human hands using painting materials: charcoal and pigments. Charcoal contains nano material graphene, a two-dimensional allotrope of carbon. Pigments are micro- and nano-powders; by mixing with water they can be converted in colloidal or clay form. Particles in colloid have a diameter between 1 and 1000 nanometers.

Many pigments change the color of reflected or transmitted light because they selectively absorb certain wavelengths of light (Cave of Altamira and Paleolithic Cave Art of Northern Spain, 2012; Orfescu, 2012). 2,000 years ago Romans used the gold and silver nanoparticles in their artwork not knowing they are so minuscule. Dated from fourth century AD base of the Lycurgus cup (now in the British Museum, London) changes color from green (when illuminated from outside) to red (when illuminated from within) because it contains particles about 70 nanometer across, of gold and silver; followers couldn't recreate this effect.

Medieval artists from the 500–1450 period used to add nanoparticles of gold to create stained glass windows; they produced colors from yellow-orange (with silver nanoparticles) to ruby red (with gold nanoparticles). The Renaissance (15th-16th centuries) Italian pottery makers from Deruta Ceramists (2019), Umbria produced iridescent or metallic glazes using copper and silver particles: light bounces off the particles' surface at different wavelengths giving metallic or iridescent effect. Irish stain glass designers and the Damascene masters of sword making also applied nanoparticles materials (PennState Modules, 2011; Goodsell, 2006).

Photographic film is covered with gelatin containing silver halides and a base of transparent cellulose acetate. Light decomposes the silver halides producing nanoparticles of silver – the pixels of the photographic image. In 1827 Joseph Niépce used material that hardened when exposed to light. Louis Daguerre (1839) continued this work after Niépce died. Michael Faraday prepared first metallic (gold) colloids in 1857. Colloidal systems have now numerous applications. Gustav Mie's developed in 1908 a theory about why light scatters from particles more efficiently at short wavelengths. Thus, scientists learned why the size of particles would determine the visible colors. For example, air particles scatter blue light more efficiently than red light (blue light has a shorter wavelength than red light), and so the sky is blue.

Advances in biology come after a progress in technology. Gaining a new perspective regarding our milieu due to the advances in technology, we are able to notice that the science of biology is going through the same kind of transformation as other disciplines. For example, we have to examine with the new understanding the traditional division into phylogenesis – the evolutionary development resulting in growing diversity of species of organisms (e.g., from single-cell organisms to apes and humans), and ontogenesis – the development of every single organism or its features from the earliest stage to maturity (for example, from an egg in a frogspawn to an adult frog). We can see what's new about our ontology: that it is created from large new datasets and shows properties and relations between organisms within a broad scale of sizes and with reference to the new body of knowledge.

## Our Bodies Make a Universe for Smaller Creatures

We may apply the concept of the scale to cell biology by examining structures in a human cell in micro- and nano-scale. A cross section of a human cell presents its compositional elements (Figure 4). A cell is surrounded by a cell membrane. The cytoplasm lies within the plasma membrane of lipids (fat) and protein. Most cells have a single nucleus, which contains nucleoli. Nucleus embodies most of the cell's genetic material in chromosomes containing DNA and proteins; it directs the activity of the cell. Some other organelles are: complex sets of membranes called endoplasmic reticulum (with ribosomes, numerous tiny particles consisting of RNA and proteins, which control protein synthesis), a Golgi apparatus (part of endomembrane system that processes proteins for further secretion), mitochondria (with an outer membrane and a convoluted inner membrane, a site of respiration and energy production in the cell), and centrioles near the nucleus (which play a part in cell division).

Generally, the size of a human cell is between 4 μm ($4 \times 10^{-6}$ m) and 135 μm. Blood cells are about 2.5 μm. For comparison, the ostrich egg is the largest known cell and weights over 3 pounds (over 1360 grams). Paramecium (a single-celled freshwater animal) is about 60 μm wide and 50 to 350 μm long. The size of a skin human cell is about 30 μm. Water molecule (hydrogen

*Figure 4. Compositional elements of a cell*
(© 2012, A. Ursyn. Used with permission)

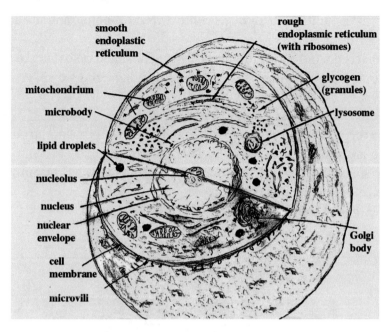

oxide $H_2O$ consisting of two hydrogen atoms and one oxygen) is about 0.29 nm. A flu virus has diameter about 100 nm.

Most of the structures inside the cell belong to the nano world. For example, a molecule of the deoxyribonucleic acid, DNA is 2.5 nm wide (it is millions of atoms long). Mitochondria range from .5 to 1 μm and ribosomes are between 25 and 30 nm in diameter. Microtubules in a cytoskeleton (a scaffolding of a cell's cytoplasm) may be 25 micrometers long, with diameter about 25 nm. Microfilaments in a cytoskeleton have individual subunits of microfilaments in the actin filaments that measure approximately 7 nm, and their bundles separate filaments by ~35 nm. In many cells one may find plasmids, which are not considered alive; they are the DNA molecules separate from the chromosomal DNA. In our body, there are several types of cells that circulate in blood: red and blood cells including lymphocytes, granulocytes, monocytes, macrophages, and more.

Popular literature, as well as the American Academy of Microbiology informed us in 2014 that there are about ten times more microbial cells living in our bodies than we have our own cells: around 100 trillion bacterial cells versus around 10 trillion human cells. However, more recent estimates reduced this ratio to 1-to-1: about the same number (Sender, Fuchs, & Milo, 2016).

Figure 5 presents work by Anna Ursyn titled "Fuzzy Logic." Nano photographs were juxtaposed with photographic material, sketches, and codes in order to capture some swift in context. Nano photograph used courtesy by Cris Orfescu.

But that is not the end of this story. First of all, bacteria belong to microbes or microorganisms, which is a big group of living beings comprising of six major types:

- **Bacteria**: Unicellular organisms having cell walls but not any organelles and an organized nucleus; 0.2 to 10 micrometers.
- **Archae**a: Single-cell microorganisms; prokaryotes, meaning having no cell nucleus; mostly 0.1 to 15 micrometer diameter and up to 200 micrometer long.

*Figure 5. Fuzzy Logic*
*(© 2018, A. Ursyn. Used with permission)*

- **Fungi**: Which may be unicellular with a cell nucleus, multicellular, or making a mass of syncytium; 2 to 10 micrometers in diameter and different length. Yeast living in or on human body may measure single micrometers in diameter.
- **Protozoa**: Single-cell eukaryotes having a nucleus; in humans are often pathogenic; 1 to 50 micrometers.
- **Algae**: Single cells or a chain of cells; 0.1 to 15 micrometers.
- **Viruses**: Infective agents with a nucleic acid molecule in a protein coat, which live and reproduce only inside the cells; 20 to 400 nanometers. Viruses are a few nanometers long; they have a protein shell.

Thus, they differ in size, structure, and in many other respects; they live as single cells, multicellular organisms, or as cell clusters. Figure 6 shows a work by Anna Ursyn entitled "Threat."

Researchers found more than 10,000 microbial species inside the human ecosystem. Most of them are beneficial to our life, but some can cause serious harm. Some microorganisms can produce metabolites that harm human hosts. Many microbes symbiotically cooperate with our cells, which benefits to both sides, like when a hummingbird pollinates a dianthus while drinking from it. Microorganisms reside on or within our tissues and biofluids, including the skin, mammary glands, placenta, seminal fluid, uterus, ovarian follicles, lung, saliva, mucous membrane inside the mouth, and also covering the front of

*Figure 6. Threat*
*(© 2018, A. Ursyn. Used with permission)*

the eye and the inside of the eyelids, as well as the biliary and gastrointestinal tracts. Apart from the world of microbial inhabitants of our bodies there is also another world of beings that are living outside.

**Viruses** are a few nanometers long; they have a protein shell. Oncologists are working on using the virus shells to target cancer cells. They remove the viral material from the virus shell and replace it with chemotherapy drugs, antibodies, and nanoparticles. Patient's healthy cells are programmed to die when infected by a virus, because this prevents the virus spreading to other parts of the body. But a cancerous cell is immortal, so if a virus infects a cancer cell, it could continue to replicate inside it and cause the cell to die. The progeny viruses then spread to cancer cells nearby and repeat the process. A virus becomes, in effect, a cancer of cancer. Figure 7 presents an image of a virus imagined by Alejandra Ramos.

According to National Cancer Institute (2019), "tumors have the ability to develop their own blood supplies, manipulate the immune system to tamp down immune responses, and recruit normal cells to help them grow. Just as important, tumor cells can ignore signals that normally tell old or damaged cells to die." Researchers and physician-scientists developed targeted therapies: treatments that target the specific proteins that underlie the

*Figure 7. Virus*
*(© 2018, A. Ramos. Used with permission)*

growth and development of cancer. Surgery, radiation therapy, and standard chemotherapy will continue to play an important role in treating cancer, but treatment options are enhanced by targeted therapies and immunotherapies, which harness the power of the immune system to fight cancer (National Cancer Institute, 2019). In a figure 8 Alejandra Ramos presents a character as a fictional rendition of a cancer tumor.

It is possible to modify properties of a virus and target the viruses to cancer cells, so the engineered viruses can infect cancer cells. When injected into a cancer patient, virus shells would seek out the cancer cells and inject the chemotherapy medication directly into them. Viruses can be modified by genetic engineering or chemical modification. With this targeted approach, a benign nanoscale virus called bacteriophage MS2 was utilized in studies of disease transmission and for therapy (Aanei et al., 2016). The MS2 is a single-stranded RNA virus about 27 nm in diameter that lives in human gut and infects the bacterium Escherichia coli. MS2 uses protein markers to identify a host cell and then attaches itself to it and injects its RNA genetic material into the cell. (RNA, a ribonucleic acid is one of the nucleic acids that, along with lipids, carbohydrates, and proteins are essential for life). MS2 shells were combined with antibodies to construct nanoparticles targeted toward breast cancer cells in vitro. Also, radiolabeled shells were injected into mice and examined with the positron emission tomography-computed tomography (PET/CT) and scintillation (emitting flashes of light) counting

*Figure 8. Cancer tumor*
*(© 2018, A. Ramos. Used with permission)*

*Figure 9. Bacteriophage*
*(© 2018, M. Zilkenat. Used with permission)*

method. Targeted nanoparticles are good diagnostic and therapeutic carriers because they can increase the signal-to-background ratio of imaging agents, improve the efficacy of drugs, and reduce adverse effects by concentrating the therapeutic molecule in the region of interest (Aanei et al., 2016). Computer-based models allow studying how viruses attach to cell surface proteins. Figure 9 shows an imaginary bacteriophage as seen by Max Zilkenat.

## Project: Robots vs. Microbes

This project can be considered futuristic. The task is to picture a fight where specially designed micro robots and transformers struggle tenaciously with large forces of harmful microbes and viruses, and thus defend a human organism battling against its illness.

## Drawing Comics About Fictional Battle Going Inside of a Body

You may want to resolve this project with creating comics about the fight with microbes and cancer cells. This project will be composed of following stages:

1.    Develop several characters based on pictures of microbes. First, develop characters based on pictures of microbes. Draw a character representing a bacterium causing a disease and a virus.

Figure 10 presents an unreal representation of a microbe created by Tatiana Ingino Silberberg.

2.    Define distinctive features, properties, and attributes characteristic of robots you will design. Create some tiny micro robots possessing particulate powers, which are designed to fight bacteria and viruses in our body. Each robot will have several (1 to 10) properties such as speed, power, intelligence, attention span, persistence, hardness, flexibility (shape-changing), and more. They will add to each robot's total potential, with the total value of the robot's powers equal to 10.

Figure 11 shows a robot designed by Morgan Hurtado.
Figure 12 presents a mini robot drawn by Alejandra Ramos.
Create several kinds of robots that may impersonate leukocytes, white blood cells engulfing, devouring, eating bacteria and viruses. Leukocytes circulate in the blood and body fluids and are involved in counteracting foreign substances and disease. There are different types of leukocytes, all amoeboid cells with a nucleus: they are lymphocytes, granulocytes, monocytes, and macrophages. Microphages engulf and digest foreign objects, microbes, cancer cells, especially at sites of infection, so they are part of the immune system,

*Figure 10. A microbe*
*(© 2018, T. Ingino. Used with permission)*

*Figure 11. HumanBot*
*(© 2018, M. Hurtado. Used with permission)*

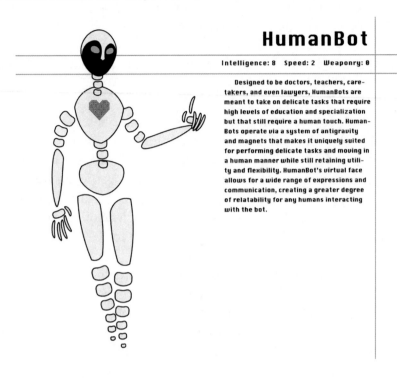

## HumanBot

Intelligence: 8    Speed: 2    Weaponry: 0

Designed to be doctors, teachers, care-takers, and even lawyers, HumanBots are meant to take on delicate tasks that require high levels of education and specialization but that still require a human touch. Human-Bots operate via a system of antigravity and magnets that makes it uniquely suited for performing delicate tasks and moving in a human manner while still retaining utility and flexibility. HumanBot's virtual face allows for a wide range of expressions and communication, creating a greater degree of relatability for any humans interacting with the bot.

*Figure 12. Mini robot*
*(© 2018, A. Ramos. Used with permission)*

support tissue healing and regeneration. Your robots will have abilities similar to those of leukocytes, and thus they will be designed to fight different types of invaders: microbes or viruses.

3.   Create a storyboard about actions taken by your robots. Use your knowledge about microbes and human blood cells.
4.   Made comics showing the fight between robots and structures inside a body.

Your micro robot may be equipped with applications of current technologies; it may use fiber optics to transmit light signals and communicate, sensors to detect microbes and their chemical or electrical signaling, and effectors that act in response to the enemy's actions. You may also plan to create cooperation with good bacteria that live in the host, and also use emptied virus shells to deliver medicine that is good for the disease treatment or drugs that fight the harmful bacteria and viruses. Figure 13 presents a mini robot "Cheatbot" drawn by Sami Lee.

*Figure 13. CheatBot*
*(© 2018, S. Lee. Used with permission)*

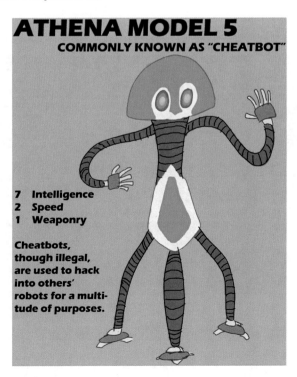

Some techniques involve hiding a medication into a shell of a virus. Scientists are able to place a medicine inside of an emptied shell or a skin of a virus, or into a medical fiberoptic. The treatment is aimed at a cancerous cells without affecting the other cells and functions of a body. Therefore, you may need to create several kinds of your robots as transformers that would distract, mislead the enemy, and penetrate into inaccessible areas. Figure 14 presents "Nanotransformers" by Anna Ursyn.

- Picture an RNA molecule as a transformer who carries molecules of a tumor-killing drug. Nanoparticles can be designed so they attach exclusively to cancer cells. They can carry drug molecules.
- Another transformer may represent an engineered virus filled with a drug or a radioactive material inside.
- Translate into a transformer the application of the gold nanoshells, that can enter a tumor cell in a macrophage; nanoshells can selectively link to cancer cells, delivering therapeutic treatment directly to kill tumor cells without harming neighboring healthy cells.
- Show the monocytes containing drugs that can serve for nanoparticle transport into tumor regions that are inaccessible to cancer therapies.

*Figure 14. Nanotransformers*
*(© 2018, A. Ursyn. Used with permission)*

Figure 15 presents "Transformers" drawn by Jeremy Rice.

Feel free to select an environment where your robots will exist: would it be located on Earth, Moon, Mars, or elsewhere? In that case you may consider other forms of life, not necessarily based on proteins, with carbon as a backbone of molecules, but for example there may be sulfur-based life forms. Sulfur-based bacteria live on Earth in hot springs and hydrothermal vents. They represent ancient type of metabolism that maybe as old as dated from 3.5 billion years ago. Some scientists tell about silicon-based life, where

*Figure 15. Transformers*
*(© 2018, J. Rice. Used with permission)*

This is the Snail Wrangler. Once a full grown man making his way out west during the gold rush, he fell into a mysterious canyon that appeared out of nowhere causing him to go through a wormhole and shrinking him down to the size of an eraser on the end of a wooden pencil. He utilizes his previous cowboy knowledge to tame the creatures of the microscopic world.

This is a lightning eel. It lives at the deepest parts of the ocean. Its skin lights up brightly with neon colors to attract its prey. The size of its teeth allows it to kill prey much larger than itself. Once its prey is close it lights up 5 times brighter, blinding its prey like a deer in the head lights.

This is a lantern fish. It has tentacles like an octopus but they act as though of a jelly fish. It tentacles are used to swim as well as shock its prey and pull it into the inner shell for consumption. They only come close enough the the surface at night to hunt.

silicon is incorporated into carbon-based molecules (Kan, Lewis, Chen, & Arnold, 2016). Figure 16 presents a work "The Real World" by Anna Ursyn. Nano photographs were juxtaposed with photographic material, sketches, and codes in order to capture some swift in context. Nano photograph used courtesy by Cris Orfescu.

## Project 'Battlefield'

## Making Video About Fictional Battle with Cancer Cells

The task of this project is to create a metaphor of a battle by comparing a defense of a country to a defense of a living organism. Imagine a biology-inspired scenario with the new types of treatment using nano technology. Offer the basic understanding how we can fight cancer. Your visual response to the theme may inform the viewers how nanotechnology may have an impact on fighting an illness.

A subchapter "Our bodies make a universe for smaller creatures" provides some information supporting this project. As you probably already read, researchers found more than 10,000 microbial species inside the human bodies. Most of them are beneficial to our life, but some can cause serious harm. First, create several fictional characters that would represent real microbes.

*Figure 16. The Real World*
*(© 2018, A. Ursyns. Used with permission)*

This project may be seen as a group effort. In that case, individually created comics would be followed by a group video. Figure 17 presents a fictional bacterium as seen by Alejandra Ramos.

Apart from the world of microbial inhabitants of our bodies there is also another world of beings that are living outside. In our body, there are several types of cells that circulate in blood including red and blood cells including lymphocytes, granulocytes, monocytes, macrophages, and more. Oncologists are working on using the virus shells to target cancer cells. They remove the viral material from the virus shell and replace it with chemotherapy drugs, antibodies, and nanoparticles. Figure 18 presents microbes imaged by Jakob O'Grady.

Create a storyboard about a battle based on your knowledge about microbes and human blood cells, and then make a video depicting the enemy of a cancer cell. The cancer cells are multiplying. There are several possibilities to present this battle. Chemotherapy, drugs, and nanotechnology are your weapons. Cancer cells are aggressors that are difficult to destroy without

*Figure 17. Bacterium*
*(© 2018, A. Ramos. Used with permission)*

*Figure 18. Microbes*
*(© 2019, J. O'Grady. Used with permission)*

destroying the environment and its inhabitants. Devices that can transfer an image can be placed there. This way a shell of a virus can perform a certain set of medical tasks.

Present visually how the help may come from the outside of the body when a chemotherapy and radiation therapy is applied. Chemotherapy agents kill cancer cells but they also harm normal cells. For this reason, you need to show a targeted therapy. Show the monocytes containing drugs that can serve for the nanoparticles' transport into tumor regions that are inaccessible to cancer therapies.

A mini robot fighting cancer drawn by Max Zilkenat is shown in Figure 19.

Work on video editing by applying your characters and other images to your footage and then adding music to your video. Feel free to act, record images, and record motion using various cameras, microscopes, lighting, and other equipment.

You will need a background scene for a battlefield. Place in your battlefield the healthy cells that make a quiet, free from hardship environment. Show how the abnormal cancer cells spread, invade, and consume the healthy ones. Use color-coding to enhance the dramatic, frightening situation. Picture how body's immune system produces more white blood cells to defend body against intruders. The body recognizes cancer cells and their products as alien.

*Figure 19. Cancerbot*
*(© 2018, M. Zilkenat. Used with permission)*

## Comparison Between Historical Battlefields and Your Fictional Scene in a Human Body

While working on a comparison of the defense of a country with the defense of a living organism, several examples of battles led in unexpected ways may provide inspiration for completing the project.

The Trojan Horse was used as a disguised gift. This tactic in fighting is often used as a metaphor of a successful trick or stratagem that causes that a foe can enter a protected space. The ancient Greeks constructed a hollow wooden horse, which enabled them to enter and destroy the city of Troy and end the Trojan War. The only evidence that the Trojan horse really existed is in written and pictorial sources. This metaphor is often applied to describe deceitful computers programs or applications that are really harmful; it is used in political disputes, as well as in describing the strategies in fighting cancer. The earliest picture of the Trojan horse can be seen on a vase ca. 670 BC. A painting by Giovanni Domenico Tiepolo (1727-1804) presents the Procession of the Trojan horse into Troy can be seen at: https://www.nationalgallery.org.uk/paintings/giovanni-domenico-tiepolo-the-building-of-the-trojan-horse

The Battle of the Ice took place at Lake Peipus in 1242 between forces of the Russian Republic of Novgorod and the Teutonic Knights (Roman Catholic Northern Crusaders consisting of Germans and Estonians). This example shows how knowledge about the terrain allows the right choice of tactic. 20 years old prince Alexander Nevski and his 1,000 soldiers defeated

5,000 Teutonic crusaders when he made the knights rally at the far side of the lake. Many knights drowned when the thin ice gave way under the weight of their heavy armor. Russian film director Sergei Eisenstein glorified this event in 1938 in his drama 'Alexander Nevski.'

Polish Hussars were the cavalry undefeated in battle and regarded as the most powerful cavalry formation between16th and 18th centuries. The hussars were famous for their huge wings. A wooden, and then metal frame carried eagle feathers, and sometimes ostrich or swan feathers. Wings were originally attached to the saddle and later to the backs of the riders, which were covered with plate metal body armor. The possible purpose to use the wings was that they made a loud, clattering noise, which made it seem like the cavalry was much larger than in reality. The wings were also made to defend the backs of hussars against swords and lassos. Maybe, they were worn to make their own horses more fearless, insensible to noise made by the wooden noisemakers used by the Turkish Ottoman and Crimean Tatars. The other army's horses were afraid of noise caused by the hussars' wings.

Napoleon's Russian campaign of 1812 illustrates a misfortune coming out of a lack of knowledge about the region. In 1869, Charles Joseph Minard created his famous 'Carte Figurative' picturing this epic disaster; later on, Edward Tufte (1983/2001) made this graphics famous by describing it in his writings. Menno-Jan Kraak (2014) described the work of Minard in his monograph entitled "Mapping Time: Illustrated by Minard's Map of Napoleon's Russian Campaign of 1812." Napoleon's army consisting of 422,000 soldiers retreated from Moscow in the cold winter (-36 F, on December 6, 1812) and only 4,000 soldiers survived the campaign, with 45% captured, 29% killed in battle, and 24% were those who died of hunger, cold, and sickness.

## 1.2. IN NANOSPHERE, LIGHT AND ORGANIC MATTER CONNECT

### Soft Matter

We all can be called soft matter. When we look at things at the nano scale, we can credit a great amount of everyday things as soft matter including food, soap, ink, paint, cosmetics, putty, and gels. Research community has studied nanoparticles for several decades. Scientists and practitioners explore complex soft matter in order to understand general principles that drive behavior and properties of the nanoscale structures. They develop measuring tools, new chemical structures and new technologies, and examine processes going at the nanoscale.

The soft condensed matter is in a state neither liquid nor crystalline. Liquid crystals, biological tissues: cells, and a cytoplasm, biological membranes, microfilaments and filamentous networks, e.g., a cytoskeleton present in all cells, molecular mono-layers, polymers and biopolymers (such as DNA or filaments in neuronal or muscle fibers), and also liquid crystals are called soft matter.

## Liquid Crystals

Physicists call as liquid crystal such a matter that flows like a liquid but has its molecules somewhat ordered and arranged. Liquid crystal changes shape like a liquid, but its molecules may be oriented in a crystal-like way. It is an organic compound usually structured as rods oriented along a common axis; it has positive and negative charges separated, so responds to electric and magnetic fields. Thus, liquid crystal is a fourth state of matter besides the solid, liquid, and gas states.

According to Ivan Smalyukh (2019), "liquid crystals, nano-structured, biomolecular, and other soft materials are attractive not only because of the richness of observed physics phenomena but also because of the wealth of potential technological applications and because of their significance for the fields of biology, biotechnology, and medicine. These materials combine properties of crystalline solids and ordinary liquids in unexpected ways, often possessing fluidity along with orientational order and varying degrees of positional order." Small particles, both natural and engineered, range from one nanometer to tens of microns. In atmosphere, where there is from a few to a few thousands of small particles/cm$^3$, they impact both warming and cooling of the climate. In Earth sub-surface, they impact soil and water quality. Small particles have an effect on catalysis and reaction engineering, material design, and synthesis. Isotopic signature (with krypton or xenon isotopes) of some nanodiamonds indicate they were formed outside the solar system, whether in supernova or in interstellar medium.

Depending on the amount of order, liquid crystal materials have the hydrophilic (water loving) and hydrophobic (water-hating) parts. Some liquid crystals are thermotropic; they have phases: nematic, smectic, and cholesteric. Nematic liquid crystals have the molecules oriented in parallel but not arranged in well-defined planes, while in smectic liquid crystals the molecules are oriented in parallel and arranged in well-defined planes. Cholesteric liquid crystals have a helical structure, and so they are <u>chiral</u> (asymmetric, their structure and their mirror images are not superimposable). The rod-shaped liquid crystal molecules have length at least 1.3 nanometer.

In lyotropic liquid crystals, for example in a mixture of oil and water, heads of molecules are in contact with water, while the tails are immersed in oil. They are abundant in living organisms, mostly as phospholipid bilayers in biological membranes of eukaryotic organisms and cell membranes. Liquid crystals are used in polarizers (optical filters), color LCD systems with color filters used to generate red, green, other optical devices, and blue pixels, liquid crystal thermometers, liquid crystal lasers, and many other applications.

## Colloids

A colloid is a suspension of ultramicroscopic particles of one substance in another substance. Colloidal mixture is resistant to filtering or centrifuging and it does not settle. It may form a colloidal suspension of:

- A solid in liquid: As in an Indian ink you draw a picture with.
- Liquid in liquid, an emulsion, as in a mayonnaise.
- Gas in liquid, foam of gas in liquid: As in beer or soap bubbles making foam.
- There could be also gas in solid, like in a bath sponge or ice cream.

Colloidal systems are objects of intensive research, mostly as a part of nanoscience. In colloids at least a part of a system has a dimension of one micrometer or less, so it has to be examined it in the nanoscale. Aerosols are particles suspended in the air. Aerosols scatter light producing urban haze and photochemical smog; they reflect sunlight so less sunlight reaches Earth's surface. They also act as seed particles for the formation of cloud droplets. Without aerosols, there would be no clouds, and the Earth's climate would be very different. Aerosols thus change the global energy balance and climate.

Knowledge of particle shape, size, and size distribution is critical for creating new materials that are useful and safe for environment health. Research on the role of aerosols in climate involves modeling the particle formation in polluted atmosphere, where newly formatted particles may act as the cloud condensation nuclei. Research on aerosols pertains to air pollution, potential bioterrorism, climate change, and diesel engines related pollution with exhaust. Mixtures of particles that form clusters come from organic vapors from vegetation, dust, industrial sulfur dioxide emissions, biomass burning, ocean sea salt, and other sources.

Colloidal systems are used in fabrication of photonic crystals, which are natural (for example, a gemstone opal) or artificial optical nanostructures such as plasmonic circuitry. There are also applications such as nanoantennas, and plasmonic sensors. Plasmons are quasiparticles existing as plasma oscillation in solid matter. Plasmonics is a field of research on light–metal interaction: for example, surface plasmons are oscillations of electrons on a metal surface excited by electromagnetic radiation. Plasmonic nanostructures serve for designing photonic circuits, miniature optical devices, sensors, colloidal and soft lithography, and more. They can be applied to medical diagnostics, therapeutics, and nanofabrication methods. Scientists has already created a biosensor made from plasmonic nanohole arrays, to detect molecular binding on the membrane surface, such as of viruses like Ebola (Yanik, Huang, Kamohara, Artar, Geisbert, Connor, & Altug, 2010). Virus, a package having a diameter 20 to 300 nm and containing proteins, genetic material, and often lipids, may reorganize itself after entering a living cell, whether a mosquito cell or a human cell, where it may mutate, replicate, and spread into new cells.

Synthetic supramolecules are promising new advances for optical and biomedical materials. Trivedi, Klevets, Senyuk, Lee, & Smalyukh (2012) work on achieving sparse colloidal assemblies that can be controlled at will due to tunable interparticle separations. The Soft Matter Physics Research Group led by Ivan Smalyukh (2019) works toward achieving the fundamental understanding of nanostructured liquid crystals and their practical utility in enabling a new breed of inorganic–organic composite materials. As claimed by Smalyukh, some biological macromolecules can control their own assembly into elegant hierarchical structures. Authors (Peng, Yu, Chen, Xue, Liao, Zhu, Xie, Smalyukh, & Wei Yen, 2019) examine physical behaviors and functional properties of liquid crystalline nanocolloids, which comprise nanoparticles and a liquid crystal host. The liquid crystalline nanocolloids can be assembled into ordered structures through phase separation induced by holographic photopolymerization. Reconstruction of high-quality switchable and unclonable colored images promises a host of advanced applications (e.g., anticounterfeiting).

Scientists work on designing the packaging of small particles as dry fine powders. Applications for packaging include metallurgy, agricultural, pharmaceutical and food products, fertilizers, detergents, catalysts, and other applications (Challenges, 2012: James Litster). Scientists study bioavailability and bioaccumulation of nanomaterials, their possible toxicity, and interaction with bacteria and other microorganisms. Studies are conducted to design simulations and models of nanomaterial interaction with biological structures, especially the cell membrane lipids and the lung surfactant lipids. Other groups examine the sea salt 100-nanometer to 100-micron aerosol droplets, their effect on atmosphere, and interactions with biological structures. Sea salt particles coated with organic material in smog can increase ozone levels (Challenges, 2012: Douglas Tobias).

Nanoscale devices are man-made constructs made with carbon, silicon, and other materials that have the capability to monitor the biological phenomena and relay information to the medical care provider. Devices are one hundred to ten thousand times smaller than human cells, similar in size to large biological molecules such as enzymes and receptors. Nanoscale devices smaller than 50 nanometers can easily enter most cells, while those smaller than 20 nanometers can move out of blood vessels as they circulate through the body. Nanoscale devices can interact with biomolecules on both the surface and inside cells. They can detect disease and deliver treatment.

## Wavelengths and Spectra

General topics such as light and wavelength refer to objects and events belonging to various categories, starting with history of the universe or focusing on the micro and nano applications in medicine. While exploring studies about events and processes occurring in nature we can see greater than before emphasis placed on the study of light, apart from the focus on matter and materials. For example, light can be applied to modify DNA and other types of nanoparticles for the purpose of inquiring into ways to prevent and cure diseases such as cancer (Vogt, 2018). Light and organic matter are coupling at the nanoscale. The coupling can modify optical, electronic, and chemical properties of systems.

Electromagnetic radiation has dual properties: it behaves as a particle (called a photon) and at the same time as an energy wave. Electromagnetic radiation, as a wave, can be described by its wavelength $\lambda$ (Greek lambda), frequency $v$ (Greek nu), and amplitude. The wavelength is the distance between one wave maximum to the next. The frequency is the number of wave maxima passing by a given time; it is usually measured per second, in hertz, Hz: $1\ Hz = 1\ s^{-1}$. The amplitude means a height of a wave measured from its midpoint to the maximum. The intensity of radiant energy is proportional to the square of the wave amplitude (McMurry, 2015). Energy wave travels with a speed of light. This results from the equation: wavelength x frequency = speed. It can be written as: $\lambda$ (m) x $v$ (s$^{-1}$) = $c$ (m/s).

Visible light is one of several electromagnetic waves listed in order of their length: long electric waves, radio, television and radar, microwaves, infrared waves (felt as heat), visible light, ultraviolet (invisible), X rays, and cosmic and gamma rays.

Table 1 shows in meters wavelengths of different kinds of electromagnetic radiation.

Figure 20 presents infographics "*Electromagnetic Spectrum*" done by Amanda Betts.

*Table 1. Wavelengths (in m) and communication*

| $10^{-16}$ | Gamma rays | Information about Cosmos |
|---|---|---|
| $10^{-12}$ | X rays | Instruments for gathering and communicating information … |
| $10^{-8}$ | Ultraviolet | Some animals, e.g., bats, dolphins, sharks |
| $3.8 \times 10^{-7} – 7.8 \times 10^{-7}$ | Visible light | Visual communication |
| $10^{-6} – 10^{-4}$ | Infrared light | Some cold-blooded animals: frogs, snakes, blood-sucking insects, and fish. Warm-blooded animals cannot see infrared light because their own bodies release heat (Tali, 2018). |
| $10^{-4} – 10^{-2}$ | Microwaves | |
| $10^{-2}$ | Radio waves | Sound and verbal communication; radio; drums as a code; music and visual music. The radio spectrum is the part of the electromagnetic spectrum with frequencies from 3 Hz to 3 000 GHz (3 THz). |

*Figure 20. Electromagnetic Spectrum: Wavelengths in meters*
*(© 2018, A. Betts. Used with permission)*

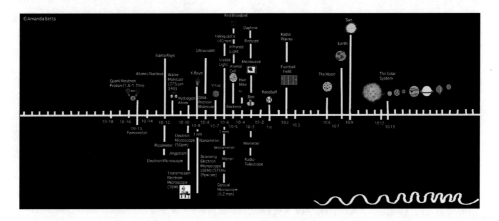

**Techniques** that are possibly most effectively used to determine the structure of organic compounds include mass spectrometry, infrared spectroscopy, nuclear magnetic resonance spectroscopy, and ultraviolet spectroscopy. According to McMurry (2015) mass spectrometry (MS) allows measuring the mass, and thus getting information about the molecular weight and a formula of a compound. Infrared spectroscopy (IR) informs what functional groups are present in a substance, Nuclear magnetic resonance spectroscopy (NMR) may determine what carbon–hydrogen framework is present. Ultraviolet spectroscopy (UV) can tell about the presence of a conjugated $\pi$ electron system. While mass spectrometry involves bombarding a sample by a stream of high-energy electrons, infrared spectroscopy, nuclear magnetic resonance spectroscopy, and ultraviolet spectroscopy involve interaction of molecules with electromagnetic energy (McMurry, 2015).

**Infrared light** is a part of spectrum of light. Infrared-transmitting optical materials include short-wave infrared (SWIR) or a near-infrared light (NIR) light of 0.75 to 3 micrometer, the mid-wave infrared (MWIR), which covers 3 to 5 micrometers, and the long-wave infrared (8 to 14 micrometer). Materials for optical systems are also made in the UV band of 0.1 to 0.4 micrometer. When molecules absorb the IR radiation, vibration amplitude increases in those molecules that have their characteristic frequency matching this IR radiation (McMurry, 2015).

NIR light has been used for at least fifty years to treat pain, inflammation, and healing wounds. Scientists gained knowledge about the effects of particular wavelengths, power density, and total energy, along with the understanding of the mechanism of action. The near-infrared light acts on photoreceptors in the mitochondrial respiratory chain, mostly cytochrome c oxidase subunit IV. It was reported that shining a NIR light on the head of somebody with a brain disorder may become an effective treatment for a several ailments: neuro-degenerative diseases, brain damage or injury, psychiatric disorders such as depression, anxiety, addiction, or PTSD, and neuro-developmental conditions for example, autism and ADHD (Hamblin, 2018). For example, a portable NIR fundus camera can capture detailed images of the interior lining of an eye – the only place allowing observation of blood vessels from outside of the body. The infrared sensors can detect how active substances affect the structure and behavior of proteins, thus supporting the development of new drugs (No author, Photonics showcase, 2018). Infrared spectroscopy, for example Fourier transformation IR (FTIR spectroscopy) enables looking inside neurons and performing diagnostics of degenerative diseases, diabetes, and cancer (Mann, Kötting, & Gerwert, 2018).

Light emitting diodes (LED) convert electrical energy into light energy. LED semiconductors emit light in three wavelengths: ultraviolet, visible light, and infrared. These colors of light result from material and composition of semiconductors.

Electrons can tunnel through a barrier formed by potential at semiconductor junctions. Leo Esaki and Ivar Giaver were awarded Nobel Prize for a discovery of the tunneling phenomenon. Visible light has a wavelength $\lambda$ between 400 and 750 nanometers. It is larger than the radii of nanostructures. Specific wave properties of the soft matter are caused by the size of nanostructures that is smaller than the wavelength $\lambda$ of visible light, so light interacts with nanostructures (scatters and diffracts) differently.

**Laser** (Light Amplification by Stimulated Emission of Radiation) was introduced about 60 years ago. Lasers generate very short pulses of different kind – below $10^{-16}$ second. Most common forms of energy source for stimulating laser emission are optical and electrical energy. Contrary to conventional light all laser photons are in phase with each other, share the same wavelength, and all the emitted light travels in the same direction as an intense beam. The laser beam can be a continuous, pulsed, or ultrafast wave (Photonics Handbook 2019c).

Laser technologies involve a wide spectrum of disciplines and applications. Ultrafast (ultrashort-pulse) lasers are used for biomedical discovery in the fields of nonsurgical vision correction, multiphoton imaging, neuronal optogenetics, and more. Nearly 60% of the adult U.S. population requires some form of vision correction. A technique for vision correction uses a femtosecond (one quadrillionth of a second) laser, not only as a cutting tool but to strengthen eye tissue. A femtosecond pulse sends enough photons to create ionization without disrupting a tissue. Optogenetics is a technique that uses light to control living cells (mostly neurons). Pulses of light delivered to the brain can affect behavior. Genes for light-sensitive proteins and their ion channels are modified and then introduced to selected brain cells to learn how they communicate. Researchers use Ti:sapphire fiber lasers and ytterbium fiber lasers for generating ultrashort pulses (Ahmed, 2019). With the use of optogenetics light can control, with spatial and temporal precision, specific cell groups and could offer effective treatment of neurogenerative diseases. Hybrid robots consisting both of electronics and living cells can be remotely controlled by illumination (Gutruf, 2019). High-power lasers serve in surgery to cut and burn to stop bleeding. They also serve for medical endoscopes. Currently, lasers are used for fraying and fading jeans, and even decorating them with flowery patterns.

Many applications of laser technologies for microscopy include:

- Super resolution techniques used in nanoscopy for switching on and off single-molecule fluorescence (emission of light by substance that absorbed radiation).
- Improving spatial resolution by deterministic photo switching in space and time (e.g., STED stimulated emission depletion microscopy).
- Stochastically (random) switching single-molecular fluorescence on and off in space (e.g., d-STORM– direct stochastic optical reconstruction microscopy.
- Multiphase applications in optogenetics, neuroscience, and clinical use. Optogenetics enables scientists to manipulate activity of nerve cells in animal brain. Opsins – gene-encoding proteins act as gates for ions: Na+, K+, Cl-, or other charged ions, so they flow across a membrane and change its electric membrane potential. Opsins can be controlled by pulses of light. When placed in a nerve cell, pulses of laser light from an implanted optical fiber can turn cell activity on (Deisseroth, 2018). Ultrafast lasers with high power and short pulse duration can provide in vivo imaging of multiphoton excitation (MPE), manipulate, and monitor activity of single-neurons. This can be combined with patch clamp electrodes to monitor electrical activity of single neurons.

## Features of the Quantum World

Classical knowledge about electromagnetism and Newtonian mechanics describes deterministic explanation of physical world: no randomness may influence future states of the system. However, phenomena occurring at a very small distances and energy scales are not deterministic (may depend on initial conditions) and are often counterintuitive. Behavior of very small objects and events called 'quantum systems' cannot be perfectly described by the equations of classical physics.

Quantum mechanics, a subfield of physics examines the behavior of very small particles. This theory and a model for explaining the physical world is not deterministic but probabilistic as it allows some uncertainty. A quantum object does not generally exist in a completely determined and knowable state. Every time somebody observes a quantum object it looks like a particle, but when it is not being observed it behaves like a wave. This is so-called wave-particle duality (Grumbling & Horowitz, 2018). Quantum objects can exist in multiple states at the same time, with the states adding together and interfering like waves. The overall state of the quantum system is described as 'wave functions,' with only of them can be observed at one time.

Quantum mechanics proposes that a quantum object has both wave- and particle-like properties – it displays a wave-particle duality. Quantum system can exist in two or more states at once, which is called a 'superposition state.' Measurement of a quantum system fundamentally changes it. Disrupting of a quantum state by a measurement is called 'collapsing the wave function. After the measurement, the wave function of the quantum object has the state that was detected but not that from before the measurement. Entanglement occurs when a measurement of the state of one particle collapses the state of the other particles, even if the particles are far apart with no apparent way to interact

Photons, plasmons, and elementary particles belong to topics that are fundamental in many branches of knowledge and are examined with different methods depending on the way of thinking and exploring this science. Plasma, an ionized state of matter consists of positive ions and free electrons. In plasma, plasmons oscillate at a given frequency. In most metals the plasma frequency is in ultraviolet range and is shiny; in some metals such as copper and gold the plasma frequency is in the visible range. Photons' oscillation produces light. Light with a frequency below the plasma frequency is reflected by the material, because electrons screen the electric field. Light of frequency above the plasma frequency is transmitted.

## History of the Universe: Quantum Physics for Visualizing Astrophysics

Quantum mechanics supports visualizing astrophysics. Astrophysicists analyze spectra that contain information about composition and temperature. They believe the universe is at least ten billion light-years in diameter and is expanding since its beginning. Below is a description of first events in the universe as seen by an astrophysicist Neil deGrasse Tyson (2017).

The beginning of the Universe occurred between 10 and 20 billion years ago. It has been called the Big Bang – a giant explosion. First, in a very short Planck era lasting from $t=0$ to $t=10^{-43}$ sec, gravity dissolved from other forces and the universe expanded.

Then during time $t=10^{-35}$ sec, universe still expanded and thus energy became less concentrated. Forces split into the electroweak force and the strong nuclear force, which binds the atomic nucleus. Electroweak force split then into the electromagnetic force, which binds the molecules and the weak nuclear force, which controls radioactive decay. Gravity bids the bulk matter.

When time was $t=10^{-12}$, one trillionth of a second from the time $t=0$, matter as subatomic particles and energy as photons (light energy without mass, rather waves than particles) interplayed. I was the era when the universe consisted quarks, leptons, their antimatter siblings, and boson. Photons converted their energy into the matter – antimatter pairs; they annihilated and their energy returned to photons according to the $E=mc^2$ equation. Quarks are elementary particles that combine their charges in thirds to form hadrons. Astrophysicists discern six flavors of quarks: up, down, strange, charm, top, and bottom. There is asymmetry of quark–lepton and antimatter: a billion and one particles of matter correspond to a billion of particles of antimatter.

When time was $t=10^{-6}$, one millionth of a second from the time $t=0$, there were hadrons –heavy particles created from quarks, but also protons, neutrons, and other particles. Asymmetry was passed to the pairs hadron–antihadron, and those hadrons which did not annihilate created matter: galaxies, stars, planets, and all other things. Asymmetry was an important factor because without asymmetry annihilation would be complete, and only photons would exist in the universe.

When time was 1 second old since the beginning, the universe was a few light-years wide and about a billion degrees hot. Asymmetry was acting for electrons: electrons and positrons annihilated in a sea of photons, and so only one in a million survived. When time was 2 minutes old since the beginning, universe was a hundred million degrees hot. Atomic nuclei were then forming, mostly (90%) of hydrogen, helium, deuterium, tritium, and lithium: 1 electron fused with 1 proton and neutron added.

During next 380 000 years, temperature of a particle soup of electrons and photons fell below 3 000 K (which means a half of the Sun's surface temperature). Free electrons could combine with nuclei. There was visible light.

For the first billion years the universe continued to expand and cool. A hundred billion of galaxies formed, with stars inside. Thermonuclear fusion occurring at the star cores produced elements. High-mass stars exploded providing materials for molecules, and then organic molecules. Anaerobic bacteria appeared, and then their by-product was oxygen: $O_2$, $O_3$, forming a

*Figure 21. The Starflake*
*(© 2018, A. Ursyn. Used with permission)*

shield from the ultraviolet. Carbon-based molecules appeared, and then entered organic life. The Yucatan asteroid could probably end the life of dinosaurs, allowing the existence of mammals including humans.

Figure 21 presents a work of Anna Ursyn titled "The Starflake." The image is unified with a text entitled "The King of Shapes."

## The King of Shapes

A triangle rules because in Euclidian space, all polygonal shapes derive from the triangle:

- A circle.
- A rectangle.
- A square.
- An octagon.
- A parallelogram.

- A dodecagon.
- A trapezoid.

or any form:

- A sphere.
- A cube.
- A toroid.
- A cylinder.
- A pyramid.
- A box.
- And all polytopes,

and it can even stand for itself.

The existence of gravitational waves could be detected and thus confirmed with the use of photonics. All mass, as small as our actions or as large as colliding black holes, create gravitational waves. Dark matter material is believed to make up about 85% of the mass of the universe but is not readily visible because it neither emits nor reflects electromagnetic radiation such as light or radio signals. Its presence supposedly explains some gravitational effects: the existence of gravitational waves would explain anomalies seen in the motion and distribution of galaxies. The Laser Interferometer Gravitational-Wave Observatory (LIGO) has been built after tens of years' collaboration of over 1000 people and the funding of about $500 million from the National Science Foundation. In 2017, Rainer Weiss, Barry C. Barish, and Kip S. Thorne were awarded the Nobel Prize in Physics "for decisive contributions to the LIGO detector and the observation of gravitational waves." Now the Advanced LIGO gravitational wave detectors are built for the two LIGO observatories in Hanford, WA and Livingston, LA, USA (Aasi et al., 2015). Both have two perpendicular arms, each one measuring 4 kilometers. They enabled the scientists to confirm general relativity and expand knowledge about gravitational events, black holes, and neutron stars (Coffey, 2018). These detectors will help to explore essential questions in basic physics, astrophysics, and cosmology. Isotopic signature using krypton or xenon isotopes indicates that nanodiamonds were formed outside the solar system, whether in supernova or in interstellar medium. In the same time as the nanodiamonds were formed, the $^{60}C$ cage monolayers of carbon were trapped there together with the noble gas atoms such as neon.

On April 10, 2019, the astronomers published the first image of a black hole, a bright ring formed as light bends in the intense gravity around a black hole, which is 6.5 billion times more massive than the Sun. This black hole resides 55 million light-years from Earth in the center of the galaxy Messier 87 in the nearby Virgo galaxy cluster. In order to capture the first direct visual evidence of a supermassive black hole and its shadow, researchers initiated international collaboration, making The Event Horizon Telescope (EHT) observations – a planet-scale array of eight ground-based radio telescopes. The EHT astronomers wrote, "The shadow of a black hole is the closest we can come to an image of the black hole itself, a completely dark object from which light cannot escape. The black hole's boundary – the event horizon from which the EHT takes its name – is around 2.5 times smaller than the shadow it casts and measures just under 40 billion km across." (Event Horizon Telescope, 2019). Six papers have been published in a special issue of The Astrophysical Journal Letters. The authors report, "Supermassive black holes are relatively tiny astronomical objects – which has made them impossible to directly observe until now. As a black hole's size is proportional to its mass, the more massive a black hole, the larger the shadow. … Although the telescopes are not physically connected, they are able to synchronize their recorded data with atomic clocks – **hydrogen masers,** which precisely time their observations. Each telescope of the EHT produced enormous amounts of data – roughly 350 terabytes per day – which was stored on high-performance helium-filled hard drives" (Doeleman, 2019).

Figure 22 presents a work by Anna Ursyn entitled "Invented Space" Nano photographs were juxtaposed with photographic material, sketches, and codes in order to capture how quantum physics and astronomy work together to describe the Universe. Nano photograph used courtesy by Cris Orfescu.

## Nature Inspired Explanations and Solutions

Scientists and engineers often draw their technological solutions from biology-inspired processes. Themes include evolutionary computing, soft computing, quantum mechanics related solutions, attempts to create quantum computers, among many others. Natural mechanisms detected in plants and animals may inspire scientists to create biophotonic apps. Examples may include models such as artificial joints. Chemistry studied at the micro- and nano-technology level, as well as organic chemistry such as carbon and coal related technologies, industrial applications such as stains, materials, fabrics, cosmetics, and

*Figure 22. Invented Space*
*(© 2018, A. Ursyn. Used with permission)*

plastics examine the ways the materials science draws from solutions found in nature. Projects about advances in chemistry and pharmacology refer to achievements in therapy. Many studies examine changes: mechanical (e.g., hardness), thermal, and electrical in properties; some depend on the size of material. Possibility of creating nanostructures allows exploring soft matter, liquid crystals, nanoparticles, nanotubes, and nanoshells. Nano art projects can be now seen at the nano art exhibitions.

Insects can produce colorful structures, for example, scales composed of a 3D photonic crystalline chitin. In some species larger scales reflect red light while smaller scales with smaller volume of chitin reflect blue light. Uncovering the mechanism of color tuning supports investigation on biophotonic nanostructures to develop bioinspired applications. Some beetles display brilliant colors of nano materials present in their hard cuticle. The iridescent, rainbow-hued scales are due to a 3D photonic crystal network of chitin. A study of biophotonic nanostructures (Wilts, & Saranathan, 2018) may result in bioinspired and biomimetic applications such as synthesis of photonic crystals at visible length scales. Demosponges, a species of sponges have sharp spicules and internal axial filaments. Scientists created models and three-dimensional reconstructions of these crystal structures to shape highly regular glass architectures (Schoeppler et al., 2017).

The electricity-making organs of electric eels inspired scientists to create artificial battery-like devices made up of water-based polymer mixes called hydrogels (Schroeder et al., 2017). In an eel's electric organ, rows of cells called electrocytes generate a voltage of about 150 millivolts across each cell, when an eel zaps its prey. Potassium and sodium atoms inside and between these cells flow toward the eel's head, making its front end positive and tail end negative. The voltages of these electrocytes add up, so eel's electrocytes can generate hundreds of volts. The environmentally friendly artificial energy sources created after eels' electric organs may power soft robots or next-generation wearable and implantable technologies.

A bio-inspired adhesive, surgical glue that could hold wounds together as strongly as stitches and staples, has been created by Jianyu Lu and colleagues at McGill University in Montreal (Lu et al., 2017). The chemical structure of the adhesive resembles that of a slime that slugs exude when they're startled. Deep learning is one of methods of machine learning, which is based on representation of learning data. It allows computational models to learn representations of data with multiple levels of abstraction. Deep learning methods support the speech recognition, visual object recognition, object detection, drug discovery, and genomics, also discovering intricate structure in large data sets (LeCun, Bengio, Hinton, 2015). Deep learning, often used in computer vision and image recognition, is getting closer to the concept of AI thanks to the evolution of graphics processing unit architectures and parallel computing. Many other species such as mussels or marine sandcastle worms can strongly cling to boat hulls and slippery rocks due to their sticky secretions.

## Intelligent Decisions

Scientists design and build autonomous agents that live and interact with large numbers of humans and other intelligent agents. In a near future artificial systems will work effectively with humans to accomplish tasks; they will adapt to changes in environment and co-exist with humans as partners.

New methods to work with data include representing it, discovering patterns, interacting, managing, and making decisions. According to Lev Manovich, artificial intelligence and data visualization play major roles. In cultural sphere, the development of data art, projects that use big data, is a new artistic medium (Manovich, 2019). As stated Capece, Erra, & Scolamiero (2017), the aim of applying artificial intelligence is to recognize and make an intelligent decision based on data provided as input. Several applications that use artificial intelligence include self-driving cars, speech recognition, antispam filters, and image recognition. However, while machine learning and artificial intelligence (AI) studies are developing fast, some mathematical models become biased or opaque, which has an impact on our lives, but big companies developing them show no interest in fixing the problem. Hidden biases in algorithms may be used in financial and legal decisions: who gets a loan, a job interview, or will be granted parole. Researchers instigated The AI Now initiative to study and address these problems (Knight, 2019).

## New Materials in Research, Production, and Sustainability

Adaptive materials and structures can sense external stimuli and react by changing their organization. Changes toward a desire state can be calibrated, which results in an altered shape, compliance, or appearance. Tsukruk (2013) provides examples of the natural adaptive materials and systems:

- Adaptive colors in butterflies and octopuses provide photonic, sensing, and camouflaging abilities.
- Dynamic adhesion in gecko feet allows climbing and holding.
- Self-healing biological parts produce self-healing materials.
- Reptilian locomotion allows movement on complex terrains.
- Dogs and other canines present the remote trace chemical sensing.
- Silk materials comprise tough lightweight nanocomposites.
- Night vision in some species is possible due to the thermal sensors.
- Wave tracking in seals and fish means underwater monitoring.
- Spider hair air flow receptors are the mechanical sensors.

Materials science draws information from physical chemistry, chemistry, applied physics, electronics, engineering, and nanoscience. The field of material science concerns crystalline materials, quasicrystals, polymers, fibers and bio-based fibers, ceramics and amorphous materials (such as glass), composite materials, thin films and coatings, and newly made materials.

Methods applied in materials science belong to the solid-state physic disciplines such as classical and quantum mechanics or thermodynamics, along with mother disciplines. Metamaterials are engineered; they have properties that are not found in naturally occurring materials. For example, Russian scientists are developing nanofabricated, perforated silicon metamaterial to be used in solar cells and in nano optics (Ospanova, Stenishchev, & Basharin, 2018). Studies include also soft matter, colloids, smart quantum materials, and many experimental methods.

Implementations of new materials include novel superconductors, photonic materials, lasers and opto-electronic devices, imaging devices, and microelectronics. They advance progress in sustainable, eco-friendly green materials engineering. Both technologies aimed at human wellbeing and disruptive technologies comprise robotics, intelligent and smart materials (including nanomaterials), AI and deep learning, 4D printing, wearables, spatial computing, and more. For example, wearable patch sensors allow users monitor their level of exposure to sunlight (UV), hydration, heartrate, oxygen saturation, breathing rate, and temperature (BioPhotonics, 2019, p. 28). A graphene-based sensor built in a camera consists from hundreds of thousands of photodetectors sensitive to ultraviolet and infrared light; it could be used for driving in a dense fog or test the freshness of fruits in a supermarket.

Sensors of many types are needed for the developing autonomous cars industry. They include lidar, multiple cameras, radar, and ultrasonic, to resolve car performance pertaining temperature, illumination, reflectivity, navigation, and cybersecurity. While radar (radio detection and ranging) uses radio frequency (RF), lidar uses light from a laser for surveying objects. Compared to RF, light has much smaller wavelength, and thus provides higher resolution. A pulsed scanning lidar and a frequency-modulated continuous wave (FMCW lidar) provide a 3D image of the environment and can discern highly diffused surfaces such as animals and clothing. They make travel by air, water and air safe, preventing hundreds of thousands of accidents and fatalities (Asghari, 2019). According to Hogan (2018), cars are currently staying idle 22 out of every 24 hours. Fully autonomous self-driving cars may be running 20 plus hours a day. Maybe in the near future smaller amount of cars would be produced for every member of the family and replaced with new ones every few years.

Production of biomimetic and smart biomaterials results in large measure from inspiration from living beings. There are structures in biology that can be used or industrially recreated. Gel-like substances secreted by spiders, insects, or termites make the best source of inspiration for creating glues and microgels. Spiders produce webs that harden, become strong, and can support very heavy objects. Scientists produce many kinds of chemical counterparts for diverse applications in engineering, medicine, electronics, failure analysis, nanotechnology, or crystallography. They work on computers made of soft materials resembling biological gels to study what lays at the basis of natural substance's strength, durability, endurance, hardness, and the ability to withstand long use. Then they are able to improve production of earthquake resistant buildings or bulletproof vests. Studies on bio-inspired materials comprise computational solutions, biomaterials used in the life forms, reinforced textile technologies, electronic and magnetic materials, and pervasive computing, among more fields. Advances in materials science make possible constructing biology-inspired soft materials based on nanotechnologies. Studies on materials science are also changing our perception of human-machine interaction.

## Sapphires

Sapphires – precious gemstones of various colors consisting mostly of aluminum oxide – have optical properties that transmit wavelengths from 150 to 6,000 nanometers and have hardness 9 on the Mohs hardness scale (1 to 10) testing the resistance to being scratched. Sapphires are thus used as optical components for medical, laser, defense, and industrial markets. As sapphires combine strength when thinned, precision, and wear resistance, they are used for ornamental and non-ornamental purposes, for example as infrared optical parts, very thin electronic wafers for insulation, wristwatch crystals, bearings, and durable window panels.

## Flexible Glass

Flexible glass substrates enable new applications. In portable electronics, displays, and many other applications glass (typically as rigid sheets >0.3 mm thick) has been used as substrates, backlights, and protective covers. The roll-to-roll (R2R) processing of flexible glass allows manufacturing curved, lightweight applications. For example, Corning's flexible Willow Glass is made with a width >1 meter, a Thickness <200 micrometers, and a length 300 meters (Garner, 2017, 2018). These glass substrates include vacuum deposition, photolithographic and laser patterning, printing, solution coating, and lamination. Also, interactive walls or smart surfaces connect devices with the environment by integrating flexible glass touch sensors, photo-voltaic devices used as energy sources, displays as active matrix liquid crystals, antennas, and other options.

## Additive Manufacturing, 3D Printing

The 3D printing technology is based on the rapid prototyping process. According to Formlabs, a 3D printing developer and manufacturer (2019), 3D printing or additive manufacturing technologies create three-dimensional objects; the 3D printing processes start from a computer-aided design (CAD) model – the mathematical representation of any 3D surface or they are developed from 3D scan data. The model is then sent to software to prepare the design: to specify print settings and slice the digital model into layers that represent horizontal cross-sections of the part. Each object is created by successively adding material layer-by-layer according to a computer program, and solidifying resin or sintering powder. The parts are then removed from the printer and post-processed for the specific application. Some 3D printers use a laser to cure liquid resin into hardened plastic, and others fuse small particles of polymer powder at high temperatures to build parts. In a post-process, the printed parts may require rinsing in isopropyl alcohol to remove any uncured resin, post-curing to stabilize mechanical properties, manual work to remove support structures, or cleaning with compressed air or a media blaster to remove excess powder.

The 3D printing technologies have been around since the 1980s. Advances in machinery, materials, and software have made 3D printing accessible to a wider range of businesses: engineering, manufacturing, dentistry (dentures), healthcare, education, entertainment, jewelry, and audiology: custom ear buds are made by casting biocompatible silicone in 3D printed hollow molds. Shoe companies like New Balance and Adidas will produce 3D printed custom shoe midsoles. Other companies include aerospace, automotive, defense, consumer goods, medical, and more industries. Formlabs (2019) claim that the benefits of 3D printing are speed, low cost, design freedom, reduced risk, and customization. Compact, desktop 3D printers have become capable. The 3D printing market has sales of $6 billion in 2017, to reach a market size of $22 billion by 2022. Alas, additive manufacturing is becoming a serious threat to our environment, as it provides great amount of pollution with discarded materials. Figure 23 presents a board with an unconventional set of chess figures that were 3D printed by Oksanna Worthington.

*Figure 23. Chess*
*(© 2018, O. Worthington. Used with permission)*

3D Printing Technologies include stereolithography and selective laser sintering. Stereolithography 3D printing, including high-resolution 3D printing and recently Low Force Stereolithography technology for large format printers, uses a laser to cure liquid photopolymer resin into solid isotropic parts. The print is built in consecutive layers less than a hundred microns thick. Stereolithography is ideal for rapid prototyping, functional prototyping, concept modeling, short-run production, dental applications, and jewelry prototyping and casting. Selective laser sintering 3D printers use a high-power laser to sinter small particles of polymer powder into a solid structure. The laser scans a cross-section of the 3D model fusing the particles into layers between 50 to 200 microns. Selective laser sintering is ideal for functional prototyping, end-use parts, and short-run, bridge, or custom manufacturing. Draft Resin can balance the speed with prototyping accuracy needs, and it prints three to four times faster than Standard Resins and has a 300-micron layer height. Benchtop selective laser sintering 3D printers produce nylon parts (Formlabs, 2019). Key trends in additive manufacturing include compact, modular systems for plastic and also metal 3D printing, which is expensive. Labor is the costliest component of most processes.

With immediate design, 3-D Printing is now close to $60 billion global eyeglass-frame market. Printed frames made, almost without waste, of layers of metal or plastic powder cost $100 to $500 – about 1.5 billion frames annually for eyeglasses, and Editors of the Wired Magazine (January 2019, pp.18-19) describe a snow rover, which is 3d printed from plastic and powered by sun heating the infrared windows and solar vacuum tubes designed to boil water from snow. The 3D printed rover will be used in Antarctica – the driest, highest, windiest, and coldest continent. NASA backed a project of the Research and Architecture Studio AI Space Factory, which has designed 3D-printed houses for the surface of Mars. Each house that looks like a beehive can accommodate four astronauts (Wood, 2018).

3D printing technologies are now serviceable for fabricating microscale objects with highly integrated systems such as miniaturized photonic chips, cameras, high-speed telecommunications, ultra-compact imaging systems, and more. Miniaturization down to the microscale increases the performance of devices and products, for example mobile devices and medical instruments at the point of care. To assemble a microchip, the 3D micro-printers can fabricate micro parts directly on a photonic integrated circuit, without any need for assembling or aligning (Rodriguez, 2018).

Using an infrared camera, 3D images of a printing process are available in nearly real time, which allows detecting defects in the process of printing (Greco, 2019). Custom 3D printed objects produced under surveillance of thermal imaging (IR, infra-red cameras) combined with x-ray imaging techniques serve for making prosthetics, personalized medicine, and medical devices. The 3D printing instrument supports laser bed powder fusion; laser melts and fuses metal or polymer powder and builds an object layer by layer. Researchers from academia, industry, and government investigate 3D printing methods using IR and x-ray imaging.

## Bioprinting in 3D

Stereolithography based bioprinters serve for building biomaterials for artificial tissues developed for regenerative medicine at the University of California, L.A. A 3D printer has a microfluidic chip with multiple inlets for different materials and bio-inks. Hydrogels have been used to regulate cell behavior as well as to model and microfabricate artificial tissues with the use of 3D printing. Hydrogels form scaffolds into which tissue can grow (Miri et al., 2018). Other 3D tissue printing companies are starting to develop microvasculature and scaffolding for human tissues. Printed capillaries supply oxygen and nutrients to tissues (BioPhotonics, September 2018, p. 21). An array of 3D-printed light receptors on a hemispherical surface is a first step toward creating a bionic eye, which in future would serve visually impaired people (Park & al., 2018). Scientists successfully completed high-sensitive polymer-based photoreceptors when they converted light into electricity with 3D printed semiconductors. Hand-held scanning laser device enables cellular-level ophthalmic imaging.

## Housing on Mars: a 3D Printed Habitat Challenge

According to Jeffrey Bezos, a technology entrepreneur, investor, and philanthropist, people will soon start packing for Mars. There might be a stop at the Moon. He sponsors the NASA-based 3-D printed housing that will be waiting for the new explorers. The shape of these constructions might remind us of the nests of the termites, or scientific observatories with giant telescopes, which teams from the US, Europe, and Latin America have been placing high in the mountains. One can also think of the Anasazi dwellings in Arizona, Utah, New Mexico, and Colorado, as well as South American Inca architecture or the Egyptian Pyramids. The NASA-sponsored contest called 'The 3D printed habitat challenge' is a competition to build a 3D-printed habitat for deep space exploration. In 2015 the teams submitted architectural renderings. In 2017 the competition focused on creating material technologies and structural components. Currently, there is the On-Site Habitat Competition to fabricate habitats on three construction levels and two virtual levels. On March 27, 2019 NASA determined top three teams who shared a prize in complete virtual construction level of 3D printed habitat (NASA, 2019, Latest Updates). 3D printers programmed with blueprints will create construction material out of the regolith – the dust, rock, and other local indigenous materials.

## Who and Why Would Visit These Hotels?

There may be a need for several types of houses for various teams, where team members may want to work and live in their specialized hotels designed for a particular purpose. We may imagine sets of hotels combined in a future Martian village. For example:

1. Some astronauts will go to one hotel to explore Mars and expand human habitat.

2.  Computing scientists and communication specialists will stay at the second hotel in order to establish communication with Earth, the satellites orbiting around Mars and Earth, and then secure sensory (visual and auditory) communication with the Earth. Teams of specialists are competing to build a satellite network that can deliver internet anywhere in the world. Building space stations and other spacecraft orbiting a planet is crucial to delivering information. There are two current orbits: Low-earth orbit with satellites up to 1,200 miles high that orbit the Earth in 100 minutes, and geostationary orbit with telecommunications network, about 22,000 high. A low-earth orbit satellite is the new cable guy, wrote the Wall Street Journal on April 12, 2019. The fast online access will be ready in 5–10 years. Now, satellites that provide internet need half second to bounce a signal from Earth. Satellites on low-earth orbit will do it in a tenth of that time. Companies such as Facebook, Google, and Amazon are already competing. The Defense, Government, civil and commercial agencies are launching satellites, with the cost of launching to low-earth orbit, being thousands of dollars per pound.

3.  Businessmen and geologists will occupy the third hotel in order to find treasures: scientists think that the most abundant chemical elements in the Martian crust are iron, magnesium, aluminum, titanium, and chromium, besides silicon and oxygen. There is also hydrogen present as water, ice, and hydrated minerals, and carbon as carbon dioxide ($CO_2$). Professionals specializing in deep drilling will work onto harvesting resources and rare elements found on Mars. Helium-3 (He-3) is valued at $5 billion per metric ton, while gold is valued $42 million per metric ton. He-3 is used in fusion power.

4.  Transportation specialists will go to research and apply methods for transportation of the rare findings from Mars to Earth and deliver all necessities to Mars.

5.  Social, health, and knowledge sharing specialists will stay in the Hotel 5. Medical practitioners will assemble an emergency room to help in cases of sickness, accidents, and issues such as burning or freezing of one's limbs. Social workers will control medicine and drug intakes and would arrange social encounters instead. Health specialists will make exercising possible and enjoyable. Educators will help with collaboration and cooperation to keep learning and exchanging various types of knowledge. Everything on Mars is different, from gravitation, pressure, temperatures, to atmosphere, and even dirt. People will need to learn about the new materials.

6. Artists will go to the Hotel 6. They will create art based on new materials, technologies, and ideas, and serve as visual communicators. Performing artists will entertain and serve as culture organizers.

7. Cooks, chefs, and nutritionists will be developing ways to enrich the packaged food by growing bacterial cultures such as kefir bacteria or applying yeasts and mushrooms.

8. Waste management and recycling specialists will occupy Hotel 8. They will also work on models for energy conservation.

9. Wearable computing specialists will solve human related problems by making costumes with wearable apps that inform, warn, alert, and even restrain people from doing anything not appreciated by the Mars community, and still remain fashionable.

10. Robot makers will collaborate with everyone else to create custom based robots for the group and individual needs.

11. Translators and language specialists will help people communicate with other people and with machines.

12. Encryption and security specialists working on information shared between Mars and Earth will cooperate with quantum computers specialists.

13. Insulation and clothing specialists will work together on developing the light and durable, but also breathable and pressure-controlled insulation, both of costumes and buildings. This will involve designers working on comfort and safety of a wearer.

14. Microbiologists will make sure that microbes (bacteria, amoebas, fungi, viruses and more) brought from the Earth or new locations would stay under control.

15. Safety and warning systems people will research possible blasts of asteroids, comets, meteoroids, volcanic eruptions, and more.

16. Visual documentation specialists will work on creating films, videos, cartographic maps, infographics, seismic information, and more.

17. Writers will work on writing all sort of interactive stories and documentations.

Preparations for the Moon and Mars exploration involve creating models of tentative structures. Teams from around the world have proposed several models.

The modular model consisting of 3 hexagonal structures would contain the living space in the center (with a large window to hydroponic garden, which produces greenery and oxygen), a laboratory, and the crew' space:

small bedrooms with viewports to the outside and composting toilets. The storage on a ceiling produces radiation shield.

The giant dome was designed in the Mars Science City in the Emirati desert. Community with 1.9 million square feet of space, with pressured biospheres tied and inflated. Robot machinery works for water, regolith, and more, dig down, and builds up (3D prints). Multilayered buildings shield against radiation, with underground floors being the safest. There will be indoor foliage, a space museum, and research place, to live there for one year. Super strong tori would welcome more than a million people to one community. Figure 24 shows imaginary rendition of water on Mars, entitled "Flying Water" by Aaron Richardson.

The inflatable city designed by Sir Norman Foster would consist from small pre-made modules installed inside 3D-printed anti-radiation barrier on Mars, and then inflated, and connected with air-locked tunnels. White walls and transparent touch screens would be next to hydroponic gardens. A massive wall made by swarms of robot-printers as movable modules, from local a

*Figure 24. Flying Water*
*(© 2018, A. Richardson. Used with permission)*

soil would protect entire communities from sun's radiation and meteorites. Suitports – spacesuits are sealed to the outside surface and accessible from the inside of the habitat.

The sky-scraper 'Marsha, AI Space Factory' – a multilevel cylindrical building made of two shells: an exterior wall (a shield) and interior space for humans: four levels with a long spiral staircase, the ground-level garage for rovers, a lab, a kitchen, and a main communal space. Above are private bedrooms, and a garden. On the top floor, under a skylight is a place for exercise and relaxing. Space between shells diffuse light and has its own air and temperature regulation. Internal, regulated lighting system secures a normal circadian schedule.

A robotic tail 'SpaceHuman' designed to use in zero gravity is inspired by the anatomy of a seahorse. A trio of ribbed tubes made of translucent, flexible silicone have 36 air chambers inflated in different configurations by 12 battery-operated air pumps attached to a belt, so the tail can curve or lengthen, grab onto surfaces, act like a rudder, and pick up objects. The SpaceHuman has an array of sensors on the tail and body and an object-tracking camera on the back. Figure 25 presents a part of a group project "Mars" created by Tatiana Ingino Silberberg.

As a preparation, 12-foot machine 'Icefin,' a torpedo-shaped robot controlled and monitored from above the ice is drilling through 1,100-meter-thick ice. It has cameras and sensors that measure under ice salt content, pressure, oxygen, levels, temperature, and more. Under the West Antarctic Ice Sheet scientists found microbes living in a sub glacial lake. They live in extreme cold and in the darkness; they must get their energy from the earth (Pierce, 2019).

## Project: A 3D Printed Home on Mars: An Egg-Shaped Hotel

A project "An egg-shaped hotel" offers inspiration coming from the developments in new materials in the fields of biology, chemistry, and physics, with themes related to architecture in space. It tells first about biology of an egg in several animal groups, ponders on a chicken or the egg causality dilemma, tells about egg culture related to traditions, language, food, and applications, and then invites the reader to design a model for a livable space on Mars. First, you may want to make a cartoon strip or a funny story about planning a trip to Mars. It would answer questions about who, when, why, etc. Figure 26 presents a sketch by Larry Ward Jr. showing life on Mars.

*Figure 25. Library on Mars*
*(© 2018, T. Ingino Used with permission)*

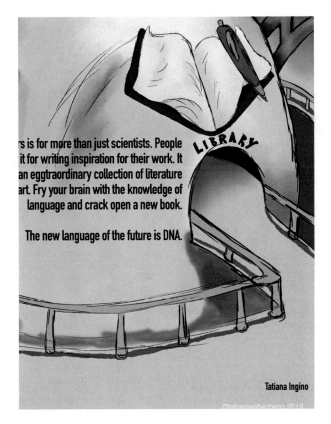

When accomplished as a group project, it may take form of a model for future colony on Mars. Figure 27 is a part of a group project "Mars" presented as a video: Alejandra Ramos, "Coming to Mars – Hotel."

Then it would be a time to link information from the fields of biology, chemistry, physics, and new architecture, and to create a project "An egg-shaped hotel." The first eggs were laid, fertilized, and hatched in the ocean about 250 million years ago. An egg is one of essential biological structures present in majority of animal species including many invertebrates (which have no spine) such as insects, spiders, mollusks, and crustaceans. For this reason, researchers specializing in sciences such as genetics, endocrinology, and zoology study the mystery of this ovoid or round object. Figure 28 shows a work by Ali Alzaid, "Coming to the Egg Hotel."

While working on this project, it's good to know about a visionary architect Paolo Solieri who works on arcology (architecture + ecology) and on a

*Figure 26. Life on Mars*
*(© 2018, L. Ward Jr. Used with permission)*

*Figure 27. Coming to the hotel on Mars*
*(© 2018, A. Ramos. Used with permission)*

*Figure 28. Coming to the Egg Hotel on Mars*
*(© 2018, A. Alzaid. Used with permission)*

futuristic utopian city in Arizona desert. Arcosanti – an urban laboratory (https://arcosanti.org/) begun in 1970 and continues to be developed as an experiential learning center and walk-through demonstrations of how to pursue efficient "lean" alternatives to urban sprawl.

Curvature of an egg puzzles mathematicians and topologists. A chicken eggshell has an asymmetric shape close to an oval. In geometry, an oval is a two-dimensional closed curve that may have one or two axes of symmetry. The three-dimensional surface is called ovoid; it can be made by rotating an oval curve around one of its axes of symmetry. With two axes of symmetry, the figure looks similar from both ends, while with an only one axis of symmetry it resembles a chicken eggshell, having one end somehow pointed. An egg shaped in plaster serves as an assignment in sculpting at art departments aimed to develop in students' capability to attain a demanded shape, in accordance with Michelangelo's saying that a sculpture is hidden in a block of a marble and an artist must extract it from the inside of it.

For those interested in ethnography and cultural anthropology egg is a theme existing in celebrations, festivities, and decorations. In everyday conversations, there are sayings about eggs, such as 'an egg smarter than a hen,' or 'what was first: an egg or a hen?' A saying, 'he is a good egg' means that this person has a special quality. Decoration of eggshells or hard-boiled eggs is popular in many parts of the world: in Central and Eastern Europe, also in countries that are influenced by the culture of Persia; eggs are decorated with dyeing, painting, or spray-painting. By decorating the hollow shell, one may make an imitation of Fabergé eggs, jeweled eggs created in 1885-1917 by Peter Carl Fabergé (Faber, 2008). Patterns with ovoid shapes can be found in the Fin-de-Siècle Art, Art Deco, and also Surrealism.

A form of an egg is very fragile but at the same geometry behind its construction makes it sturdy and hard to break. Following this idea an Italian architect from the Renaissance Filippo Brunelleschi constructed a dome, a cupola for the Florence Cathedral. The shell supports an access for the air, and thus permits the natural growth of an embryo. Also, a white part of an egg makes great glue, while a yellow part mixed with some pigment creates old-fashioned tempera paint. The egg tempera paints are still made and used. The egg base colors don't decay like the water-based paints; they can be still seen in museums. Eggs consolidate also foods such as meat pie. The role of yolk in eggs may vary in different types of animals. Scientists believe that a yolk in human eggs is a remainder of phylogenetical processes going in the earlier types of animals. To scientists, phylogenesis is a process of evolutionary development of organisms. Phylogenetics studies this process through the molecular sequencing data, and by collecting morphological data about the species, populations of organisms, and relations between their structures.

One may ask, when nutrition from the yolk is necessary. On the one hand in non-mammalian vertebrates (such as birds, reptiles, amphibians, and fishes) the development of the offspring depends on nutrients stored in egg yolk. Thus, the food source for the developing chicken embryo is the yolk of an egg, which nourishes the embryo as it grows. On the other hand, mammals nourish their developing offspring during pregnancy through placenta, and later on due to the lactation. The eggs of mammals, developing after fertilization from the immature oocytes show evidence of a loss of yolk-dependent nourishment. By means of comparative analyses concerning evolution of genomes and simulation of evolutionary processes, Brawand, Wahli & Kaessmann (2008) evidenced a loss during mammalian evolution (30-70 million years ago) of three ancestral genes encoding the egg yolk precursor protein, vitellogenin, while the milk resource genes appeared in the common mammalian ancestors about 200-310 million years ago. However, the preserved yolk sac in mammals is crucial for the early embryonic development and survival. It transfers to the embryo nutrients and other substances that control its differentiation and functions. Errors in yolk sac development and function could contribute to embryonic malformation, miscarriage and growth diseases (Freyer &

Renfree, 2009). Thus, quite different factors may determine the development of offspring – the subjects in your project. At the same time, contrasting the mammalian and non-mammalian eggs would serve for creating a metaphor in our project. The hotel analogy may be suitable for a chicken egg, while it is the mother's organism that hosts the embryo in mammals.

To begin working on a project, think about eggs of a snake, an ostrich, a cuckoo, or a dinosaur. Think about the egg's structure, and its mechanical, chemical, immunological, antibacterial and thermal features; then translate information gathered about an egg into a concept of a hotel. Choose two kinds of eggs: the first one that has been laid by a bird and the second one belonging to a turtle; turtles dig in holes in wet sand to hide their devoid of eggshell eggs. Mentally inspect these types of eggs from the inside. You will find several kinds of matter and various structures; you can find reasons why their properties have developed in a specific way. An eggshell contains mostly calcium carbonate, and a cuticle – an outer membrane on the eggshell protects an egg from bacteria. Membranes inside the shell also form barriers to bacteria. Figure 29 presents a ER room drawn by Sarah.

In models for the Mars housing one may think about shields against radiation and layers securing temperature regulation. Albumen, an egg white, protects the yolk and the embryo against stress and shocks; this factor is truly important on Mars. A yolk feeds the developing embryo; also, it contains an

*Figure 29. An ER on Mars*
*(© 2018, S. Hiller. Used with permission)*

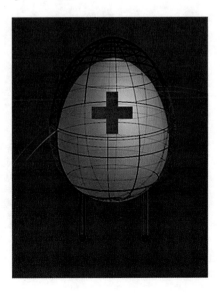

**antibody** called antiglobulin (IgY) that protects the embryo and hatchling from the microorganism invasion. Think how these concerns can be solved in the projects for Mars. Figure 30 shows another work from a group project – the Artist Lounge in a Hotel 6 on Mars.

Environmental concerns may become vital on Mars. The eggshell removal problems on Earth result from the fact that the US food industry generates hundreds of thousands of tons of shell waste a year. Waste eggshells are used in many ways by pharmaceutical and food industries, as soil conditioner and supplement, animal feed supplement, coating pigments for inkjet printing (Yoo, Kokoszka, Zou, & Hsieh, 2009), low-cost solid catalyst for biodiesel production (Wei, Li, & Xu, 2009), and for adsorbing carcinogenic dyes in wastewater (Ee, 2013). Several ways of the eggshell reuse are advised (Yeager, 2015) such as adding crushed eggshells to coffee grounds to make them less bitter and then composting them and thus adding calcium to the soil; using crushed eggshells as a nontoxic pest control, as a drain cleaner;

*Figure 30. A Group project: Artist Lounge in Hotel 6*
*(© 2018, A. Ursyn. Used with permission)*

*Figure 31. Mars dwelling*
*(© 2018, J. O'Grady. Used with permission)*

when transplanting tomatoes putting crushed eggshells into the hole to prevent the plant ends rot, along with other possibilities. Figure 31 presents another project for a Mars dwelling created by Jakob O'Grady.

Decide what analogy you will create to compare an egg with a hotel on the basis of their common makeup, functions, and processes going on in both these structures. This analogy should be helpful in understanding the underlying biological, physical, and chemical concepts you would picture in both cases. Consider individual organisms inhabiting an egg contrasted with the guests of a hotel. On Figure 32, Moises Gomez proposes including observatory, housing, technology room, food farm, and energy core as main parts of the Egg structure on Mars.

Characterize objects serving to host these subjects. The design of a hotel on Mars may depend on gravity, temperature, climate, and other conditions, with a need of thermal insulation and solar heating. On Figure 33, Kate Bierschwale presents solar heating panels for a hotel on Mars.

Protection from danger provided by an eggshell can be thus compared to accommodation offered to the hotel guests on Mars. The outside walls of the egg are the insulation of the hotel. Metaphors may also include blankets and comforters compared to fat and fatty acids contained in yolks. Figures 34 and 35 present models of dresses for Mars inhabitants.

*Figure 32. Egg Hotel on Mars*
*(© 2018, M. Gomez. Used with permission)*

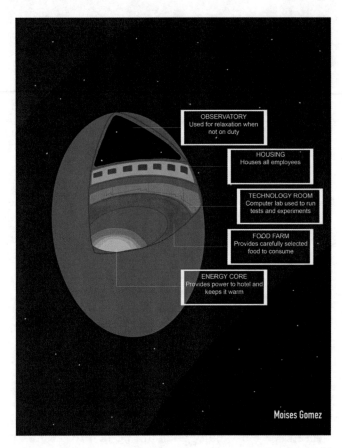

*Figure 33. Solar heating for a home at Mars*
*(© 2018, K. Bierschwale. Used with permission)*

*Figure 34. Dress to Eggspress*
*(© 2018, M. Zilkenat. Used with permission)*

An analogy may be created between the nutrients in the egg yolk for the chicken embryos and the meals served on the hotel premises. Looking at the egg's internal structure one may design a hotel consisting of a large central area set up as a restaurant, which is surrounded by quiet, soundproof rooms providing safe environment for resting. Elevators connecting various areas of the hotel could be compared to the egg's chalazae – structures resembling ropes that keep the yolk centered.

## Nanofabrication: Making Nanoscale Structures

Microelectronics is changing into nanoelectronics. Production of nanoscale structures serves the semi-conductor industry to fabricate integrated electronic circuitry. By making nanoscale sized circuits engineers can put millions of transistors per square inch. This provides more processing per square inch,

*Figure 35. Dress for a Space Hotel*
(© 2018, E. Funk-Breay. Used with permission)

more memory, and faster communication, so computers become faster. Scientists design biologically inspired models, materials, applications, tools, and devices; they apply nanoparticles using advances in nanotechnology. For example, graphene – a form of carbon – is considered the thinnest and the strongest material that can sustain great densities of current, has great thermal conductivity, stiffness, and is impermeable to gases.

Nanoceramic filters allow water purification pushing water through nanotubes or the $10^{-9}$ m to $10^{-11}$ m membranes. In a study on molecular and cellular biology Selvin and his group developed a method for recording the walking motion at a distance of 74 nm for the biggest motor (myosin V), and 16 nm for the smallest motor (kinesin). Dynein takes part in many cellular processes including organelle transport and cell division. The dynein motor converts chemical energy of the ATP hydrolysis to mechanical work (ATP – adenosine triphospate transports energy within cells for metabolic processes)

(Yildiz, Forkey, McKinney, Ha, Goldman, & Selvin, 2003). Yuan, Abuhaimed, Liu, & Smalyukh (2018) consider biological motors the marvels of nature. The authors created molecular bio-inspired motors, which have the comparable nanoscale dimensions, high efficiency, and diverse functions. They describe a self-assembled colloidal motor with a repetitive light-driven rotation of transparent micro-particles immersed in a liquid crystal and powered by a continuous exposure to unstructured ~1 nW light. The liquid crystal's optical axis mechanically couples to the particle's surface, and they jointly rotate as the light's polarization changes.

Nanoparticles can be produced with a "top down" strategy by the mechanical crushing of source material into nanosize bits using a milling process, or a "bottom up" method where structures are built up through chemical processes by growing molecules like crystals in controlled conditions (NanoWerk, 2019). These approaches can be combined into a hybrid nanofabrication.

With a top-down approach, material is removed or added in layers using mechanical or chemical means, such as lithography. Process starts from a large piece and subsequently uses finer and finer tools for creating correspondingly smaller structures (La Rosa, Yan, Fernandez, Wang, & Zegarra, 2013). Basic steps involve deposition causing the film growth, material modification, etching, and lithography, writing where material should be added or removed. Nanolithography is the fabrication of nanometer-scale structures, patterns between 1 and 1,000 nm. Usually, computer programming provides the content for transfer. In some cases there is inherent pattern, such as the self-assembling of an antigen and antibody due to shape, size, and chemical bonding.

With the bottom-up approach, which can often be seen in nature, small components of atomic or molecular dimensions self-assemble together, according to a natural physical principle or an externally applied driving force, to give rise to larger and more organized systems (La Rosa, Yan, Fernandez, Wang, & Zegarra, 2013). Nano structures are built from atoms, molecules, particles, their combinations, and layers. They grow molecule-by molecule and have often the ability to self-assemble spontaneously in response to a trigger. The bottom-up approach involves chemical or physical self-assembly, catalyzed nano-wire (nanotube, about 1.3 nm in diameter) growth, colloidal characterization with the use of optical means, scanning probes, and electron microscopy (NSF NACK Center, 2012). For example, with a bottom-up nanofabrication sequence a nanoparticles may be synthesized made functional, linked with antibodies, or attached to the antigen (PennState modules, 2011).

## Project: A Tale About New Materials

Based on the previous text, write a tale about people who live in a world that is 3D printed of new materials. Tell how they become aware and conscious of their new possibilities. Below is a story about fictional characters, which was imaged by a person who learnt about the ubiquity of new materials.

## New Materials: A Story

A large group of students arrived at the lab after their teacher introduced some new materials and then announced a new tool orientation session. They started using the tools after the teacher's short introduction Their teacher said, "You have to go around that structure because the entrance in this wall is closed," One student reached without effort to a top of an oversized white wall, three times taller than him, and led his own finger straight down to the floor. He thus created in the wall a long bruise, which suddenly widened itself.

As it happened, the tall opening became a source of an unknown material with the changing texture, which allowed the students to cover themselves with it and at the same time to control the form and functioning of this material. Students could monitor its movements and the ways it was changing. When they coated themselves with this strangely changeable matter, they noticed that this textured material was constantly evolving into all sorts of tentacle-like tools, some resembling wings, feel-related apparatuses, appendages, antennas, and also swords.

The surroundings became silver-grayish and at the same time beautifully colorful within a sub-colored grayscale but the metallic tones were not glittery. The material was slowly pouring out; it enveloped the group allowing everybody to create objects, which instantly transformed into applications. Some students used this material like the precious metal clay. For other ones, this stuff resembled and acted like wearable computers and other devices. Students were making imaginative, almost impossible things: they were taking pieces of material coming out of the wall to create objects or decorative elements. One could take a shapeless chunk of this to form a cube, a prop, a feathered wing, an art form, or to create whatever one wished for. Each object started then to do something, and almost perform.

Students looked like warriors when enhanced by structures that were differentiated and varied. They set these forms to motion according to their individual wills. Soon, group choreography became evident in their common march around a constantly expanding courtyard. All students unknowingly formed a random parade and kept waving their hands in a coordinated pulsating unity. They all were moving there together, everyone waving one's own tentacles and appendages in a different fashion, yet in a highly coordinated way. Some could describe it as an octopus's parade, a beautiful ocean polyp, or a medusa with many limbs. Parts were moving, but some bigger force coordinated the overall effect. There wasn't any sign or feeling of aggression; the event was closer to a festivity, celebration, or a parade than a military action.

Suddenly the gap in the wall closed, and all went back to normal. The students started to take their notes supported by visual documentation of their memories. Each one wrote a different story and created a unique set of sketches. "We will move to the geology lab now," the teacher announced.

## 1.3. CARBON AS AN OLD AND A NEW MATERIAL

### Carbon Isomers

Isomers of carbon compounds may have the same molecular formula but different arrangements of atoms in a molecule. There may be also isomerism of atoms, when they have the same atomic number and mass but differ in the energy states. There are two isomers: butane with a straight-line carbon chain and isobutane with a branched carbon chain would have the same formula $C_4H_{10}$. Carbon isomers have different physical properties: melting points, boiling points, densities, and heats of formation.

### Carbon Allotropes

Carbon exists in several physical forms with different molecular configurations, which are called allotropes. They have different physical properties. Carbon has eight different structural forms (allotropes); four of them are common: graphite, diamond, amorphous carbon such as coal, and graphene. Figures 37–40 presented below are infographics by Zahra Alsukairi based on internet encyclopedia: Wolke, R. L. (2014). Carbon. In K. L. Lerner & B. W. Lerner (Eds). The Gale Encyclopedia, 5th Ed., Vol. 2, pp. 777-780. Farmington Hills, MI: Gale.

## Graphite

Graphite is a lattice of forms with six straight sides and angles. Carbon as graphite is the softest of natural substances. Each carbon atom is bonded to three other carbon atoms and arranged at the corners of a network of regular hexagons with a 120-degree C-C-C bond angle. These planar arrangements form a horizontal, hexagonal array (Rossi, 2007). Natural graphite may be crystalline flake graphite arranged in a honeycomb lattice, amorphous, and lump graphite. Natural graphite, mined and then refined, may contain up to 98% of carbon. It is opaque, black, and conducts electricity well so is used, for example in arc lamp electrodes. Natural and synthetic graphite is a good dry lubricant. Graphite, which was earlier called black lead or plumbago has been used in steelmaking, brake linings, as a recyclable anode in batteries, as a lubricant in air compressors, railway track joints, ball bearings, for lining molds for cannonballs, and also in food industry. Graphite has been used for decorating pottery since the 4th millennium B.C. Now synthetic graphite serves as a matrix in nuclear reactors. Carbon nanotubes reinforce plastics and thus many commercial articles. Figure 36 presents an infographic "Graphite" by Zahra Alsukairi.

*Figure 36. Graphite*
*(© 2018, Z. Alsukairi. Used with permission)*

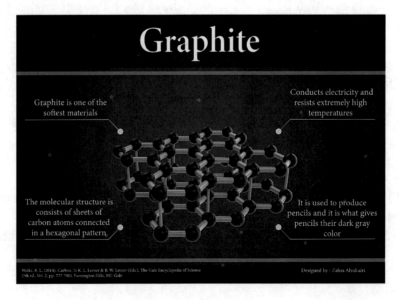

## Diamond

Atoms of diamond make a lattice of triangular pyramids arranged as tetrahedrons, so each atom of carbon is attached to four other carbon atoms (Rossi, 2007). Diamonds were known in China about 2500 BC. Carbon as diamond has the highest thermal conductivity of all materials, poor electrical conductivity, is transparent, and the hardest of natural substances. Diamond is hard and coarse, so it's highly abrasive. Carbon atom in a diamond has covalent bonds with four other carbons; it means each carbon atom bonds to four other carbon atoms, which makes tetrahedrons that form hexagonal rings; this makes diamond extremely strong. Because of its tetrahedral structure, diamond also shows a great resistance to compression (Rossi, 2007). Of the mined diamonds, 80% (20 tons annually) are for industrial use and are unsuitable as gemstones; from the 1950s, tons of synthetic diamonds are produced annually. Synthetic nano crystalline diamond is the hardest material known (Irifune, Kurio, Sakamoto, Inoue, & Sumiya, 2003). Diamond anvil cells using boron-doped metallic diamond electrodes covered with undoped diamond insulating layers serve for electrical transport measurements under high pressure (Matsumoto et al., 2018). Figure 37 presents an infographic "Diamonds" by Zahra Alsukairi.

*Figure 37. Diamonds*
*(© 2018, Z. Alsukairi. Used with permission)*

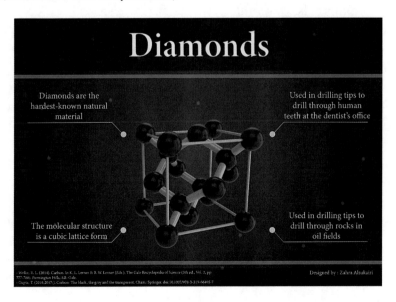

*Figure 38. Amorphous Carbon*
*(© 2018, Z. Alsukairi. Used with permission)*

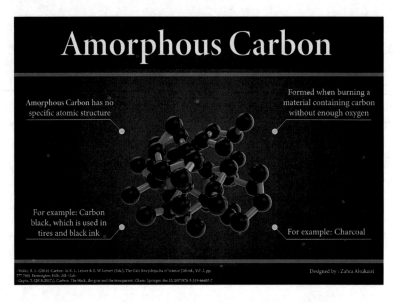

## Amorphous Carbon, Coal

Amorphous carbon, such as coal has no clearly defined form or structure of its particles. Many times amorphous minerals change under high temperature and pressure into metamorphic rocks such as kimberlite – an igneous rock containing diamonds, or granite.

Coal is usually amorphous, without crystalline structure. Coal and powdery or flaky soot (a product of pyrolysis - decomposing by heat) are amorphous forms of carbon. The coal grades in industry depend on the carbon content and include anthracite (about 90% carbon), bituminous coal (75–90% carbon), and soft, brownish lignite (about 55% carbon, often containing traces of plant structures), to say nothing about brown, soil-like peat (turf). Figure 38 presents an infographic "Amorphous Carbon" by Zahra Alsukairi.

## Graphene

Monolayer graphene membranes, and also monolayers of carbon atoms on silicon dioxide, are considered one of the strongest materials ever measured. Graphene can carry electric charges far faster than currently used materials. Graphene has been used as 'electrodes' for solar cells. Thermal conductivity of suspended graphene exceeds that of diamond and graphite, so graphene can be useful in nanoelectronics. Graphene nanoelectronics becomes effective, as nanographene can be carved lithographically and then sandwiched between protective layers (Gomollón-Bel, 2019). Graphene is a sheet of carbon atoms arranged in tightly bound hexagons. Graphene is almost unbreakable, tougher than a diamond, and stretchable like a rubber (Palmer, 2012). A Russian-Dutch scientist Andre Geim and a Russian-British scientist Konstantin Novoselov discovered graphene in 2004, and then shared the 2010 Nobel Prize for physics for studying behavior of this one atom thick sheet of carbon. According to Geim & Novoselov, graphene is a flat monolayer of carbon atoms tightly packed into a two-dimensional (2D) honeycomb lattice, and is a basic building block for graphitic materials of all other dimensionalities. It can be wrapped up into 0D fullerenes, rolled into 1D nanotubes, or stacked into 3D graphite. Geim and Novoselov were praised for playfulness of their approach that involved producing flakes of graphene using sticky tape: they extracted the material from a piece of graphite that can be found in ordinary pencils using adhesive tape, and repeating the tape-trick until they got miniscule flakes of graphene. Three million sheets of graphene loosely held together on top of each other produce 1mm of graphite. Scientists are able to fabricate molecule-scale structures and devices in graphene with atomic precision. The ice-assisted e-beam lithography can be used to pattern very thin materials deposited on substrate surfaces. The procedure can be performed *in situ* in a modified scanning electron microscope. A low energy focused electron beam can locally pattern graphene coated with a thin ice layer. Moreover, photons, x-rays generated by atoms may also come back (which is used in X-ray spectroscopy). Figure 39 presents an infographic "Fullerenes" by Zahra Alsukairi.

The scanning probe tools use the nanoscale probe (a small, sharp tip on the end of a lever that is dragged across a nanoscale object) for the scanning probe microscopy. Nanoscale beams or probes interact with a nano material generating signals that can be processed by a computer into pictures. Examples of such tools are the atomic force microscope AFM that measures forces between atoms, and scanning tunneling microscope STM that uses quantum mechanical tunneling between atoms of the probe and atoms on the scanned surface. The nano-scale tips on scanning probe microscopes (SPMs) allow us to even "see" atoms (PennState modules, 2011). Atoms on the probed surface may be arranged by an STM into a quantum corral, which is about 14 nm in diameter. Christopher Lutz, Donald Eigler, and Michael Crommie

*Figure 39. Fullerenes*
*(© 2018, Z. Alsukairi. Used with permission)*

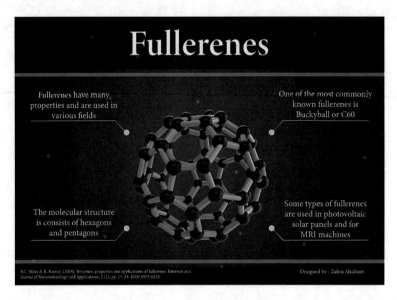

demonstrated for the first time the quantum corral in 1993 by using an elliptical ring of iron atoms on a copper surface. The STM tunneling current can be turned by a computer into a false color STM image of the quantum corral.

A single-layer, two-dimensional graphene interacts wavelengths ranging from ultraviolet to microwave (Xia, Watson, Yan, & 2013). Two-layer graphene may serve as a semiconductor, creating an energy gap between layers, tuned with the electric field. Bi-layer graphenes serve for measuring cosmic microwave background radiation) and for creating photo-thermo-electric detectors working in the far-IR or terahertz region. Terahertz waves are used in airport body scanners and imaging.

A carbon nanotube is a molecule of carbon in form of a hollow cylinder. A carbon nanotube has a diameter of around one or two nanometers; they can be seen using a scanning tunneling microscope. One nanometer (nm) is one billionth, or $10^{-9}$ of a meter. Typical carbon-carbon bond has the length about 0.12-0.15 nm; a DNA double helix has a diameter around 2 nm. Nanotubes and fullerenes are present in structures such as inorganic carbon, DNA, and cell membranes. Both carbon nanotubes and graphene products (such as graphene foams, nanowires, sieves, graphite nanoparticles, or porous carbon) are offered for sale online.

Carbon nanotubes have the nanoscale cross-section areas but they may be many micrometers up to centimeters long. This shapes cause unusual chemical bonding and physical properties, such as great strength: carbon nanotubes are the strongest known materials. Carbon nanotubes may form single wall and multi-wall structures. Nanotube sheets are 250 times stronger than steel and 10 times lighter; they are also stretchable. Many magazines quoted James Hone, Columbia University saying, "It would take an elephant, balanced on a pencil, to break through a sheet of graphene the thickness of Saran Wrap [cling film]" (Mirsky, 2011). As claimed by Richard Van Noorden, "According to the Nobel Prize committee, a hypothetical one-metre-square hammock of perfect graphene could support a four-kilogram cat - the hammock would weigh 0.77 milligrams, less than a cat's whisker, and would be virtually invisible" (Hudson, 2011).

The cylindrical structures of carbon nanotubes have exceptional electrical and thermal properties along with superior mechanical strength. The fabrication of carbon nanotubes serves a variety of applications. Carbon nanotubes are used in the production of memory chips, batteries, and many consumer products such as tennis rackets, badminton rackets, bicycles, compounds to manufacture cars and airplanes, and so forth. Carbon nanotubes distributed on small cement grains provide superior strength of concrete. New methods for producing carbon nanotubes are capable of reducing their price.

## Carbon as Soft Matter

Carbon exists the nanoscale dimension as graphenes, carbon nanotubes, liquid crystals, nanoshells, and other soft matter. Fullerenes, which have atoms arranged in closed shells, include buckyballs (particles that have millions of atoms, with dozens of concentric shells like a set of Russian dolls that fit one into another from the smallest to the biggest one), carbon nanotubes, nanofibers, and carbon nanobuds.

In both the micro-scale and the macro-scale dimensions, pure carbon has the diamond-type bond and the graphite-type bond between carbon atoms (existing for example, in pencil lead). At the nanoscale, carbon develops a specific type of bonding: buckyball bonding, typical of the carbon nanotubes. Covalent bonds between carbon atoms make buckyballs very strong, so they are used to strengthen composites (PennState modules, 2011).

In 1996, nanotech pioneers Richard E. Smalley, Harold Kroto, and Robert Curl won the Nobel Prize for Chemistry for their discovery of a new allotrope of carbon. In 1985, they discovered a molecule made of 60 carbon atoms, about 1 nm in diameter, which Smalley called a buckminsterfullerene or a buckyball because it resembled geodesic domes created in the 1960s by the architect Richard Buckminster Fuller. This discovery opened a new section of chemistry, with applications in astrochemistry, superconductivity, and chemistry/physics material science, for example for catalytic methane activation.

Fullerenes have atoms bonded in a form of an empty sphere, ellipsoid or a tube. Examples of fullerenes are buckminster fullerenes (or buckyballs, spherical molecules where carbon atoms are connected in a pattern of hexagons and pentagons) and carbon nanotubes. The most common buckyball contains 60 carbon atoms and is called C60. Carbon nanotubes are cylindrical fullerenes, usually a few nanometers wide (tens of thousands times smaller than the diameter of human hair) but they may be micrometers up to centimeters long. Single walled carbon nanotubes are the rolled sheets of graphene. Multi-walled nanotubes take form of the parchment or Russian doll (Matryoshka doll) model; their production is cheaper.

Smalley envisioned a power grid of nanotubes that would distribute electricity from solar farms. He believed nanoscale missiles would target cancer cells in human body. He spoke this on June 1999, but he died of non-Hodgkin lymphoma on October 2005. The IBM Research–Zurich scientists Gross, Mohn, Moll, Liljeroth, & Meyer provided images of single carbon molecules and their chemical structure with unprecedented atomic resolution by probing the short-range chemical forces with use of noncontact atomic force microscopy. They could imagine not only the physical shape of a single carbon nanotube but even the bonds to the hydrogen atoms could be seen (Palmer, 2009).

Fullerene C60 is a black solid that sublimes at 800 K and is soluble in common solvents such as benzene, toluene or chloroform. Nasibulin et al. (2007) synthesized NanoBuds – a hybrid material that combines fullerenes and single-walled carbon nanotubes into a structure where the fullerenes are covalently bonded to the outer sidewalls of carbon nanotubes. Nanobuds have combined mechanical and electrical properties of both these structures. Buckyball bonding is a specific type of bonding typical of the carbon nanotubes.

Natural and engineered small particles range from one nanometer to tens of microns. In atmosphere, where there is from a few to a few thousands of small particles/cm$^3$, they impact both warming and cooling of the climate. In Earth sub-surface, they impact soil and water quality. Small particles have an effect on catalysis and reaction engineering, material design, and synthesis. Isotopic signature (with krypton or xenon isotopes) of some nanodiamonds indicate they were formed outside the solar system, whether in supernova or in interstellar medium. The noble gas atoms such as neon can also be seen in a monolayer of carbon when it is trapped inside $^{60}C$ cages that were formed at the same time as the nanodiamonds.

The developments in nanoscale and molecular-scale technologies let us study the nanoscale objects: liquid crystals, soft matter, nanoshells, and carbon nanotubes. We may learn about structures and actions going in the nanoscale and how can we use nanoparticles and nanotechnology. These technologies make a background for progress in energy conservation in micro and nano scale. Nanotechnology can impact cancer treatment, clinical neuroscience, tissue engineering, drug delivery, and diagnostics.

## Carbon in a Nanoscale: Nano Computers

Carbon in the nanoscale dimension in the form of carbon nanotubes plays some role in designing nanocomputers. A nanocomputer has its parts no bigger than a few nanometers. There are no commercially available nanocomputers yet; they exist now both in computer science laboratories and in science fiction. Nanocomputers might be built using mechanical, electronic, biochemical, or quantum mechanics principles. Nanosize chips would hold thousands of bits of memory. That would involve thousands of junctions, each of which would represent a "0" or "1" in digital language. Individual junctions would open and close billions of times per second, hundreds of gigahertz. A hybrid approach would allow making the nanotube junction switches by combining silicon nano wires with carbon nanotubes, to make it easier to connect switches on a chip and chips in the computer.

Till now, chips have been made of silicon, which is the main ingredient of sand and is available in large quantities on Earth. Now, silicon will have to be replaced in order to further miniaturize electronic systems and make them faster. Silicon transistors in computers may be replaced by transistors based on carbon nanotubes. Application of carbon nanotubes circuit will possibly provide a ten-times improvement in energy efficiency over silicon. However, nanotube transistors display material imperfections inherent to carbon nanotubes. Some carbon nanotubes are semiconducting and they can be used in transistors. Metallic carbon nanotubes (that are not semiconducting) may often cause short circuits, excessive power leakage, and susceptibility to noise. Existing nanotube synthesis techniques do not produce exclusively semiconducting nanotube solutions. Teams of engineers are now working on securing the carbon nanotubes' viability to complement silicon. Connecting nanotubes to form large circuits creates problems with manufacturing good metal contacts for the tubes. Concerns are also about the perfect alignment of nanotubes.

## Carbon in New Materials

Carbon is often present in synthetic fibers, which may comprise small molecules or polymers, mostly synthesized ones. They include mineral fibers such as made of carbon, glass, basalt, or some metals, as well as polymers, which include acrylic, aramid, microfiber, nylon, polyester, polyethylene, spandex, and several other materials. Some fibers have been also artificially made from cellulose, for example acetate and triacetate, art silk, bamboo derived cellulose products, and rayon of several kinds. Synthetic fibers are usually formed through the melt-spinning process or by forcing synthetic materials through holes to make threads.

## Carbon Isotopes

Carbon has three naturally occurring isotopes (isotopes have in their nuclei equal numbers of protons but different numbers of neutrons), with $^{12}C$ and $^{13}C$ being stable; carbon $^{14}C$ is a radioactive isotope decaying with a half-life of about 5,730 years (half-life tells time isotope falls to half of its original radioactivity).

Radiocarbon dating, invented in 1949 by Willard Libby (the 1960 Nobel Prize) is a $^{14}C$-based radiometric method of estimating the age of materials aged up to 58,000–62,000 years. Older samples contain too small number of remaining intrinsic $^{14}C$ carbon. Carbon dating allows estimate the age of organic remains and artifacts, objects of cultural or historical value, if they contain carbon. Scientists collected wood of the same age (based on the tree ring analysis) to increase accuracy of the technique. They have also measured radiocarbon in stalactites and stalagmites (called speleothems) using both $^{14}C$ carbon dating method and the uranium-thorium dating to obtain radiocarbon calibration curves (Hoffmann et al., 2010). Ancient fossilized animal and human footprints in Acahualinka, Nicaragua has been first estimated as 5,000 years old and later determined as 2,100 years old.

# $^{14}$C in Art History: Carbon Footprint

The carbon dating and lead dating supports scientists in estimating the age of earliest known drawings from 30,000 to 10,000 B.C, which were found on the walls of caves in France, Spain, Sulawesi in Indonesia (Marchant, 2016), and also cross-hatched etchings in South Africa from 10,000 to 70,000 years (Stezano, 2018). The Chauvet-Pont-d'Arc Cave in the southern France, discovered in 1994, contains the rock art, a treasure trove of Paleolithic masterwork paintings, prints, charcoal drawings of different animal species such as horses, lions, rhinos and bears, etched into the cave's walls, and also fossilized remains, and markings of animals, some of which are now extinct (Herzog, 2019; 2012). Findings based on an analysis called geomorphological and chlorine-36 dating ($^{36}$Cl Cosmic Ray Exposure) shown that most of the art works were created by people who lived 28,000 to 40,000 years ago, in the Aurignacian culture of the early stages of the Upper Paleolithic, Late Stone Age; later on, an overhanging cliff began collapsing 29,000 years ago and did so repeatedly over time, definitively sealing the entrance to humans around 21,000 years ago. "This study confirms that the Chauvet cave paintings are the oldest and the most elaborate ever discovered, challenging our current knowledge of human cognitive evolution" (Sadier et al., 2012; Agence France-Presse, 2012). Bon et al. (2008) wrote, "We collected bone samples from the Paleolithic painted cave of Chauvet-Pont d'Arc (France), which displays the earliest known human drawings, and contains thousands of bears remains. We selected a cave bear sternebra, radiocarbon dated to 32,000 years before present, from which we generated overlapping DNA fragments assembling into a 16,810-base pair mitochondrial genome. ... our study establishes the Chauvet-Pont d'Arc Cave as a new reservoir for Paleogenetic studies".

A film director Werner Herzog created in 2010 a documentary film about Chauvet Cave, *Cave of Forgotten Dreams* (Herzog, 2019) and won Best Documentary Award by several film critics groups. He rendered in 3D the curvature of the rocks to enhance the texture and depth of the art works on the cave walls. As described on his webpage, Herzog had been mesmerized, as a boy in his native Germany by a book about cave paintings that he saw in a store window. He wrote, "The deep amazement it inspired in me is with me to this day. I remember a shudder of awe possessing me as I opened its pages." (Herzog, 2012). Cave of Forgotten Dreams was triggered by a Judith Thurman's article in The New Yorker based on photos and interviews. Herzog became the first filmmaker permitted by the French Ministry of Culture to enter the cave, however under restrictions. All people had to wear special suits and shoes that have had no contact with the exterior, stay on a two-foot-wide walkway, using only a small 3D-camera rig and three battery-powered light sources. Because of near-toxic levels of $CO_2$ and radon in the cave, the crew could enter the cave for only a few hours each day. The cave explorers found, among rock paintings on a cave wall, some hand imprints with one finger shorter than others. This could be considered the first signature in art. In his film "Roma (1972) awarded at Festival de Cannes, BAFTA (British Academy of Film and Television Arts), and other festivals, an Italian film director and scriptwriter Federico Fellini devoted one episode to a sudden discovery of ancient Roman frescoes and sculptures that would conceivably happen during digging a tunnel for an underground metro. When the workers stunned by the majesty of the portraits on the frescoes pointed their flashlights toward the paintings in the newly discovered chambers, the faces on the walls became slowly bleached, whiten by exposure to light, and finally they disappeared. We experience this trauma when we lose our unsaved data due to a power failure and all we worked on for hours becomes a fraction of our memory.

The radiocarbon dating provided a key marker for the disastrous volcanic eruption (Minoan eruption of Santorini) that devastated the island of Santorini (also called Thera) close to the coast of Crete, and implications for the chronology of the Eastern Mediterranean cultures from the Bronze Age in the second millennium BC. The radiocarbon dating analysis of an olive tree buried beneath a lava flow from the volcano indicate, that the eruption occurred between 1627 BC and 1600 BC with a 95% degree of probability (Friedrich et al., 2006; Manning et al., 2006).

The carbon dating and lead dating mean a set of radioactive dating methods. They have been used to verify authenticity of paintings, and thus public appraisal of the rendering talents of copyists, imitators, and forgers diminished with the improvement of technologies. Talents of the Dutch forger Han van Meegeren who painted 'just discovered unknown works' of Vermeer were appreciated in his times, in both the artistic and deceptive terms, as equally skilled as those of the Masters; he was selling his paintings at high prices after he was unmasked as a counterfeiter. Van Meegeren created 'new' Vermeer's, Frans Hals' and other masters' paintings on old canvases from the old times and applying similar chemicals. Investigations made after his death with the use of the radioactive lead dating method revealed small differences in isotope composition of lead. It was caused by additional trace elements that were different in the 17th century than those that are present in contemporary lead pigments. Other investigations, including a gas chromatography method confirmed the forgery. One may ponder why talented people like van Meegeren preferred to forge and sign masterpieces instead of developing their own style, and whether they would still like to do it having a computer as a tool, when computers make possible to do the task even without so great manual dexterity. Han van Meegeren and many other producers of counterfeits have been selling their works for millions until they were recognized as frauds; then the buyers felt they lost millions while still being the owners of these so-called original works.

## Carbon in Cosmos

Carbon is one of the most plentiful elements in the universe after hydrogen, helium, and oxygen (by mass). There is a lot of carbon in the Sun, stars, and comets. Because of this relatively short half-life, $^{14}C$ is virtually absent in ancient rocks (half-life is the amount of time required to reduce a quantity by half). It develops in atmosphere at altitudes of 9–15 km by interaction of nitrogen with cosmic rays. Formation of the carbon atomic nucleus occurs within giant and supergiant stars in extreme temperatures, in a triple alpha process, a set of nuclear fusion reactions where three alpha particles (helium-4 nuclei) are transformed into carbon. The shortest-lived of isotope is $^{8}C$, which has a half-life of $1.98739 \times 10^{-21}$ seconds (Barwinski, 2019).

Stars are spheres of plasma made of ionized molecules and atoms of gas, and consisting mainly from hydrogen and helium. Interstellar CO molecule is the most abundant molecule after hydrogen both in atomic or molecular form $H_2$. The CO molecule is asymmetric and thus it radiates spectral lines easier to detect than hydrogen lines (Combes, 1991, p. 195). In astrophysics, it is commonly used tracer of molecular gas in the interstellar medium of galaxies and provides information about the molecular clouds in which stars emerge.

In 2012, carbon monoxide in the cosmos has been mapped for the first time (http://www.bbc.co.uk/news/science-environment-17027949) and the first map was made, of carbon monoxide in the cosmos. The Planck space telescope, which was designed to look at the background glow in the cosmos in an effort to understand how it formed, can help spot star-forming regions where carbon monoxide glows brightly.

Figure 40 presents a work entitled "Winter Solstice" by Anna Ursyn. The day of winter solstice is the shortest, and we have the least sunlight in the year.

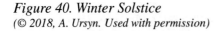

*Figure 40. Winter Solstice*
*(© 2018, A. Ursyn. Used with permission)*

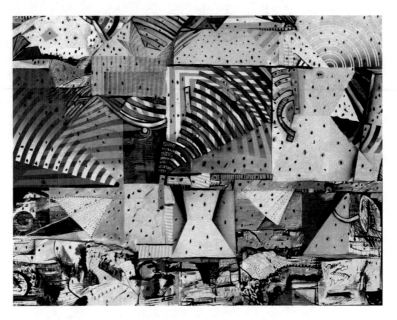

## Organic Carbon

Organic chemistry is about carbon containing compounds and thus it is also about us. Scientists described almost ten million organic compounds formed by carbon. On the Earth carbon is the main constituent of many minerals and biological molecules. Inorganic carbon is contained in carbonate rocks: the hard sedimentary rocks such as limestones, the translucent sedimentary rocks dolomites, white crystalline marbles, and in carbon dioxide ($CO_2$); it occurs in organic deposits such as coal, peat, oil, and a natural gas methane hydrate. Carbon is present in all life forms and is crucial for life on Earth because it forms many bonds to form complex organic molecules (carbon makes up to four bonds per atom). Strong carbon-carbon bonds to other carbon atoms combine into long, strong, stable, rich in energy chains and rings, such as in a DNA that is made of two intertwined molecules built around a carbon chain. The carbon exchange results from the chemical, physical, geological, and biological processes.

Carbon exists in the atmosphere as carbon dioxide (810 gigatons of carbon; one gigaton $= 10^9$ metric tons, $= 10^{15}$ grams), in water bodies (36,000 gigatons of carbon), and in the biosphere (1,900 gigatons of carbon). The amount of carbon in simple organic compounds (carbon plus hydrogen) of hydrocarbons, such as coal, petroleum, and natural gas, is around 900 gigatons. Carbon dioxide is the most important human-contributed greenhouse gas (which absorbs and emits infrared radiation) resulting in the greenhouse effect.

Carbon combines with hydrogen and oxygen into carbohydrates, which are present as soluble, crystalline sugars, starch, and cellulose; plant lignans; chitins found in exoskeletons (external covering of bodies, in contrast to internal skeletons such as in humans) of crabs, lobsters, shrimps, insects, shells of mollusks, and forming walls of fungi. Carbohydrates are present also in alcohols, fats, aromatic esters, carotenoids - pigments found in plants, fungi, and bacteria; and terpenes produced by many plants (especially conifers) and insects such as termites and some butterflies.

A chemical element carbon C has atomic number 6. Carbon nucleus contains 6 protons (subatomic particles present in atomic nuclei, having positive electric charge equal to the negative charge of an electron) and 8 neutrons (which have the mass similar to that of a proton, but do not have an electric charge). Carbon isotopes have 2–16 neutrons. As a nonmetallic element, carbon in its solid form is dull and brittle, forms acidic molecules with oxygen, and has a tendency to attract electrons, making four electrons available to form very strong covalent chemical bonds (with pairs of electrons shared between atoms). It does not react with oxidizers at room temperature; when heated, it forms carbon oxides, which are used in the iron and steel industry. Carbon atoms can form covalent bonds to many other types of atoms and form many materials such as wood or body cells.

## Reservoirs of Carbon: The Biosphere

The exchange of carbon includes:

- Respiration.
- Transpiration.
- Combustion.
- Decomposition.

The biosphere contains organic carbon in living and dead organisms, as well as in soils: about 500 gigatons of carbon is in plants and other living organisms and approximately 1,500 gigatons in soil. Carbon in the terrestrial biosphere is mostly organic; the soil contains also inorganic carbon such as calcium carbonate ($CaCO_3$). Combustion and respiration cause the release of organic carbon into the atmosphere. Organic carbon may turn into the inert carbon in soil and then be washed into oceans or return to the atmosphere.

Humans influence the carbon cycle by changing the terrestrial and oceanic biosphere. By affecting the ecosystem's productivity they change its ability to remove carbon from the atmosphere. They modify the land use, change the land cover, and reduce the ecosystems' biodiversity and resilience to environmental stresses. Forests hold large amounts of carbon; removing them for agricultural, industrial, or urbanization related purpose causes that more carbon stays in the atmosphere. Air pollution, temperature increase, agricultural practices, and land erosion are increasing decomposition processes and washing carbon out of soils to the atmosphere.

Carbon (as $CO_2$ and CO) returns to the atmosphere after burning of a substance such as coal, wood or an active volcano content. Ash is another residue left after burning, as a solid remains of fire, incineration, or combustion; for example, in a fireplace or at the end of a cigarette. Ash remaining after a scientific sample is burned is used in analytical chemistry to get information about its content. One may find many cultural and social connotations in literature, religions, and cultural rituals, related to ash and the remains left from cremation.

## Reservoirs of Carbon: The Air

The atmosphere contains two main forms of carbon: carbon dioxide ($CO_2$) and methane ($CH_4$) both absorb and retain heat intensifying the greenhouse effect. $CO_2$ is more important greenhouse gas because methane is more short-lived and its concentration is much lower. Plant respiration produces $CO_2$, which falls in raindrops and reacts with the atmosphere's water forming carbonic acid ($H_2CO_3$). This acidifies rocks and increases the ocean acidity, which affects ocean biosystems and slows the biological precipitation of $CaCO_3$. By burning fossil fuels, manufacturing concrete and other materials humans increase the amount of carbon in the atmosphere, mostly as $CO_2$.

## Reservoirs of Carbon: Hydrosphere

The hydrosphere includes fresh water systems and the oceans with inorganic carbon dissolved in water and contained in living and dead marine biota. Oceans contain almost as much carbon as the lithosphere. The surface and the deep layers of the oceans contain dissolved $CO_2$ from the atmosphere and rivers (turned into $H_2CO_3$) and organic carbon, which is produced by organisms through photosynthesis, exchanged throughout the food chain, or settled in the ocean's deep, carbon rich layers as dead soft tissue or in shells as $CaCO_3$. Absorption of $CO_2$ in oceans limits its rise in the atmosphere caused by humans. Humans affect the oceanic carbon cycle. Higher ocean temperatures due to the human-induced climate change modify ecosystems. Acid rain and polluted runoff from agriculture and industry have devastating effects on sensitive ecosystems such as coral reefs. It limits both the ocean's ability to absorb carbon from the atmosphere and reduces oceanic biodiversity.

## Carbon Monoxide (CO)

Carbon monoxide (CO) has no color, odor, or taste, and is slightly lighter than air. Atoms of carbon and oxygen are connected by a triple bond. However, when in air, carbon monoxide combines with oxygen and forms carbon dioxide $CO_2$ and ozone $O_3$; it is part of photochemical smog and also increases ground ozone level according to reaction $CO + 2O_2 > CO_2 + O_3$. It occurs naturally in the lowest parts of atmosphere due to photochemical reactions that produce about $5 \times 10^{12}$ kilograms per year; daytime concentration in atmosphere is twice more during a day than in darkness (Weinstock & Niki, 1972). It is dissolved in molten volcanic rock at high pressures in the Earth's mantle. It is also present in forest fires, man-made fires, and other forms of combustion associated with vehicles, generators (many of cases occurring during power outages due to severe weather), furnaces, ranges, fireplaces, water heaters, room heaters, or mowers. It is also temporary pollutant in some urban areas. Carbon monoxide forms due to incomplete burning of wood, coal, charcoal, oil, paraffin, propane, natural gas, and trash, when there is not enough oxygen to produce $CO_2$.

CO normal level in human blood is 0% to 3% and is higher in smokers. In higher concentration, it is toxic to humans and animals because it combines with hemoglobin (protein that transports oxygen in blood of vertebrates) to produce carboxy-hemoglobin, which cannot deliver oxygen to tissues and also to myoglobin (a red protein in muscle cells that delivers and stories oxygen) and mitochondrial enzyme cytochrome oxidase. Therefore, there is a danger of poisoning when coal is burning in a stove or a car is idling in a closed garage. On average, hundreds of people in the United States die every year from CO produced by non-automotive consumer products. Previously, coal gas containing CO was used for domestic lighting, cooking, and heating, and now iron smelting in steel plants still produces CO as a byproduct, blast-furnace gas, which is flammable and toxic (Ayres & Ayres, 2010, p. 36). Some microorganisms (bacteria and archaea) living in extreme conditions can metabolize carbon monoxide.

Carbon monoxide is produced in organism as part of normal metabolism (when produced during hemoglobin breakdown) and may possibly have biological functions as a biological regulator of several functions: as a vascular growth factor, anti-inflammatory agent, and blood vessel relaxant. CO is associated with many functions in the immune, respiratory, reproductive, gastrointestinal, kidney, and liver systems. According to Wu & Wang (2005), communication inside a cell and also among cells occurs by conducting mechanical, electrical, or chemical signals. Chemical communication includes hormones (acting on distant targets via circulation in endocrine mode), autacoids (that act on the same cells from which they are produced, such as prostaglandins, adenosine, and platelet-activating factor), and transmitters (regulation for adjacent cells or cells where transmitters are produced).

Physiological functions of CO involve acting as a signaling molecule in the neuronal system: neuronal activities such as regulation of neurotransmitters (ACH, catecholamines, serotonin, histamine, glutamate, glycine, GABA, and ATP or its metabolites), neuropeptide release, learning and memory, and odor response adaptation. Abnormalities in CO metabolism have been linked to a variety of diseases including neuro degenerations, hypertension, heart failure, and inflammation (Wu & Wang, 2005).

Solomon Snyder & Christopher Ferris examined carbon monoxide CO, nitrogen monoxide (nitric oxide) NO and d-serine as candidate neurotransmitters and offered insights regarding novel definitions of neurotransmitters or neuromodulators. As described by the authors, a transmitter is a molecule, released by neurons or glial cells (non-neuronal, connective cells that support and protect neurons) that physiologically influences the electrochemical state of adjacent cells. Outside the CNS, those adjacent target cells need not be neurons and, in most instances, would be smooth muscle or glandular cells (Snyder & Ferris, 2000, p. 1750).

Industrial carbon monoxide's production includes many methods for obtaining CO under different names. A producer gas, a low-grade fuel containing nitrogen and carbon monoxide, is formed during passing air or air-and-steam through red-hot carbon. Water gas, a fuel gas consisting mainly carbon monoxide and hydrogen, forms during passing steam over incandescent, white-hot coke. Synthesis gas, a mixture of hydrogen, carbon monoxide, and sometimes also carbon dioxide, serves for producing synthetic chemicals such as ammonia or methanol that are used for making feedstock – raw material for manufacturing industrial, chemical, or pharmaceutical products. Several laboratory methods also allow obtaining carbon monoxide. As an industrial gas, it has many other applications in bulk chemicals manufacturing, for example, for producing fuels used as replacement for petrol, or as color additive in meat and fish packaging, to keep them looking fresh (because it combines with myoglobin – oxygen carrying and storing red pigment, a protein similar to hemoglobin, present in muscle tissues).

The consumption of fossil fuels results in energy-related carbon dioxide ($CO_2$) emissions. According to EIA, U.S. Energy Information Administration, concentrations of $CO_2$ in the atmosphere have increased by about 40% since the mid-1800s (EIA, 2018). According to the Intergovernmental Panel on Climate Change in the United Nations (IPCC, 2019), concentrations of $CO_2$, $CH_4$, and $N_2O$ now substantially exceed the highest concentrations recorded in ice cores during the past 800,000 years. The mean rates of increase in atmospheric concentrations over the past century are, with very high confidence, unprecedented in the last 22,000 years.

Greenhouse gases in an atmosphere trap heat from the sun and warm the planet's surface. They are mostly water vapor ($H_2O$), carbon dioxide ($CO_2$), methane ($CH_4$), ozone ($O_3$), and nitrous oxide ($N_2O$). Nitrogen ($N_2$ comprising 78% of the dry atmosphere) and oxygen ($O_2$ comprising 21%) exert almost no greenhouse effect. Most of the U.S. greenhouse gas emissions are related to energy consumption, and most of those are $CO_2$. Greenhouse gases absorb and emit thermal infrared radiation (with longer wavelength than that of visible light). The greenhouse effect results from this: absorption and re-radiation of heat toward the Earth surface and lower atmosphere, and the following elevation of the Earth temperature. In the United States, about three-quarters of human-caused greenhouse gas emissions came from the burning of fossil fuels in energy use driven by economic growth, heating and cooling needs, and electricity generation. Energy consumption causes 87% of the U.S. greenhouse gas emission, which is growing by about 1% per year. Levels of greenhouse gases have increased by about 40% since industrialization began around 150 years ago. A cap-and-trade program (which increases the costs of using fossil fuels) places a limit (or cap) on the total amount of emissions, to reduce polluting emissions through a system of allowances that can be traded to minimize costs to affected sources. Artificial photosynthesis could possibly help limit carbon emissions (BioPhotonics, 2019, 23).

## The Fast and Slow Carbon Cycles

Scientists describe the fast and slow carbon cycle.

### The Fast Carbon Cycle

Processes going in the carbon cycle regulate the $CO_2$ concentration in the atmosphere in a natural way. Carbon geochemical cycle describes the processes that sustain life on Earth. It is generally accepted that the rising levels of $CO_2$ concentration from 280 ppm in 1800 to almost 400 ppm (ppm, a measure of concentration means 'part(s) per million') result in global warming, so lowering the amount of $CO_2$ in the atmosphere may re-balance the carbon cycle. The fast carbon cycle moves $10^{16}$ to $10^{17}$ grams of carbon per year (NASA Earth Observatory, 2019).

The fast carbon cycle includes the plants and phytoplankton (microscopic organisms in the ocean); they are the main components of the fast, biological/physical carbon cycle, which operates at the time scale of days to thousands of years. The fast carbon cycle presents the movement of carbon through life forms or the biosphere such as animal tissues, between land, atmosphere, and oceans, in billions of tons of carbon per year (with diurnal and seasonal oscillations). It is caused both by natural fluxes and human actions.

### The Slow Carbon Cycle

The geological component of the carbon cycle operates at a slow pace, at the time scale of 100-200 million years, yet it determines the amount of carbon in the atmosphere, and thus of global temperature. On average, $10^{13}$ to $10^{14}$ grams (10–100 million metric tons) of carbon move through the slow carbon cycle every year (NASA Earth Observatory, 2019). Tectonic activity, that may last hundreds of millions of years, moves great amounts of carbon between rocks, soil, ocean, and atmosphere. There is carbon stored in lithosphere as rocks from the time when the earth was formed, and the organic carbon, mostly as limestone and its derivatives resulting from the sedimentation of $CaCO_3$ stored in the shells of marine shell-building (calcifying) organisms (such as corals) and plankton (like coccolithophores or foraminifera), which sink after death to the seafloor. Calcium ions combine with carbonic acid into calcium carbonate that becomes limestone or its metamorphic form, marble. There are also fossilized organic material and sediment buried under high heat and pressure, some fossils aging millions, sometimes hundreds of millions of years. Carbon moves with rain from the atmosphere to the lithosphere as carbonic acid ($H_2CO_3$) and causes chemical weathering: calcium, magnesium, potassium, or sodium ions flow in rivers to the ocean.

Humans strongly alter the carbon cycle, mostly through $CO_2$ emissions into the atmosphere that are exceeding natural fluctuations (NASA Earth Observatory, 2019; Falkowski et al., 2000), altering weather patterns, influencing oceanic chemistry, and affecting global climate, especially temperature. The use of fossil fuels has accelerated since the industrial revolution and increased carbon accumulation in the atmosphere.

Scientists estimate there is organic matter beneath the Antarctic Ice Sheet, up to 14 kilometers thick and weighting billions of tons, possibly the same order of magnitude as in the Arctic permafrost. It contains metabolically active Archaea (single-cell microorganisms) that support the degradation of organic carbon to methane. That means organic carbon is probably being metabolized beneath the ice by microbes to carbon dioxide and methane gas. It may play a part in the global climate warming because of the ice-sheet deterioration.

## Carbon in Fossil Fuels

Carbon is the 15th most abundant element in the Earth crust, present in great amounts in fossil fuels – coal, petroleum, and natural gas. Fossil fuels result from decomposition of the large quantities of organisms, mostly zooplankton, algae, and plants. Microorganisms break down organic matter in the absence of oxygen (which is called anaerobic digestion). Organisms and resulting fossil fuels, mostly buried below the Earth surface underneath sedimentary rock, undergo intense heat and pressure. They are up to 650 million years old (Halbouty, 2004). Decomposing organic matter provides an abundance of hydrocarbons – organic compounds built from hydrogen and carbon. They can be gaseous like methane or propane, liquid such as benzene, solid (for example paraffin wax), or polymers (e.g., polyethylene or polystyrene). Saturated (without double or triple bonds in a molecule) hydrocarbons, along with other organic compounds, occur in abundance in crude oil and are basis of petroleum fuels existing in geologic formations. Oil provides 93% of the energy used for transportation, but only about 1% of the energy used to generate electric power.

## Carbon in Living Organisms

We are all made of carbon (and of water as well). Carbon is second element (18% by mass) after oxygen (65% by mass) that makes human body. Human cells consist of 65-90% water; apart from it they are composed of organic molecules containing carbon. Organic carbon is a crucial component and a source of energy stored in carbon bonds and used by all living beings. Organisms (called autotrophs) extract carbon from the air in the form of $CO_2$ converting it into organic carbon and building nutrients. Using the sunlight's energy plants and plankton absorb and combine $CO_2$ and water to form sugar ($CH_2O$) and oxygen: $CO_2 + H_2O + energy = CH_2O + O_2$. Glucose, fructose, and other sugars, through processes such as respiration, create fuel for further metabolic processes. Plants can break down the sugar to get the energy. Other organisms (called heterotrophs) cannot fix carbon and must obtain organic carbon by consuming other organisms.

In chemical reactions, also those involving carbon, matter releases or absorbs energy. For example, energy release in the form of heat or light happens when methane $CH_4$ is combusted in the presence of oxygen $O_2$ into carbon dioxide $CO_2$ and water $H_2O$ ($CH_4 + 2O_2 > CO_2 + 2H_2O + energy$). Energy absorption happens for example, during electrolysis of water, when water $H_2O$ plus energy changes into hydrogen $H_2$ and oxygen $O_2$ ($2H_2O + energy > 2H_2 + O_2$).

Animals (including people) can get energy from breaking down the plant or plankton sugar; they have to eat it first. Nutrition consumed by animals provides compound substances for further processing. Oxygen combines with sugar to release water, carbon dioxide, and energy: $CH_2O + O_2 = CO_2 + H_2O + energy$. Then, carbon (as $CO_2$) returns to the atmosphere because plants and plankton die and decay, bacteria decompose dead organisms, or fire burns out plants. Such chemical reactions may explain why compost, a decomposed and recycled organic matter used as a fertilizer, releases heat during breaking down the organic materials.

## Carbon in a Human Cell (in Micro- and Nano-Scale)

Carbon exists in organic molecules such as fats, amino acids and proteins, sugars. We are built of carbon.

Structures such as inorganic and organic carbon, DNA, and parts of cell membranes contain nanotubes and fullerenes. They are subject of the inquiries made with nanotechnologies, for example molecular electronics, nanolithography, or nanorobotics.

In order to visualize the sizes present in cell biology, we can compare some structures. The size of a human cell is between 4 μm ($4 \times 10^{-6}$ m) and 135 μm. Blood cells are about 2.5 μm. For comparison, the ostrich egg is the largest known cell and weights over 3 pounds (over 1360 grams). Paramecium (a single-celled freshwater animal) is about 60 μm wide and 50 to 350 μm long. The size of a skin human cell is about 30 μm. Water molecule (hydrogen oxide $H_2O$ consisting of two hydrogen atoms and one oxygen) is about 0.29 nm. A flu virus has diameter about 100 nm.

Scientists examine metabolism, excretion, and toxicity of fullerenes C60 and their derivatives because they have potential biological applications, such as enzyme inhibition, antiviral activity, DNA cleavage, photodynamic therapy, electron transfer, and other in vitro and in vivo biological effects. Buckyballs can act in a body as antioxidants. Antioxidant is a molecule that can add an electron and neutralize a free radical. Free radical is a molecule or atom with an unpaired electron. Free radicals may react with cells in the body and cause many types of cancer. Buckyballs may connect a drug with a molecule that reacts to changes in pH (pH is a measure of the acidity in a solution). As the harmed tissues have different pH levels than the healthy areas, buckyballs may deliver drugs directly to harmed areas of the body. Thus, by using buckyballs researchers can create drugs that are only released at the infected area.

# REFERENCES

Aanei, I. L., Elsohly, A. M., Farkas, M. E., Netirojjanakul, C., Regan, M., Taylor Murphy, S., O'Neil, J. P., Sen, Y., & Francis, M. B. (2016). *Biodistribution of antibody-MS2 viral capsid conjugates in breast cancer models.* doi:10.1021/acs.molpharmaceut.6b00566

Aasi, J., Abbott, B. P., Abbott, R., Abbott, T., Abernathy, M. R., Ackley, K., ... Zweizig, J. (2015). Advanced LIGO: The LIGO Scientific Collaboration. *Classical and Quantum Gravity*, *32*(7), 074001. doi:10.1088/0264-9381/32/7/074001

Agence France-Presse. (2012). France cave art gives glimpse into human life 40,000 years ago. *National Post*. Retrieved from http://news.nationalpost.com/2012/05/07/france-cave-art-gives-glimpse-into-human-life-40000-years-ago/

Asghari, M. (2019). Integrated Photonics Looks to Advance Safety for Lidar. *Photonics Spectra, 55*(7), 50–55.

Ayres, R. U., & Ayres, E. (2010). *Crossing the Energy Divide: Moving from Fossil Fuel Dependence to a Clean-Energy.* Pearson Prentice Hall.

Barwinski.net. (2019). *Links to various web databases. Use query for carbon-8.* Retrieved from http://barwinski.net/isotopes/query_select.php

Bon, C., Caudy, N., de Dieuleveult, M., Fosse, P., Philippe, M., Maksud, F., ... Elalouf, J.-M. (2008). Deciphering the complete mitochondrial genome and phylogeny of the extinct cave bear in the Paleolithic painted cave of Chauvet. *Proceedings of the National Academy of Sciences of the United States of America, 11.* doi:10.1073/pnas.0806143105 PMID:18955696

Brawand, D., Wahli, W., & Kaessmann, H. (2008). Loss of Egg Yolk Genes in Mammals and the Origin of Lactation and Placentation. *PLoS Biology, 6*(3), e63. doi:10.1371/journal.pbio.0060063 PMID:18351802

Capece, N., Erra, U., & Scolamiero, R. (2017). Converting night-time images to day-time images through a deep learning approach. *Proceedings of the International Conference on Information Visualisation, 21.*

Cave of Altamira and Paleolithic Cave Art of Northern Spain. (2019). *Unesco World Heritage Centre.* Retrieved from http://whc.unesco.org/en/list/310

*Challenges in Characterizing Small Particles: Exploring Particles from the Nano- to Microscales.* (2012). Chemical Sciences Roundtable & National Research Council, The National Academies Press.

Coffey, V. C. (2018, Nov.). LIGO Continues Making Waves. *Photonics Spectra*, 34–37.

Combes, F. (1991). The SAO/NASA Astrophysics Data System. *Annual Review of Astronomy and Astrophysics, 29*(A92-18081 05-90). 195-237. Retrieved from http://articles.adsabs.harvard.edu/full/1991ARA%26A.29.195C

Corkery, R. W., & Tyrode, E. C. (2017). On the colour of wing scales in butterflies: Iridescence and preferred orientation of single gyroid photonic crystals. *Interface Focus*, *7*(4), 20160154. doi:10.1098/rsfs.2016.0154 PMID:28630678

Cox, D. J. (2008). Using the supercomputer to visualize higher dimensions: An artist's contribution to scientific visualization. *Leonardo*, *41*(4), 390–400. doi:10.1162/leon.2008.41.4.390

Davidson, M. W. (2019). *Molecular Expressions*. Retrieved from http://micro.magnet.fsu.edu/primer/java/scienceopticsu/powersof10/

De Grand, A., & Bonfig, S. (2015, Jan.). Selecting a Microscope Based on Imaging Depth. *BioPhotonics*, 26-29.

Deisseroth, K. (2018). Article. *BioPhotonics, 2018*(9), 18-19.

Deruta Ceramists. (2019). Retrieved August 26, 2012, from https://www.thatsarte.com/handmade-italian/region/deruta

Doeleman, S. (2019). *Focus on the First Event Horizon Telescope Results*. Retrieved from https://iopscience.iop.org/journal/2041-8205/page/Focus_on_EHT

Ee, C. C. (2013). *Removal of Dye by Adsorption of Eggshell Powder*. Technical University.

EIA. (2018). *U.S. Energy Information Administration; Greenhouse Gases' Effect on the Climate*. Retrieved from https://www.eia.gov/energyexplained/index.php?page=environment_how_ghg_affect_climate

Event Horizon Telescope. (2019). Retrieved from https://eventhorizontelescope.org/

Faber, T. (2008). *Faberge's Eggs: The Extraordinary Story of the Masterpieces That Outlived an Empire. Random House*. Retrieved from http://en.wikipedia.org/wiki/Faberge_egg

Falkowski, P., Scholes, R. J., Boyle, E., Canadell, J., Canfield, D., & Elser, J. (2000). The Global Carbon Cycle: A Test of Our Knowledge of Earth as a System. *Science*, *290*(5490), 291–296. doi:10.1126cience.290.5490.291 PMID:11030643

Formlabs. (2019). *Additive Manufacturing: Industry Trends and Outlook.* Retrieved from https://formlabs.com/3d-printers/

Freyer, C., & Renfree, M. B. (2009, Sept. 15). The mammalian yolk sac in placenta. *Journal of Experimental Zoology. Part B, Molecular and Developmental Evolution, 312*(6), 545–554. doi:10.1002/jez.b.21239 PMID:18985616

Friedrich, W. L., Kromer, B., Friedrich, M., Heinemeier, J., Pfeiffer, T., & Talamo, S. (2006). Santorini Eruption Radiocarbon Dated to 1627-1600 B.C. *Science, 312*(5773), 548. Retrieved from http://www.sciencemag.org/content/312/5773/548

Garner, S. M. (Ed.). (2017). *Flexible Glass Enabling Thin, Lightweight, and Flexible Electronics.* Hoboken, NJ: Wiley-Scrivener. doi:10.1002/9781118946404

Garner, S. M. (2018, Nov.). Flexible Glass Substrates Enable Large-Scale Integration. *Photonics Spectra*, 42–45.

Gomollón-Bel, F. (2019). Graphene and boron nitride 'sandwich' key to new electronics. *Graphene Flagship.* Retrieved from https://graphene-flagship.eu/news/Pages/Graphene-boron-nitride-%E2%80%98sandwich%E2%80%99-key-to-new-electronics.aspx

Goodsell, D. S. (2006). Fact and Fantasy in Nanotech Imagery. *Leonardo Journal, the International Society for the Arts, Sciences and Technology, 42*(1), 52–57.

Greco, M. (2019, Apr.). IR Light illuminates Biotech Manufacturing. Biophotonics, 49.

Grumbling, E., & Horowitz, M. (Eds.). (2018). *National Academies of Sciences, Engineering, and Medicine. In Quantum Computing: Progress and Prospects.* Washington, DC: The National Academies Press. doi:10.17226/25196

Gutruf, P. (2019, Apr.). The digital tech, biological system blend. *BioPhotonics*, 7.

Halbouty, M. T. (2004). *Giant Oil & Gas Fields of the Decade - 1990-99 (Aapg Memoir 78).* American Association of Petroleum Geologists.

Hassanzadeh, P., Fullwood, I., Sothi, S., & Aldulaimi, D. (2011). Cancer Nanotechnology. *Gastroenterology and Hepatology from Bed To Bench*, *4*(2), 63–69. Retrieved from www.ncbi.nlm.nih.gov/pmc/articles/PMC4017405/ PMID:24834159

Herzog, W. (2012). *Werner Herzog: The artist's website*. Retrieved from http://www.wernerherzog.com/index.php?id=64

Herzog, W. (2019). Cave of Forgotten Dreams. In *Wikipedia, the free encyclopedia*. Retrieved from http://en.wikipedia.org/wiki/Cave_of_ Forgotten_Dreams

Hoffmann, D. L., Beck, J. W., Richards, D. A., Smart, P. L., Singarayer, J. S., Ketchmark, T., & Hawkesworth, C. J. (2010). Towards radiocarbon calibration beyond 28 ka using speleothems from the Bahamas. *Earth and Planetary Science Letters*, *289*(1–2), 1–10. doi:10.1016/j.epsl.2009.10.004

Hogan, H. (2018, Dec.). For Self-Driving Cars, Sensors Galore. *Photonics Spectra*, 48–51.

Hudson, A. (2011). Is graphene a miracle material? *BBC News*. Retrieved from http://news.bbc.co.uk/2/hi/programmes/click_online/9491789.stm

IPCC. (2019). *Intergovernmental Panel on Climate Change in the United Nations*. Retrieved from https://www.ipcc.ch/

Irifune, T., Kurio, A., Sakamoto, S., Inoue, T., & Sumiya, H. (2003). Materials: Ultrahard polycrystalline diamond from graphite. *Nature*, *421*(6923), 599–600. doi:10.1038/421599b PMID:12571587

Irvin, D., & Koenning, T. (2015, Jan.). Line-Narrowed Laser Module Enables Spin-Exchange Optical Pumping. *BioPhotonics*, 36-39.

Kan, S. B. J., Lewis, R. D., Chen, K., & Arnold, F. H. (2016). Directed evolution of cytochrome c for carbon–silicon bond formation: Bringing silicon to life. *Science*, *354*(6315), 1048–1051. doi:10.1126cience.aah6219 PMID:27885032

Knight, W. (2017, July 12). Biased Algorithms Are Everywhere, and No One Seems to Care. *MIT Technology Review*. Retrieved from https://www. technologyreview.com/s/608248/biased-algorithms-are-everywhere-and-no-one-seems-to-care/

Kraak, M.-J. (2014). *Mapping Time: Illustrated by Minard's Map of Napoleon's Russian Campaign of 1812*. Esri Press.

La Rosa, A., Yan, M., Fernandez, R., Wang, X., & Zegarra, E. (2013). *Top-down and Bottom-up approaches to nanotechnology. An overview in the context of developing Proton-fountain respond to chemical and electrical stimuli.* Portland State University. Retrieved from https://www.pdx.edu/pnna/sites/www.pdx.edu.pnna/files/%282013%29_Top-down_Bottom-up_Approaches_to_Nanotechnology__An_overviwe_in%20_the_contect_of_PEN%20Lithography.pdf

LeCun, Y., Bengio, Y., & Hinton, G. (2015). Deep learning. *Nature, 521*(7553), 436–444. doi:10.1038/nature14539 PMID:26017442

Lu, J. (2017, July 28). Tough adhesives for diverse wet surfaces. *Science, 357*. doi:10.1126cience.aah6362 PMID:28751604

Maine, R. (2019). Airglow. *Photonics Spectra, 53*(5), 66.

Mann, D., Kötting, C., & Gerwert, K. (2018, Nov.). FTIR Spectroscopy: A Comprehensive Biological Investigator. *BioPhotonics*, 30-35.

Manning, S. W., Ramsey, C. B., Kutschera, W., Higham, T., Kromer, B., Steier, P., & Wild, E. M. (2006). Chronology for the Aegean Late Bronze Age 1700-1400 B.C. *Science, 312*(5773), 565–569. Retrieved from http://www.sciencemag.org/content/312/5773/565

Manovich, L. (2019). AI, Data Visualization, Data Art. Workshop at the Central Academy of Fine Arts (CAFA), Beijing, China.

Marchant, J. (2016). A Journey to the Oldest Cave Paintings in the World. *Smithsonian Magazine*. Retrieved from https://www.smithsonianmag.com/history/journey-oldest-cave-paintings-world-180957685/

Matsumoto, R., Yamashita, A., Hara, H., Irifune, T., Adachi, S., Takeya, H., & Takano, Y. (2018). Diamond anvil cells using boron-doped diamond electrodes covered with undoped diamond insulating layer. *Applied Physics Express, 11*(5), 053101. doi:10.7567/APEX.11.053101

McMurry, J. (2015). *Organic Chemistry* (9th ed.). Brooks Cole.

Miri, A. K. (2018). *Microfluidics-Enabled Multimaterial Maskless Stereolithographic Bioprinting.* Wiley Online Library. doi:10.1002/adma.201800242

Mirsky, S. (2011). No title. *Scientific American*, *305*, 96. doi:10.1038cientificamerican1111-96

NanoWerk. (2019). *Nanoparticle production: How nanoparticles are made.* Retrieved from https://www.nanowerk.com/how_nanoparticles_are_made.php

NASA. (2019). *Latest Updates from NASA on 3D-Printed Habitat Competition.* Retrieved from https://www.nasa.gov/directorates/spacetech/centennial_challenges/3DPHab/latest-updates-from-nasa-on-3d-printed-habitat-competition

NASA Earth Observatory. (2019). Retrieved from https://earthobservatory.nasa.gov/

NASA Earth Observatory. (2019). *Carbon Cycle.* Retrieved from https://earthobservatory.nasa.gov/features/CarbonCycle

Nasibulin, A. G., Pikhitsa, P. V., Jiang, H., Brown, D. P., Krasheninnikov, A. V., Anisimov, A. S., ... Kauppinen, E. I. (2007). A novel hybrid carbon material. *Nature Nanotechnology*, *2*(3), 156–161. doi:10.1038/nnano.2007.37 PMID:18654245

National Cancer Institute. (2019). *Cancer treatment research.* Retrieved from https://www.cancer.gov/research/areas/treatment

NSF NACK Center. (2012). *National Center for Nanotechnology Applications and Career Knowledge.* Penn State University Center for Nanotechnology Education and Utilization. Retrieved August 20, 2011, from http://www.nano4me.org/

Orfescu, C. (2012). NanoArt: Nanotechnology and Art. In A. Ursyn (Ed.), *Biologically-Inspired Computing for the Arts: Scientific Data through Graphics.* IGI Global. doi:10.4018/978-1-4666-0942-6.ch008

Ospanova, A. K., Stenishchev, I. V., & Basharin, A. A. (2018). *Anapole Mode Sustaining Silicon Metamaterials in Visible Spectral Range.* Wiley Online Library; doi:10.1002/lpor.201800005

Palmer, J. (2009). *Single molecule's stunning image*. Retrieved from http://news.bbc.co.uk/2/hi/science/nature/8225491.stm

Palmer, J. (2012). *Graphene transistors in high-performance demonstration*. Retrieved from http://www.bbc.co.uk/news/science-environment-18868848

Park, S. H., Su, R., Jeong, J., Guo, S.-Z., Qiu, K., Joung, D., . . . McAlpine, M. C. (2018). *3D Printed Polymer Photodetectors*. Wiley Online Library. Retrieved from https://onlinelibrary.wiley.com/doi/pdf/10.1002/adma.201803980

Parker, S. & Marson, M. (2018, Oct.). DNA Is the Next C++. *Wired*, 48-49.

Peng, H., Yu, L., Chen, G., Xue, Z., Liao, Y., Zhu, J., … Wei, Y. (2019). *Liquid crystalline nanocolloids for storage of electro-optic responsive images*. *ACS Applied Materials & Interfaces*. Retrieved from https://pubs.acs.org/doi/10.1021/acsami.8b22636

Penn State Modules. (2011). *Nano4Me.org. NACK educational resources*. The Pennsylvania State University. Retrieved from http://nano4me.live.subhub.com/categories/modules

Photonics Handbook. (2019a). *Superresolution Microscopy. An Imaging Revolution* (65th ed.). Photonics Media.

Photonics Handbook. (2019c). *Lasers. Understanding the Basics* (65th ed.). Photonics Media.

Pierce, D. (2019, Apr.). Welcome to your home on Mars. *Wall Street Journal*.

Rodriguez, S. (2018). Ultraprecise 3D Microprinting for Optical and Photonic Components. *Photonics Spectra*, *52*(12), 40–43.

Rossi, M. (2007). How can graphite and diamond be so different if they are both composed of pure carbon? *Scientific American*. Retrieved from https://www.scientificamerican.com/article/how-can-graphite-and-diam/

Sadier, B., Delannoy, J.-J., Benedetti, L., Bourlès, D. L., Jaillet, S., Geneste, J.-M., ... Arnold, M. (2012). Further constraints on the Chauvet cave artwork elaboration. *Proceedings of the National Academy of Sciences of the United States of America*. doi:10.1073/pnas.1118593109 PMID:22566649

Sandros, M. G., & Adar, F. (2015, Jan.). Raman Spectroscopy and Microscopy: Solving Outstanding Problems in the Life Sciences. *BioPhotonics*, 40-43.

Schoeppler, V., Reich, E., Vacelet, J., Rosenthal, M., Pacureanu, A., Rack, A., Zaslansky, P., Zolotoyabko, E., & Zlotnikov, I. (2017). Shaping highly regular glass architectures: A lesson from nature. *Science Advances, 3*(10). Doi:10.1126ciadv.aao2047

Schroeder, T. (2017). An electric-eel-inspired soft power source from stacked hydrogels. *Nature, 552.* Retrieved from https://www.nature.com/articles/nature24670

Sender, R., Fuchs, S., & Milo, R. (2016). Are We Really Vastly Outnumbered? Revisiting the Ratio of Bacterial to Host Cells in Humans. *Cell, 164*(3), 337–340. doi:10.1016/j.cell.2016.01.013 PMID:26824647

Smalyukh, I. I. (2019). *Soft Matter Physics Research Group.* Boulder, CO: University of Colorado. Retrieved from https://www.colorado.edu/soft-matter-physics/

Snyder, S. H., & Ferris, C. D. (2000). Novel Neurotransmitters and Their Neuropsychiatric Relevance. *The American Journal of Psychiatry, 157*(11), 1738–1751. doi:10.1176/appi.ajp.157.11.1738 PMID:11058466

Stezano, M. (2018). Earliest Known Drawing Found: Is It the First Hashtag? *History.* Retrieved from https://www.history.com/news/prehistoric-hashtag-stone-age-painting

Tali, D. (2018). Animals That Can See Infrared Light. *Sciencing.* Retrieved from https://sciencing.com/animals-can-see-infrared-light-6910261.html

Tesa, M. (2019, Apr.). Upconversion Materials: Empower Thermal Bioimaging. *BioPhotonics*, 34-38.

Trivedi, R. P., Klevets, I. I., Senyuk, B., Lee, T., & Smalyukh, I. I. (2012). Reconfigurable interactions and three-dimensional patterning of colloidal particles and defects in lamellar soft media. *Proceedings of the National Academy of Sciences of the United States of America, 109*(13), 4744–4749. doi:10.1073/pnas.1119118109 PMID:22411822

Tsukruk, V. (2013). Learning from Nature: Bioinspired Materials and Structures. In *Adaptive Materials and Structures: A Workshop Report.* Washington, DC: The National Academies Press.

Tufte, E. R. (1983/2001). *The Visual Display of Quantitative Information.* Cheshire, CT: Graphics Press.

Tyson, N. d. G. (2017). *Astrophysics for People in a Hurry*. Thorndike Press.

Vogt, A. K. S. (2018, Nov.). A Biophotonics Revolution. *BioPhotonics*.

Weinstock, B., & Niki, H. (1972, April 21). Carbon Monoxide Balance in Nature. *Science*, *176*(4032), 290–292. doi:10.1126cience.176.4032.290 PMID:5019781

Wilts, B. D., & Saranathan, V. (2018). A Literal Elytral Rainbow: Tunable Structural Colors Using Single Diamond Biophotonic Crystals in *Pachyrrhynchus congestus* Weevils. *Small*, *14*(46). doi:10.1002mll.201802328 PMID:30112799

Wolke, R. L. (2014). Carbon. In K. L. Lerner & B. W. Lerner (Eds.), *The Gale Encyclopedia* (5th ed.; Vol. 2, pp. 777–780). Farmington Hills, MI: Gale.

Wood, B. (2018). *NASA backs designs for 3D-printed homes on Mars*. Retrieved from https://www.cnn.com/style/article/nasa-3d-homes-mars/index.html

Wu, L., & Wang, R. (2005). Carbon Monoxide: Endogenous Production, Physiological Functions, and Pharmacological Applications. *Pharmacological Reviews*, *57*(4), 585–630. doi:10.1124/pr.57.4.3 PMID:16382109

Xia, F., Watson, T. J. H., Yan, H., & Avouris, P. (2013). The Interaction of Light and Graphene: Basics, Devices, and Applications. *Proceedings of the IEEE*, *101*(7), 1717–1731. doi:10.1109/JPROC.2013.2250892

Yanik, A. A., Huang, M., Kamohara, O., Artar, A., Geisbert, T. W., Connor, J. H., & Altug, H. (2010). An optofluidic nanoplasmonic biosensor for direct detection of live viruses from biological media. *Nano Letters*, *2010*, 5. doi:10.1021/nl103025u PMID:21053965

Yeager, J. (2015). *12 Eggscellent Things You Can Do with Eggshells*. Retrieved from http://www.goodhousekeeping.com/home/green-living/reuse-eggshells-460809

Yildiz, A., Forkey, J. N., McKinney, S. A., Ha, T., Goldman, Y. A., & Selvin, P. R. (2003). Myosin V walks hand-over-hand: Single fluorophore imaging with 1.5-nm localization. *Science*, *300*(5628), 2061–2065. doi:10.1126cience.1084398 PMID:12791999

Yoo, S., Kokoszka, J., Zou, P., & Hsieh, J. S. (2009). Utilization of calcium carbonate particles from eggshell waste as coating pigments for ink-jet printing paper. *Bioresource Technology, 100*(24), 6416–6421. doi:10.1016/j.biortech.2009.06.112 PMID:19665373

Yuan, Ye., Abuhaimed, G. N., Liu, Q., & Smalyukh, I. I. (2018). Self-assembled nematic colloidal motors powered by light. *Nature Communications,* (9). Retrieved from https://www.nature.com/articles/s41467-018-07518-x

# Chapter 2
# How Do We Communicate

## ABSTRACT

*This chapter examines our modes of imparting or exchanging facts and opinions. After discussion of the role of electromagnetic waves in our sensory perception, further text describes the ways we and other living beings gain information through the senses, especially when enhanced with technology. Finally, communication between people, with computers, and with other living things is described, especially when animal communication involves senses unavailable to human beings. Emphasis is put on visual communication, some basic notions about semantics, and also visualization techniques and domains. Basic art concepts, elements of design in art, and principles of design in art serve as background information, followed by learning projects.*

## INTRODUCTION

First of all, electromagnetic waves of different wavelengths serve as a medium and thus make a worthwhile contribution to our perception and means of communication. Many kinds of human and animal senses operate as a source of gathering information, and then cognitive abilities support our sensing of numbers and spoken or written language. The following text discusses a notion of semantics as it tells about visual communication through images, art, and signs of different kinds. Visualization with its techniques and domains, along with some other ways of sharing data support these actions. Technologies that enhance our senses and means of communication involve our communication with computers. Humans have been exposed to encounters

DOI: 10.4018/978-1-7998-1651-5.ch002

with threats of different kinds from the very beginnings of history. Knowledge about acute abilities of animals enhances our communication, defense, and attack capabilities related to many spheres of life. In some of these cases, communication happens to be unilateral.

## 2.1. MODES OF GATHERING INFORMATION

### Wavelengths: Sources for Our Perception

Describing senses in separate groups may be seen improper because senses are interconnected in many ways. Communication may mean an exchange of sensory information from different kinds of perception. Signals coming from the senses are often combined to convey a clear message. For example, we can receive information about numbers from various senses, looking at patterns, listening to sounds, feeling vibrations, or reading numbers.

In general terms, senses provide input to an organism due to their physiological capacities. Our senses can identify distinctive electromagnetic wavelengths. The electromagnetic spectrum might best characterize our world (Table 1). It includes, from longest wavelength to shortest: radio waves, microwaves, infrared, visible light, ultraviolet, X-rays, and gamma rays. We can detect only a small fragment of the electromagnetic spectrum as sounds, heat, or light. A lot of applications and tools serve for light transmission, amplification, signal processing, and other kinds of manipulation. These interacting electric and magnetic currents or fields have distinctive wavelengths, energy, and frequency. Living beings gather information and communicate by responding to electromagnetic waves, cymatics (wave phenomena, vibration of matter that makes sound visible), the pitch response, the senses of vision, smell, touch, and taste, and more.

Signals become stimuli that cause physical or physiological reflex responses, which may be performed without our consciousness or as intentional reactions; they also cause psychological reactions. Our communication may involve many internal and external senses: a sense of temperature, kinesthetic sense that gives us balance, a sense of motion, a sense of acceleration and velocity changes (e.g., pressure caused by the wind), proprioception that allows sensing the relative position and movement of parts of the body, a feel of direction, responsiveness to pheromones, and sensitivity to pain. We are constantly processing sensory information coming from our external and internal receptors that respond to and transmit signals about our body. We may sense someone's feelings or mood through the tone of their voice, body language, even from the look in their eyes; it may happen also in our communication with animals. Our own feelings, for example a feeling of being tired, exhausted, hungry, or just thirsty and dehydrated after a vigorous physical exercise or after a long discussion, can add or subtract the intensity of the sensory perception. For this reason, information coming to us from our senses might be discussed in diverse frames of reference: physiological, physical, technological, and aesthetical. Some hold that humans, and maybe some animals are experts (without training) of picking up emotional expression in faces (Loizides, 2019). The answers depend on the sensitivity of our senses or our organism.

We are able to capture light – photons or energy; we recognize, name, and categorize it with our senses. We observe, study, and record nature in terms of making inventions. For example, we use wind for such purposes as sailing, harvesting energy, and converting it into different forms. We produce photographic recording of movement, frozen in time or moving in films and movies. From the theoretical study that is possible by applying mathematics, we can develop areas for research that make the unseen, unfelt, or unheard converted into the visible, palpable, or sending sounds. From there, we go from the physical to digital or vice versa. We examine these capacities and use this information for theoretical, practical, and computational solutions within the domains of physiology, neuroscience, cognitive science, cognitive psychology, sociology, anthropology, medicine, computer science, but also human perception, philosophy, and art.

While we can get a candle smelling like rain, we cannot obtain a library of smells and create a smell-sense related composition. We can think how to code smells, so one could develop a composition taking the audience through the journey of various smells, or to go even farther and to create an IMAX like experience, when images, movies, and stories would be supported by this experience. How about an email attachment that smells? Of course, there are many not so nice smells, so we should think about how those would be used, for example as a warning, or for making a spam on the internet.

We make research to transform information into visual forms. For example, we examine history and future of computer graphics in service of information graphics, and investigate into internet data to find a source for inspiration, transformation, translation, or copying images. These sources are augmenting our bank of information. We also use the nature- and science-based data for performing one's own experimental study or production. Finally, we apply visualization of scientific and abstract concepts, events, and processes as a learning tool with explanatory power.

For some people sensitivity is considered a weakness, especially in boys. Some boys are often trained to be insensitive to be considered strong, and thus they may develop a wide spectrum of unfriendly attitudes toward highly sensitive people. In many instances boys are encouraged to shoot, hunt animals, and fish. They are trained to be insensitive to pain coming from sport games and competitions. Military training, especially intelligence services and espionage training comprise exercises focused on building insensitivity to own or others' pain. Many domains of art that require sensitivity (and sensibility) often evoke hostile reaction and a need to deny the meaning and value of these qualities. On th other hand, the role of the sensory input in art may pertain in some extent to individual curiosity and sensibility.

Animal senses may often act differently, as it for instance happens with worms, butterflies, or birds. Some animals may receive ultrasound signals, some have more acute sense of smell, some have better balance, and other have the wider or more narrow ranges of frequencies used for vision and hearing. Many kinds of animals have also other kinds of senses, different ways of interpreting data from the environment such as echolocation, and different kinds of receptors such as electrically sensitive electroreceptors found in sharks, electric eels, catfish, and other fish (Wueringer, 2019; Wueringer, Squire, Kajiura, Hart, & Collin, 2012). In a saw of a sawfish (all species of sawfish are critically endangered), an elongated cranial cartilage with teeth is covered in a dense array of electroreceptors. The sawfish's saw is unique in its use for both detecting and manipulating prey (Wueringer et al., 2012). Sharks, rays, and some other aquatic animals generate bioelectric dipole fields created by the opposite electromagnetic charges separated by a small distance; they can detect such fields and attack their prey. Figure 1 shows a water creature imagined by Cassidy Stratton.

Creatures that live in the darkness of the deep sea wouldn't seem to have need for eyes, or the ability to see color. However, some dragon fish, as well as by other deep-sea creatures have evolved from blue-light sensitivity to red-light sensitivity, and then back to blue. The force driving these changes is likely the bioluminescence produced by the dragon fish themselves. Dragon fish can see and emit far red light using organs called photophores placed below its eyes. Bioluminescence – the production and emission of light by a living organism occurs widely in marine vertebrates and invertebrates, in terrestrial invertebrates such as fireflies, as well as in some fungi and microorganisms. Also the light is produced by symbiosis between some

*Figure 1. A Creature: Life in Water*
*(© 2018, C. Stratton. Used with permission)*

*Figure 2. Tolerance*
*(© 2018, A. Ursyn. Used with permission)*

animals and bioluminescent bacteria (Parry, 2014). Figure 2 shows a work by Anna Ursyn entitled "Tolerance."

We are still not sure which senses we had already lost, and which ones we ignore or are not aware of. Sometimes our senses are below par with the animal senses. For example, we cannot sense from a distance the body heat of people or animals, and cannot perceive the signals related to the degree of water pressure or water current. However, we lack senses or not have enough sensitivity to detect many physical or chemical qualities. We seem to lack the sense of ultrasounds, we are unsure (in variable degree) about our circadian rhythms (biological processes recurring on a 24-hour cycle and influenced by the environment), our sense of time, our body temperature, or physiological responses to our emotions. Some animals have strong geospatial sense of the direction; we do not navigate like earthworms, fish, bees, or birds do. We cannot measure with our senses the strength of electric and magnetic fields, and also week electromagnetic fields, in spite of the warnings that electromagnetic fields produced by such human-made devices as mobile phones, computers, power lines, and domestic wiring might have harmful effects on living organisms: cell membranes, DNA, metabolism, and also neuronal activity. Also, we do not estimate without tools the air pressure or our blood pressure, to name a few. Therefore, we have to rely on man-made sensors and devices.

When we think about a threshold intensity for a stimulus that is needed to evoke a reaction, we can see that sensitivity to particular kinds of stimuli such as visuals, sounds, or smells varies greatly, both between species and among individual people. Not only most of animals are more sensitive than humans, for example to a smell, but they also produce and release chemical substances that cause physiological and behavioral reactions in others members of their species or in different living beings.

A growing number of studies focus on the relationship between human decisions and the levels of biologically active substances in blood. Both the hormones released into the blood and the pheromones (substances produced by organisms, e.g., of mammals and insects) can affect human physiology and behavior. Other studies support the idea that online relationships can be associated with the release of oxytocin. Several companies started production of pheromone substances containing oxytocin. One may think about factors promoting or inhibiting the release of biologically active substances; for example, how particular colors, traditionally ascribed to the mood changes, would contribute to the release of these compounds to the bloodstream. Video game designers create numerous genres of first-person-shooter or survival-horror action games. On the recipients' side, emotional problems in social relations often arise when gamers become addicted.

Pheromones are carriers of information that activate biochemical, physiological, and psychological reactions. They activate not only the organ of smell but also many other structures in the brain. In case of pheromones the threshold level is usually so low that single molecules can evoke reaction.

Possibly, a dog can gather information about the gender, size, age, etc. of another dog that left some substances behind a tree trunk, while a newborn infant cannot recognize mother by sight but can smell her pheromones.

While constructing models of animal behavior it is important to incorporate variables such as internal states: hunger, sex, drive, and higher functions: learning, memory, and personality. Most models focus on social systems. Computing scientists examine social insects, which display behavior of individuals that does not require centralized command. Packs of wolf, schools of fish, flocks of birds, and other social animals are a source of biology inspired solutions. Signals may last long, for example, chemical signals, or may be transient like the acoustical ones. Animals communicate with members of their own species and with another species. They convey information about actions such as foraging and predator defense. Some signals may differ from those used by humans: they may include chemical substances, electrical, and seismic signals (for example, when blind mole rats transmit signals over long distances by thumping on burrow walls).

Social insects working in swarms can manage complex situations (Schmickl & Hamann, 2011). Animals developed senses into highly sophisticated devices by joining and combining their sensors. Social insects developed also methods of acting on their environment, for example, by determining ant trails or building termite mounds; the swarm's behavior may change the environment and the changed stimuli from the environment may in turn alter the swarm's behavior (Schmickl & Hamann, 2011, p. 100). The authors adapted the rules of interactions inside the swarm; information about these rules may be valuable in constructing swarm robots. The principles of swarm intelligence, where the colony agents cooperate to achieve a common goal without a higher supervision, apply to the mould building capability of termites.

A lost worker ant will mimic the task that the successful one is performing, which means a worker ant can assess its own success. In social insects, many individuals respond to stimuli in a similar way. The resulting quality, referred to as swarm intelligence, has been compared to distributed, parallel computing. Social insect inspired meta-heuristic optimization solutions have been based on ant colony, wasp swarm, termite mould, honeybee hive, and genetic algorithms, among other optimization solutions (Hartman, Pinto, Runkler, & Sousa, 2011). Biologically inspired evolutionary robotics (ER) is a powerful approach for the automatic synthesis of robot controllers. Creation of collective and swarm robotics may be inspired by a feature that the behavior of a social group results from the control and communication rules followed by each individual.

## Project: Pattern and Order

Some individuals move independently in the same direction, indifferent to others' goals. On the road, a speed limit, a slope and turns of a highway determine the cars' performance. Swarm computing examines several kinds of collective behavior. Individual members of a swarm assume repetitive configurations without orchestration imposed by any conductor. There is no leader in this case, in contrast to organized events that are commanded by a leader, such as in case of marching in a military manner, being a part of an air force squadron, walking together during weddings, funerals, or participating in a circus caravan. Yet another way of an animal collective movement may result from chemical cues produced by members of a swarm in case of ants, may be measured by a distance between individuals' wings in a flock of birds, or may be caused by the smell of food attracting bees. Collective behavior of

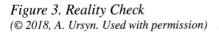

*Figure 3. Reality Check*
*(© 2018, A. Ursyn. Used with permission)*

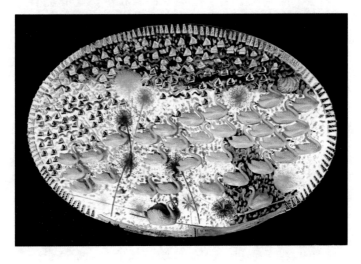

animal species often serves as inspiration for designing mechanical systems that function like living organisms.

Figure 3 shows a work by Anna Ursyn entitled "Reality Check."

Depict animals showing collective way of life. Create a multiple-horizon environment on many levels, with inhabitants moving in a particular order and obeying their specific rules. It may be the world of various kinds of birds, fish, insects, bats, four-legged animals, and also humans. Think about the ways you will apply to indicate patterns and order existing in such flocks, schools, swarms, packs, herds, crowds, battalions, and other formations. Show differences one can see between the species' behavior and the ways they form collective actions.

## Sensory Enhancement by Technologies

Human sensory experiences are expanded by the developments in current technologies including quantum physics and nanotechnology. We use our sensory information for theoretical, practical, and computational solutions within the domains of physiology, neuroscience, cognitive science, cognitive psychology, sociology, anthropology, medicine, computer science, philosophy, and art. One may say that art media of the 21$^{st}$ century including music, theater, interactive media and installations are inspired by the input from our

*Figure 4. Stellar Music*
*(© 2018, A. Ursyn. Used with permission)*

senses, and also incorporate the viewers' senses. They often visualize the unseen and give the viewer the phenomenal, immediate experience. Figure 4 shows a work by Anna Ursyn entitled "Stellar Music."

Portable devices act as an extension of human senses. Bio-interfaces have been used as wearable devices to provide organic interaction between man and machine. Developers and designers search for computational solutions and applications that enhance sensitivity and improve emotional wellbeing of the user. Within the scope of interaction with games, the wearable computers allow the users to interact with digital games through their physiological and cerebral signals. Forms of interaction include the use of mice, keyboards, joysticks, or touch screens, as well as participation by adding voice, changing position, face expression, or gesture.

## GATHERING INFORMATION THROUGH THE SENSES

### Hearing: Sounds as Electromagnetic Waves

Sounds evoke our sensory response. Sound waves cause that the ear structures pass and translate vibrations into neural messages sent through the auditory nerve from about 25,000 receptors to the brain. The ears contain also semicircular structures that provide the feeling of balance. Sensory responses to electromagnetic waves include, music and various types of communications. Musical sound is produced by continuous, regular vibrations, while noise is not regular. Electromagnetic waves, seen as energy and matter, conduct the waves as repetitive oscillations. That means the system (for example, molecules, drums, pipes, bridges, or houses) displays sinusoidal motion with a given frequency and pattern. Music, speech, and sound effects go together in a sound studio for a broadcast production, film, or video. Artists translate musical compositions into visual imagery and thus create visual music. A growing number of musical events (such as Eurographics – European Association for Computer Graphics, Imagina, or Ars Electronica) incorporate varied kinds of media: performances, live action, interactive installations, and movies.

### Pitch

Absolute (perfect) pitch is the ability to recognize and remember a tone without a reference. It's a great asset for musicians who just know the exact tone they hear and name exact notes and chords by ear. Many musicians have no pitch recognition – they have relative pitch – an ability unique to people to identify pitches in relation to other pitches. Many hold that a great deal of newborn babies have absolute pitch: they prefer to respond to absolute rather than relative pitch differences. This ability may possibly cease to exist in early maturation when absolute pitch would interfere with language perception. Infants learn to understand what their parents say; they are focusing on the content – the language perception. However, the pitch and the timbre (a tone quality of a sound that helps distinguish it from other sounds of the same pitch and volume) of the female or male voices are of no importance and of no use in this difficult task. Absolute pitch is prevalent among those who speak tonal languages where high/low pitch combinations are important (such as happens in Mandarin or Cantonese languages). Perfect pitch perception is present in many members of animal kingdom. Some animal species display ability to learn songs. Vocal learners that gain vocalization through imitation have been found in three groups of mammals (humans, bats, and cetaceans – dolphins) and three groups of birds (parrots, hummingbirds, and songbirds).

Humans hear sounds of about 12 Hz to 20 kHz. Dogs have their hearing superior to human hearing, with a range 40 to 60 kHz (dog whistles are set at about 44 kHz). Dogs can convey a lot of information and emotions through their barking. Also bats have sensitive hearing, between 20 and 150 kHz; they use it for navigation and echolocation for locating and tracking their prey. Mice hear sounds of about 1 kHz to 70 kHz. They communicate using high frequency noises partially inaudible by humans. Marmots and ground squirrels, groundhogs, squirrels, and prairie dogs all are highly social; they whistle when alarmed to warn others. Chameleons can sound frequencies in the range 200 to 600 Hz.

## Vision

The part of the electromagnetic spectrum that can be seen by human eye is in the range of 370-750 nm. There are about 150 million light-sensitive cells. Rods identify shapes, especially in dim light. Three different kinds of cones are sensitive to different wavelengths: long (~564-580 nm – perceived as red), middle (~534-545 – green), and short (~420-440 – blue color space). That means they identify colors (if light is bright enough). A term hue identifies a color or a shade of an object. Images are then sent to the brain's visual cortex, the outer layer of the cerebrum composed of grey matter that relates to vision.

Photoreception in other species differs from that of humans. Human vision is imperfect in comparison to many animals, such as owls, which can see in a dim light a mouse moving in a distance over 150 feet away. Contrary to us, many animal species such as a horse have night vision. Eyes positioned on the sides of the horses' heads allow them seeing in a range of about 350°, while humans have about 180° field of vision. Part of vision that is outside of the center of our gaze is called peripheral vision; it is weaker in humans than in many animal species.

Within the 370-750 nm part of a spectrum, humans and animals react to light by seeing colors. While light in a single wavelength is monochromatic, most colors are polychromatic – contain two or more colors. Our eyes, optic nerve, and visual cortex react to light and lighten surfaces of objects by creating mental images of colors. However, about 7% of male population is color deficient, mostly for red-green discrimination, so many visualization designers are avoiding the red-green color contrasts. People developed also several conventional mental models about colors, by considering a given color as a warm, cool, pleasant, or sad one. Humans developed several mental models of colors. In the RGB additive color model is about light emission; red green, and blue light can be added to produce various colors. The RGB model serves for sensing, representing, and displaying images in computers, television, and traditional color photography. Representations of the RGB color space model designed for the purposes of computer graphics include the HSL (hue, saturation, lightness) and the HSV (hue, saturation, value) models. The CMYK model is about light absorption and the subtractive mixing process in printing, when the cyan, magenta, yellow, and black colors are used in color printers. The CIE 1931 defines colorimetric properties of the color spectrum and a link between the spectrum wavelengths and color perception.

Some painters (and not only painters) have perfect color feel and color memory, in a similar way, as some musicians (and not only musicians) possess perfect pitch. They have an ability to recognize and remember color without an external reference for making a comparison, so they do not need to bring a color sample to a store in order to choose the right color of paint. For most people, the visual system perceives the light frequencies in terms of luminance (as in gray scale seen by the rods). Hence, to pick colors for visualization, it's good to use a few distinctive colors and have a high luminance contrast between foreground and background. Thus, the lightness is important, in addition to color.

Humans and animals are able to encode several variables, such as a shape, size (length or area), color hue and color saturation, texture, value (density), and orientation of an object as seen in a 2D image; also, form, position and volume when seen in 3D.

## Smell

The sense of smell, called olfaction can convert chemical signals into stimuli for our perception. Separate systems detect airborne substances and fluid stimuli. For example, pheromones – chemical substances produced mostly mammals and insects and released into the environment trigger specific social responses. Depending on the type of a pheromone the response is in the form of aggregation of individuals, flight, aggression, but also attraction of mates or babies, and changes their activity, behavior, or physiology. As for the matters of smell and taste, people can tell the difference between 4,000-10,000 smells, and they have close to 10,000 taste buds in their mouths. In most cases those living in big cities may desire to have a quality of smell displayed by people living in pristine conditions, such as members of tribes living in the Sahara Desert or the Aboriginal people living in Western Australia.

A single receptor recognizes many odors. Odors are translated into patterns of neural activity and the olfactory bulb, olfactory nerve, and then the olfactory cortex interpret the patterns. Olfactory sensory neurons are replaced throughout life. Richard Axel and Linda B. Buck were awarded the Nobel Prize in Physiology or Medicine 2004 "for their discoveries of odorant receptors and the organization of the olfactory system." A big part of an olfactory receptor is placed outside the cells, another part is inside a cell membrane, and the inner part is in a cell. The outer part of the receptor changes its shape when it binds with an odor molecule, and the olfactory cell sends a message to a brain. Andreas Mershin and some researchers pose that olfaction may be both a physical sense (detecting molecular vibrations of odors) as well as a chemical sense by sensing shapes of odorant molecules). While vision and hearing are vibration-based senses, taste is a purely chemical one (Franco, Turin, Mershin, & Skoulakis, 2011). In 2017, Maniati, Haralambous, Turin, and Skoulakis concluded that the character of odorant functional groups in Drosophila is encoded in their molecular vibrations.

The smell cells in dogs are 100 times larger than human cells. Dogs have about 1 million smell cells per a nostril and therefore dogs are so keen to go for a walk to detect (perceive) and mark their messages. Army and police forces train dogs to sniff out and track bodies, drugs, and bombs. Later on, researchers found that dogs can detect many more. Some diseases, for example prostate cancer, are difficult to detect. Methods of detection, which include biopsy or testing patient's blood for specific agents, are often not satisfactorily accurate. However, a considerable number of cancer and many other diseases give rise to a volatile signature present in human body, which is discernible for a dog. When trained to detect cancer, dogs can detect a prostate cancer in human urine with over 90 percent accuracy, can sniff out cancer in blood with nearly 100 percent efficacy 18 months before medical tests (Newsmax Health, 2019), smell the early onset of melanoma, breast cancer, lung cancer, colorectal cancer, and ovarian cancer (Harrison, 2019). However, not only dogs can be trained to detect diseases in humans. In Tanzania (Africa), scientists have trained rats to detect tuberculosis (TB) by smelling saliva samples. While laboratory workers could analyze with microscopes twenty samples per day, a trained rat, attached to a leash, can examine 120-150 samples in a half hour. The African rat can also sniff TNT – the explosive used in mines, and detect mines. It is too light to set off a mine; as a reward, the handler gives the rat a banana, a pat, and some kind words (Marrin, 2006).

Detecting smells may become the better way for finding hidden events that are illegible to people without expensive tools such as gas chromatography or mass spectrometry, or painful procedures, for example biopsy. Scientists are currently trying to gain understanding how is the sense of smell working, in order to create robots that can sniff as well as dogs. At the MIT (Massachusetts Institute of Technology) they conduct research toward developing artificial olfaction and create a Nano-Nose – a sensing device and a diagnostic tool. Researchers promise that we will be "Smelling skin cancer with your smartphone" (Franco et al., 2017). Researchers are training the AI system on a data gathered from trained dogs, to decide what receptors they need to develop. They are working on running a kind of Turing test for smell by imitating the Medical Detection Dogs' results until they could not be differentiated between the Nano-Nose's reactions and their canine's (Harrison, 2019). Medical Detection Dogs is a group in UK that trains animals to be able to sniff out cancers.

## Taste

Taste: A physical ability to discern flavors is one of the senses; however, gustatory perception securing us a sense of taste can hardly be considered a tool for building communication. We can feel a specific taste when a substance in the mouth reacts chemically with taste receptors on the taste buds. Taste, smell, and activation of trigeminal nerve determine altogether the flavors.

Perception of taste is provided by the gustatory cortex. Five basic tastes include saltiness, sweetness, sourness, bitterness, and umami – a savory taste found in broths, cooked meats, soy sauce, and tomatoes.

Herz, Schankler, & Beland (2004) have shown that the senses of smell and taste are uniquely sentimental, prompting the feelings because they "are the only senses that connect directly to the hippocampus, the center of the brain's long-term memory (while) all our other senses (sight, touch, and hearing) are first processed by the thalamus, the source of language and the front door to consciousness." The sense of smell is well connected to our memory. As often quoted in numerous books, French writer Marcel Proust (1871-1922) described the power of his early sensory experiences when he translated the taste of the madeleine pastry and the smell of the tea he remembered from his childhood. In a book "Proust was a neuroscientist" Jonah Lehrer (2007) wrote that Proust intuited a lot about the structure of our brain. The insight of the writer was that senses of smell and taste bear a unique burden of memory.

## Touch

The sense of touch is of special importance for some people, which can be illustrated by the bringing the virtuoso musician's hand in contact with an instrument, the distinctive manner of performing a surgical operation, or the faculty of reading by touch (for example, Braille), and perception through physical contact. An eye surgeon Vladimir Petrovich Filatov was famous for his ability to cut a stack of ultra-thin tissues used for rolling tobacco cigarettes for a depth (for example, 100 layers) requested by an audience, so everybody could count and check the number of the cut tissues. The sense of touch is located in the dermis – the bottom layer of skin. About twenty different types of nerve endings in the dermis carry to the spinal cord and further to the brain information coming from the heat, cold, pressure, touch, pain, and other receptors, especially from the most sensitive body areas: hands, lips, face, neck, tongue, fingertips and feet. One may say our sense of touch may impose our need for creating the palpable, three-dimensional art forms; we can go around, and touch them.

## The Sense of Numbers: Communication Using Numerals

The sense of numbers involves numerical and verbal cognition and communication with the use of numerals. Many studies and publications explore the sense of numbers as a nonverbal counting and search whether there is thought, especially math thought, without language. Howard Gardner considered those processing capabilities being the environmental information processing devices. For example, he considered the perception of certain recurrent patterns, including numerical patterns, to be the core of logical mathematical intelligence (Gardner, 1983, 2011; 1993, 2006; 1999). As stated by Rudolph Arnheim (1969, 1974), perceptual sensitivity is the ability to see a visual order of shapes as images of patterned forces that underlie our existence. This approach to perceptual sensitivity somehow corresponds to the way computer scientists talk about the codes in terms of patterns. One may also ponder about programming languages such as HTML or Processing as the information and communication tools related to the numeral perception and serving for nonverbal communication between individuals and computers, as well as for human-computer interaction.

## The Numerical and Verbal Cognition

The numerical cognition involves mental processes of acquiring and processing knowledge and understanding of numbers. Adults, infants, and animals have already revealed a shared system of representing numbers as analog magnitudes (that contain information on a continuous scale not restricted to a specific set of values). Children count first without naming, then with names spoken or read, or seen as written. How do you know without counting that a mosquito bites you three times or you hear a whistle two times? Numbers can be received by various senses: the same message can be received visually with flags, dots and dashes, or with sounds (long–short or sharp–dull, by pressing 3x3, etc.).

Scientists look for correlations between verbal (language dependent) and nonverbal number knowledge. According to Bar-David, Compton, Drennan, Finder, Grogan, & Leonard (2009), the number concepts can be categorized into two major conceptual camps: language-independent model that claims that nonverbal number concepts are not shaped or created by verbal number understanding and abilities, and the language-dependent model that claims that the use and development of number in verbal activities enables children to become proficient (conceptually and procedurally) with numbers. There is an opposition between Symbolist theories, which pose that the thinking occurs in mental symbols, and Conceptualist theories considering mental symbols as products of the thinking about conceptual and abstract entities.

## The Language-Dependent Model

One hypothesis is that language is necessary to produce thought and children are unable to think about exact number quantities without first learning and mastering verbal counting. Gordon (2004) and then Frank, Everett, Fedorenko, & Gibson (2008) examined connections between language and numbers in the Piraha people, an indigenous hunter-gatherer Amazonian tribe mainly located in Brazil. The Piraha have a counting system with words for "one," "two," and "many" but no exact verbal number words for numbers higher than two; the lack of language for exact large numbers affected the Piraha's numerical cognition and performance with numbers higher than three (according to Bar-David et al., 2009).

It is believed that, in contrast with the Arabic decimal system used today almost everywhere, the Mayans counted with fingers and toes and thus they used the Maya vigesimal system based on groups of twenty units (Maya Mathematical System, 2016). One may wonder whether the covering of toes with shoes might influence the developing of counting systems by limiting possibility to use this counting tool to ten. The Maya discovered a notion of zero, and thus the 20 units meant [0-19] with a significant zero, while in the decimal system we apply [0-9] as a placeholder. Each number, from zero to 19, had its name. They only used three symbols: an ovular shell for a zero, a dot, and a dash, alone or combined, and wrote them vertically or horizontally.

Ancient Egyptians performed division as multiplication in reverse: they repeatedly doubled the divisor to obtain the dividend. Actually, we often avoid using exact verbal number words when we say, some, less, a few, several, many, numerous, or a couple. A rosary designed as a string of beads for keeping count in practicing devotion, a calculating tool abacus, the secular strings of worry beads komboloi used in Greece and other countries, and Hindu prayer beads can be seen as examples of numerical cognition processed without verbalizing.

## Numerical Representation Without Language

On the other hand, there is evidence for precise numerical representation in the absence of language, indicating that language is not necessary to represent small exact numbers or large approximate numbers, and one does not have to know language to understand number. Researchers explored the counting systems in native tribes of South America, and indigenous Australian

Aborigines looking for languages that encode the linguistic as well as numerical information. The quipu, a system of knotted cords, is a numerical recording system that was used in the Inca Empire in the Andean region in the 15th and 16th centuries. Gary Urton, a specialist in Andean archaeology, posed that this combination of fiber types, dye colors, and intricate knotting contains a seven-bit binary code capable of conveying more than 1,500 separate units of information. According to Marcia and Robert Ascher (1980, 1997), most information on quipus is numeric, and these numbers can be read. Each cluster of knots is a digit, and there are three main types of knots: simple overhand knots; "long knots", consisting of an overhand knot with one or more additional turns; and figure-of-eight knots. Butterworth, Reeve, Reynolds, & Lloyd (2008) questioned claims that thoughts about numbers are impossible without the words to express them, that children cannot have the concept of exact numbers until they know the words for them, and adults in cultures whose languages lack a counting vocabulary similarly cannot possess these concepts. They have shown that children who are monolingual speakers of two Australian languages with very restricted number vocabularies possess the same numerical concepts as a comparable group of English-speaking indigenous Australian children.

Dunn, Greenhill, Levinson, & Gray (2011) pose that cultural evolution, rather than innate parameters or universal tendencies is the primary factor that determines linguistic structure and diversity, with a current state shaping and constraining future states. Data collected by Gelman and Butterworth (2005) imply that numerical concepts have an ontogenetic origin (resulting from the development of an individual organism) and a neural basis that are independent of language. They question theories about the necessity of using language to develop numerical concepts, both in the case of the child developmental psychology and the counting systems in Amazonian cultures that have very restricted number vocabularies, with the lack of language for exact large numbers.

Preverbal humans and animals can represent number through analog magnitudes. Adult people, when told to tap 15 times with their finger while blocking out the counting system through verbal interference, can usually perform 15 taps, showing that humans can approximately map the number 15. As subjects try to tap higher numbers, responses become less precise (Carey, 2011). According to Varley, Klessinger, Romanowski, & Siegal (2005), the numerical reasoning and language are functionally and neuro-anatomically independent in adult humans. They demonstrated a dissociation between grammatical and mathematical syntax in patients with brain damage who suffered from severe aphasia, preventing them from understanding or producing grammatically correct language. Models of number processing, which are language-independent, indicate that number concepts exist prior to verbal counting (Bar-David et al., 2009).

## Supporting Our Senses With Technologies

Animals are able to detect and locate environmental changes, so the scientists are working on finding biology-inspired computational solutions that improve our ability to control our external and internal environment. For example, we apply echolocation, ultrasound imaging, and gather thermally conveyed information, which allows us to see from a helicopter whether an object is alive, dead, or inanimate. Communication satellites include civilian and military Earth observation satellites, weather satellites, research satellites, GPS navigation satellites, space stations and other spacecraft orbiting a planet. People are competing to build a satellite network that can deliver internet anywhere in the world. The orbit used is crucial to delivering on the vision. There are two current orbits: low-earth orbit, up to 1,200 miles high and geostationary orbit, about 22,000 high.

Figure 5 shows work by Anna Ursyn titled "Waiting for Rain." Amid drought, people wait as quiescently as the golden soil does.

*Figure 5. Waiting for Rain*
*(© 2018, A. Ursyn. Used with permission)*

Sensors inform us about levels of substances that are crucial factors in our metabolism such as glucose level in our blood, or are vital components of our environment such as air pressure or information about time and position. Biosensors are used as input channels for galvanic skin response sensor (measuring the electrical conductance from skin), blood volume pulse sensor (that uses photo-plethysmography to detect existing blood pressure), breathing sensor (monitoring the individual's thorax or diaphragm activity), and electromyogram sensor (that captures the electrical activity produced by a muscle at the moment of contraction).

Works on enhancing human sensitivity continue from the seventies. A Canadian Steve Mann is one of the pioneers of wearable, mobile, wireless computing, and he also worked on augmented reality and computational photography. A wearable computer is included into the personal space of a user and controlled by the user. Mann built the WearComp with display and camera concealed in ordinary eyeglasses, so the wearer had increased awareness of the environment. WearCam was one of the first cameras transmitting images on the web. Janzen & Mann (2017) introduced a feedback-control method to automatically adjust multiple exposure settings for assembling sensor information, such as images or audio, from multiple "strong" and "weak" samplings or sensor snapshots, whose sensitivities drift and change over time. The system responds in real-time to changing ambient conditions and sensor motion. Janzen, Yang, & Mann (2018) introduced a "veillogram," a measurement of sensing or perception of physical objects. A veillogram is a detailed sensory map, 3D sensory measurement space, which is transformed and rendered onto physical objects, so it indicates sensory attention accumulated over an object's surface. Applications can include the assessment of control panels in aircraft cockpits, automobiles, and industrial control rooms.

Connectivity among humans and their environment is enhanced with accessories such as bands, watches, glasses, clothing and implants. Graphene is becoming part of wearable smart health devices or environmental sensors thanks to its sensitivity to subtle variations in its surroundings (Graphene Flagship, 2019). Wearable sensors, when attached to skin or a fingernail, record our movements and provide medical information about our bodies telling about our heart rate, blood oxygenation, possible arterial blockade or other peripheral arterial disease. Optoelectronic sensors can detect muscle contractions, and then a robotic arm can mimic a recorded movement (Ahmed, 2019a, 2019b).

Applications designed to power human senses take a form of small gadgets, such as a smart phone or a smart watch, which tracks sleep patterns (deep versus light sleep, awake time, and overall sleep quality), has a silent vibrating alarm, a motion sensor (that counts your steps on a track), and more. For example, smart watch designed by Apple relies on its wireless connection to an iPhone. It can track health activity using built-in sensors (e.g., a heart-rate sensor), communicate with others, run a wide range of apps, and make retail payments. Users can send and receive messages by dictating them or selecting from preset options. There's a built-in speaker and microphone for phone calls; one can draw on the watch's screen. A personal assistant can take dictations, give directions, or perform local searches.

There are also numerous applications aimed at powering human actions. Hiroo Iwata, Yu-ta Kimura, Hikaru Takatori and Yu-ki Enzaki constructed and exhibited, at Post City of Ars Electronica 2015 Festival, a project that was conceived as a human-centered computing. A Big Robot, a large humanoid interactive robot on wheels places the pilot at 5m-height position. Thus, the pilot, who can ride and move, feels as if his/her body were extended to 5m giant. Even a novice rider can walk on the Big Robot Mk.1A. It was then exhibited at the SIGGRAPH 2016 Conference.

## Micro- and Nanoscale Structures and Applications

We can see now the world in a changed way due to advances in microscopy and spectroscopy that allow discoveries in a nanoscale. We can study nanoscale objects: liquid crystals, soft matter, nanoshells, and carbon nanotubes; we can learn about nanoparticles and processes going in the nanoscale. Possible uses of nanotechnology, especially nanophotonic techniques serve in biomedical and clinical research, cancer treatment, clinical neuroscience, tissue engineering, drug delivery, and diagnostics. They allow biosensing of various molecular processes occurring in nanostructures in live cells. Nanophotonic biosensors enable scientists to study proteomes – complements of proteins expressed by cells, detect viruses and their functions, and create new diagnostic tools (Li, Soler, Yesilköy, & Altug, 2018). Electroceramics such as piezoelectric materials make possible to break nanometer resolution barrier. Imaging and visualization of small particles in cells can be now done with the use of computed tomography, to know how nanoparticles interact, undergo changes, and deliver drugs into a cell or on a cell membrane.

## Fiber Optics

Optical fibers have usually diameter of human hair and may have length of many miles. They are made from glass or plastic. They transmit light along the center of the fiber. Total internal refraction keeps light inside the fiber's core. Optical fibers are better than metallic conductors as they transmit signals with more information, the wide bandwidth of light wavelength. They are light, they are immune to tapping, do not need grounding, do not react to nor create electromagnetic interference. Optical fibers serve for communication by transmission of voice, data, and video, but also for sensing pressure, temperature, or spectral information. They deliver power (e.g., for laser cutting, welding, or drilling), illuminate (for example, an inside of human body), and display signs or decorations (Photonics Handbook, 2019b). Gigabit-capable optical fibers are used for phone and data communications. First trans-Atlantic fiber optic communication system was led in1988. Over 90% of the world international digital data goes through under water fiber optics, with over a million kilometers of submarine cable in service globally (Petrie, 2019). Currently hollow-core optical fibers deliver ultrashort pulses in the visible and near-infrared light.

## Photonics and Biophotonics Support Vision and Serve Science and Medicine

Optical components and optical fibers include sensors, microscopes, lasers, cameras, and more. They all support us in drawing information from our surrounding environments and other living beings. The science of photonics (as the science of photons) serves for studying the visible and invisible light detection and generation. Photonics and biophotonics are examples of current areas that involve a great number of disciplines. Understanding of this field seems important because of its wide spectrum of applications. Photonics techniques support telecommunication, information processing and computing, lighting, spectroscopy, holography, agriculture, and robotics. In metrology, photonics enabled updates in measuring time and determining precisely how much is a meter. In military technology, these techniques lead to many solutions such as jackets giving the soldiers invisibility. Laser material processing offers changing the properties of materials. Art diagnostics with the use of infrared reflection from the material, x-rays, ultraviolet fluorescence, and x-ray fluorescence are other examples.

Biophotonics and optical artificial materials result from bio inspiration from living organisms; solutions involve also bioinspired colors, pigments, and structural colorations. Molecular biomimetics are materials based on studying biological molecules. Organic materials for photonics can be tuned by adjusting their structure when organic photovoltaics (OPV) turn light into electricity. A sea mouse (Aphrodita aculeata) is an example of biophotonic engineering by a living organism: it has deep red spines that become green and blue when the light shines on them (Encyclopedia Britannica, 2018). Communication rates of organic semiconductors enable 1 gigabite/second communication rate. Organic materials can be coupled with organic laser sensors (Freebody, 2017).

Biophotonic technologies serve many medical purposes including endoscopy, vision correction, and surgery. They are largely aimed at imaging tissues. Computational imaging uses hardware and software to provide high-resolution 3D imaging systems. Biophotonic applications are used in laboratory results, clinical diagnoses, and treatment. Portable cameras as the compact modules can be now mounted on a smart phone to monitor our health at home. Technologies used in laboratories include X-rays, computer tomography scans (CT-scans or CAT-scans), magnetic resonance imaging (MRI), and positron emission tomography (PET-scans). Clinicians make use of fluorescence imaging and sensing techniques combined with advanced microscopy. For example, three-dimensional organization of live tissue structures can be captured by SHG (second harmonic generation) microscopy (Alonzo, 2018). Biological specimens can be also seen in 2D by combining light sheet fluorescence microscopy with super-slow-motion imaging. Results can be correlated with physicochemical data such as oxygen concentration or pH. Due to the biophotonic revolution a considerable shortage of skilled technicians caused that there is more openings than people to fill them, and there are not enough graduates to fill the open technical positions worldwide (Vogt, 2018).

There is considerable difference between temperature of mammals and their environment, which makes possible to make heat signatures of animals in a complex structure of their habitat. Scientists are using drones (remotely piloted aircraft systems) equipped with thermal imaging and object detection algorithms to detect wildlife populations including koalas (Maine, 2019).

## Modes of Our Communication With Humans, Computers, or Other Living Beings

Communication involves our senses, as our exchange depends on what is the content of information we have already gathered. We develop technologies to extend our senses beyond what we can see, feel, or hear. Also, we benefit from inspiration coming from studying our living environment, and then mimicking solutions used by small and big living beings. In most cases, communication requires the use of a language to send or receive information. However, it may be successful through the use of images or other modes of exchanging information.

Figure 6 shows a work "Weekday, 5 p.m." by Anna Ursyn.

*In a cycle of city life, twice a day:*
*At midday and in the afternoon*
*The City becomes vibrant with life*
*Organized around people*
*Reflecting them in its stone-and-glass walls.*
*The overall vitality of the City, its cars, lights, windows*
*Become the focus of their attention.*

*Figure 6. Weekday, 5 p.m.*
*(© 2018, A. Ursyn. Used with permission)*

We may use our communication skills to share or exchange information with fellow humans, computers, or other living beings. Visual and verbal codes support a notion that if something exists, there can be a function, and vice versa. The following text examines modes of our exchange of ideas.

## 2.2. HOW DO WE COMMUNICATE WITH PEOPLE

We may envision a range of possible ways of communication:

- Visual communication may refer to visual semiotics, signs, symbols, analogies, icons, visual plus verbal imaginative metaphors, and visualizations, but also to the robotic vision integrated with sensors, and computer vision applications (Chen, 2011).
- Communication through art involves the process of creating an artwork, conveying a message through an artwork, and receiving a message by viewers.
- Verbal communication may involve semantics, abstract ideas and messages, and also storytelling, using a story as a container (a setting appropriate for telling the same story in another, particular medium) or for an interactive novel (where a user is given a power to dictate how the story would unfold); at the same time, websites, especially those containing games, are illustrated.
- Nonverbal communication includes gesture, face expression (used by software designers for creating glyphs), body language, and pitch, among other means of expression.
- Communication through numbers, with more than one sense (and brain areas) is involved in numeral activities.
- Sound and visual music, which combines sensory modalities such as acoustical, visual, oral, and gestural.
- Temperature and thermal information.
- Other ways to communicate may involve faculties usually described as senses, which include many internal and external receptors answering to changes in environment.
- Computer languages allow communicating with a machine by using programs as instructions. For example, HTML (HyperText Markup Language) allows displaying information on the internet, e.g., on the websites or in web browsers. HTML allows transformation of communication resulting from developments in ubiquitous portable

apps, smart apps, and smart phones. Processing, an open source programming language and integrated development environment is not only a programming language but also a source for creating an online community. Environment for developments supported by haptic actions and data or info collection are possible with the Arduino boards.

## Semantics

Semantics defines the role of meaning in a sign or a sentence. Semanticists analyze also the structural features of sentences, for example location of the sign in a text. The search for information goes through making associations (relations between topics) and linking the topics. Semantic networks comprise knowledge about interconnected categories, from taxonomies of knowledge about animals and plants to multimedia communication. Semantics make such network of topics meaningful.

Semantics (from the Greek semantikos, 'significant') is a linguistic and philosophical study of meaning in languages, programming languages, formal logics, and semiotics. Semantics applies the concepts of signifiers (words, phrases, signs, and symbols) and their denotations (what they stand for). The formal semantics studies the logical aspects of meaning, while the lexical semantics studies word meanings and word relations, and conceptual semantics studies the cognitive structure of meaning. In computing, semantics denotes the meaning of language constructs, while syntax indicates their form.

Alfred Korzybski, who initiated the movement called General Semantics, drew attention to a difference between a thing and a word. According to Korzybski, language comes between someone and the objective world, sometimes causing the confusion between the signifier and the signified. Because of that, we allow language to take us up the 'ladder of abstraction'. A well-known example of the levels of verbal abstraction of categories in relation to a cow called 'Bessie' has been transferred from Korzybski via Hayakawa (1973).

The denotative and connotative meanings are two main forms of the sign meanings in semiotic analyses.

Denotation means that the meaning is translated to a sign in literal way, not admitting other meanings. Connotation may be composed of associated meanings. With connotative meanings, associations usually coexist and add nuances to the sign meanings. The word 'heart' taken alone has a denotative meaning, but when it is used in a context it may carry many connotations characteristic of distinct cultures, and not necessarily relevant directly to a part of an organism. Figure 7 presents a work of Alicia Baeza entitled "Signs."

*Figure 7. Signs*
*(© 2018, A.Baeza. Used with permission)*

Visual semantics is used in design and in presentation of three-dimensional objects, for example, in experimenting with the design of utility products. We apply semantics in practice by describing purpose, function, and qualities of the product. Symbols can be pictorial drawings, everyday pictographs such as street signs; they can be ideograms presenting an idea or an abstract concept, e.g., mathematical symbols or Egyptian hieroglyphs. Both pictograms and ideograms convey semantic content often enriched with the emotive component. According to Danesi (2017, p. 55), nuances in the symbolic meanings built in pictorial messages such as emoji can result in a 'thesaurus effect' of encoding various connotative meanings defined by the author as a "potential set of related cultural and symbolic concepts" used in some specific context. Semantic structure of a sentence is often offered from a specific perspective depending on a sender's frame of mind. The message can be interpreted differently when received by somebody who is accustomed to a dissimilar cultural context. While posting pictorial messages into the networked world, we cannot assume that the internet-savvy recipients will understood them universally.

In the semantic web, an extension of the World Wide Web, computers can read the data in web pages. According to Sir Tim Berners-Lee who started the World Wide Web and its evolving extension – the semantic web, information can be expressed in a format that is readable and usable not only for humans but also for the software applications. The Data Web and the Web 3.0 are aimed to grow as a universal database, a medium for data, information, and knowledge exchange (Wikipedia, 2019). A Web3D Consortium is working on transforming the Web into a series of 3D spaces, realized also by the Second Life. Topic maps help navigate on the web. Topic maps bridge knowledge representation and information management by building a structured semantic network above information resources.

## Communication Through Images

Visual communication may involve images as well as written texts. Communication through images may take various forms: two-dimensional images such as drawings, art works, graphs, graphics, or typographic prints, among others; three-dimensional forms – such as architectural or sculptural works; 4-dimensional time-based media – such as moving images. Communication through images can be interactive with the viewers; it can be also virtual. Communication and collaboration within 3D virtual worlds may occur by interacting with the help of customized avatars in three-dimensional graphical settings. Virtual setting enables bringing content to life, sharing and using 3D objects and thus augmenting immersion.

Visual information is often presented as numerals, graphics, or diagrams; it may be shown as a sketch, drawing, plan, outline, image, geometric relationship, map, music and dance notation, object, interactive installation, or a story. Nonverbal means of communication is of utmost importance because we are constantly immersed in interactive contact with others through social networking that uses multimedia to convey information through combinations of forms such as still images, animation, video clips, or interactive media.

Imagery refers to mental images in everyday conversation, which involves cognitive processes. Mental imagery may be visual, auditory, tactile, olfactory, gustatory, or kinesthetic. Images are the mental models for thinking; they influence language, concepts, and values, and support reading comprehension. Images and mental imagery are important in developing skills, concepts, problem solving, explaining life, and may assist in understanding forms and patterns to make discoveries. Students' learning can be mightily supported by visual display of the learning content, for example by applying color coding, interactivity (e.g., by showing interactive links in blue color or underlined), using micro/macro display (Tufte, 1983/2001, 1990/2005), or in many other ways. Visual communication techniques often include small multiple drawings that represent the sets of data with miniature pictures, to reveal repetition, change, pattern, and facilitate comparisons (Tufte, 1990). Since their introduction, cartoon faces evolved into a tool for presenting data as empathic facial expressions (Loizides, 2019).

The cognitive approach to visual thinking stimulates the progress in many disciplines, such as graphic presentation of quantitative and qualitative information, structural analysis, semiotics, computing, and also art inspired with generative algorithms, cellular automata, emergent systems, or the A-life systems. Education, computer science, business, and marketing are becoming increasingly visual, especially in the web space context, as they offer both visual and verbal types of communication. Product design and advertising depend on visual thinking. Industrial design uses applied art and science to improve aesthetics, design, ergonomics, and usability of products, such as the Bauhaus products. Images serve as models for thinking and discussing imagery as a medium for thought. Integrative fields combine literature, poetry, sociology, psychology, social anthropology, art, and music with any discipline related to the media techniques. Visual thinking applied to practice serves as an information tool. Even bank reports are often shown as pictures, possibly as an artwork.

## Communication Through Art

### Basic Art Concepts

Many concepts about art may stem from a statement that every artwork should fulfill general principles related to its design, editing, and presentation. For example, a good graphic project should enhance complexity, dimensionality, density, and beauty of communication (Tufte, 1983; 1990). Basic art concepts, which can be applied to any work of a visual arts help in analysis of a work, especially of its beauty and aesthetics of display. For example, while creating an artwork representing an apple, they support us in making certain decisions. Below the theme about apple will be further discussed. Basic art concepts include the type or form of art, subject matter, style, medium, and design.

1.  The type or form of art describes the kind of art or art products, the schemes used to classify art, and the functions art products serve; an artwork may be described as a drawing, a painting, a sculpture, etc. Would we paint, sculpt, draw an apple, or erect an architectural structure in the form of an apple?
2.  The subject matter defines the meaning of the work of art; the theme, topic, or motif represented as a person or object; it may be a portrait, a landscape, a still life, an abstract work, etc. Would we represent an apple as a part of a still life, a portrait of a man or a woman eating an apple, a landscape such as an orchard with small, multiplied images of an apple, an abstract artwork about an apple, or an almost abstract image of a close-up of the apple skin or showing an apple's interior.
3.  The style tells about the traits and resemblances within a group of works of art, the visual similarities influenced by the time, place, or personal manner of the artist. We'd need to decide if an apple would be seen as a geometric form, as the cubist artists would see it; if we 'd work on the scenery issues, like in paintings from the Renaissance or Mannerism periods; if we'd focus on light and paint related work, as it was done by the Impressionist artists; or if we'd create pop art, or a generative artwork using programming or software.
4.  The medium informs about the materials, tools and procedures the artist uses to create the work of art. For example, medium can be described as: 'oil on canvas mounted on panel,' 'acrylic on canvas,' 'marble sculpture,' 'paper, pen and ink over chalk drawing,' or 'polychrome woodblock print on paper.' We need to secure proper materials, tools, and apply selected techniques for our representation of an apple. We may choose to use Adobe Photoshop filters and effects for a painting, or apply additive and subtractive sculpture chisel. The medium can depict the differences resulting from a particular use of materials and tools. For example, an oil-on-canvas painting will look differently than an oil-on-paper painting because a canvas would repel paint, while paper would absorb it. That is while we refer to the artwork as 'oil-on-canvas painting' rather than just 'oil painting.'

5.   The design specifies the visual elements and principles used in the artwork; the planned organization of the visual phenomena the artist manipulates. We can cut an apple in half and focus on pips (seeds) and how they are placed inside five carpels arranged in a five-point star. We can picture the repetition of lines and dots on the apple skin or exaggerate irregularities in its design.

## Project: An Apple

Project about an apple may be solved in many ways: it may be a still life with apples on a plate, a portrait of a man or a woman eating an apple, landscape with apple trees, or abstract cross section showing the geometrical character of the apple carpel and the seeds arrangement. This project may take form of a book for children about an apple. In that case you may reuse your images by for example, placing the same apple many times on a tree, or on your still life. Selections from images can serve as illustrations. Figure 8 shows a computer graphics made by my student Tatiana Ingino as a part of the story.

*Figure 8. Grasping an apple*
*(© 2018, T. Ingino. Used with permission)*

After making decisions described above we may examine further properties of an artwork about an apple, for example, composition – the arrangement of visual elements in a work of art, the construction and layout of a work that defines how everything is put together using thoughtful choices. In graphic design and desktop publishing, composition is usually called a page layout. Now we would decide on the arrangement and style treatment of our image of an apple. Also, iconography is important: visual signs, symbols, and icons contained in the work. In case of an apple there is extremely rich set of meanings, connotations, cultural traditions, legends, and fairy tales. Connotations may be related to the old scripts (such as the biblical accounts about Adam and Eve), scientific research and experiments (Newton's apple), art works (Claes Oldenburg), legends (a Swiss folk hero Wilhelm Tell as an expert shot with the crossbow), symbols (an apple for a teacher), fairy tales (Snow White), artistic exaggeration (Giuseppe Arcimboldo), companies (Apple computers), places (Big Apple), many literary and cinematic works, and colloquial expressions (an apple of my eye, an apple a day keeps the doctors away). Figure 9 is a work by Ethan (the) Funk-Breay – page 4 of a story about apple.

After completing your artwork you may feel ready to write a short poem about an apple as a transformation from the visual mode of thinking to the verbal expression of your thought. Choose a form for your short verse: it may be a rhymed poem or a blank verse with a few metrical lines; or, a free verse having no fixed meter and no rhymes. You may as well prefer to write a pun – a short, humorous word play that suggests two or more meanings, or to create an apple out of letters and numbers. Make decisions about typography – the style and appearance of your work. You may also want to combine your visual and verbal solutions into one work, with the text and image well balanced. It can become a book for children about an apple.

## Elements of Design in Art

Elements of design refer to what is available for the artist/designer or any person willing to communicate visually, while principles of design describe how the elements could be used (Goldstein, Saunders, & Kowalchuk, 1986). We usually consider line, color and value, shape and form, space, line, and texture as the design elements. By applying elements and principles of design we may expand our art beyond just depiction of reality and invoke aesthetical and intellectual sensations. Fine art, web production of all kinds, utilitarian

*Figure 9. A story about apple*
*(© 2018, E. Funk-Breay. Used with permission)*

pictures, posters, and commercials are evaluated in terms of the elements and principles of design. These elements are just the fundamentals for all works of art. Also, they are applied for data presentation in all branches of knowledge. In the same way, basic kinds of picturing in art, such as still life, portrait, landscape, and abstract obey the design elements and principles. All of these elements exist in nature and in the environment we create. Depending on the kind of an artwork and the message it conveys, particular elements take over the overall composition.

- **Line:** As the shortest path between two points, line leads the eye through space. Thus, line can be a record of movement and can create illusion of motion in a work of art. Lines define an enclosed space. In a drawing or a painting, line may be used both in a functional and imagined way and may represent anything: an actual shape, a person, or a building.

Lines may be thick or thin, wavy, curved or angular, continuous or broken, dotted, dashed or a combination of any of these. There are many ways in which we can vary a line by changing its width, length, curvature, direction, or position. The use of line in art involves selection and repetition, opposition, transition, and variety of length, width, curvature, direction, and texture. Movement shown by a line is considered a principle of art. Examine short sketches and explore by drawing how different lines can show emotion. Draw and title expressive lines: draw happy lines, excited lines, stressful lines, dramatic lines relaxed lines, pathetic lines, and boring lines.

Norton Juster created "The Dot and the Line: a Romance in Lower Mathematics" (1963) using line drawings for his amazing storytelling. The title is considered a reference to a book "Flatland: A Romance of Many Dimensions" by Edwin Abbott Abbott (1994/2008). This book is easy to find online, in bookstores, or libraries. A 10-minute animation by Chuck Jones of Juster's book won the 1965 Academy Award for Animated Short Film. It can be seen online and it still attracts tens of thousands of visitors.

- **Color and Value:** A band of colors called a spectrum is formed when the light passes through a prism. Sir Isaac Newton discovered in 1704 that all colors of the rainbow are contained in white light such as sunlight. Newton also invented a color wheel: color dimensions in pigment. He put the three primary colors: red, yellow and blue, and the three secondary colors: orange, green, and violet, in an outer circle. Black is the sum of all of these colors. Intermediate colors are the additional hues, which fall between the primary and secondary colors. The mixture of adjoining primary and secondary colors can produce intermediate colors.

The source of color is light – visible radiant energy having various wavelengths. We see color because light reflects from the object. Color is a property of the light waves reaching our eyes, not a property of the object seen. The white light of the sun contains all wavelengths of light. When light falls on a surface that reflects all white light, it appears white. When the surface absorbs all the white light, we see the object as black.

The primary colors of pigment are derived from mixtures of pigment primaries. A pigment primary is caused by the reflection of two light primaries. The pigment primaries are red (magenta), yellow, and blue (a blue-green referred to as cyan). Colors of light are derived from mixtures of light primaries. A primary color of light is caused by the reflection of two pigment primaries. The light primaries are green, red-orange, and blue-violet. This means that a pigment primary is a secondary color of light.

The value of color is its lightness and darkness. Colors can be made lighter or darker by adding either white or black. To lighten value, add white. Lightening (any color plus white) produces a tint. To produce a shade, add black: any color plus black is a shade. Black plus white makes gray. A color plus gray is called a tone. Black, white and gray are called neutrals. Hue, a synonym for color, is a particular quality of a color (full intensity, tint, tone, or shade). In order to change the hue of a color, we add the neighboring color. Primary hues are: red, yellow, blue. Secondary hues are: orange, green, and violet. Intermediate hues are: yellow-green, blue-green, etc. Intensity means the purity or strength (also called chroma). To change intensity and produce a tone, add a complementary or gray color. Gray is a color without hue, made from black and white. On Figure 10, Jeremy Blue Rice presents colors that are usually seen as a color wheel.

- **Psychological Aspects of Color:** According to Tufte (1983; 1990), color is used in printing to gain attention, to be legible and comprehensible, and to make an impression. Tufte provides some helpful hints about using color:
  - **To Attract Attention**: Warm colors are higher in visibility than cool colors; contrast in values (light versus dark) is greater than contrast in hues (blue versus yellow); the darker the background, the lighter a color appears against it.
  - **To Produce Psychological Effects**: To convey coolness, warmth, action, purity, etc.
  - **To Develop Associations**: Do not use green when advertising fresh meet.
  - **To Build Retention**: Color has high memory value, especially in repeated messages.
  - **To Create Aesthetically Pleasing Atmosphere**: Poor choice is worse than the use of no color at all. The use of elements and principles of design is effective for this purpose.
- **Shape and Form:** Shapes describe two-dimensional (2D) configurations; they have no volume. In an outline drawing we only show the shape. An ambiguous shape is doubtful, uncertain, or open to more than one interpretation. A favorite textbook example of ambiguous space is a vase/profile, and an old/young woman. Form describes and

gives a three-dimensional (3D) feel and look of an object. In drawing and painting, we may use shading and highlighting of an outline drawing to show this. Forms have volume – a word that describes the weight, density, and thickness of an object. The solidness or volume of the form could be obtained by using highlights on one side of each object and shading on the opposite side. Shapes are geometric (such as triangles, squares, circles, etc.) or organic (such as leaves). Forms also are geometric (such as pyramids, cones, cubes, spheres, etc.) or organic – natural (like trees). They can be irregular (like clouds).

Space is the void between solid objects (forms) and shapes. Everything takes up space, whether it's two-dimensional, like drawing and painting, or three-dimensional, like sculpture and architecture. Paintings, drawings, and prints take up 2D space. In a painting, it is limited to the edges of the canvas. Sculpture and architecture take up 3D space. Music and literature take up time. Some arts, such as film, opera, dance and theater take both space and time. We talk about positive and negative space when space describes the void between solid shapes and forms. The solid shape or form is called a positive space. The space within the drawn objects is a positive space; a doughnut has a positive shape or form. The space between the objects is a negative space; the doughnut hole is a negative shape or space.

*Figure 10. A Color Wheel*
*(© 2018, J. Blue Rice. Used with permission)*

- **Perspective:** Is the appearance of depth or distance on a flat surface. We are picturing a 3D world of depth and distance on a 2D surface of a sheet of paper or a computer screen. With perspective, we show objects and scenes as they appear to the eye, with relation to implied depth on a flat surface of the picture. Designing a 3D display involves visual thinking. Perspective drawing is one of the solutions, often with orthographic projection or the bird's eye view. We can display data in 3D as cardboard models or on the surfaces of a polyhedron – a solid body bounded by polygons. Other presentation techniques include architectural miniatures, stereo illustrations and slides. Three-dimensional graphics are designed with the use of programming strategies or 3D graphics software packages; data can be presented as holograms, video, stereo illustrations, and slides. Maybe the most impressive is a computer-based immersive multi-wall virtual reality and interactive visualization environment. Thus, we can show a 3D object as a 2D image when we draw a perspective drawing, a shaded drawing, or create a painting or a sculpture, but we do not achieve it by designing a map. We can consider a geometrical cardboard model a 3D form of display, but we cannot say this about a musical score, a railroad schedule, a periodic system of elements in chemistry, or a tabular array of numbers.

Figure 11 presents work of Anna Ursyn entitled "Viewpoints."

Several methods help us to create an aerial perspective, the representation of objects and scenes according to their distance: overlapping, vertical positioning, graying colors, varying details, varying size, and converging lines. By overlapping objects, we may create an illusion that the partially hidden object is more distant. Vertical positioning lets us believe that objects placed higher are at a considerable distance and those positioned lower are closer in space. Gradation of the strength of light and colors of objects, and showing objects in grayed colors makes them look remote. We may show less detail on an object to make it more distant than another, as well as drawing distant objects smaller and nearer objects larger. Converging lines is the most frequently used method that can be achieved by drawing lines closer and closer together in the distance.

Cognitive perception addressed by painters was not always derived from an analysis of traditional rules governing the composition of an artwork. Many times, the masters chose the perspective according to their cognitive perception. Sometimes, it was an isometric method of drawing, so that three

*Figure 11. Viewpoints*
*(© 2018, A. Ursyn. Used with permission)*

dimensions were shown not in perspective, but in their actual size. For example, interiors painted by Vincent Van Gogh were not fully based on the familiar Euclidian perspective. Cezanne's paintings reflected the way the viewer perceives reality. Areas where the viewers were supposed to direct and focus their eyes were painted in a three-dimensional perspective with greater detail and enhanced color in the center (and blurred lines at the edge). The rest of the painting addressed peripheral vision and so it was flat.

- **Pattern:** Is an artistic or decorative design made of lines; thus, pattern is a repetition of shapes. Patterns make a basis of ornaments, which are specific for different cultures. Owen Jones (1856/2010) made a huge collection of ornaments typical of different countries. He wrote a monographic book entitled "The Grammar of Ornament."
- **Texture:** Is a general characteristic for a substance or a material. It can be either actual (natural, invented, or manufactured) or simulated texture (made to look rough, smooth, hard or soft, or natural). Simulated textures are made to represent real textures such as a smooth arm or rough rock formation. But they are not actual textures, and if you touch the picture you feel only the paint or the pencil marks.

## Principles of Design in Art

Principles of design that are most often used in visual arts are: balance, emphasis, movement, variety, proportion and unity. These principles may vary according to the person using them. For example, some textbooks discuss also contrast, rhythm, and repetition (Goldstein, Saunders, & Kowalchuk, 1986). The skillful use of elements and principles of design may enrich the work of art beyond just depiction of reality and invoke aesthetical and intellectual sensations of pleasure, appreciation, or repulsion.

- **Balance:** Is an arrangement of lines, colors, values, textures, forms, and space, so that one section or side of the artwork does not look heavier or stronger than another. We can see in art three main types of balance: formal (or symmetrical, for example two people of the same weight at two ends of a see-saw), informal (or asymmetrical, for example, when a person on a see-saw who weighs more sits closer to the center and the lighter person sits farther out on the end), and radial balance, a circular balance moving out from a center of an object (for example, when only one object is centered in a picture).
- **Emphasis:** Is way of bringing a dominance or subordination into a design or a painting. Major objects, shapes, or colors may dominate a picture when they are larger and repeated more often, by being heavier in volume, or by being stronger in color and color contrast than the subordinate objects, shapes, or colors. Without a balanced relationship between the dominant and subordinate elements there is too much emphasis.
- **Movement:** We may achieve the illusion of movement by the use of lines, colors, values, textures, forms and space to direct the eye of the viewer from one part of the picture to another. For example, the feeling of movement can be suggested by circular, diagonal or vertical arrangements; we may also create illusion of movement that goes back into the distance, both by diminution of sizes and similarity of shapes.
- **Composition:** Is orderly arrangement, a proper combination of distinct parts so they are presented as a unified whole. To develop composition in a drawing or painting, we have to select the objects we want to show, then create a center of interest and find out balance among the objects. Good composition may involve movement, rhythm, and well-arranged positive and negative space.

It took many years to develop routine features of books, with page numbering, indexes, tables of contents, and title pages. Web documents undergo a similar evolution and standardization in order to define the way information is organized and made available in electronic form. Visual composition of a website and its graphics is an important part of the user's experience. In interactive documents, the interface design includes the metaphors, images, and concepts used to convey function and meaning of the website on a computer screen.

In accordance with Edward Tufte (1990), every graphic presentation, as well as every project should fulfill general principles related to its design. Tufte taught that information should enhance complexity, dimensionality, density, and beauty of communication. Good information display should be: documentary, comparative, casual and explanatory, quantified, multivariate, exploratory, and skeptical; it should allow comparing and contrasting. When envisioning statistical information, such display should insistently enforce comparisons, express mechanisms of cause and effect quantitatively, recognize the multivariate nature of analytic problems, inspect and evaluate alternative explanations.

- **Variety and Contrast:** An artist uses elements of design to create diversity and differences in an artwork. Contrasting colors, textures, and patterns all add interest to the artwork. Highlights of color to the corners or edges of some shapes may be used to add contrast.
- **Proportion:** The size of one part of an artwork in comparative relation its other parts is called proportion. Artists use proportion to show balance, emphasis, distance, and the use of space. Sometimes, for example in medieval religious paintings, saints were pictured out-of-proportion to emphasize their importance: some donors were painted bigger and humble donators smaller.
- **Unity:** Unity is the result of how all elements and principles of design work together. All parts must have some relation to each other. They must fit together to create the overall message and effect.

## Project: Crowd

This learning project is about creating art works as a means of communication and introduces information about creating pictures that communicate message to the viewers. This activity serves as introduction to the cognitive way of learning by creating visual presentation of knowledge. First, you are invited to draw several sketches: first a shoe, then a manikin, and finally a group of people. Read about the elements and principles of design in arts as well as in other disciplines, and explore by sketching the positive–negative space relations. Consider links of drawings, architecture, and design with mathematics, physics, and the functioning of the brain and body (Halpers, 2015). Sketching has a cognitive power as it enhances the mind–brain–eye–hand coordination. Write your own statement on this theme.

First, draw some basic lines: thick, thin, wavy, curved, angular, continuous, broken, dotted, dashed. Start with ovals, and then work like a sculptor by removing unwanted parts and adding lines bringing depth and character to your drawing. Change line's width, length, curvature, and texture. Now, draw some geometric sketches.

## Sketching a Shoe

This part of a project is designed to exercise in capturing an essence of an object. Take off your shoe and make sketches of the shoe done in 3 minutes, and then 2 minutes, 30 seconds, and in 10 seconds. This last sketch would take only 10 seconds, so you'll need to eliminate what is not relevant. Examine all your sketches. Which one is the best? Many would say this is the last one. Anyway, we have a camera when we need a detailed picture.

When you have less time each time for drawing lines, you make fast decisions what is really crucial for a depiction of your shoe, by drawing only important characteristics that make it your own shoe. Repetition of lines without erasing them shows the shoe's weight and implies motion, so your drawing will be more imaginative. A unique portrait of your shoe, almost a caricature, will show its specific features exaggerated in a funny way. Explore the ways a line can function in a work of art showing not only forms but also the meaning and emotion.

## Drawing a Manikin

Familiarize yourself with sketches made by artists such as Chris Lester, Danny Coleman, and Ken Bernstein. This part of a project involves drawing a manikin that serves for learning drawing or a mannequin usually used for displaying garments on it.

Draw an image of a person while looking at a wooden manikin. There are three ideas you might want to consider:

1.  **Proportion**: The head of a man fits seven to eight times in the entire body. Look at the manikin and think of its head as a unit. Make a mental or sketched division of your entire paper, so eight heads would fit in. This way you will make a grid, a network of lines that cross each other to form rectangles.

2.  **Geometric Approach**: Examine your model. It is made out of geometric forms; in computer world it is referred to as primitives. Those are the 3-D objects. Start with thinking in terms of 2D objects: an oval, a trapezoid, a circle, a rectangle, etc. By looking at the initial grid you created, start inserting an oval for the head, another one for the neck, a trapezoid for a torso, etc., till you see the whole figure drawn. Make your own individual decisions about dividing your paper with lines and placing shapes into the rectangles of the grid. Draw only absolutely necessary lines to convey the essence of the human shape.

3.  **Positive and Negative Space**: Consider all the space that belongs to your manikin a positive space and all that does not, a negative space. For example, its leg will form a positive space, while the space between an arm and its torso will be considered a negative one. Now, examine the relationship between the positive and the negative space. Like a subtractive sculptor working with clay, keep polishing your lines by making darker those lines that better define your shapes. Do not erase lines, and don't get upset if your hand guides the pencil in an unwanted direction. The triad of lines with different shades of gray will build the depth in your object. Your drawing will not appear flat anymore, but will show an illusion of depth.

To summarize, define proportion of the body parts to the whole picture: a head, as a unit, fits 7-8 times in the entire body. Insert geometric forms: an oval for a head, another one for a neck, a trapezoid for a torso, etc., till you see the whole figure drawn. Figure 12 shows a manikin drawn by Erin McClintock.

## Drawing a Group of People

Create a crowd scene by multiplying and then placing human figures in a background. Repeat these steps, so you have a scene with people crowding. Unless you have drawn your manikin using any image editing software, you may either scan your drawing or photograph it. Open your file in any image editing software, for example in Adobe Photoshop (you may try this

*Figure 12. A manikin*
*(© 2018, McClintock, E.. Used with permission)*

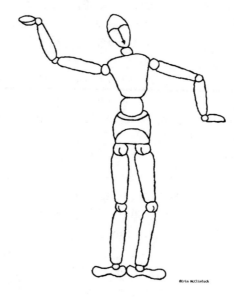

program for 30 days, before buying it by registering and downloading from the Adobe.com website). Select your manikin, copy it, then paste on a new canvas. Figure 13 shows a scene with manikins drawn by Alejandra Ramos.

Change the size, transform it by rotating, skewing, or applying perspective, so a manikin that is further away from you will appear smaller than the one that is right in front of you. When you repeat these steps three times, you will have a scene with four people, for example crowding in an elevator. Create an impression of motion by slanting the whole bodies of your figures, and changing position of their limbs. Your picture will show the dynamics of a group gathered with an unknown common purpose: it might be an attempt to make a performance or to dance. Figure 14 presents a work of Nicolas Kunkel entitled "A crowd on a roof" where a solitary viewer watches a crowd on a screen.

## Drawing a Background That Explains Why These People Are Together

Create a background, showing the reason why these people are gathered. At this moment, your human figures are no longer unidentified, nameless figures – they acquire meaning. The relation between human figures and a

*Figure 13. A workout*
(© 2018, A. Ramos. Used with permission)

*Figure 14. A crowd on a roof*
(© 2018, N. Kunkel. Used with permission)

background in your project can be compared to the relation between the data and information gained when you conduct a search. The data itself has no meaning – it contains just numbers; the numbers gain meaning in a context of your search and just become meaningful information. Draw scenery for your visual story, and at the same time create a clear message. Many artists use deliberately open messages using symbols or signs that could be freely interpreted and also generated cooperatively by the viewer. Abstract artists choose their own means of expression, so their paintings gain a feature of an ambiguous, open work with loose relation between signs and meanings. Thus, the paintings of Rothko, in spite of their recognition in the world of art, may be annoying for someone who can see there only the colorful rectangles. Figure 15 shows a composition with manikins by Mary Jo Lasky entitled "Who killed Mr. Green?"

Design a background as a visual clue. It can be a concert hall, a field game scene, a roof to take shelter from rain, or an approaching bus during a rush hour. Depending on the background, the crowd becomes the audience at the concert, viewers of the circus performance, soldiers serving in an army, players, contestants, or competitors. Draw your visual story, and create a message by adding patterns, colors, densities, and sizes.

You have just created a composition that is self-explanatory and can be classified as a closed message rather than an open message, because everyone will see what you described visually. This is an example of an artwork with an explanatory power because the viewer can look at your composition and understand why those people are there. Figure 16 presents a work by James Reiman entitled "Packed train."

*Figure 15. "Who killed Mr. Green?"*
*(© 2018, M-J. Lasky. Used with permission)*

*Figure 16. Packed train*
*(© 2018, J. Reiman. Used with permission)*

# Metaphor

The use of signs and metaphors in art, graphic design, and visual storytelling supports visual communication. Learning and understanding of abstract ideas and processes can be easier when difficult concepts are presented through visual metaphors – a basic structure for communicating a message. Visual metaphors, which make difficult concepts visible, help us to abstract the essence of an idea. Metaphors focus people on an issue and facilitate understanding of the idea. They enable us to translate abstract knowledge into a realm of familiar actualities that we can experience or see (Ursyn & Lohr, 2010). A metaphor describes relations among data, organizes information in a meaningful way, and combines creative imagery with the analytic rationality of conceptual diagrams. Visual metaphor indicates one thing as representing another, difficult one. In a metaphor, a feature of an object or a word belonging to a particular object is applied to another thing, concept, or idea. Metaphors enable making mental models and comparisons, so a basic structure of visualization is metaphorical. The word 'metaphor' has been created in ancient Greece where 'μεταφορά' (*metaphorá*) meant 'carrying over' or 'transferring' and then used in Latin as 'metaphora' – a transfer (Online Etymology Dictionary, 2014).

To create a visual metaphor, we can use natural objects or phenomena (e. g., mountains, tornados), artificial, man-made objects (e. g., a bridge, a temple), activities (climbing), or concepts (war, family). Metaphors structure information, organize knowledge in visualizations, and thus originate an insight. Metaphors may convey disparate topics such as theological events or encyclopedias' entries, or serve as classification systems (Lima, 2011, Lima, 2019). Manuel Lima called the tree figure the most ubiquitous and long-lasting visual metaphor, "through which we can observe the evolution of human consciousness, ideology, culture, and society" (Lima, 2014, p. 42). Therefore, hierarchical structures are most often analyzed with the use of a tree metaphor.

Digital images, sounds, or animations can be analyzed as metaphors and seen as important sign systems working beyond the literary culture. Linking a culture of the image and of the text, for example sending messages containing words, images, sounds and objects, makes a synesthetic mode of cognition which operates outside the language-based thinking. Messages conveyed as the non-verbal, visual media are often more abstract and more interactive with the viewer. By crossing senses, viewers construct their perception of the reality that has been communicated by an artist in their own art-historical and cultural contexts. Visual metaphor may support conveying meaning when a notion defined and verbalized in one language has quite different meaning when transferred into another language, alphabet, and culture. Application of the visual metaphor may eliminate such differences in understanding concepts. Many times this happens through the use of a meta-language, as in case of blogs.

Figure 17 shows a work of Anna Ursyn titled "Urban Masquerade."

*Dream you can fly.*
*You can mold everything you dream into an amazing form*
*You can create other cities in your dreamy wonderings*
*And know kin souls' lingo.*
*It happens. You have double force now,*
*Uncanny might, potent, ongoing, supernatural command.*
*All because of computers.*

*Figure 17. Urban Masquerade*
*(© 2018, A. Ursyn. Used with permission)*

## Pretenders, Misleaders, and Informers

When we communicate online, send a voicemail, or use visualization, we want to be understood exactly as intended. However, addressing user's need for joy is equally important. In contrast to generally accepted philosophy that the best design is self-explanatory, every day we encounter objects that challenge our sagacity, entertain us by mimicking other things, mislead us about their function, or about the material they are made of. Some objects are designed to inform and entertain at the same time, by mimicking other objects' characteristics. Some of them are made to mislead us. The thinking behind this design is aimed to entertain, make the day brighter, or make a product more attractive, while fulfilling its purpose.

- **Pretenders:** Products that show metaphorical likeness to other forms and 'pretend' to be something else can be called pretenders. For example, a candle may be shaped like a cactus, a cat, or anything else. One may say about Las Vegas, Nevada that a whole Las Vegas Strip is a big pretender, with Paris, Venice, and ancient Egypt recreated inside of it. Many times, ample semiotic content is needed in product design to make it easy to understand, rather than metaphorical likeness of a product to something else. In fact, there are a lot of gift products with the appearance of another well-known object and it is difficult to guess what it is for or how to use it. On the other hand, the Apple Company ensures that the design of the connectors does not allow plugging them in the wrong way. One may see pretenders in everyday life. Healthy food products are often designed to pretend something else, for example meatless meatballs. Hamburgers made of portabella mushroom 'pretend' they are made of meat. There are even human pretenders – when a person wears a costume and advertises a product, for example pretending to be a Mexican taco. Toys are often designed as transformers and pretenders. Toys called Transformers (introduced in 1988) and the Ultra Pretenders featured a large exterior vehicle shell, then a secondary humanoid shell (which could also transform), and within that, the miniature interior robot. A puppet often hides another character within itself. The notion of pretenders is somehow related to the concept of camouflage. It could be understood as the disguising forms, patterns, or coloring that enables to blend with the surroundings. Figure 18 presents a candy box pretender.

- **Misleaders:** We may think about some products as misleaders, when objects are designed to look like one thing while they are serving quite another purpose, for example, you may think it's a book but it is a CD cover. Some souvenir products lack the product semantics, as they have an appearance of another well-known object as a disguise; it prevents the viewer from understanding what it is for or how to use it. For example, candles that are made in a shape of fruits or toys, and therefore do not look like candles, are misleaders. Figure 19 displays a container pretending to contain mushrooms while it is empty (mushrooms make a cover).

The most dramatic example of a misleader comes from the Bronze Age, when a huge figure of a wooden horse, with a force of men hidden inside, allowed the Greeks to enter the city of Troy (Figure 61). After the Greeks pretended to sail away, the Trojans pulled the wooden horse into their city as a gift and a victory trophy. Then, at night, the hidden soldiers came out of their wooden structure, opened the city gates and let the Greek army get in and take over the place. Many times, one material pretends to be another, for example, traditionally designed laces threaded in a web-like pattern are actually made of a synthetic material, not even knitted with thread but polymerized as

*Figure 18. A bus: A candy box pretender*
(© 2019, photographed by A. Ursyn. Used with permission)

*Figure 19. A pretender: Mushroom storage. pretender*
(© 2019, photographed by A. Ursyn. Used with permission)

a whole. A 'crystal' vase is often made of plastic. A countertop in a kitchen may be made of another plastic material that pretends to look like marble. Figure 20 shows a small figurine of a Trojan Horse.

- **Informers –Hidden Messages**: Objects may have hidden messages. For example, when car dealers want to make you feel powerful, they show a lion or a tiger and transfer this feeling on a car. Other objects

153

*Figure 20. A figurine of a Trojan Horse as a misleader*
*(© 2019, photographed by A. Ursyn. Used with permission)*

carry the hidden messages to help to use products. Such objects that have an easy recognizable shape are called canonical objects. In spite of the new line in a design of cellular phones, we still draw an old-style telephone with a round dial to signal where we can find the phone booths with the more modern touch-tone ones. We use symbols and link-node diagrams for abstract concepts in graphic languages.

The developments in product semantics put the designers on guard about the role of images as cognitive reflections of real world. Hence, aesthetics in marketing became important. Designers and advertisers began to consider visual imagery as a form of non-verbal processing. They became aware that products might be better remembered as easy to evoke images, so they started to apply imagery as a mnemonic strategy. Quite often, objects carry hidden messages: to attract prospective buyers, phone may take a shape of something else, for example, a pet animal. Figure 21 presents an informer – a container for a tomato.

Thus, there is a link from iconic, well known content to a hidden content of a commercial, but designers must know the audience they are talking to evoke expected reaction. Also, CD covers send hidden messages through images, sexual, political, or other, to address visually a selected group of listeners. Many times color takes as a message using generally accepted associations, such as green = calm and soothing, red = hot and violent, etc.

*Figure 21. A tomato container as an informer–pretender*
*(© 2019, photographed by A. Ursyn. Used with permission)*

Thus, commercials present a product along with a hidden message that provides the viewer with aesthetic sensations, emotional associations, and the producer's promises that supplement the product itself. Designers and advertisers began to consider visual imagery as a form of non-verbal processing. They became aware that products might be best remembered when they evoke images, so they started to apply imagery as a mnemonic strategy. Designing informers and pretenders may be somehow related to entertainment: objects one can play with and laugh at may be useful in marketing.

There are many camouflage restaurants blended with the surroundings or pretending they are something else by applying unusual decor. Also, hundreds of hotels defy convention, hosting quests in the cars, aircraft, in a prison, a lighthouse, a tree house, underground, underwater, on the top of cranes, and in other unusual places. In terms of product design, when discussing pretenders and misleaders we may think about their look, functionality of the product and its effectiveness in terms of cost, maintenance, or ecology, messages it conveys, joy, fun, and emotions they evoke. We may ponder why the pretenders and misleaders are so ubiquitous and what kind of needs they satisfy. Maybe, they quench our inclination toward spontaneous playfulness. If so, we may seek advantages of applying them in communication, product design, and in instruction. We may use their ludic character relating to play or playfulness properties to entertain, evoke attention, emotion, and curiosity, and thus enhance the attractive qualities of a product or motivation of the learner. With cognitive approach to mental imagery, one can include pretenders as tools to visualize a concept and create image representation of it. Thus, we may make pretenders, misleaders, and informers a tool for instruction, as well as the product design and it's marketing; they convey both emotion and poetry, and make us aware of the artistic context of material culture of the products.

Figure 22 shows a playful misleader: One may think it is possible to write on this mug, so it would be useful for making notes.

## Emoji

The main use of emoji is in sharing informal messages and bonding with others, mostly friends (as in F2F – friend-to-friend computer networks), family, and acquaintances. Web users add various kinds of emoji into their phone messages, Facebook pages, Twitter postings, Instagram uploads, websites, and internet domains. The word Emoji corresponds to a Japanese word containing notions of a picture (e) and a letter or character (moji). Manga comics have been the main source of inspiration for creating the Emoji code.

*Figure 22. A mug as a misleader–pretender, standing on another pretender: A laptop cover*
*(© 2019, photographed by A. Ursyn. Used with permission)*

Emoi characters make up a common visual alphabet, the universal set of characters for the languages of the world. They are standardized in the Unicode Standard, with its recent version 12.0, by the Unicode Consortium, which specifies and maintains 150 modern and historic scripts, as well as symbols and emoi. As we don't draw emoji ourselves but we select them from a standardized set, so they do not reveal our subjectivity.

Emoji are mostly adjective to the main message; they enhance mood of the receiver, add emotions to communication, and emphasize remarks or comments it contains. Many times, they save the effort of writing full phrases, as it happens when they replace salutations or punctuation in informal writing. Emoji are added to make a message more positive, joyful, and amusing but also sometimes ironic or sarcastic. The hybrid emoji text produces writing blended with pictorial system, and thus emoji as metaphorical pictures produce a new kind of meaning (Danesi, 2017). Many keyboards have emoji characters included. Apple is adding 50 emoji to its latest keyboard iteration, so do Google & Instagram. However, writing emoi-only texts or even sentences engenders considerable difficulty to decode for older generation not trained in communicating visually but popular with teenagers intuitively comfortable in today's image based environment.

Emoji are different from emoticons, which are pictorial representations of facial expressions using keyboard characters such as punctuation marks, letters, and numbers. Probably the most used emoticon is a smiley face. For example, emoji of a smiley-face is a picture ☺, while the analogous type-based emoticon looks like:–). While they are concise in a graphic form, emoji can convey complex emotions through their symbolic expressions, somehow in a way a chemical formula or a mathematical equation represent complexity of natural forms in a compact way. However, the same emoji may invoke unexpected connotations and arouse unpredicted emotions because people develop various conceptual meanings for signs and symbols according to their cultural background (Danesi, 2017). Figure 23 presents a work done by Karli Cumber titled "Karli's Monday Routine."

*Figure 23. "Karli's Monday Routine"*
*(© 2019, K. Cumber. Used with permission)*

## Synesthesia

Synesthesia is a neurologically based condition that results from the merging of two or more sensory or cognitive pathways. It happens when stimulation of one sense leads to experiences in another sensory pathway: one may taste some shapes or hear color. Visual perception may involuntary accompany sensations of taste, touch, pain, smell, or temperature. Synesthesia may be induced with drugs. The most common types of synesthesia are: the word-to-color association and colored hearing, when someone is seeing colors when hearing a musical tone; usually the lower a musical note, the darker is the color. Therefore, synesthesia can be seen as a metaphor for transferring sensations typical of one medium into another. Thus, the notion of synesthesia incorporates elements of design, optics, neurology, physiology and psychology.

Synesthetic ways of expression are applied in electronic art, performance arts, data presentation, technical implementations, design, advertisement, visualizations and simulations for scientific and educational purposes; they interact with the varied audience. A Russian painter and art theorist Wassily Kandinsky claimed he experienced synesthesia. Several writers, such as Edgar Allan Poe or Arthur Rimbaud described synesthetic experience and even linked it with memory. Some poets state they hear sounds or musical tones when they see words, images, and colors. Some musicians interpret their color experience in terms of musical keys or associate their mood or feeling with musical keys; they assert that they see colors assigned to particular tones or musical passages. Interactive multimodal data presentations are of interests to scientists. Strong aesthetic experience elicited by synesthetic art may result in a sensation of increased artistic potential and a need for doing one's own artwork. Examples of visual presentation of music and sound include artwork sonification and environmental problems sonification.

## 2.3. VISUALIZATION OF NATURE AND KNOWLEDGE AS COMMUNICATION

Visualization means the communication of data, information, and knowledge with graphical representations. It changes numerical data into graphs, clouds (Chen, 2010, 2011), tree visualizations (Shneiderman, 2014; Lima, 2014), network data, time-based, interactive, metaphorical visualization designs, and other formats. We can see and understand our data more deeply and this understanding may help us make first-rate decisions. Many times, a good visualization changes the way how one thinks about the topic.

We can create visualization of our concepts by drawing basic shapes like squares, triangles, and circles connected by lines and arrows, and then inserting simple drawings inside of these shapes. Graphs, diagrams, or animations can visualize messages as well. Other examples are multimodal interactive data presentations, sonifications, and haptic/touch interfaces. Visualization has also been considered a semiotic process because of the use of signs to present ideas. According to Manuel Lima (2011), visualizations fall into three categories: science, design, and art; they are used as a tool for understanding data – i.e. discovering patterns, connections, and structure. For example, one can adopt a visualization workflow with components: data sources (data base, programs, files) – data transformers (filters, spreadsheet formulae, file format converters) – data visualizers (graphical representation of results) (Benoît, 2019).

Visualization enhances communication through information display with the use of letters, numerals, art, graphic design, visual storytelling, signs, symbols, and application software. Visualization in the form of a diagram may change information into plots, line-graphs and charts, or the engineers or architects' blueprints. Diagram is rather abstract than illustrative. Presentations of data organization and interpretation such as governmental statistics are easier to comprehend in a graphic than in a numerical form. Graphics serve as explanatory tools for the data sets. Visualization usually means using the computer, which transforms data into information, and then visualization converts information into picture forms. Graphic images and symbols convey and express the meaning of abstract data, which lets us comprehend data and make discoveries, decisions, or explanations about patterns or individual items (Shneiderman, 1996). Thus, communication through visualization is at the same time pictorial and linguistic. It is socially and culturally conditioned, based on familiar linguistic patterns, as in a 'pie chart' metaphor for market shares, or a 'starry night' metaphor showing data in 3D (Bertschi & Bubenhofer, 2005).

Visualization assists practitioners in creating communication media-art, installations, animated video or film, architectural projects, designing newspapers and magazines, or working on website design. Users apply. Visualization helps to analyze huge resources of information such as libraries, email archives, or things such as a blog, a wiki, and a tweeter feed (Ward, Grinstein, & Keim, 2010, p. 291). These applications are running the World

Wide Web – an information space containing web resources accessible over the internet with the use of software called a web browser. Visualizations help users to understand how data analyses and queries relate to each other. From simple charts and data graphics to 3D multi-user virtual reality environments happening in real time, with human interaction possible, visualizations let us fly around the organized data, comprehend, and make decisions (Chen, 2010, 2011).

According to Lev Manowich (in Lima, 2011), there are important features that make information visualization unique: projects are visually dense, with more data; they show relations between data; in aesthetical terms, they show complexity (chaos theory, emergent complexity theory) rather than reduction (breaking down into the simplest elements). As a scientific tool, information visualization serves for discovery of new knowledge; as a design tool it facilitates the perception of patterns and evokes emotions in the viewers; as art it is a technique to produce something non-utilitarian and aesthetically interesting (Lima, 2011, p. 12).

Visualization projects often include icons. Images of iconic objects are familiar to all viewers, such as an old-style electric bulb, a DNA double helix, or a telephone handset. To convey a message visually with an icon, we take in those features that best identify an object, and suppress those features that are not basic to comprehending it, thus showing the scissorness of the scissors. In order to give a meaning to our image, we get rid of similarities and features (visible or semantic) that are not crucial. For example, knife and fork belong to 'silverware' - does not matter if it is green or wooden. Most often, these are icons referring to concrete objects; however, many icons stand for abstract ideas. For example, an old-style electric bulb shining above one's head is often meant to stand for a bright idea. Many icons have a longer life than the shapes of the objects they stand for; we already seldom use the old-style phones with a round dial but we can see this icon when we look for a phone booth. In the same way, in spite of the developments in robotics, a picture of an anthropomorphic, humanoid robot still serves as an icon for industrial, servicing robots designed for specific tasks, or bots (virtual software agents), which do not resemble humans. By the way, the word "robot" was coined in 1920, in the course of conversation between the Czech writer Karel Čapek and his brother, the cubist painter and writer Josef Čapek (Zunt, 2005); it was given to an artificial man that could be mistaken for humans. The U.S. writer of Russian origin Isaac Asimov introduced to the readers the term 'robotics' in 1941, building on Karel Čapek's concept of the robot.

Visualization of large data sets is in demand because the web became the main carrier of information. When we use the search engines, there is too much data to be scrolled on the screen; a search can be done with the use of information visualization, data mining, and semantic web. A big set of data can be presented in an interactive way on more than three axes. Users can navigate across big data sets, find patterns, relationships, and structures, and then examine their dynamic factors, resulting changes, and effects in real time. All that would be invisible if presented numerically.

Pedagogical qualities of visualizations involve their visual, verbal, auditory, haptic, and other features, along with the easiness of learning about their use. Visualization is a way of learning, teaching, or sharing the data, information, and knowledge because it supports cognition, outperforms text-based sources, and increases our ability to think and communicate.

In the field of product design, product visualization supports market research and advertising; a grasp of visualization technologies is a requisite for designing effective visual marketing. Various trends in product design aim for comfort, simplicity, elaboration, or fool proof and easiness of use. Designers and advertisers consider visual imagery as non-verbal processing. By applying icons in design designers can support our learning of using a complicated product, so it's easy to answer a question, for example, "How to open this thing?" The best design is often self-explanatory. Information visualization communicates with users through shortcuts. It uses signs, symbols, icons, metaphors, connotations, and associations. We can create open or closed messages, whether we intend the user to understand the info as close to what is being sent, or we'd allow for imaginative interpretation. Object design has to fulfill functional, ergonomically oriented, aesthetic, material and space related demands, as well as match the area of joy of the user.

Product visualization can show high-quality features of products in a way that everybody can apprehend the product's values and buy the marketed article. The objectives of aesthetic studies move toward the effectiveness, efficiency, and easiness to understand (at a low cognitive cost) of visual presentation, not exclusively the beauty of an image. Informative art works are not only aesthetical objects but also contain information. Users tend to associate aesthetics with readability, and readability with understanding.

Traditionally, visualization meant the intuitive use of visual presentation of concepts. There are anecdotes about famous inventors such as Friedrich Kekulé, Albert Einstein, and many other scientists. Friedrich Kekulé formulated an idea of four covalent bonds between a carbon atom and four hydrogen atoms. He supposedly visualized the theory of chemical structure as the dancing atoms and molecules while he was riding in 1855 on the upper deck of a horse-drawn omnibus in London (Rocke, 2010). Kekulé also discovered the ring-shaped structure of benzene (Kekulé, 1865). It is said that he had a daydream of a snake seizing and eating its own tail resembling the ancient symbol ouroboros depicting such a serpent or dragon. These cases may serve as examples of knowledge inspired by mental visualization on the subconscious level. The imagining such things might be stimulated by the long hours of learning and working in a lab. Asking the challenging and puzzling questions may evoke curiosity in students.

- **Tools for Visualization:** Serve as cognitive instruments such as utilization of metaphors, simulations, or the use of layers, details, and complex presentations in a website. Tools and instruments for visualization are derived from many domains; they may include scanners, microscopes, and cameras, micro agents, or bots, along with many kinds of applications for recording and measuring in real time. One may apply computer graphics tools such as Adobe Photoshop, Adobe Illustrator, Adobe Dreamweaver, and more, along with the computer networking related concepts such as cloud computing. Also, geographic maps, heat maps, and graphical representations such as flow or fever charts, and sparklines often serve for visualization of events. Clustering technique (clusters as subsets of observations) is used in data mining for statistical analysis, pattern recognition, and bioinformatics.

- **Simulation:** Takes the appearance of a process or system to create a model and represent the real world by a computer program, if events can be presented as mathematical data. Thus, simulation creates computer-generated environment or virtual environment. The values of certain variables can be changed to simulate and measure the effect of the variable of interest, for example the effect of a price change on a market.

This allows predicting the behavior of the system. Simulations describing the space phenomena can be enhanced with the use of mapping colors. With this pseudocolor technique, complex waveforms are converted to a composite color map; it can show variables such as amplitude, frequency, and phase. This method allows the user immediate visual feedback and is also an effective educational tool. Interactive simulation including human operators is used in virtual reality techniques, as it happens in the aircraft flight simulator (equipment which represents real conditions in an aircraft or spacecraft used by people learning to fly) or an electronic circuit simulator. Immersive, interactive VR systems are used as a public display medium in common spaces, such as museums, galleries, conferences, and festivals. The projection-based VR bring forth artistic and educational experiences in entertainment and museum settings and serve the research community. Simulation has been applied to analysis of the dark matter. Various kinds of simulation support works performed in different domains: in petrology, to understand the origin and properties of rocks; in aerodynamics to study gases in motion; in biology to study homology, the similarities in structure or function in different species; in archeology, art, and architecture, to support reconstruction of medieval mosaics, mural works and mosaic floors; in mathematics, simulations support analysis of axioms and logical methods; in neural network, simulation of neural networks imitate the brain's ability to sort out patterns and extract the relationships; in object-oriented programming and in software design, simulations support combining data and procedures; in multimedia, software and applications are often simulated, that combine text, sound, two- and three-dimensional graphics, animation, photo images, and full-motion video; and in many other fields. Simulation video games copy the real-life actions for entertainment, training, analysis, or prediction.

## Visualization Techniques

To create visualizations, computing and technical persons have to study graphics, while art and design individuals should study data (Benoît, 2019). Tools for creating visualizations include libraries such as a W3C Architectural domain, which provides a Document Object Model (DOM) – a platform and interface that allows programs to access and update documents. Also, a D3.js is a JavaScript library for manipulating documents based on data, using HTML, SVG, and CSS.

Visualization techniques often include small multiple drawings that represent the sets of data with miniature pictures, to reveal repetition, change, pattern, and facilitate comparisons. The pioneer in the field of data visualization Edward Rolf Tufte is an expert in the presentation of informational graphics, visual literacy, and visual communication of information. For Edward Tufte (1983, 1990), good design has two key elements found in simplicity of design and complexity of data. He described the collecting of small, sequential changes as the time series, and then drawing explanatory conclusions (Tufte, 1983,

1990, 1997, & blog 2006). Data can be presented in many ways, for example they can be ordered by the value of a variable, displayed as a stem-and-leaf exploratory analysis invented in 1977 by John Tukey (1977), or as time series plots, which were first drawn in 1785 by William Playfair (1805/2005; 1807/2005). Currently, animations and movies effectively present the causal factors. In his book entitled "Envisioning Information" (1990/2005) Tufte wrote that vision is the only universal language: "the world is complex, dynamic, multidimensional, and all the interesting worlds are inevitably and happily multivariate in nature, having many values and dimensions." He taught that information should enhance complexity, dimensionality, density, and beauty of communication. Good information display should be: documentary, comparative, casual and explanatory, quantified, multivariate, exploratory, and skeptical; it should allow comparing and contrasting. In accordance with Edward Tufte (1997), the good design means that "information is effectively arranged and empty space is used properly due to contrast, comparison, and choice, to allow reasoning about information."

In visualization domain, interactive visual metaphors enable us converting abstract knowledge into familiar facts that we can experience or see. A fisheye view (visual distortion creating a hemispherical or panoramic image) or a tree-map (a display of hierarchical data with the use of ordered, nested items) are examples of classic representations used for pictorial data presentation. Glyphs – graphical units that portray many variables by adapting their properties – can display much more in a small space than abstract presentations, just helping to overview, examine details, and abstract information about the very large, multi-variate data sets. An early example was developed by Chernoff who represented multi-variable data through face expressions as a way of displaying interactive content. Thus, by observing data points represented on a glyph, such as a sphere or a "bubble," one can determine the quality and quantity of the links within a website, because they are displayed in five dimensions by the position (x, y, and z), size, shape, and color of the sphere. Tag maps – visual representations of text in geographical space – are used in social software (where users can interact and share data) for labeling digital content of websites. They are also useful when we are browsing for topics; importance of a tag is depicted by a font size, color, popularity, or content.

Metaphors may link the sender and the viewer by conveying not only perception but also the meaning. We can think in pictures, in addition to a linear, sequential fashion that is typical of talking. With images, linear information can be translated into spatial one. Graphic imaging is considered a means to reason about an arrangement of data, to communicate, document, and preserve knowledge. Visual metaphors serve for labeling various Web services, such as photos (Flickr, Instagram, Pinterest), videoclips sharing (YouTube), microblogging platforms (Twitter), making the www. bookmarks (delicious.com), as well as using services like MySpace, Blogger, Facebook, or professional networking (LinkedIn), and collecting online content (Twine, Dropbox). The internet portals and communication media, such as the Web, videoconference software, and search platforms (e.g., Wikipedia) became more visual interdisciplinary and more interactive.

Most metaphors originate from biology-inspired thinking. Nature-derived metaphors support data visualization, information and knowledge visualization, data mining, semantic web, swarm computing, cloud computing, and serve as the enrichment of interdisciplinary models. In many cases they are used as tools for visualization techniques such as data mining, clusters and biclustering, concept mapping, knowledge maps, network visualization, web-search result visualization, open source intelligence, visualization of the semantic web, visual analytics, and tag cloud visualization, along with music visualization.

We haven't developed a nomenclature specific for computing. Instead, we apply names of familiar items and actions as metaphors, which serve to organize computing-related items and activities. Thus, we open a new window or a file with a mouse, put them in a folder, we cut, copy, and paste, place icons on a desktop, use tools and search engines, canvas, mailbox, documents, in-and-out boxes, and a web portal. The desktop metaphor is now fading because cell phones and tablets are replacing PCs as the main gateway to the internet. When describing photographic images, we talk about clouds and fluid metaphors: there is image flow in the JavaScript image gallery, a photo stream in Apple's photo storage software, and photo streams in a viewing page for photographs hosted on Flickr (Henning, 2018).

Since people are familiar with general concept of a parking lot or a skyscraper, this type of environment is being used to create metaphors for large web data organization. For instance, data are structured toward metaphorical representation of a building. Floors, rooms, elevators, or corridors are being used as visual interpretation of subsets of a data set. Thus, by imaginative tour of a skyscraper, one may create connotations about each subset and its relationship to the whole set of data and its links.

*Figure 24. Uptown*
*(© 2019, A. Ursyn. Used with permission)*

*Go uptown at night to eat and shop,*
*Meet artists and musicians,*
*Visit local bistros and bars.*
*Homeless people spend their days here,*
*And then leave to find quiet sheltered areas.*
*Young professionals look for trendy addresses.*
*What a diverse community!*

The choice of a metaphor for data visualization depends on the kind of connections existing between the data. Information can be looked at from various angles, so the user has an understanding of the hierarchy of the web site and its topology. For example, we may use a city metaphor with districts, blocks, houses, buildings, with a height dimensionality. When the data are organized into ranks with each level subordinate to the one above, a tree metaphor with a hierarchy of its limbs, branches and twigs would be helpful. For a hierarchical presentation of a concept, a description of the animal kingdom may also serve well. The division in biological classification comprises its phyla (such as Chordata), classes (such as Mammalia), orders (such as Carnivora), families (such as Canidae), genera (such as Canis - Latin 'dog'), and species (such as doglike species - dogs, wolves, jackals, coyotes, and foxes). If the connections among concepts are not hierarchical, we may draw a garden and arrange various plants, shrubs, and trees in a specified relation or order. When we can list many kinds of equally important data, we may need to describe the structure and the relations among these data, which means, explore their topology. A parking lot metaphor could be useful for this purpose. For example, metaphors used for multiple visualizations applied topological view with conetrees, workstation view as a solar system, file system view as pyramids, geographic view as a landscape, temporal view as a library, and a site view as a pyramid.

## Project: Portrait as Visualization

Now, create a visualization using metaphors for a set of factors that make up a visual portrait or a verbal profile of a person. It may be your portrait or you may choose to portray a person of your choice. You may do it in two ways – the journalistic way by writing a profile (verbal portrait), and the artistic way by graphically conveying a mental image (visual portrait). Depending on the kind of a profile you will work on, whether it be a personal, cultural, social, political, or psychological portrait, you will cope with a different set of variables you will have to take into account. For this reason, you will have to structure them toward different metaphorical representations. Figures 25 a, b, c show three computer graphics made with different approaches to the task of creating a self-portrait, solved by Computer Graphics students Shauna Pitzer, Oksanna Worthington, and Jenny Lee.

We may examine pictures portraying people in terms of the content (what does this portrait say). Portraits may serve various purposes, such as in works of artists:

- Social, for example, painted by William Hogarth or Francisco Goya.
- Political, such as by Jacques-Louis David.

*Figures 25. Three self-portraits*
*(© 2019, © S. Pitzer, O. Worthington, and J. Lee. Used with permission)*

- Erotic, as in Agnolo Bronzino.
- Religious, such as Francisco de Zurbaran.
- Ironic, as in William Holman Hunt.
- Enigmatic, such as by Andy Warhol.
- Psychological, e.g., Christian Schad.
- Experimental, for example, Hans Holbein.

Figures 26 and 27 present two portraits of other people. Figure 26 shows a portrait of a neighbor sketched by Katherine Ashcraft, while figure 27 presents a portrait of an elderly man drawn by Anna Ursyn.

We may also examine pictures portraying people in terms of the artistic process applied by the artist (how does this portrait look). A portrait may be made as:

- **A Caricature**: Which deliberately exaggerates the subject's distinctive features or peculiarities. A caricature could be made with a number of approaches to original works including humor, symbolic or metaphorical interpretation, satirical intent of the pastiche creator, or visualization of one's needs and dreams, as at the George Grosz' "Berlin Street scene."
- **An Assemblage**: An arrangement of miscellaneous objects, such as fruits and vegetables in works of Giuseppe Arcimboldo.

*Figure 26. Portrait of a neighbor*
*(© 2018, K. Ashcraft. Used with permission)*

This is Moises and he loves owls listening to music, and eating Italian food.

©KT Ashcraft

*Figure 27. Portrait of an elderly man*
*(© 2018, A. Ursyn. Used with permission)*

- **A Pastiche**: A work that imitates other artists, made with a number of approaches to original works including humor, symbolic or metaphorical interpretation, satirical intent of the pastiche creator, or visualization of one's needs and dreams (e.g., Francis Bacon, "Study after Velasquez's Portrait of Pope Innocent X")
- **A Grid of Assemblage Units**: As in photorealistic portraits by Chuck Close

Figure 28 shows a triptych over time created by Kate Bierschwale.

Design a portrait using a metaphor for its organization. Explore and communicate your art concepts about portraying people and the relevance of various solutions to one another. This project provides a good occasion to apply your visual literacy and exercise cognitive processes related to imaging. It may serve well to enhance your familiarity with art, both passive and active,

*Figure 28. Self-portraits: As a kid, now, and in the future*
*(© 2018, K. Bierschwale. Used with permission)*

Kate Bierschwale      Triptych Over Time      2018

| Past | Present | Future |
|---|---|---|

As a kid, I was a bit of an oddball although to be fair, I still am. I dressed eclectically, loved the outdoors and hiking, and loved playing make belive during recess. When I was a kid I liked believing I could control the weather. I've been a creative type since birth.

At this point in life I'm definitely still pretty weird, but I'm more confident about it now. I love listening to music, making art, and hiking, which were also important elements of my childhood. I'm still trying to find myself completely, and although I believe I'm closer than I was when I was a kid, I'm still growing.

In the future, I hope that I'm better at taking care of plants than I am right now! If I could keep my air plant alive until I look like this I would be very proud. I hope that I understand myself and learn how to share myself with the world more easily, along with continuing to be the amicable person I try to be currently.

when you act both as a perceiver, when you look at art works on a computer screen or in books, and a creator. Works of art are available in abundance at the internet-based sources such as the websites of.

Figures 29 a, b show two self-portraits by Jeremy Rice: first is current, and a next one shows his vision of himself as an old man.

In a similar way, Evan Van Dyke reflects on evolution of his image against time presenting on Figure 30 three stages of his life along with objects telling about him.

## Visualization Domains

The most important domains in visualization are: data visualization, information visualization, and knowledge visualization.

- **Data Visualization**: Presents the sets of data in a visual form, and thus enables us to go from the abstract numbers in a computer program (ones and zeros) to visual interpretation of data. Sabol (in Bertschi,

*Figure 29a. Two self-portraits: A current one*
*(© 2018, J. Rice Used with permission)*

*Figure 29b. Two self-portraits: A prediction of future*
*(© 2018, J. Rice Used with permission)*

*Figure 30. A triptych*
*(© 2018, E. Van Dyke. Used with permission)*

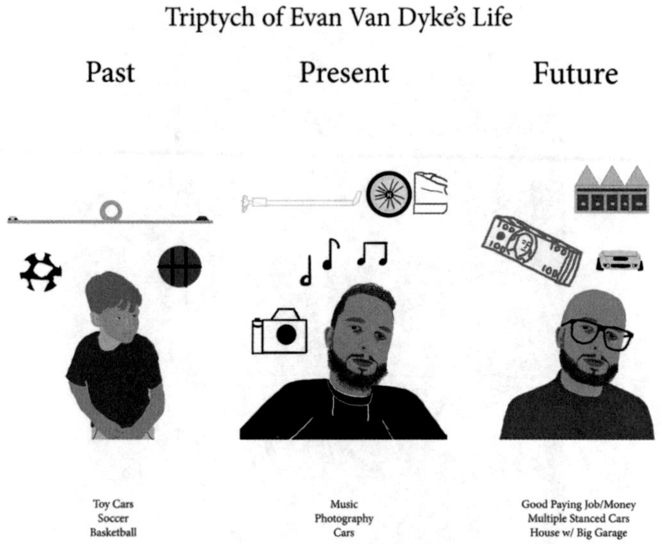

Triptych of Evan Van Dyke's Life

| Past | Present | Future |
|------|---------|--------|

Toy Cars
Soccer
Basketball

Music
Photography
Cars

Good Paying Job/Money
Multiple Stanced Cars
House w/ Big Garage

Bresciani, Crawford, Goebel, Kienreich, Lindner, Sabol, & Moere, 2011, p. 333) describes data as "sequences of numbers or characters representing qualitative or quantitative attributes of specific variables." Moreover, data may result from facts, products, but also from naming these products. Many types of physical or numerical data may include 1D linear, 2D with horizontal and vertical axes (e.g., a map), 3D world including depth on the z-axis (e.g., molecule or architectural models), multidimensional, often presented in an interactive form (scattergrams, clusters), and other types. Data visualization applies tools that have been listed as techniques for spatial and geospatial data, imaging multivariate data, visualization of trees, graphs, and networks, text representations, and interaction techniques (Ward, Grinstein, & Keim, 2010). Data provide us a raw material that has no meaning if we do not process it. To obtain information, data is processed and brought into a context where it gains a specific meaning and becomes understandable to users. About 80% of sensory input comes from our visual system (Hartman & Bertoline 2005). Text visualization means converting textual information into graphic representation, so we can see information without having to read the data; we can see tables, histograms, pie or bar charts, or Cartesian coordinates.

- **Information Visualization** (IV): Happens when somebody presents what has been done with the data. It gathers information and puts it in a visual format. It is often characterized as graphic representation of data plus interaction, which means the use of computer-supported, interactive visual representations of abstract data to amplify cognition (Bederson & Shneiderman, 2003). It thus provides the visual insight into sets of data. Due to our visual perception capabilities we can recognize patterns and extract knowledge from raw data and information. In structural modeling of data we can detect, extract, and simplify relationships and structure in a graphical form, and then examine them visually, often interactively. Creating visualizations includes transforming raw data (that may be abstract, semantic, or verbal information that is present in hypertext, www, or other text documents) into structured forms as data tables, converting data for calculations of their attributes, and visual mapping of important structures into the abstract visual structures.

The strong point in information visualization is that it could be (and should be) interactive. Interactive information visualization combines interaction design, exploratory data analysis, and graphic design (Benoît, 2019). Interactivity in visualization means that specific data are analyzed in exploratory way to allow creating web- and computer-based info graphics that can serve the information visualization. Users transform structures on a screen changing their shape, color, size, or location. Biomolecular structures were first visualized as balls connected with sticks, and then as spheres with rods; visualizers generate now images from an electron microscope, thus providing information visualization (Ward, Grinstein, & Keim, 2010, p. 24). We can visualize information as graphs, trees, or cones; detect proximity and connectivity; cluster and classify using word search; scale in multi-dimensional way; perform network analysis; design glyphs, charts and graphs; create virtual structures; apply complex network theory, and make network representations (Chen, 2010). Information visualization as a tool for visual communication helps to locate data and explore its structure, understand its complexity, communicate and navigate, for instance on the web. We can communicate visual messages showing events and their patterns for further analysis. With computer programs, abstract data is identified and gathered, selected, transformed, and manipulated directly from the data into pictorial form. Then textual labels and related information are combined with visuals to be published online.

Information visualization supports applications of graph theory, geometric modeling and imaging, visual analytics, virtual environments, geo-analytics, biomedical informatics and visualization, web visualization, cultural heritage knowledge visualization, aesthetics, visualization in software engineering, architecture, visualization in built and rural environments, and many other fields. It serves for conveying information in online journalism, business management, technical writing, social networks, and education.

Web search engines, a software system for searching information presents its results often as a mix of web pages, images, and other types of files. According to the eBusiness Guide (http://www.ebizmba.com/), the most popular search engines are: Google with 1,800,000,000 monthly visitors, Bing with 500,000,000, Yahoo! with 490,000,000, Baidu with 480,000,000, and Ask with 300,000,000 estimated unique monthly visitors (eBizma/MBA, 2019). Visual search engines use information visualization, data mining, and semantic web. Visual queries help us to find patterns in node-link diagrams in software architecture. Web architectures use search engines, manage large databases, and create web interfaces based on the concept of the semantic web. Surfing the web involves visualizing and manipulating data in multiple dimensions, using Java, 2D and 3D interaction metaphors, and data mining. Visualization techniques support clinical studies including cancer treatment. While information visualization supports the retrieval and organization of large data sets about facts and numbers, knowledge visualization helps to augment communication about knowledge-related relations and principles.

- **Knowledge Visualization**: Is a general concept underlying an action of gathering of data, interpretation, creation of a new visualization, and sharing knowledge in a visual format. Knowledge visualization has been defined as the presentation of pictures showing easy-to-recognize objects, which are connected through some well-defined relations, to amplify cognition. It uses visual representation to transfer insights to create, integrate, and apply knowledge between individuals; it focuses on the recipients, other types of knowledge, and on the process of communicating different visual formats (Burkhard, Meier, Smis, Allemang, & Honish, 2005). As Jean Constant (2019) put it, "The concept of Knowledge Visualization, more framework than theory, affects all areas of science such as mathematics, physics, engineering, chemistry, biology as well as medical and social sciences, art and the humanities. Techniques are aimed at explanation and presentation of knowledge, so they enhance cognitive processes of users and reduce cognitive load for working memory. Knowledge visualization can be created without the use of a computer. A cave drawing, a map, or a mind map drawn with a pen on paper may serve as examples of knowledge visualization generated without a computer. Knowledge visualization has been present in different disciplines and in various modes since early days of civilization. Many kinds of tables preserved since ancient times, the Near East Akkadian clay tablets, Sumerian accounting tables, Aztec calendars, or the Egyptian stele Rosetta Stone, as well as the medieval chronicles, canon tables, and calendars are representations of early genres of knowledge visualization. Analysis of these tables demonstrates the constant need to visualize abstract data, information, and knowledge.

Cognitive solutions for knowledge visualization take form of a selection of science-based problems using computer graphics, computer art, images, algorithms, animations, or web art. Knowledge visualization specialists use computer-based (and also non-computer-based) graphic representations, such as information graphics (infographics), objects, sketches, conceptual diagrams, concept maps, interactive visualizations, storyboards, and visual metaphors to produce solutions concerning readability, simplification, and effectiveness of presentation for a wide spectrum of users. Designers co-work with communication science specialists for social network users (such as cell phone users, e-mail archives, criminal networks, or underage audience sensitive messages). Knowledge visualization could contribute design- and user-specific representations, e.g., a map, metro, aquarium, solar system, or flower metaphor for users with limited visual literacy (Kienreich, in Bertschi et al., 2011). We often utilize current technological appliances and applications without thinking about scientific disciplines that have been necessary to create them; on the other hand, our knowledge of science disciplines paves the way for creating nature inspired solutions to high-priority problems.

- **Scientific Visualization**: Is a field in computer science that encompasses user interface, data representation, processing algorithms, visual representations, and other sensory presentation such as sound or touch (McCormick, DeFanti, & Brown, 1987). Abstract or model-based scientific visualizations present real objects in a digital way. Scientific visualization means mapping from the computed to perceptual representations. Physically based data are defined, selected, transformed, and represented according to space coordinates, such as

175

geographic data or computer tomography data of a body for medical use. Analysts, decision makers, engineers, or emergency-response teams depend on the ability to analyze information contained in the data; they also search how users navigate the database.

- **Concept Mapping**: Shows the structure of information, and builds knowledge models useful for strategic planning, product development, market analysis, decision-making, and measurement development. Concept maps support the learning, construct knowledge, reduce cognitive load, and improve recall of information. Knowledge maps visualize knowledge by showing changes and interrelationships; they help us design strategies and build assessment. Network and web-search result visualization became the important carrier of information.

- **Visual Analytics**: Provides automated analysis of large amounts of dynamic information. The closed loop approach uses visualization and interaction of multi-touch surfaces; combine mobility s computational and visual methods using visualization, data mining, and statistics; uses abstract visual metaphors, mathematical deduction, and human intuitive interaction. Visual analytics serves for studying the entire genome of an organism at many abstraction levels: cells, organisms, and ecosystems, in formats and scales such as molecules, gene networks, and signaling networks. It also serves medicine, environmental investigation, and national security. Tag cloud visualization is a text-based visual representation of a set of tags.

Currently, technology is used for genome editing. CRISPR (Clustered Regularly Interspaced Short Palindromic Repeats) has been developed as a coding language of DNA to edit the genome, the organism's hereditary information. It has potential to make it easier to write new code in the language of genetics (Parker & Marson, 2018). CRISPR/Cas9 is an enzyme that can be used to edit genes within organism, to confer resistance to foreign genetic elements and provide a form of acquired immunity (CRISPR, 2018). CRISPR scissors show potential to cut the some DNA and insert a new gene. Scientists perform experiments both on gene editing and building chimeras. The epigenetic editing is a variation of CRISPR that modulates, rather than cuts away the DNA sequences. With a chimera approach, the gene editing technique is being used to grow human organs on animal bodies (Hayasaki, 2019). However, these developments in biology of gene expression – signals that govern the organs' development – are a subject of fervent discussion in terms of ethics and safety.

- **Information Aesthetics**: Combines information visualization and visualization art. Ward, Grinstein, & Keim (2010, p. 366) stressed that the effectiveness of visualization depends on its aesthetics. Visual appeal of visualization may depend on drawing the user's focus to the most important parts, balance of the screen space, and simplicity of presentation provided without information overload and graphical gimmicks. The authors provide several design rules for creating effective visualizations. These include the use of intuitive data-graphic mappings; providing multiple views of the data; a careful use of color and grids without occluding the data; creating attractive but not misleading design with semantic meaning and compatible units; providing the user an access to the raw data; and designing visualizations of the relative rather than absolute judgment (Ward, Grinstein, & Keim, 2010, p. 374).

A large number of scientists perceive the visualization techniques as a chance to show what is invisible – translation of mental, abstract, formal concepts into images: pictures or graphs (Lima, 2011). Visualization not only makes the unseen visible; it builds a meaningful net of associations and connotations. Information visualization often represents data in pleasurable and intelligible way. Computing technology may cause that aesthetics of knowledge visualization may be measured as the balance between art literacy and technological literacy: visual competence in the art, design, and technological solutions in visualization. Aesthetic values are considered important in mathematics, science, and computing, including the aesthetic computing and aesthetic issues related to digital environment.

## Other Forms of Sharing Data

- **Infographics:** Are tools and techniques used in graphical representation of data, information, and knowledge, mostly in journalism, art, and storytelling. For example, representing information management may involve data presentation, mapping, and issues related to the temporal dimension. Infographics can tell a story, reveal relationships, and show structure. A model may mean a scaled copy of some object (often using interactive modeling systems), or a mathematical model describing physical laws and the behavior of physical objects.

- **Instagram**: Is a social networking service own by Facebook, for sharing photos and videos. Uploaded material can be edited with filters, and then organized with tags and location information. The instagram egg, a photo of a brown egg, posted on 14 January 2019 on this social media platform by the account @world_record_egg, gained the most-liked online post on any website in history. According to The New York Times, on January 13, 2019 this instagram gained 53,393,058 likes (Victor, 2019).
- **A Radar Chart**: is also called a spider chart or a star chart. It presents multivariate data in the form of a two-dimensional chart of variables presented on axes starting from the same point. The radar chart consists of a sequence of spokes called radii. Each spoke represents one of the variables. The length of a spoke is proportional to the magnitude of the variable. A line connects the data values for each spoke.

## Calligraphy

Handwritten lettering is considered art in many cultures. This visual art of decorative writing gives "form to signs in an expressive, harmonious, and skillful level" (Mediaville, 1996, p.18). Figure 31 a b presents works of my doctoral student Fatma Alabdullaziz who juxtaposed an Arabic script and old cultural symbols with the quick response code (QR code) matrices, thus blending Islamic cultural icons with the contemporary QR matrix barcodes.

Calligraphers create inscriptions, which are often considered fine art works. Calligraphic inscriptions are made in service of font design and typography, graphic design, and logo design. They are present in cut stone inscriptions, maps, memorial documents, religious art, film and television, wedding

*Figure 31a. Kufic, the oldest calligraphic form of various Arabic calligraphic scripts combines a geometric discipline with a dynamic rhythm*
*(© 2015, F. Alabdullaziz. Used with permission)*

*Figure 31b. Kufic, the oldest calligraphic form of various Arabic calligraphic scripts combines a geometric discipline with a dynamic rhythm*
*(© 2015, F. Alabdullaziz. Used with permission)*

and other events announcements, birth and death certificates, and other testimonials (Geddes & Dion, 2004). The following figures, figure 32a, 32b, 32c, and 32d are created by my student Jingying Zhen as a visual counterpart of selected calligraphic scripts of Chinese characters. The calligraphy of Chinese characters carried artistic expressions of emotions. Jingying Zhen have been studying characteristics of calligraphy by personifying calligraphy as humans: characters with personalities.

Tools serving for calligraphers include broad tip instruments, brushes, fiber tip pens, reed pens, fountain pens, dip pens, quills, steel or copperplate nibs, or other writing tools (Harris, 2003). Origins of calligraphy come from the visual context, with nature-based depictions gradually changing into abstract shapes symbolizing objects existing in nature.

*Figure 32a. Visual counterpart of a Chinese calligraphic script*
*(© 2018, J. Zhen. Used with permission)*

*Figure 32b. Visual counterpart of a Chinese calligraphic script*
*(© 2018, J. Zhen. Used with permission)*

*Figure 32c. Visual counterpart of a Chinese calligraphic script*
*(© 2018, J. Zhen. Used with permission)*

In many countries calligraphy is considered a measure of culture, and a person who writes beautifully in a rigorous way is valued as someone with integrity and artistic talent. Calligraphy masters perfected their strokes to express the structure and harmony in a single character by exerting force and transpire emotion; at the same time they focused on overall composition of the work, which led to developing the individual character of the artist.

*Figure 32d. Visual counterpart of a Chinese calligraphic script*
*(© 2018, J. Zhen. Used with permission)*

There are several calligraphic styles, some coming from ancient times. Arabic scripts include Islamic calligraphy, Coptic Christian, and Kufic script, which is the oldest. Arabic calligraphy draws from Arabic alphabet. Persian (or Iranian) calligraphy, respected and admired as art, has developed several styles with more letters than the Arabic handwriting, including many contemporary artistic movements and styles. There are four Tibetan calligraphic traditions, mostly created with a reed pen. Chinese artistic writing and painting, playing string instruments, and the game go are celebrated as forms of artistic expression. There are several transcriptions, traditional or simplified. Related art forms are seal carving, ornate paperweights, and ink stones.

Japanese calligraphy with Chinese roots dates from the twenty-eight century BC, while the first calligraphic Japan text was written in early 7th century. The Hiragana and Katakane are distinctive Japanese kana syllabaries (characters representing syllables). Five types of Korean script are derived from Chinese calligraphy; artists are developing their own Korean style. Indian scripts have been mostly Buddhist religious texts. European calligraphy mostly used the Latin script serving for sacred texts, often decorated with illuminations. Font families used in computers for software such as Adobe InDesign, Microsoft Word, or Apple Pages draw from past calligraphic tradition as well as from contemporary typeface designers. Current computer writing systems have been standardized by the Unicode Consortium, which has published on March 2019 the *Unicode 12.0.0* containing a repertoire of 137,993 characters covering 150 modern and historic scripts, as well as multiple symbol sets and emoji (http://www.unicode.org/versions/Unicode12.0.0).

## Ethical and Legal Issues: Copyright

Ethics in communication and the use moral reasoning in a variety of contexts is often an important factor, when one has to take into consideration legal rights and copyright laws, or learn how to defend one's ethical decisions. Bioethics examines issues concerning the ethical, legal and social implications of advances in biotechnology and biomedicine. From stem cell research to health care reform, these topics involve critical dilemmas at the intersections of law, society, culture, public policy, philosophy, religion, economics, and history.

Some examples of such issues might involve history-based trading (software helping with stocks, retirement, or house mortgage rates). Transparency in the open source companies becomes an important issue. For example, Aleph Object, the producer of 3-d printers that also print themselves, Lulzbot has open source policy allowing anyone to learn all about their work, from collaboration, ideas, inspirations, to materials, techniques and processes. Medical, criminal, family data becomes a growing issue on several levels. Crime and solutions are yet another topic: private detectives using the internet, security cameras (miniaturization).

Apps devised for everything are changing business models, from taxi to Lyft, with the internet shopping resulting in reducing the number of such stores such as Toys R Us and closing bookstores. Those movements are removing many social opportunities from the global map, some believe. Gaming is becoming extremely collaborative across the globe, too.

## 2.4. HOW DO WE COMMUNICATE WITH COMPUTERS

### Interface

A notion of interface is important for successful communication. When we talk about an interface we use a preposition 'between.' The term interface, usually denoting any type of connection or interaction between two units (which may be subjects, organizations, physical or electronic systems) is used every day in many contexts and meanings. In social science, we can talk about social interface. Physicians tell about interface as a boundary between matter or phases of mater such as solid, liquid, and gas. For example, aerosol presents a gas-liquid interface. Such interfaces may cause optical effects such as for instant refraction. Optical lenses create interface between glass (or plastic) and air. This term also describes connections in electrical circuits.

An interface in computing denotes a point of interaction at the level of both hardware and software. For example, a graphics card (hardware) and an internet browser (software) may use interfaces to communicate with other components. Most computer interfaces are bi-directional. A computing interface may provide communication between the computer and the user with a monitor and a keyboard. Interface with the internet may go through the Internet protocol. Computing specialists would program user interface between a user and a computer allowing the user to communicate with the operating system, human-computer interface (using touch, visual, auditory, olfactory, balance, or taste), or an interaction and thus communication between items of hardware, software, or their combination. They make network interfaces and protocol interfaces in a computer network to pass messages, or connect and disconnect communication between computer peripherals. Graphical user interface (GUI) uses visuals and graphical icons instead of texts as user interfaces. GUI allows users to interact with electronic devices using images rather than text commands. It can be used in computers, portable devices, and appliances, using graphical icons rather than text based interfaces.

Many kinds of user interfaces are realized in visual, auditory, or tactile domains. The haptic/touch interfaces, for example pressure sensitive interfaces, exemplify a kind of multimodal data presentations. The interface between software and hardware means a set of instructions represented by binary codes. Codes make up a machine language that is then decoded by a computer. Assembler is a program that converts assembly language to binary digits. Compilers are programs that convert commands into computer codes (Kerlow & Rosebush, 1994).

Biointerfaces and brain-computer interfaces enable communication between humans and machines and/or humans-machines-humans. Biointerface means contacts between organic materials such as biomolecules, tissues, or cells with inorganic matter. These interfaces translate biological functions into numerical data and then computer systems interpret them and display the results. For example, electrophysiological functions of a brain are gathered as electroencephalographic activities. Biosensors placed on a skin register galvanic skin response measuring the electrical conductance from the skin. Blood volume pulse sensors detect changes in blood pressure (e.g., as photoplethysmography). Breathing sensors monitor one's thorax or diaphragm activity. Electromyogram sensors capture the electrical activity produced by a muscle at the moment of its contraction.

Biointerfaces can also transform electrophysiological signals from the brain and physiological information about the user into commands that produce actions performed by the hardware and software. This may aid failing human senses and bio-regenerative medicine by enhancing potential of individuals with social and/or motor disabilities, severe muscle disorders such as lateral amyotrophic sclerosis, cerebral hemorrhage, and muscle damage. Interest in biointerfaces is now important in biotechnology, medicine, for creating new materials, bioengineered products, nano and micro contact methods, nanotube and nanoparticle interfaces, and in many other disciplines. Bio-interfaces can be used as wearable devices that provide organic interaction between man and machine. This area of study involves different fields of knowledge, such as neurobiology, psychology, design, engineering, mathematics, and computer science.

Biointerfaces also enable applications in the areas of design, art, education, and games. They allow participation and audience's interaction with art works, design projects, and games. They connect participants' physiological and brain activities with the therapeutic, educational, or entertainment games, so the participants feel and act as co-authors.

## Classical Computers

Apparently, the world's first mechanical computer had been built sometime between 200 and 70 B.C. and was discovered 117 years ago off the coast of the Greek island Antikythera. It is called Antikythera Mechanism, and it shows the engineering prowess of the ancient Greeks as well as their impressive knowledge of astronomy. This clock-sized device contained about 30 interlocking, spinning gears that controlled dials tracking the Sun, the Moon, eclipses, planets, and the schedule for the Olympics (Becker, 2017). Archeologists believe it was sunken with the ship carrying it to Rome, and possibly the dark ages ended its future existence (Pruitt, 2016).

Before the advent of nanotechnology and works on designing a nanocomputer, when one talked about computers one might mean an original mainframe computer, a mini computer, or a microcomputer. The powerful mainframe computers served for statistics, planning, and processing of big data sets such as those concerning the census, government, industry, or consumers. They included the central processing unit, main memory, hosted multiple operating systems, and operated virtual machines – the guest operating systems with software implementation of a computer enabling the execution of the operating system or running programs aiding the single processes.

Mini computers, introduced in mid-1960s were priced at about $25,000; they had input-output devices such as a teleprinter and memory capable of running higher-level language programs such as Fortran or Basic.

Microcomputers, often called personal computers and designed for individual users, did not need big cabinets or special rooms. They contained a microprocessor, a central processing unit (CPU), a power supply unit, RAM memory, memory storage devices combined with the CPU, batteries, and integrated or separate input/output devices for conveying information such as monitors, keyboards, printers, and other human interface devices. Some of them became personal computers.

Classical computers convert information to binary digits (bits); thus, the state of a classical computer is determined by the binary values of bits. Each bit has only two possible values, 0 or 1. Computers operate on bits using integrated circuits containing billions of transistors. They manipulate binary representations to process algorithms, assembly codes, text documents and spreadsheets, games, videos, and the Web-based services. Transistors are used to build integrated circuits, where they are connected with wires and send electrical signals. When signals are analog, their values change smoothly. The values of these signals may depend on changes in environment creating noise. Transistors that create circuits sending digital binary signals (around two Boolean states – either 0 or 1) form 'digital gates' which send electrical signals as binary values.

## Quantum Computers

Nanocomputers might be possibly built using quantum mechanics principles. Richard Feynman introduced the field of quantum computing in 1982. Quantum computing combines physics, mathematics, and computer science. In the same way as a bit which can only be 0 or 1, a qubit can represent the values 0 or 1; but the fundamental premise of quantum mechanics poses that a qubit may be a superposition of both such states at the same time. Thus, at the level of quantum mechanics particles of matter can exist in multiple, simultaneous combinations of states (0 or 1). The qubits have both digital and analog character, and quantum phenomena manifest as noise. Qubit is the quantum analogue of the bit. The basic paradigm for quantum algorithms involves the quantum circuit model composed of the basic quantum units of information (qubits) and their basic logical manipulations (quantum gates represented by matrices).

As for now, groups of scientists are striving to build small quantum computers by creating and controlling 'qubits' – units of quantum information. They are now working on building small demonstration quantum computing systems, which are based on two technologies, one uses trapped ionized atoms (trapped ions) and the other uses artificial 'atoms' generated by miniature superconducting circuits (Grumbling & Horowitz 2018). Earlier attempts included developing a quantum computer that utilized properties of superconductor circuits, trapped ions, quantum dot charge based semiconductor, nuclear magnetic resonance on molecules in solution, fullerene-based (electronic spin of atoms or molecules encased in fullerene structures), or a diamond based quantum computer.

Nanoscale computers would be tentatively faster and combine high computing power with low electrical requirements. Nanotubes allow reducing the size of chips and lowering physical limitations. Grids of nanotubes may form memory and very fast operating circuits. Researchers are developing quantum computers based on light rather than electricity. At Stanford, new materials could be the key to progress in this field. With the Stanford team's approach, quantum computers work by isolating spinning electrons inside a new type of semiconductor material. When a laser strikes the electron, it reveals which way it is spinning by emitting quanta or particles of light. Those spin states replace the ones and zeros of traditional computing (Abate, 2017). Zhang et al. (2016) present diamonds as quantum emitters, where semiconductor-based quantum photonic structures contain negatively charged silicon-vacancy color centers. These hybrid quantum photonic structures result from combining the growth of nano- and microdiamonds on silicon carbide substrates. Color centers are incorporated in diamond during its synthesis from molecular diamond seeds (diamondoids), with no need for ion-implantation or annealing. Thus, high quality color centers can be incorporated into nanophotonic structures synthetically. Applications comprise both classical and quantum information processing.

According to the 2018 report from the National Academies of Sciences, Engineering, and Medicine, "quantum computers are unlikely to be useful as a direct replacement for conventional computers, or for all applications;

rather, they are currently expected to be special-purpose devices operating in a complementary fashion with conventional processors, analogous to a co-processor or accelerator. Apart from the problems with logistics and costs, it may soon change so workstations will be terminals & quantum computers will operate server side, in the cloud. Perhaps the best-understood application of quantum algorithms is in the field of cryptography (specifically, defeating it), an application based directly on mathematics" (Grumbling & Horowitz 2018). The cryptographic methods are used to protect government and civilian communications and stored data. Investigations into quantum computing offer promises to solve these civilian and national security purposes.

## Programming Languages

To communicate with a computer, we use a language that is understandable for the machine. Computers that do not consist of hard-wired algorithms have to understand the language in which their algorithms are given. The algorithm is a process involving a set of rules. A program combines several algorithms, and the language in which it is given is called a programming language. A computer must have the ability to access (read and manipulate) the representation that is us ed by the algorithm (it operates on) and affect it's required changes (Erwig, 2017). Programming languages are discussed with two broad perspectives involving the examination of their syntax and semantics. The syntax of a programming language defines the structure of the code and its form of expression. The semantics relates to the meaning of the code. A sign communicates a meaning; it is a representation of something else. For example, we can design a road sign "left turn" and then by crossing this sign we will make a new sign "no left turn." Manipulating such representations means computation. By writing a combination of signs we can produce an algorithm. By providing interpretation needed to understand these signs or transformation of signs we perform computation. Writing an algorithm is a method for sending a set of instructions and solving a particular problem. Each algorithm can be then executed many times. In computer science, each use of algorithm is called a computation, thus computation is algorithm execution (Erwig, 2017).

- **Hypertext Markup Language (HTML):** Is the core language of the World Wide Web. It makes the structure of a web page explicit and presented in unambiguous way allowing only one interpretation. Uniform Resource Locators identify documents and other web resources.

HTML documents represent a media-independent description of interactive content. HTML documents might be rendered to a screen, through a speech synthesizer, or on a Braille display. HTML represents information but does not describe computation.

- **JavaScript:** Is a language that defines the dynamic behavior of web pages (Erwig, 2017). Visual types of programming may involve object oriented programming – language oriented toward objects and data, more than actions or logic. Hyper Text Markup Language (HTML) is a set of tags used for describing web pages and building web applications (HTML W3C, 2016). Markup language is a system for tagging a document to indicate its logical structure (such as paragraphs). Tags replace text providing typesetting instructions. Markups instruct the software about electronic transmission and display of the text (Merriam-Webster, 2019).

- **HTML5 Canvas:** Element is used to draw graphics on a web page via JavaScript, for example color or multicolor shapes, gradient colors, or multicolor texts. Canvas has several methods for drawing paths, boxes, circles, text, and adding images. Canvas is a container for graphics; so using JavaScript is needed to actually draw the graphics (HTML.5 Canvas, 2019).

- **Processing:** Was created by the MIT alumni Ben Fry and Casey Reas for the electronic arts and visual design communities. Processing, which is based on Java, is a flexible software sketchbook and a programming language for learning how to code within the context of the visual arts (Reas & Fry, 2015). This award-winning program serves for anyone willing to try one's exploratory way of programming. In the program, the image, animation, or an interactive work is presented along with a code, and the user is welcome to alter the code and see the changes made to the visual data provided by the authors, or write the own code following the rules provided in the added manual. An open source programming language Processing.org can be downloaded without any charge (https://processing.org). Since 2001, Processing has promoted software literacy within the visual arts and visual literacy within technology. There are tens of thousands of students, artists, designers, researchers, and hobbyists who use Processing for learning and prototyping. However, Casey Reas & Ben Fry (2007, p. 5) express their dissatisfaction, "there have been very few classes that strive to integrate media arts knowledge with core concepts of computation."

Processing won a 2005 Golden Nica award at Prix Ars Electronica – International Competition for CyberArts, which incorporates varied kinds of media: performances, live action, interactive installations, visual music, and movies.

## Biologically Inspired Models for Nano Computing

As a Nobel laureate in chemistry Frances Arnold put it, DNA was discovered about 50 years ago, genetic engineering 30 years ago, and in the last 10 years scientists learn how to synthesize DNA. By using evolution, we are doing what nature does—just faster and more targeted. While natural evolution takes for millions of years, new biological molecules and organisms are much faster created in the laboratory by forcing their evolution. Synthetic biologists are working on identifying genomic parts to build biological systems, improving functioning of existing biological parts, engineer microbes to produce enzymes and natural products, and learn to construct simple genomes of natural bacteria (Biotechnology Innovation Organization, 2019).

Nano computing can be produced by various nanoscale structures including biomolecules such as DNA and proteins. As DNA functions through a coding system of four nucleobases it is suited for application in data processing. Practical applications of this theoretical technology will require the ability to control and program DNA flexibly. Applications of DNA to computing will likely be in the form of transistor switches overcoming current microcomputing problems such as transistor tunneling. Biomolecular switches will be able to control electron flow for computation through a change in composition of the DNA molecules or by adapting the amount of light scattered by the biomolecules (AZoNano, 2017). Alternative transistors have already been developed using DNA for biological nano computers. The DNA switch could be genetically programmed to produce or inhibit the production of a protein.

Many people strived for over 50 years to build, using DNA, a molecular scale of the universal Turing machine (UTM). According to Currin, Korovin, Ababi, Roper, Kell, Day, & King (2017), DNA is an excellent medium for information processing and storage because it is stable, can be copied reliably as many genes remain unchanged for millions of years. Thus speed, energy efficiency, and information storage are advantages of DNA over electronics. Authors work toward engineering a general-purpose way of controlling cells. In living organisms, cells are controlled by a combination of DNA, RNA, protein interactions, and chemical interactions. The authors' approach is to develop a DNA non-deterministic UTM (NUTM) that would enable arbitrary biological processes to be programmed and executed. According to authors, a desktop DNA NUTM could potentially utilize more processors than all the electronic computers in the world combined, and thereby outperform the world's current fastest supercomputer, while consuming a tiny fraction of its energy.

Scientists from the Massachusetts Institute of Technology (2019) and the Arizona State University have created a computer program that can translate drawings of arbitrary shapes into two-dimensional structures made of DNA. According to Jun, Zhang, Shepherd, Ratanalert, Qi, Yan, & Bathe (2019), "until now, designing such structures has required technical expertise that puts the process out of reach of most people. Using the new program, anyone can create a DNA nanostructure of any shape, for applications in cell biology, photonics, and quantum sensing and computing, among many others." The shape can be sketched in any computer-drawing program and then converted into a computer-aided design (CAD) file, which is fed into the DNA design program. Quantum dot are used for labeling and tracking individual pollen grains transported by bees (BioPhotonics, 2019, p. 11).

Bio-inspired models utilize information gathered from animal social systems. Artificial life (ALife) denotes the creation of synthetic life on computers to study, simulate, and understand living systems. ALife application fields include robot control, robot manufacturing, practical robots, computer graphics, natural phenomenon modeling, entertainment, games, music, economics, internet, information processing, industrial design, simulation software, electronics, security, data mining, and telecommunications. Methods for designing such applications include evolutionary computation, swarm intelligence, artificial immune network, and agent-based modeling. Biologically inspired evolutionary robotics (ER) is a powerful approach for the automatic synthesis of robot controllers. Drawing from the object-oriented and functional programming languages allowed creating programs as polypeptides: object-oriented combinator chemistry, an artificial chemistry with composition devices (Williams, 2016).

The study of biological networks may result in creating biologically inspired models for information and communication networking (Liu & Leibnitz, 2011). In problem optimization, basic families of social insects: ants, wasps, bees, and termites were used as an inspiration source for designing challenging computational models (Hartmann, Pinto, Runkler, & Sousa, 2011). For example, ants in ant colonies can indicate the shortest path from a food resource to the anthill by depositing pheromones on the trail, so other ants can sense their high concentration and follow this trail. Mathematical models of real colonies serve the authors in developing optimization algorithms. The way these social insects interact to efficiently carry food to the colony served as inspiration for writing meta-heuristic, approximate algorithms and creating mathematical models of ant colony that served the purpose of problem optimization (Hartman, Pinto, Runkler, & Sousa, 2011). According to Liu & Leibnitz (2011), cells interact with each other by transmitting the first messenger signaling molecules from a cell membrane to another cell's membrane receptors. Receptors activate the signaling proteins within the cell that are referred to as secondary messengers. Due to a signaling cascade of reactions the signal arrives to the nucleus, activates a specific gene in the DNA causing the gene expression – the production and release of the protein it encodes.

Many times a solution is needed very soon, even if the optimality of the solution is not guaranteed. For example, a car-navigating system (GPS) should respond quickly to a driver's mistake in selecting a route, so the driver wouldn't need to stop the car while waiting for computation of the new solution and new directives about the corrected route. A compromise between optimization and effectiveness and speed is needed. Observation of ants' behavior serves for creating the biologically inspired models, which are aimed at finding approximate algorithms providing good, even if not very meticulous solutions in a short computation time.

## The Next Industrial Revolution

According to Christopher Mims (2018), "the first three industrial revolutions were driven by coal, and steam, then electricity and the automobile, then computing. Now we may be witnessing the rise of the fourth: an economy powered by the mobile internet, automation and artificial intelligence." For example, in 2015 global shipments of smart phones exceeded 1,500 million (the smart phone is the first and only computer for many people); in US there were 340 000 active cell sites; E-commerce sector has created more jobs than brick-and-mortar retailers have lost; in 2016 estimated global shipment of industrial robots amounted to 400,000; in academic papers mentioned about 90 000 smart machines learning (AI). However, it is predicted, China will surpass US in spending on RD at the end of 2018, as the pace is quicker there (Mims, 2018). And, as the President of Mexico Enrique Peña Nieto (2018) stated, "Mexico is one of the only nations whose constitution recognizes the right of its people to a broadband internet connection" which may be the DSL (Digital Subscriber Line), fiber-optic, cable, and satellite connection.

The fifth-generation wireless system networks (5G) are expected to be 100 times faster than 4G networks we have today. The country that takes the lead in 5G will enable its companies to access powerful technologies sooner than rivals from other countries. The convergence of AI with internet-connected machines and superfast 5G wireless networks opens possibilities on Earth and in space to transform industrial technology. There is no need to build fiber optic networks. Internet-connected devices will transmit information more quickly. The Internet of Things links technology with 5G and networks of online-capable devices.

The founder of the World Economic Forum Klaus Schwab (2017) explores how it will be fundamentally changing the way we live, work, and relate to one another. According to the author, previous industrial revolutions liberated humankind from animal power, made mass production possible, and brought digital capabilities to billions of people. This fourth industrial revolution provides new technologies that are fusing the physical, digital, and biological worlds, impacting all disciplines, economies, and industries, and even challenging ideas about what it means to be human (Schwab, 2018).

## Heuristic Methods

Self-discovery and practical methods that may be not perfect (called, heuristic techniques for problem solving and learning) may ease the cognitive load of making decisions, such as in case of making an educated guess, an intuitive judgment, stereotyping, or using a common sense. Metaheuristic strategies apply search and optimization algorithms. Many times finding solutions for problems in accordance with the computational complexity theory is not efficient when time is important. For example, with the use of the global positioning system (GPS), quick compensation for the driver's mistakes in the car route are more desirable than having the driver to stop the car and wait for an optimal solution, so trading optimality for efficiency is preferable (Hartmann, Pinto, Runkler, & Sousa, 2011). For example, Ant Colony Optimization is a bio-inspired metaheuristic that examines how ants keep supplying lines excreting the chemical factors pheromones (Dorigo & Stützle, 2004); coordination between termites for building their mounds goes by the use of pheromone traces; hierarchical organization of wasp colonies provides combinations of factors such as reduced risk from predators, easier access to food, increased productivity, and availability of mates; and bee colonies, simulated by the Artificial Bee Colony (ABC) communicate by performing a waggle dance (Hartmann et al., 2011).

## Deriving Solutions From Biology for Production

The use of bio-inspired way of developing new solutions applies to a number of venues. Bio-inspired technologies change the way people think in the fields of computing, software management, material science and material design, resource management, developments in computer technologies, and many other fields. Scientists focus on biology-inspired research to understand how biological systems work, and then create systems and materials that would have efficiency and precision of living structures. Current bio-inspired modeling approaches apply models based on four families of social insects (ants, wasps, bees, and termites) and non-insect models for communication and robotics, including primates and other socially complex mammals as biological models. Inventors develop systems inspired by structures that can be seen in nature, such as optical fibers, liquid crystals, or structures that scatter light. Many times designers combine biomaterials with artificial ones to create hybrid materials and technologies. The National Research Council of the National Academies (2008) provided examples of three strategies for creation of new materials and systems: (1) bio-mimicry, (2) bio-inspiration, and (3) bio-derivation.

1. Bio-mimicry involves designing structures that function in the same way as living systems and creating synthetic materials that respond to external stimuli. Visualization of living systems is aimed at achieving similar functions in synthetic material and creating new materials, which would mimic cells in their response to external stimuli; this strategy may serve for detecting hazardous biological and chemical agents and strengthening national security systems.

2. Bio-inspiration means developing systems performing the same function, even with different scheme than the living systems. For example, the adhesive gecko foot, the self-cleaning lotus leaf, and the fracture-resistant mollusk shell are examples of inspiring structures. The optical technology solutions can be found in animals as well: multilayer reflectors, diffraction gratings that spread a beam of light waves, optical fibers, liquid crystals, and structures that scatter light. For instance, Morpho butterfly has

iridescence sparkle and blue color visible from hundreds of meters due to periodic photonic nanostructure in scales on wings that responds to specific wavelengths of light without any dye involved.

3.  Bio-derivation means incorporating biomaterials into human-made structures: using existing biomaterial to create a hybrid with artificial material. For example, incorporation of a protein into polymeric (that has many similar units bonded together) assemblies for targeted drug delivery. The photosynthesis occurs in green plants and other organisms, which use sunlight to synthesize carbohydrates as food from carbon dioxide and water. These biological structures and processes can support harvesting light and fuels by converting cellulose polymer to ethanol. Bio-derivation can advance clinical diagnostics, prosthetics, and drug delivery. Molecular motors convert chemical energy (usually in form of ATP – adenosine triphosphate) into mechanical energy. Scientists create self-evolving, self-healing, self-cleaning, and self-replicating super-materials that could mimic the ability to evolve and adapt. For example, the gecko's adhesive works in vacuum, under water, leaves no residue, and is self-cleaning; adhesion is reversible, so geckoes run up walls alternatively sticking and unfastening themselves 15 times per second.

## 2.5. HOW DO WE COMMUNICATE WITH LIVING BEINGS?

## Communication vs. Information

Either we draw information from our surrounding environment and from other living beings or we bring about changes to induce desired improvement in our surroundings. For this reason, it is important to recognize a relation between communication and information. Information is a fact we learn about something or someone but not a signal to communicate. For example, one of the ways a mother receives information about a baby is through her smell sense, while a baby communicates by voice (and mother's hearing). Communication can be visual, acoustic, chemical (e. g., pheromones produced and released by animals), tactile, electrical, or conveyed as seismic signals resulting in vibration of earth (Bales & Kitzmann, 2011). For example, a blind mole rat's thumping on burrow walls transmits over very long distances. The same message can be conveyed and received in many ways: visually with the semaphore flags (signals made with hand-held flags, rods, disks, paddles, or just hands), sonically (3 times 3 long versus short sounds: "·· — — — · ·" for the SOS, or through the international Morse code, for example as a distress signal.

Visual communication may involve the use of graphs, trees, or cones; detecting proximity and connectivity; clustering and classification using word search; multi-dimensional-scaling; network analysis; glyphs; virtual structures; applying complex network theory and network representations (Chen, 2010).

In a historical perspective, our visual communication abilities draw from the old cultural patterns including visual writings in many modes and styles, visible stories, and visual rhetoric. Yet older ways of visual communication involved cave paintings, clay tablets, hieroglyphs, knots, numbers, and their various representations. Human history was strongly influenced by the ways various senses were used in human communication. However, images change along with technical advances.

## Camouflage

According to Merilaita, Scott-Samuel, & Cuthill (2017), camouflage is an adaptation to the perception and cognitive mechanisms of another animal, in accordance to the principles of visual perception of objects; it is a suite of adaptations to reduce the signal-to-noise ratio (SNR). The authors state, "Camouflage mechanisms can be characterized as interference with the perception of primitive features, edges, surfaces, characteristic features or objects (whole animals). Camouflage acts to minimize the SNR at different stages in visual processing." The most widespread camouflage strategy is matching of the background, so animals avoid detection by having color and pattern similar to the background. However, the camouflage strategies cannot be static, as predators learn the features of their prey, and humans can also learn about the background (Michalis, Scott-Samuel, Gibson, & Cuthill, 2017).

Camouflage in the floral and animal world exists as a natural design of the outer surface; flounder can almost totally blend with small rocks at the bottom; patterns on a giraffe and zebra's skin, or the whiteness of polar bears in the winter months allow the animals to remain unnoticed or resemble something else (camouflage by mimesis). Some animals stop moving when being approached, to be confused with the background, for example pretending to be an inedible stick. Camouflage may take form of the ability to change color quickly as a means of survival, as it can be seen in chameleon, fish in coral reefs, foxes and hares in winter, and in many other cases.

People can disguise their presence, mostly for military purposes by means of a camouflage clothing, equipment, and installation. Camouflage may also mean dressing unusually and wearing masks to disguise one's identity or personality, especially during special holidays and festivities such as St Patrick's Day parade, Halloween's 'trick-or-treating activities, Venice carnivals in Italy with the costume and mask balls, Mardi Grass celebrations in New Orleans, or the forty-six days lasting Brazilian Carnival and parades. Costume design may transform a person into somebody different. A mask serves as camouflage and, at the same time a pretender, as it is aimed to blend in or stick out. Many celebrities wear dark glasses or sun glasses.

In visual arts, camouflage and pretending something else used to be applied mostly in painting. For example, the trompe l'oeil art technique created (first in the Greek and Roman times and then from the 16th century on), optical illusion of three-dimensionality with the use of exceptionally realistic imagery. One may find several other ways to pretend there is different actuality or reality disguised by camouflage, for example, the camouflage work of an artist Bev Doolittle. Craig Reynolds (2011) designed an abstract computation model of the evolution of camouflage in nature, "The 2D model uses evolved textures for *prey*, a background texture representing the *environment*, and a visual *predator*. A human observer, acting as the predator, is shown a *cohort* of 10 evolved textures overlaid on the background texture. The observer clicks on the five most conspicuous prey to remove ("eat") them" (Reynolds, 2011, p. 123). One of the proponents of Op-art Bridget Riley (2012) shows movement on still canvas. Considering that "Camouflage can be thought of as visual warfare, the Ohio State University hosts "The Camouflage Project" (https://camouflage.osu.edu/research-camo.html). Also, in his camouflage art an artist Liu Bolin (2010) turns himself into the invisible man. Inspired by how some animals can blend into their environment, Bolin uses camouflage principles to create his art.

## Animal Communication About Defense and Attack

The faculty of perceiving sounds used as a communication tool is often more acute in animals than in humans, animals having greater sensitivity to sounds than people. A Zen monk once asked, what is the sound of a cloud? Do different clouds have different sound? (Constant, 2019, personal communication). Birds communicate by sounds but they try to avoid being heard by predators. A bird may emit a very high-pitched and a very short sound, which its mate but not its predator can hear. Some species display ability to learn songs. Vocal learning is considered a substrate for human language. This trait has been found in three groups of mammals (humans, bats, and cetaceans – dolphins) and three groups of birds (parrots, hummingbirds, and songbirds). Vocal learners gain vocalization through imitation, while auditory learners do that by making associations. Perfect pitch perception is present in many members of animal kingdom. According to Slobodchikoff, prairie dogs have highly developed cognitive abilities (Jabr, 2017); they use vocal communication to describe any potential threat, send information about what the predator is, how big it is, and how fast it is approaching. As described by the author, alarm response behavior varies according to the type of predator announced. Slobodchikoff thinks that the idea that a human might have a two-way conversation with another species, even a humble prairie dog, is inevitability. According to Jabr (2017), "Over the course of a 30-year research project, an African gray parrot named Alex learned to identify seven colors, five shapes, quantities up to eight, and more than 50 objects; he could correctly pick out the number of, for instance, green wooden blocks on a tray with more than a dozen objects; he routinely said "no," "come here" and "wanna go X" to get what he desired; and on occasion he spontaneously combined words from his growing vocabulary into descriptive phrases, like "yummy bread" for a cake.

Senses may be considered the important part of the communication process, not only about food, reproduction, and family matters but also about the self-defense, group defense, and finding a prey or a competitor. Communication is an important factor in the defense systems for all populations of living things. One may say living organisms use their senses to become aware of the danger, defend their integrity, survive harsh environmental conditions, or attack other creatures in attempt to forage on them. Computing based approaches and technologies allow learning more about varied mechanisms of communication, defense, and aggression in living organisms.

When we mention defense mechanisms in plants, spines may come to mind first. Most cacti are spiny plants. Spines are modified leaves, while thorns present in many other kinds of plants are modified branches. Most of the species of a stinging nettle have stinging hairs on the stems and leaves. Venus flytrap catches and then digests (with the use of catalyzing enzymes) animal prey, mostly insects and spiders (arachnids). It does it by a complex interaction between elasticity and turgor – pressure in cell plasma.

Animals use many of their senses at the same time to develop their defense systems that fit their living conditions and their needs. The sense of smell applied as a communication tool is often more acute in animals than in humans, so most of animals manifest greater sensitivity to smells than people. Elks can smell their predators approaching against the wind at a distance of 0.5 mile. A skunk secretes a foul-smelling liquid as a defense against predators. However, many keep a skunk as a pet and playful companion because skunks are intelligent, curious, and friendly.

The sense of touch allows animals to feel the harmful things but also to develop the mechanical ways of defense and aggression. Porcupines (and also other rodents belong here, such as capybaras and agoutis) use their sharp spines or quills when necessary; they defend and camouflage them from predators. The same can be told about hedgehogs. Swordfish, which usually reach ten feet in length, use their long, flat bill to slash (but not to spear) its prey and then catch it; they are among the fastest fish. Moreover, they efficiently use their excellent sense of vision. Sea urchins, small globular animals with radial symmetry, have long protective spines. Starfish also have spines covering their upper surface and a soft bottom side.

Many species can sense changes in air pressure or react to wind. Picas defend against blowing food by wind by building walls of pebbles and storing dry plants and grasses for the cold season. Cockroaches have sensitive appendages called cerci, which can sense air motion caused by leaps of their predators such as toads.

A beak, bill, or rostrum helps a bird to eat, groom, feed its young, courtship, or manipulate objects but also fight. A shape of a beak depends mostly on a bird's feeding method. Mammals use teeth and claws both for defense and aggression. Many mammals, for example cattle, goats, and antelopes use horns to defend and attack. A horn is a projection of the skin with a bone inside. However, there are many kinds of hornlike growths. Giraffes have bony bumps, deer have antlers, and rhinoceros have keratin horns. Also chameleons, horned lizards, some insects, and even some jackals display horny growth on their heads. Many mammals, such as musk deer, wild boars, elephants, narwhals, and walruses have tusks that are oversized teeth but serve the same function as horns.

Chemical defense and attack include the ability of sensing smells but also secreting, excreting, and in some cases injecting harmful substances. Jellyfish can sting their prey and inject venom; some of them may even kill a grown man. Puffer fish not only uses its external, spiky fins combining it with sudden speed burst, but it also puffs up, and many of them contain neurotoxins (tetrodotoxin) in their stomachs, ovaries, and livers that have lethal effect.

Spiders use chemical sensors providing information about taste and smell and touch sensors called setae located on their bristles. They also use their four pairs of eyes, some of them very acute, to detect direction of their prey movement. Spiders defense themselves against birds and parasitic wasps by their camouflage coloration as a method of concealment. Venomous spiders have the warning coloration. Frogs defense themselves in many ways: by camouflage, making long leaps, or secreting mucus with diverse toxic substances (bufotoxins) from their parotid glands behind the eyes. Poison dart frogs use their toxins for hunting. Some Australian frogs synthesize the alkaloids that are irritants, hallucinogenic, convulsant, nerve poisoning, and vasoconstrictors, so they can severely affect humans. Poisonous mushrooms, which contain many kinds of toxins, are often looking like the edible ones and taste good. However, an edible chanterelle looks like a poisonous Jack-o-lantern. Some other examples of defense systems may include using a shell as a shield by turtles; using an exoskeleton of calcium carbonate and a single pair of chelae (claws) by crabs; applying long lasting force of jaws by a badger: their lower jaws are articulated to the upper by means of transverse condyles firmly locked into long cavities of the skull, so dislocation of the jaw is all but impossible. This enables the badgers to maintain their hold with the utmost tenacity.

## Sensing Electricity and Magnetism

An electric eel that is often over 6 feet long is capable of generating electric shocks up to 600 volts and use them for self-defense and hunting. They can stun the prey by producing either a low voltage or high voltage electric charges in two pairs of electric organs made of electrocytes – muscle-like cells. Electric eel can also use electrolocation by emitting electrical signals.

Many kinds of animals can detect the direction of the Earth's magnetic field and use this information for orientation and navigation. Those are turtles, spiny lobsters, newts (including salamanders), and birds (Lohman, Lohmann, & Putman, 2007). Also, earthworms can feel magnetic field. The directional 'compass' information extracted from the Earth's field provides the animals with positional 'map' information. It helps navigate; for example, small birds pied flycatchers navigate along the migratory pathways possibly using several magnetic navigational strategies in different parts of their journey. The tied to vision magnetic sense in the birds such as European robins, Australian silvereyes, homing pigeons, and domestic chickens allows them to sense the direction of the Earth's magnetic field and navigate when other landmarks are obscured. The magnetic compass orientation of birds is light dependent, in particular on blue-green wavelengths. The compass lies in the right eye of the robin. For example, if their right eye was blocked, they headed in random directions. Thanks to special molecules in their retinas, birds like robins can 'see' magnetic fields. Magnetic fields act upon the unpaired electrons and affect the sensitivity of a bird's retina (Stapput, Güntürkün, Hoffmann, Wiltschko, & Wiltschko, 2010).

## Camouflage as Defense

Some fish show their colorful parts of fins only to their mates and hide them in other times while trying to stay invisible. Many mammals such as polar bears or foxes change their color according to the season so they are almost invisible from a distance. Many birds have colorful feathers on their sides only, so the predators cannot see them from above.

Chameleons, which have stereoscopic vision and depth perception, can see in both visible and ultraviolet light. They can change their skin color; in three layers below their transparent outer skin they have the chromatophores – cells containing pigments (yellow, red, blue, or white) in their cytoplasm, and melanophores with a pigment melanin controlling how much light is reflected, which sets the intensity of each color. Prairie dogs use a dichromatic color vision. The common toad has golden irises and horizontal slit-like pupils, the red-eye tree frog has vertical slit pupils, the poison dart frog has dark irises, the fire-bellied toad has triangular pupils and the tomato frog has circular ones. The irises of the southern frog are patterned so as to blend in with the surrounding camouflaged skin (Beltz, 2009; Mattison, 2007). Some frogs are bluffing by inflating their body and standing on its hind legs, other 'scream' loudly or remain immobile. There are many forms of parental care in frogs.

Cuttlefish – the mollusk of the order Sepia, one of the most intelligent invertebrates, release brown pigment from its siphon when it is alarmed. The pupils of their eyes have a W shape. They do not see colors; they can perceive light polarization and contrast. The sensor cells (foveae) in their retina look forward and backward. According to Mäthger, Barbosa, Miner, & Hanlon (2005), the eyes focus by shifting the position of the entire lens with respect to the retina, instead of reshaping the lens as in mammals. Unlike the vertebrate eye, there is no blind spot because the optic nerve is positioned behind the retina. Cuttlefish can camouflage by intensity of their color. They have leucophores (the light reflectors) that help match the blue-green spectrum of their deep-sea environment.

## Other Defense Systems

Animals develop many kinds of communication through specific visual defense systems. Examples may include the bird neck swelling, chameleon color change, and even cat's fur spikes swelling.

The social grouping animals develop many kinds of the collective defense systems, for example by keeping their females and youngsters inside a herd. Animal communication in associations of animals goes often through secreted or excreted chemical factors that trigger a social response in members of the same species. Pheromones could be alarm related, food trail or sex related, evoking aggregation, attracting a mate, marking trails, defining landmarks for territory boundaries, and other types that affect behavior or physiology of a plant, an insect, a reptile, or a mammal. Also plants release pheromones to attract bees and other pollinators to their flowers.

Leukocytes, white blood cells are involved in defending an organism against infection. They evolve from a hematopoietic stem cell produced in bone marrow. The number of leukocytes in blood is an indicator of a disease. Immunology – a branch of biomedical science study the immune system that protects an organism. It is present in all organisms: phagocytosis is present in single-celled organisms, production of the antimicrobial peptides in arthropods, and the lymphatic system has developed of in vertebrates; it uses both ways of protecting an organism, phagocytosis and production of immunoactive substances.

It has been reported that many sea animals can sense the coming eruptions of submarine volcanoes, possibly through acoustic vibrations. These underwater fissures in the Earth surface located mostly near ocean ridges (tectonic plate movement areas) account for 75% of annual magma output. In the past, life on the seafloor was perishing because of the two huge volcanic eruptions; the age of dinosaurs might end about 65 million years ago for the same reason, especially due to the rise of the levels of carbon dioxide, carbon monoxide and other greenhouse gases followed by the climate warming and two mass extinctions.

# REFERENCES

Abate, T. (2017). Stanford team brings quantum computing closer to reality with new materials. *Stanford News*. Retrieved from https://news.stanford.edu/2017/05/09/new-materials-bring-quantum-computing-closer-reality/

Abbott Abbott, E. A. (1994/2008). *Flatland: A Romance of Many Dimensions (Oxford World's Classics)*. Oxford University Press.

Ahmed, F. (2019a). Wearable Sensors Challenge Traditional Medical Technology. *BioPhotonics*, *26*(1), 38–43.

Ahmed, F. (2019b, Apr.). Ultrashort-Pulse Lasers: Emerging Tools for Biomedical Discovery. *BioPhotonics*, 45-48.

Alonzo, C. (2018). SHG Microscopy Brings Live Cells into 3D Focus. *BioPhotonics*, *25*(7), 24–27.

Arnheim, R. (1969/2004). *Visual Thinking*. Berkeley, CA: University of California Press.

Arnheim, R. (1974). *Art and Visual Perception*. Occasional Paper. Berkeley, CA: University of California Press.

Ascher, M., & Ascher, R. (1980). *Code of the Quipu: A study in media, mathematics, and culture*. Ann Arbor, MI: University of Michigan Press. Retrieved from http://quod.lib.umich.edu/cgi/t/text/text-idx?c=acls;cc=acls;view=toc;idno=heb03649.0001.001

Ascher, M., & Ascher, R. (1997). *Mathematics of the Incas: Code of the Quipu*. Dover Publications. Retrieved from http://www.amazon.com/Mathematics-Incas-Quipu-Marcia-Ascher/dp/0486295540

AZoNano. (2017). *Benefits and Applications of Nanocomputing: DNA nanocomputing*. Retrieved from https://www.azonano.com/article.aspx?ArticleID=4700

Bales, K. L., & Kitzmann, C. D. (2011). Animal models for computing and communications. In *Bio Inspired Computing and Networking*. CRS Press. Retrieved from http://escholarship.org/uc/item/33t2p1nw

Bar-David, E., Compton, E., Drennan, L., Finder, B., Grogan, K., & Leonard, J. (2009). Nonverbal Number Knowledge in Preschool-Age Children. *Mind Matters: The Wesleyan Journal of Psychology*, *4*, 51–64.

Becker, R. (2017). A 2,000-year-old computer called the Antikythera Mechanism helped the ancient Greeks understand their universe. *The Verge*. Retrieved from https://www.theverge.com/

Bederson, B., & Shneiderman, B. (2003). *The Craft of Information Visualization: Readings and Reflections*. San Francisco, CA: Morgan Kaufmann Publishers.

Beltz, E. (2009). *Frogs: Inside their remarkable world*. Firefly Books.

Benoît, G. (2019). *Introduction to Information Visualization: Transforming Data into Meaningful Information*. Rowman & Littlefield Publishers.

Bertschi, S., Bresciani, S., Crawford, T., Goebel, R., Kienreich, W., Lindner, M., ... Moere, A. V. (2011). What is Knowledge Visualization? Perspectives on an Emerging Discipline. *Proceedings of the Information Visualisation 15th International Conference*, 329-336. 10.1109/IV.2011.58

Bertschi, S., & Bubenhofer, N. (2005). Linguistic learning: a new conceptual focus in knowledge visualization. *Proceedings of the Information Visualisation 9th International Conference*, 383-389. 10.1109/IV.2005.71

BioPhotonics. (2019, no author), p. 11

Biotechnology Innovation Organization. (2019). Retrieved from https://www.bio.org/articles/synthetic-biology-explained

Bolin, L. (2010). Now you see me, now you don't: The artist who turns himself into the Invisible Man. *Mail Online*. Retrieved from http://www.dailymail.co.uk/news/article-1201398/Liu-Bolin-The-Chinese-artist-turns-Invisible-Man.html

Burkhard, R., Meier, M., Smis, J. M., Allemang, J., & Honish, J. (2005). Beyond Excel and PowerPoint: Knowledge maps for the transfer and creation of knowledge in organizations. In *Proceedings of iV, International Conference on Information Visualisation*. IEEE.

Butterworth, B., Reeve, R., Reynolds, F., & Lloyd, D. (2008). Numerical thought with and without words: Evidence from indigenous Australian children. *Proceedings of the National Academy of Sciences of the United States of America*, *105*(35), 13179–13184. doi:10.1073/pnas.0806045105 PMID:18757729

Carey, S. (2011). *The origin of concepts*. Oxford University Press.

Chen, C. (2010). *Information Visualization: Beyond the Horizon* (2nd ed.). Springer.

Chen, C. H. (2011). *Emerging topics in computer vision and its applications*. World Scientific Publishing Company. doi:10.1142/8103

CRISPR. (2018). Retrieved from Wikipedia: https://en.wikipedia.org/wiki/CRISPR

Currin, A., Korovin, K., Ababi, M., Roper, K., Kell, D. B., Day, P. J., & King, R. D. (2017). Computing exponentially faster: implementing a non-deterministic universal Turing machine using DNA. *Journal of the Royal Society Interface*. Retrieved from https://royalsocietypublishing.org/doi/full/10.1098/rsif.2016.0990

Danesi, M. (2017). The Semiotics of Emoji. Bloomsbury Publishing Plc.

Dorigo, M., & Stützle, T. (2004). *Ant Colony Optimization*. Cambridge, MA: MIT Press. doi:10.7551/mitpress/1290.001.0001

Dunn, M., Greenhill, S. J., Levinson, S. C., & Gray, R. D. (2011, May 05). Evolved structure of language shows lineage-specific trends in word-order universals. *Nature*, *473*(7345), 79–82. doi:10.1038/nature09923 PMID:21490599

eBizma/MBA. (2019). *The eBusiness Guide. Search engines*. Retrieved from http://www.ebizmba.com/articles/search-engines

Encyclopedia Britannica. (2018). Retrieved from https://www.britannica.com/search?query=Aphrodita+aculeata

Erwig, M. (2017). *Once Upon an Algorithm: How Stories Explain Computing*. Cambridge, MA: MIT Press. doi:10.7551/mitpress/10786.001.0001

Flagship, G. (2019). *Wearables of the Future*. Retrieved from https://graphene-flagship.eu/exhibitions/MWC2019/Pages/Wearables-of-the-Future.aspx

Franco, M. I., Turin, L., Mershin, A., & Skoulakis, E. (2011). Reply to Hettinger: Olfaction is a physical and a chemical sense in *Drosophila*. *Proceedings of the National Academy of Sciences of the United States of America, 108*(31), E350. doi:10.1073/pnas.1107618108

Frank, M. C., Everett, D. L., Fedorenko, E., & Gibson, E. (2008). Number as a cognitive technology: Evidence from Piraha language and cognition. *Cognition, 108*(3), 819–824. doi:10.1016/j.cognition.2008.04.007 PMID:18547557

Freebody, M. (2017, Oct.). Promise of Organic Photonics Looms Large. *Photonics Spectra*, 36–40.

Gardner, H. (1999). *Intelligence Reframed: Multiple Intelligences for the 21st Century*. Basic Books.

Gardner, H. (2006). Art, Mind, and Brain: A Cognitive Approach to Creativity. New York: Basic Books, A Division of Harper Collins Publishers. (Originally published 1993)

Gardner, H. (2011). Frames of mind: The theory of multiple intelligences (3rd ed.). Basic Books. (Originally published 1983)

Geddes, A., & Dion, C. (2004). *Miracle: a celebration of new life*. Auckland, New Zealand: Photogenique Publishers.

Gelman, R., & Butterworth, B. (2005). Number and language: How are they related? *Trends in Cognitive Sciences*, *9*(1), 6–10. doi:10.1016/j.tics.2004.11.004 PMID:15639434

Goldstein, E., Saunders, R., Kowalchuk, J. D., & Katz, T. H. (1986). *Understanding and Creating Art: Annotated Teachers Edition. Book One*. Dallas, TX: Guard Publishing Company.

Gordon, P. (2004). Numerical cognition without words: Evidence from the Amazonia. *Science, 306*(5695), 496-499. doi:10.1126science.1094492

Grumbling, E., & Horowitz, M. (Eds.). (2018). *Quantum Computing: Progress and Prospects*. Washington, DC: The National Academies Press; doi:10.17226/25196

Halpers, O. (2015). *Beautiful Data: A History of Vision and Reason Since 1945 (Experimental Futures)*. Duke University Press Books. doi:10.1215/9780822376323

Handbook, P. (2019b). *Fiber Optics: Understanding the Basics* (65th ed.). Photonics Media.

Harris, D. (2003). *The Calligrapher's Bible: 100 Complete Alphabets and How to Draw Them*. B.E.S. Publishing.

Harrison, S. (2019). Right Under Our Noses. *Wired, 27*(6), 78-85.

Hartman, N. W., & Bertoline, G. R. (2005). Spatial Abilities and Virtual Technologies: Examining the Computer Graphics Learning Environment. *Proceedings of 9th International Conference on Information Visualisation*, 992-999. 10.1109/IV.2005.120

Hartmann, S. A., Pinto, P. C., Runkler, T. A., & Sousa, J. M. C. (2011). Social Insect Societies for Optimization of Dynamic NP-Hard Problems. In Bio-Inspired Computing and Networking, (pp. 43-68). CRC Press, Taylor & Francis Group. doi:10.1201/b10781-6

Hayakawa, S. I. (1973). *Language in Thought and Action* (2nd ed.). London: George Allen & Unwin.

Hayasaki, E. (2019, Apr.). Building a Trojan Pig. *Wired*, 46-48.

Herz, R. S., Schankler, C., & Beland, S. (2004). Olfaction, emotion and associative learning: Effects on motivated behavior. *Motivation and Emotion*, *28*(4), 363–383. doi:10.100711031-004-2389-x

HTML5 Canvas. (2019). Retrieved from https://www.w3schools.com/html/html5_canvas.asp

HTML W3C. (2016). *HTML 5.1: W3C Recommendation, 1 November 2016*. Retrieved from https://www.w3.org/TR/2016/REC-html51-20161101/dom.html

Jabr, F. (2017). Can Prairie Dogs Talk? *The New York Times Magazine*.

Janzen, R., & Mann, S. (2017). Extreme-Dynamic-Range Sensing: Real-Time Adaptation to Extreme Signals. *Journal IEEE MultiMedia*. Retrieved from http://eyetap.org/docs/EDRsensing_JanzenMann2017_preview.pdf

Janzen, R., Yang, S., & Mann, S. (2018). Painting with the eyes: Sensory perception flux time-integrated on the physical world. *Proc. IEEE GEM 2018*. Retrieved from http://eyetap.org/docs/veillogramAndTheory_camreadyBF.pdf

Jun, H., Zhang, F., Shepherd, T., Ratanalert, S., Qi, X., Yan, H., & Bathe, M. (2019). Autonomously designed free-form 2D DNA origami. *Science Advances, 5*(1). Doi:10.1126ciadv.aav0655

Juster, N. (2000). *The Dot and the Line: a Romance in Lower Mathematics*. Chronicle Books. (Original work published 1963)

Kekulé, F. A. (1865). Sur la constitution des substances aromatiques. *Bulletin de la Societe Chimique de Paris, 3*(2), 98–110.

Kerlow, I. V., & Rosebush, J. (1994). *Computer Graphics for Designers and Artists* (2nd ed.). John Wiley & Sons Inc.

Lehrer, J. (2007). *Proust Was a Neuroscientist.* Houghton Mifflin.

Li, X., Soler, M., Yesilköy, F., & Altug, H. (2018). Noanophotonic Biosensors Expand Live Cell Analysis. *Biophotonics, 25*(7), 28–33.

Lima, M. (2011). *Visual Complexity: Mapping Patterns of Information.* New York: Princeton Architectural Press.

Lima, M. (2014). *The Book of Trees: Visualizing the Branches of Knowledge.* New York: Princeton Architectural Press.

Lima, M. (2019). *Manuel Lima: Visual Complexity.* Retrieved from http://www.visualcomplexity.com/vc/index.cfm?domain=Art

Liu, J.-Q., & Leibnitz, K. (2011). Modeling the Dynamics of Cellular Signaling for Communication networks. In Bio-Inspired Computing and Networking, (pp. 457-480). CRC Press, Taylor & Francis Group. doi:10.1201/b10781-22

Lohman, K. J., Lohmann, C. M., & Putman, N. F. (2007). Magnetic maps in animals: Nature's GPS. *The Journal of Experimental Biology, 210*(21), 3697–3705. doi:10.1242/jeb.001313 PMID:17951410

Loizides, A. (2019). *Andreas Loizides research home page.* Retrieved from http://www.cs.ucl.ac.uk/staff/a.loizides/research.html

Maine, R. (2019, Apr.). Drones seek out cryptic koalas. Biophotonics, 58.

Maniati, K., Haralambous, K-J., Turin, L, & Skoulakis, E. M. C. (2017). Vibrational Detection of Odorant Functional Groups by *Drosophila melanogaster. eNeuro, 4*(5). doi:10.1523/ENEURO.0049-17.2017

Marrin, A., & Mordan, C. B. (Illustrator). (2006). Oh, Rats! The Story of Rats and People. Dutton.

Massachusetts Institute of Technology. (2019). DNA design that anyone can do: Computer program can translate a free-form 2-D drawing into a DNA structure. *Science Daily.* Retrieved from www.sciencedaily.com/releases/2019/01/190103142244.htm

Mäthger, L. M., Barbosa, A., Miner, S., & Hanlon, R. T. (2005). Color blindness and color perception in cuttlefish (Sepia officinalis) determined by a visual sensorimotor assay. *Vision Research*, *46*(11), 1746–1753. doi:10.1016/j.visres.2005.09.035 PMID:16376404

Mattison, C. (2007). *300 Frogs: A Visual Reference to Frogs and Toads from Around the World*. Firefly Books.

*Maya Mathematical System*. (2016). Maya World Studies Center. Retrieved from http://www.mayacalendar.com/f-mayamath.html

McCormick, B. H., DeFanti, T. A., & Brown, M. D. (1987). Computer Graphics. *ACM SIGGRAPH, 21*(6). Retrieved from http://www.evl.uic.edu/core.php?mod=4&type=3&indi=348

Mediaville, C. (1996). *Calligraphy: From Calligraphy to Abstract Painting*. Scirpus-Publications.

Merilaita, S., Scott-Samuel, N. E., & Cuthill, I. C. (2017). How camouflage works. *Transactions of the Royal Society B: Biological Sciences*. doi:10.1098/rstb.2016.0341

Michalis, C., Scott-Samuel, N. E., Gibson, D. P., & Cuthill, I. C. (2017). Optimal background matching camouflage. *Proceedings of the Royal Society B: Biological Sciences, 284*(1858). 10.1098/rspb.2017.0709

Mims, C. (2018, Nov. 13). Inside the New Industrial Revolution. *Wall Street Journal*.

National Research Council of the National Academies. (2008). *Inspired by Biology: From molecules to materials to machines*. Washington, DC: The National Academies Press.

Newsmax Health. (2019). *Dogs sniff out Cancer 18 Months Before Medical Tests*. Retrieved from https://www.newsmax.com/health/health-news/medical-detection-dogs-cancer-detection-tools/2019/04/10/id/911019/

Nieto E. P. (2018). Retrieved from https://www.weforum.org/agenda/2016/01/9-quotes-that-sum-up-the-fourth-industrial-revolution

Online Etymology Dictionary. (2019). *Metaphor*. Retrieved from https://www.etymonline.com/search?q=metaphor

Parker, S. & Marson, M. (2018, Oct.). DNA Is the Next C++. *Wired*, 48-49.

Parry, W. (2014). Red-Seeing Fish, Blue-Seeing Fish: Deep-Sea Vision Evolves. *Live Science*. Retrieved from https://www.livescience.com/43832-deep-sea-fish-vision.html

Petrie, S. (2019, Feb.). Connectivity: As above, so below. *Photonics Spectra*, 10.

Pruitt, S. (2016). *Ancient Greeks May Have Used World's First Computer to Predict the Future*. Retrieved from https://www.history.com/news/ancient-greeks-may-have-used-worlds-first-computer-to-predict-the-future

Reas, C., & Fry, B. (2007). *Processing: a programming handbook for visual designers and artists*. Cambridge, MA: The MIT Press.

Reas, C., & Fry, B. (2015). *Getting Started with Processing: A Hands-On Introduction to Making Interactive Graphics* (2nd ed.). Maker Media, Inc.

Reynolds, C. (2011). Interactive Evolution of Camouflage. *Artificial Life*, *17*(2), 123–126. doi:10.1162/artl_a_00023 PMID:21370960

Riley, B. (2012). *Brigdet Riley*. Retrieved from http://www.op-art.co.uk/bridget-riley/

Rocke, A. J. (2010). *Image and Reality: Kekulé, Kopp, and the Scientific Imagination*. University of Chicago Press. doi:10.7208/chicago/9780226723358.001.0001

Schmickl, T., & Hamann, H. (2011). Beeclust: A Swarm Algorithm Derived from Honeybees: Derivation of the Algorithm, Analysis by Mathematical Models, and Implementation on a Robot Swarm. In Bio-Inspired Computing and Networking. CRC Press, Taylor & Francis Group.

Schwab, K. (2017). *The Fourth Industrial Revolution*. Penguin Random House.

Shneiderman, B. (1996). The Eyes Have It: A Task by Data Type Taxonomy for Information Visualizations. In *Proceedings of the IEEE Symposium on Visual Languages*, (pp. 336-343). Washington, DC: IEEE Computer Society Press. 10.1109/VL.1996.545307

Shneiderman, B. (2014). *Treemaps for space constrained visualization of hierarchies*. Retrieved August 10, 2015, from: http://www.cs.umd.edu/hcil/treemap-history/

Stapput, K., Güntürkün, O., Hoffmann, K.-P., Wiltschko, R., & Wiltschko, W. (2010). Magnetoreception of Directional Information in Birds Requires Nondegraded Vision. *Current Biology*, *20*(14), 1259–1262. doi:10.1016/j. cub.2010.05.070 PMID:20619654

Tufte, E. R. (1983/2001). *The Visual Display of Quantitative Information.* Cheshire, CT: Graphics Press.

Tufte, E. R. (1990/2005). *Envisioning information* (2nd ed.). Graphics Press.

Tufte, E. R. (1997). *Visual explanations: Images and quantities, evidence and narrative.* Graphics Press.

Ursyn, A., & Lohr, L. (2010). Pretenders and Misleaders in Product Design. *Design Principles and Practices: An International Journal*, *4*(3), 99–108. doi:10.18848/1833-1874/CGP/v04i03/57886

Varley, R. A., Klessinger, N. J. C., Romanowski, C. A. J., & Siegal, M. (2005). Agrammatic but Numerate. *Proceedings of the National Academy of Sciences of the United States of America*, *102*(9), 3519–3524. doi:10.1073/pnas.0407470102 PMID:15713804

Victor, D. (2019). An Egg, Just a Regular Egg, Is Instagram's Most-Liked Post Ever. *The New York Times*. Retrieved from https://www.nytimes.com/2019/01/13/style/egg-instagram-most-liked.html

Vogt, A. K. S. (2018, Nov.). A Biophotonics Revolution. *BioPhotonics*.

Ward, M., Grinstein, G. G., & Keim, D. (2010). *Interactive data visualization: foundations, techniques, and applications*. Natick, MA: A. K. Peters, Ltd. doi:10.1201/b10683

Webster, M. (2019). *Dictionary by Merriam Webster*. Retrieved from https://www.merriam-webster.com/

Williams, L. (2016). Programs as Polypeptides. *Artificial Life*, *22*(4), 451–482. doi:10.1162/ARTL_a_00213 PMID:27824500

Wueringer, B. (2019, Aug. 10). Sawfish, the forgotten sea monsters. National Science Week.

Wueringer, B. E., Squire, L. Jr, Kajiura, S. M., Hart, N. S., & Collin, S. P. (2012). The function of the sawfish's saw. *Current Biology*, *22*(5), R150–R151. doi:10.1016/j.cub.2012.01.055 PMID:22401891

Zhang, J. L., & Ishiwata, H. (2016). Hybrid Group IV Nanophotonic Structures Incorporating Diamond Silicon-Vacancy Color Centers. *Nano Letters*, *16*(1), 212–217. doi:10.1021/acs.nanolett.5b03515 PMID:26695059

Zunt, D. (2005). Who did actually invent the word "robot" and what does it mean? *The Karel Čapek website*. Retrieved from http://capek.misto.cz/english/robot.html

# Chapter 3
# Inquiries About Cognitive Thinking

## ABSTRACT

*This chapter of the book is about cognitive processes and the ways they are related to learning and creating. The text discusses how scientific concepts can be translated to the realm of mental imagery and visual thinking and how solutions inspired by nature and science-based issues support developing sensitivity and the use of original ideas in our work. Because cognition and learning may not be limited to humans, the text examines some mental operations in animals. On the other hand, the text discusses how the science- and technology-related producers might enhance their imagination and problem solving with graphical thinking and visual literacy.*

## INTRODUCTION

Some mental processes we share with animals. Below however, a focus is placed on human cognition, abstract thinking, and processes enhancing our creative actions. Discussion about the ways to communicate is causally related to the notions of the cognitive thinking, cognitive science, and cognitive learning. The same may be said about concepts such as mind, consciousness, or even creative processes, art and the response to art. There is growing knowledge about the visual brain and its plasticity, organization of neurons, and how nervous system represents, processes, and transforms information. Many disciplines study the mind, for example psychology, linguistics, computer

DOI: 10.4018/978-1-7998-1651-5.ch003

science, philosophy, anthropology, cognitive neuroscience, and computational models of cognition. Cognitive science is the study of the mind and its processes, so it examines the nature, the tasks, and the functions of cognition.

Cognitive thinking, as the act of knowing, may relate to problem solving, hypothesis testing, and concept acquisition. People use the cognitive thinking to select and analyze information, organize it into memory store, and then retrieve from memory information picked up by the senses. They use it not necessarily consciously, for example for decision-making, in experimental research for gathering data and information, testing hypotheses, interpreting results, and providing scientific evidence for new theories.

The Human Brain Project (https://www.humanbrainproject.eu/en) is a multibillion-dollar program involving research on neuroscience, computing, and brain-related medicine conducted by over 750 scientists from more than 20 countries. The Virtual Brain is an open-source modeling platform for researching brain's structure and function. A super-resolution imaging technique developed at Purdue University provides a view of brain molecules with full 3D resolution. It helps to understand how a neuron works, how brain processes information, and allows monitoring age-related mental impairments such as Alzheimer's and Parkinson's diseases. For example, researchers have taken 3D single molecule super-resolution images of amyloid plaques associated with Alzheimer's disease in 30-micron thick sections of the mouse's frontal cortex (Wiles, 2018).

## 3.1. COGNITION AND LEARNING MAY NOT BE LIMITED TO HUMANS

Questions about animal minds and doubts cast upon whether animals think are fraught with fear that animals are unknowable. This attitude has been changing in the light of current research results made in terms of considering humans as a part of animal world. Also, biology inspired science and technology revealed new information about animal world and lowered the artificial barrier between humans and animals. We are currently learning to look at the animal world and the experience of other animals with a premise that humans are not the measure of all things, and all life is one (Safina, 2015). In this light we can acknowledge that, in the words of Carl Safina (2015), "animals know who they are; they know who their family and friends are. They know their enemies. They make strategic alliances and cope with chronic rivalries. They aspire to higher rank and wait for their chance to challenge the existing order. Their status affects their offspring's prospects. Their life follows the arc of a career. Personal relationships define them. Sound familiar?" (Safina, 2015, p. 2). Similar questions were asked about animal consciousness. According to the author, "all evidence indicates widespread consciousness" (Safina, 2015, p. 25). The same opinion about animal consciousness, emotions, feelings, empathy, playfulness, and sense of humor is shared by scientists studying behavior and personalities of elephants, dolphins, whales, wolfs, dogs, big cats, and other species (Worrall, 2015).

Possibly, the process of learning occurs in plants and animals. Many discuss whether plants display intelligent behavior: plants are as adept as animals and humans in reacting effectively to their ever-changing environment. As they are not able to move, they need to develop specific adaptations. Plant cells possess a network-type communication system at the level of the organ or entire plant. Van Loon poses that plants demonstrate intelligence when they learn from experience, and memorize previous experiences in order to adapt to environmental stresses. Especially, plants show the intelligent behavior when they deal with the exceptional versatility with abiotic stresses.

Thus, intelligence and cognition can be found in the animal and even the plant worlds. Moreover, some species belonging to early groups in evolutionary biology may display intelligent behavior. For example, the octopus (Figure 74) has notable abilities and surprisingly flexible behavior; it is considered one of the most intelligent animals among invertebrates and may have a form of primary consciousness (Anderson, Mather, & Wood, 2010; Mather, 2008). Octopuses developed intelligence, emotions, and individual personalities; they can recognize and like or dislike their trainers, remembering them for months (Montgomery, 2011).

The common octopus has about 130 million of neurons (Montgomery, 2011) or even equal to 300 million (Sinclair, 1985), while a human has 100 billion. However, three-fifths of an octopus's neurons are not in the brain but in its arms (Montgomery, 2011). Octopuses have brain lateralization similar to that of mammals and birds, ability to learn fast from visual and tactile cues, capacity to process complex information (Zimmer, 2008), and to form simple concepts. Octopuses are aware of its position and have a short-term and even long-term memory of foraging areas. They are capable of learning, remembering, and solving simple problem-solving experiments: mazes and puzzles (Smithsonian National Zoological Park, 2014). This cephalopod mollusk can learn by observing the behavior of others. Octopuses have eyes

*Figure 1. A drawing of an octopus*
(© 2013, A. Ursyn. Used with permission)

structured in a way resembling human eyes: they have transparent corneas, regulate light with iris diaphragms, and focus lenses with a ring of muscle (Montgomery, 2011). Scientists from the Woods Hole Marine Biological Laboratory and University of Washington found that the skin of the cuttlefish *Sepia officinalis*, a color-changing cousin of octopuses, contains gene sequences usually expressed only in the light-sensing retina of the eye (Montgomery, 2011). Octopuses can distinguish shapes, colors, and patterns: discern the difference between the horizontally and vertically placed rectangle, between the red and white ball, and they can even play with them, by capturing and throwing things (Mather, 2008; Hamilton, 1997) or shooting water at the bottle to send it back and forth across the water's surface (Anderson, Mather, & Wood, 2010). Octopuses were filmed while they were using a coconut as a tool for use as a shelter and protection (Edutube, 2009). Octopuses defend themselves against predators such as moray eels by jetting off fast, ejecting ink, discharging neurotoxic venom, biting and crushing enemies (or prey) with their beaks. They are using camouflage by assuming coloring or form that allows blending with the surroundings, morphing into a flatfish, several kinds of sea snakes, and a lionfish by changing color, altering the texture of its skin, and shifting the position of its body (Montgomery, 2011). They can also present deimatic (bluffing) displays by showing threatening or scaring patterns, for example resembling dark eye rings with dilated pupils or erecting papillae over their eyes. The octopus may weight a hundred pounds and extend to a length of over eight feet; however, it can squeeze its way through a hole measuring a few inches.

## 3.2. COGNITION AND MENTAL OPERATIONS

Cognitive activity involves thought processes which may involve perception, memory, comprehension, decision-making, problem solving, and reasoning; they all may occur at the individual or at the group level; they may support the understanding and knowledge. Examples of mental operations involving cognitive activity may include performing mathematical calculations, computing, recognizing symbols and signs, reading spatial maps, and writing poetry. A drudgery of bringing past things to mind or recalling old names and events may serve as another example of mental operations requiring a complex cognitive activity.

Learning depends on our attempts made by a conscious and curious mind, which has nonphysical nature hinging on the functioning and physiology of a brain. The brain makes a mind using neurons, which are the specialized cells, the basic brain structures for their activity. Neurons, mostly located in the central nervous system send signals to other neurons, muscles, different cells, and the outside world. Signals going outside and toward the brain are transmitted and transformed through synapses, the specialized areas at the ends of the neuronal extensions called axons. There are about 86 billion of individual nerve cells and trillions of the synaptic contacts in the brain. Large neural networks act as neural circuits consisting of smaller circuits. Patterns of the large networks' activity change briefly according to signals going from the body, the external world, and from the patterns of other circuits in the brain. Our environmental space may mean different things for different people. It can be pragmatic (related to where we live), perceptual (showing what we experience), existential (introducing social and cultural issues), cognitive, (based on thinking), and logical (abstract) space.

Mental operations are going by activation of neuronal networks co-working in a vertical and horizontal arrangement. They can be registered in many ways, for example with the use of functional magnetic resonance imaging (fMRI) which measures changes in the cerebral blood flow resulting from activation of a region under observation. Some cognitive tasks may activate many participating regions at a time, possibly including those involved in the previously performed tasks. It has been accepted that maintaining mental activity by performing intellectual tasks may enlarge a number of active synaptic connections in a neural network of the brain. Neuroimaging studies strengthen cognitive rehabilitation programs (Ledbetter & Lawson Moore, 2018). MRI-guided high-intensity focused ultrasound supports therapy for both ischemic and hemorrhagic stroke (Zafar et al., 2019).

## The Meaning of Our Thoughts and Actions: Semiotics

Visual communication uses visual symbols, sometimes supported with verbal symbols or words. Semiotics studies a meaning of signs, sign systems and symbols in any medium, starting from the relations between signs and the things to which they refer. According to the semiotician Roland Posner (Posner, Robering, & Sebeok, 2004) natural languages, writing systems, musical notations, vestment codes, culinary codes, and traffic signs are the examples of sign systems. The semiotic theory uses the concepts of:

- Sign with physically existing sign vehicle; it has understandable form of communication.
- Meaning as a referent, the actual thing or event to which thinking or symbolization stands for.
- Symbol and what it refers, or an artifact and what it expresses.

The name 'semiotics' comes from the Greek word 'semeion' which means 'sign.' Semiotics refers to semantic communication and sign systems in various cultures. Thus, culture and art is a series of sign systems. Some semioticians examine film as a system of signs. Meaning of a thing or a concept results from social conventions. Biosemiotics applies semiotics to biology, which may be about growth patterns, plant growth and blooming, genetics, heritage, swarms and swarm computing.

Previously, the Swiss linguistics scholar Ferdinand de Saussure posed that reality does not exist before language; also, that all signs are arbitrary. He proposed a two-part model composed of a 'signifier' – the form that the sign takes, which often has a physical form such as for example emoji (Danesi, 2017), and a 'signified' – the mental concept it represents. Concepts have a particular meaning because a community has agreed upon what they signify, not because they have some intrinsic meaning. A specific letter, for example the letter X may stand for several meanings depending on a particular convention. Some authors use semiotics as a generic tool for interpreting data (Danesi, 2017) Semiotics studies signs, their creation, functions, and behavior, so it serves perfectly for analyzing specific sets of signs.

The pragmatist philosopher and logician Charles Sanders Peirce developed a triadic model of a sign involving the cooperation of three subjects, such as a sign, its object, and its interpretant. Ogden and Richards devised a model of the semiotic triangle consisting of a sign with physically existing sign vehicle, meaning as a referent and what is about, and a symbol as a sign that represent conventional connection between the signified and the signifier.

In the animal world, researchers studying animal perception find symbolic shortcuts for making a meaning of what animals see or hear. For example, for small animals the rustle of leaves may mean danger. An elongated object on the sky that is moving along its axis (like a goose) seems safe for small animals on the ground. When this object is flying sideways (like a hawk), it can be perceived as a predator by frogs, snails, or bunnies.

Visual semiotics supports analysis of the visual way of communication and examines interaction between pictures of products or events and the audience as recipients. According to the works of Peirce from the 1860s, images serve as iconic, indexical, or symbolic signs. Communication through images uses signs, visual metaphors, visualization techniques, symbols, analogies, icons, allegories, and time-based images. We communicate not only by speaking or writing but also by using nonverbal means such as images (for instance signs, posters, or pictures), sounds (speech or music, for example), gestures (everyday expression through bodily actions with which we enhance our statements, mudra gestures in Hinduism and Buddhism), or artistic forms such as actor's gestures, body language and motions, among other possibilities. In another country, the same signs may mean something different, and one may not even know that one is conveying strong messages. To assist the tourists, the traveler's language kits in the form of wordless booklets contain pictures of items one may need when travelling in another country. We talk about signage to define the design or use of signs and symbols, for example, in designing billboards, posters, or street signs. Also, conveying meaning often links haptic (related to the sense of touch) and visual modes using dance, mime (a performance art involving body motions without the use of speech) and pantomime (a musical theatrical production using gestures and movements but not words).

Some items always look in an obvious, easy to recognize way, and they should be designed this way. For example, a fire extinguisher should not look fancy, it should be easy to find. Scissors should fit to a hand and a hammer should be easy to use. Product design is a part of material culture and so its analysis in the semiotics framework used to be made with a distinct approach. Product design, and product advertising in various media serve as a tool for marketing that conveys messages about the valuable features of products. Another approach, derived from the 19th and 20th century movements, draws attention of the users to the artistic context of material culture, and thus design is intended as Art. Semiotic content of product design, its artistic quality, and marketing effectiveness depend on its technical solutions, socio-economical messages, and aesthetic-communicative features. The design of computer graphical interfaces for industry, business, and media make a significant and quickly evolving part of material culture. Creation of programs for software involves conceptual structures of semiotics, while notions such as images, signs, icons, or metaphors server explaining abstract functions.

Objectivism and constructivism applies semiotics to the industrial design in different ways. According to Klaus Krippendorf (1990/2018), objectivism believes in an observer-independent or culture-independent objective reality, with structures, codes, and laws ready to be described. Objectivist semiotics of the design products may easily disrespect the cognitive autonomy of individuals, and of other cultures. Constructivism takes reality as residing in practice or in social practice as a circular process of perception and action of conceiving and making things. For example, a notion of a gift becomes a social construction that arises out of social practices. Key to the constructivist approach is not an objective reality but the understanding of our own experiences. We might approach a new product with curiosity, as a variation from what we already know and what we want it to be. With the constructivist approach, the semantic discussion on meaning should be embedded in human understanding and embrace others' understanding of the social practices.

We may talk about the semiotics of the street signs when we examine the design of street signs. Many tasks of such signs include regulatory signs with rules to be obeyed, warning signs about dangerous conditions, and informational signs giving directions and distances. Traffic signs include also signs telling about the priority, the prohibitory or restrictive signs, mandatory signs, and also the special signs about regulations, information, and directions. In some places sounds make additional signals for the visually impaired pedestrians. Both the sign's color and shape are important, such as in case of a red, yellow, or green streetlight, or in a case of a "no left turn" sign. The sign's color and shape must be unambiguous; what it shows has to be compatible with its conceptual meaning. Colors are often used as symbols, for example, they signal the cold-warm water on faucets. When we work on non-verbal communication applied to visualizing knowledge, the semiotic content of visual design is very important. Symbolic drawings may convey messages about universal forces of which we are not always conscious, such as in case of a ying-yang – contrasting, complementary symbol that endangers and sustains the universe.

Implementing standards on signs and their meanings secures their global, culture-independent understanding, communication and social orderliness. It is important in designing computer interface; applying icons used for manipulating computer screens, or making public traffic signs. On the other hand, interacting with technology in an engaging, playful way may create individual worlds in the design process, so there is some tension between standardization of signs and the creative approach to design. Figure 75 presents infographic by Zahra Alsukairi entitled "Semiotics."

## Project 'Finding the Way'

Choose a street crossing where you will find signs present on the streets and the roads accessing streets. Look at vertical signs and horizontal lines on the pavement along with words written on the surface of the road. Discuss the important message that may empower or misinform at the same time. After that compose an atmospheric road scene that would convey your specific mood while you travel: your comfortable familiarity of the landscape or a feeling of getting lost, excursion related excitement or a weariness because of a long travel. Select kinds of signs that would intensify your feelings.

*Figure 2. Semiotics*
*(© 2018, Z. Alsukairi. Used with permission)*

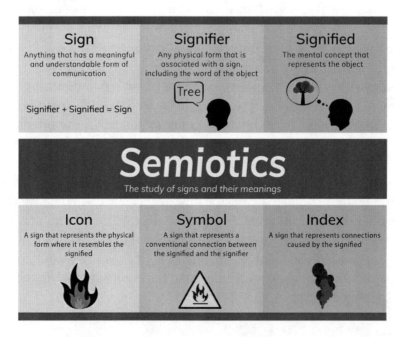

## Abstract Thinking, Abstract Art

Abstract art does not concern literal descriptions. In the arts, pictorial signs may be arbitrary, for example by showing a resemblance of a stimulus to its symbol, or conventional, which are often thematically unrelated. Art or design form can be approached in symbolic or iconic categories. Artists often apply symbolism to convey meaning. Pablo Picasso's sculpture of bull's head, which is composed of a bicycle's handlebars and a saddle, has a form which functions as a sign. This sign is composed of three parts: the material form of the sculpture carried by the 'sign vehicle' (the saddle-handlebar combination); and its meaning (a bull head); and someone who interprets it.

The abstract way of thinking is often applied to simulation and information visualization methods because it allows perceiving complex systems. Product designers use imagery as a medium for thinking about facts and data using visual connotations and associations. We use symbols and link-node diagrams for abstract concepts in graphic languages. Symbolic shortcuts in human perception make a meaning of what we see or hear. And signals of that kind are grounded deeply in neural system. While cognitive scientists usually look for the sources of human communication that are grounded in precise thinking, artists often use purposefully transformed simple signs to direct thoughts of the viewers. The existing trend in applying biology-inspired research and computing has been conducive to the advancements in biosemiotics, which examines communication and signification in living systems in terms of the production, action, and interpretation of signs; this trend approaches biology as a sign system study.

## Articulation

When we use signs to communicate or to express something, we can combine them in a system and make a code, simple or double articulated one. Semioticians use the term articulation when they are studying signs, relations between signs and meaning, codes, and communication related cultural events. Articulation describes units combined into complete structures and thus meaningfully formatted. Communication among people is possible due to articulation of the signs used. The meaning of things, concepts, and experiences may be examined in several ways, for example in terms of perception, cognition, aesthetics, technology, or art production. We may assume that structures such as natural or programming languages or biological forms are meaningfully articulated when they are combined in a set of signs that makes a code.

The term articulation may lack a common definition as it is applied in many domains. Articulation happens when we assign a form (in words, notes, or algorithms) to an idea, information, or a feeling. In linguistics articulation may refer to putting an idea into words. In human speech articulation may mean the clarity, sharpness, and expressiveness of one's pronunciation and a way of uttering sounds. Musicians articulate notes or sounds supporting their continuous transition. Specialists in telecommunication measure the articulation score as the intelligibility of a voice system. Architects use the notion of articulation to describe the styling of the joints. Articulation in anatomy tells about the ability of flexing limbs, while axle articulation in engineering means a car's ability to flex its suspension. In botany, types of joints between parts such as a leaf and a stem are described as articulation. In a graph theory, vertices in as graph are considered articulation points of the graph.

- **Double Articulation of Signs:** In natural and programming languages means that an infinite number of possible combinations may be done from a finite number of signs. A collection of signs used to communicate can be combined to make a code, simple or double articulated one. In a double articulated code communication goes on two structural levels, in a similar way as in speech. A study of syntax tells about the construction of phrases and sentences, where a great variety of sentences result from double articulation. Two types of elements interact in creating the meaning in language. Phonemes are the single units – speech sounds without any meaning. Morphemes are the smallest grammatical elements of a sentence: words or parts of words. In order to convey meaning, morphemes are developed through the combining of phonemes. A finite number of morphemes may be combined into a sentence according to the rules of syntax. An infinite number of correct sentences may be constructed this way.

Possibly, double articulation is not unique for verbal messages, so one may look for some analogy in other domains, for example, in organization of the Japanese calendar, in formation of protein molecules and a genetic code as well. Maybe organization of the Japanese calendar could be discussed as the double articulation of symbols. In the Japanese calendar a combination of 12 zodiac signs and the stems of wood, fire, earth, metal, and water may be seen as a pairing of symbols.

Molecular information processing occurring in a living cell may be interpreted as an example of a double articulation. Cells communicate by transmitting the first messenger signaling molecules from a cell membrane to membrane receptors located on other cells. Receptors activate the signaling proteins called secondary messengers, located inside of these cells. Double articulation may be also seen in a formation of protein molecules. Proteins are large biological molecules consisting of a chain (or more than one) chain of amino acids. A unique amino acid sequence specific for each protein depends on the genetic code – a three-nucleotide combination called a codon, which determines an amino acid according to the four-sign code created by four nucleotides contained in a DNA molecule. Nucleic acids contain four kinds of basic amino acids joined in triplets; they code for specific amino acids, which are the structural units that make up a molecule of a protein. Four bases assembled this way in groups of three in each triplet make possible 64 different forms of coding; however, only 20 from about 500 known amino acids (called standard amino acids) are encoded this way by triplet codons into the genetic code. A wide margin of coding possibilities makes the code open, ambiguous, so more than one coding is possible for the most of amino acids.

## Translation of Meaning

The notion of translation may include translation from nature to art (with the use of technology), as well as many forms of visual, verbal, and numeral translation. Translation from a technical description into visual or audible forms may assume various shapes. Translation of form to function is one of the ways of designing new applications and devices. It is often discussed in terms of the 'form follows function' approach; for example, by examining a symmetrical makeup of the butterfly's wings that allows flying. Nature-derived events and laws may become a source of inspiration and may result in creating bio-inspired new media art works. They are usually accomplished with the use of technologies, mainly computing (generative, genetic, biological computing, and more). On the other hand, advances in technology and the emergence of new media art are shifting our frames of reference in criticism, aesthetics, and philosophy of art. Translation of meaning can use visual rhetoric, for instance metaphors acting as explanatory analogies, making one-way or two-way connections, and performing comparisons.

Artists used to write statements and manifestos to complement their art works. They translate the visual message into literary form, and convey it to viewers, critics, and jurors. We may also see translation in the domain of art history, as well as in the work of curators who interpret works of art selected for an exhibition to supply information on labels and in catalog essays. For example, they explain a content of the paintings from the Baroque period or objects of oriental art, thus providing a translation of images into their symbolic meaning. Visual music connects tunes with corresponding images. Some composers perform music improvisation on grand piano to visual stimuli in the form of art works. Multisensory art and installations involve the use of light, sound, music, and voice including songs, haptic experiences, touch, smell, and gesture. In the course of learning, integrative instruction in science and art directs students' attention toward the essence of the concepts learned and thus support their understanding and knowledge retention. Whichever source serves for choosing the imagery, artists examine mathematical, physical, chemical, biological, and other laws that are ruling the life on our planet and search for visual language to give an account of what they find out. Examination of nature-derived events and laws may result in developing biologically inspired computer techniques (evolutionary computation, artificial life, artificial neural networks, swarm intelligence, and other artificial intelligence techniques) for the creation of artistic systems (e.g., genetic or evolutionary art) and new media art, music, design, architecture and other artistic fields. EvoStar (2019) is an international event on bio-inspired evolutionary computation.

The concept of translation has acquired varied meanings in the particular disciplines, be it geometry, fine arts, language arts and linguistics, molecular biology and genetics, philosophy, phenomenology, material science, and many technology systems.

- In geometry, translation moves geometric figure by sliding, so each of its points moves the same distance in the same direction and over the same distance, without any rotation, reflection, or change in size. Transformations of drawings, such as reflections, translations, and rotations may help extend our knowledge about geometric relationships. Fractal geometry describes self-similar or scale symmetric objects called fractals, which are ragged at every scale, not as smooth as Euclidean lines, planes, and spheres, and they do not display translational symmetry. The mathematician Benoit B. Mandelbrot coined the name of fractals.
- In computer graphics, construction methods build the solids from simpler shapes with translational or rotational symmetry. One can sweep a two-dimensional pattern or shape through space, creating solids.

- Translation was applied to the construction of early computer languages. Instructions and data were entered as punched cards, which used mnemonic symbols to represent instructions; those must be translated into machine language before being executed by the computer. Navy Commodore Grace Murray Hopper developed one of the first translation programs in 1952. The machine code was recorded on a magnetic drum.

- In linguistics, a process of translating words or text from one language to another has been expanding into many domains. The growth of social networking in the network-based environment may be conducive to the growing online readership along with the readers' interactive translation from images to words. One may notice some changes of meaning behind words used in technology, readership, and social networking, which may cause misunderstandings.

- In molecular biology and genetics translation denotes a stage in protein biosynthesis in gene expression. A molecule of a messenger RNA transfers its sequence of nucleotide triplets to amino acids, and thus takes part in synthesis of a polypeptide or a protein. Francis Crick introduced in 1958 the term 'Central Dogma' which depicted the flow of genetic information from DNA to RNA.

- Semiotic phenomenology, as a method to advance translation studies, may refer to works of Ferdinand de Saussure, Edmund Husserl, and others, and then to theories of translation such authors as a linguist Roman Jakobson and a philosopher Jacques Derrida.

## 3.3. MENTAL IMAGERY

Human cognition and memory have the verbal and imaginal systems, which are separate but interconnected. Our mind has access to internal representations. When we present scientific concepts as visual interpretations, we apply our perceptual abilities along with cognitive structures: our cognitive processes often combine with visual thought and visual problem solving. Visual reasoning, as a cognitive activity supports the simulation and visualization techniques because it brings forth an ability to perceive complex systems. Both verbal and visual analogies can be helpful in learning a code. While learning to write programs, one may make use of metaphors as well as analogies with our everyday activities.

Visual reasoning leads to concept formation, helps to comprehend logical structures, and assists in analytical learning. Imagery is the image-making function of the mind. In psychology and everyday conversation imagery refers to mental images – cognitive processes involving experiences in the mind that may be auditory, visual, tactile, olfactory, gustatory, or kinesthetic. Images are the mental models for thinking; they influence language, concepts, and values, and support reading comprehension. Images and mental imagery are important in developing skills, concepts, problem solving, explaining life, and may assist in understanding forms and patterns to make discoveries. The physical world that exists in our environment builds our mental inner reality and causes the production and manipulation of images. Thus, there is imagery that helps us form patterns and one that activates our stored visual memories.

Visual reasoning facilitates perceiving complex systems by the use of simulation and visualization techniques. Anyone with a dataset and Internet connectivity can make visualizations. Libraries, for example textures for 3D, graphic design and Adobe Photoshop (http://www.cgtexture.com/) contain collections of textures and other images, while many 3D libraries provide users with models, some applying to sound. Information visualization is often focused on visual content analysis, along with a visual and presentational exploration. This requires cooperation of researchers involved in information-rich disciplines such as humanities, psychology, sociology, architecture, natural sciences, business and management, not exclusively technology-oriented disciplines.

Mental images occur without external stimuli. Mental imagery is usually described in cognitive psychology as one's nonverbal, cognitive representation of objects, concepts, and perceptual (visual, auditory, tactile, olfactory, gustatory, or kinesthetic) experiences from the past, or images anticipated in the future, which are desired or feared. Imagery plays an indirect role in making associations – mental connections between thoughts, feelings, experiences, connections, issues, preconceptions, ideas, or sensations. We can remember (or even better, imagine) a feeling, emotion, or sensation that is linked to a person, object, or idea. For this reason, they play a pivotal role in building memory and motivation, as one feels more interested and more emotionally involved in the work by creating mental images of objects, concepts one is working on. Researchers hold that mental imagery supports recollection of verbal material, when words evoke corresponding images. Visual imagery serves for generation, inspection, recoding, maintenance, and transformation of images (Kosslyn, 1996; Kosslyn, Thompson, & Ganis, 2009).

Objects are depicted in a visual buffer or working memory – a mental space for manipulating, scanning and inspecting visual images. Our tacit knowledge about physical relations in the world supports such information Thus, knowledge is important in imagery. The visual buffer activates visual mental images induced by stored information; we may redraw maps from memory. Visual buffer can be rotated and scaled at will, but it has limited resolution. It fades if not refreshed. It may take information from long-term memory or develop a 3D model representation in a long-term memory store. Kosslyn provided a computer model of the cognitive processes involved in visual imagery. The attention window selects a region within the visual buffer for further detailed processing. The size of the window in the visual buffer can be altered and its location can be shifted. We can scan to portions of visual mental images that initially were off the screen, even when our eyes are closed, and the farther we scan across the imaged object, the more time we need. There may be a three-way link between visual perception, visual memory and control of action.

## Mapping the Images

The brain forms maps, which are concrete or abstract images (visual, auditory, visceral, tactile, etc.) that represent patterns resulting from objects and events. Cognitive mapping means mental transformations made to arrange information in everyday spatial environment. This is not a map but rather a metaphor, and a process rather than a product. Interoceptive maps provide internal feelings such as pain, hunger, temperature, itch, or visceral sensation. They can reflect physiological condition of our body tissues and organs. Proprioceptive maps reflect a state of the organism's skeletal muscles, tendons, and joints, while exteroceptive maps tell about external environment detected by senses. Our perception relies on imagery, which makes that sensations (sounds, shapes, colors and motions) convey meaning. For example, the rustle of leafs means danger for a small animal (Broudy, 1987). There is also haptic perception recognizing objects by the sense of touch, along with primitive relationships that build topological space, such as proximity and separation, order and enclosure (or surrounding), and continuity. The brain thus monitors our interior and exterior environment, produces neural foundations of our minds, and makes us conscious (Damasio & Carvalho, 2013, p. 151). While maps respond to internal and external events, mind combines the actual and recalled images; some of them may be abstract such as those active in composing music or computing.

## Emotions and Thinking

Neurophysiology of mind and behavior is focused on understanding of brain processes such as memory, language, emotions, and decision-making. Or emotions have a neural basis while emotions have a central role in cognition and decisions. While neocortex performs reasoning and analysis, it is wired up through the old biological brain (Damasio, 2012). Thus, as stressed by Ralph Lengler, "emotion leads to action while reason leads to conclusion; emotions and feelings will always be formed pre-cognitively and pre-attentively before any information processing takes place" (Lengler, 2007, p. 384). Emotional component in the arts can be seen in several media: in abstract expressionistic paintings, sculptures, dramatic performances, stage choreography, acting, improvisation, and other media allowing individual or group expression. Finding entertainment in social networking builds a need for connectivity and addiction to social media. Online relationships can be just as real as those conducted offline. Those who tweet many hours a day, when suddenly deprived of an access to the internet, get a feeling as if they were without their friends and family.

The input coming from our senses enhances our cognitive activities when making our theoretical, practical, and computational solutions. Sensory-based data is recorded and then translated into information. However, visual representations in the ventral visual stream are relevant to behavior, so human brain mapping requires complex behavioral assessment (Cichy, Kriegeskorte, Jozwik, van den Bosch, & Charest, 2017). Sensibility to our internal and external signals helps us focus our attention, remember things, enhance knowledge, and stimulate solving problems or making decisions. Investigations in the domains of cognitive science, cognitive psychology, neuroscience, physiology, sociology, anthropology, medicine, and computer science draw a great part of their data from sensory information.

This may also apply to human philosophy and art, as one may say that art media including music, theater, new media art, and design are inspired not only by information coming from our senses but also incorporate the audience's feedback based on their sensory experiences. Input coming from our senses allows us making a reconstruction of space in thought and then communicating it to others in many ways. Neural mirroring allows us to process and understand actions of other people and also our own actions. Neural mirroring is considered important for social interaction because are able to perceive and interpret the actions, intentions, and emotions of other people (Endedijk, Meyer, Bekkering, Cillessen, & Hunnius, 2017; Marshall & Meltzoff, 2011).

Recalling may evoke emotions, and a surge of dopamine that activates, as a neurotransmitter, many kinds of dopamine systems involved in motor and hormones release control or reward-motivated behavior. Dopamine is thus in important in cognition and thus in reminiscing the past and adding emotion to this activity. However, several other neurotransmitters may be also released when we feel frustration not being able to find a proper word. Emotions related to finding visual and verbal associations stimulate our higher mental activities going in the cortex. Recalling images of past events and objects (such as recall of old trees), as well as of long-forgotten names may help find a proper verb or a name. Many times, free associations may lead to unexpected mental connections between ideas and result in a creative flow of thoughts and activities such as creating an artwork.

Imprinting involves learning about the features of some stimuli. Imprinting occurs mostly at early age. Learning may happen due to enculturation coming from one's native culture. It may be episodic when is caused by a meaningful event or observational when it goes through repetition and imitation of the observed behavior.

Play is an important form of learning that is characteristic of humans (children and adults), other mammals, and birds. Play may take a form of role-playing. A rule-based play governed by codes may include construction and experimentation or may be purely physically based on movement (Lillemyr, Dockett, & Perry, 2013).

Working in literary and scientific domains includes mining for knowledge, which means making associations that are rooted in the old memory. Many times, it is difficult to call to mind a notion or a name that was stored in old memory. This task may activate neural networks by making associations with our old experiences related to senses: smell (such as description of cinnamon shops in the Bruno Schultz' "The Street of Crocodiles"), taste (for example, Marcel Proust's description of the taste of the madeleine pastry), color vision (for example, color squares of Joseph Albers, or a color of goji berries), or touch (as in the responsive sculptures or synchronicity in sculptures that are made changeable by adding an element of viewers' play).

## Visual Literacy

Visual literacy is generally described as the ability to create, evaluate, and apply conceptual visual representations. Visual literacy is the ability to understand meaning presented as images: pictures can be meaningful. The meaning of literacy has been traditionally restricted to interpretation of written or printed text. Visual literacy is now considered a skill important in creating knowledge visualizations for business, communication, and engineering. Education toward visual literacy includes the use of pictures, video clips, and animations.

The term Visual Literacy comprises different types of visual language and communication. Researchers introduced several types of visual components. In addition to generally listed types of visuals that include points, lines, shapes, masses, spaces, colors, and textures, Braden (1996) introduced categories investigated by visual literacy researchers, which are: semiotic signs, symbols, icons, illustrations, images, multi-images, and graphic representations. Graphics is an important component in visual literacy as a form of visual communication, which may apply symbols, maps, graphs, diagrams and illustrations, rendered pictures, models, composite graphics, and photographs. A researcher who in 1969 coined the term "visual literacy" was John Debes who defined this new term as "a group of vision-competencies that a human being can develop by seeing and at the same time having and integrating other sensory experiences" (Brill, Dohun, & Branch, 2007, p. 49). According to Metros (2008), visual literacy is "the ability to decode and interpret (make meaning from) visual messages and also to be able to encode and compose meaningful visual communications" (p. 103).

Visual literacy supports the quality design and product aesthetics. Critics and audience expect that an object's design answer the functional, ergonomic, aesthetic, material- and space-related demands, along with the product's comfort, simplicity, elaboration, message, or easiness of use. The goals are the effectiveness, efficiency, practicality, and manageability of the design. Frøkjær, Hertzum, & Hornbæk (2000) connected usability with effectiveness – the accuracy and completeness with which users achieve certain goals; efficiency – the relation between effectiveness and the resources expanded in achieving them; and satisfaction – the user's comfort with and positive attitude towards the use of the system.

## Sensitivity and Imagination

Is there imagination without imaging? Imagination has an image word inside of it. Imagination of musicians or mathematicians need not necessary to be visual, but many musicians think in visual terms, so do mathematicians. Jean Constant provided an interesting side comment to this: while musician describe their work in painterly terms, artists (and art critics) describe their work in musical terms. Imagination is somehow related to the old memory, to the image bank. Possibly, imagination is involved in the creative process. Also, imagination relates somehow to the senses, when soldiers, prisoners, and sailors invoke the taste of their favorite food.

Education in the arts is advised because the learning of basic skills in arts is helpful in developing the higher mental processing capabilities. Students learn to discover the power of visual forms in making decisions and find individual meaning in the art works. They improve their understanding of visual messages, take imaginative approaches in exploring scientific problems, and use their spatial abilities to recognize configurations and mathematically described relationships, for example, physical interpretations of the formulas they learn.

## 3.4. SPATIAL COGNITION

Spatial skills and abilities, described by McGee (1979a, b, 1982) mean a competence in spatial cognition. Two kinds of spatial skills have been discussed in literature. Spatial visualization is an ability to mentally rotate, twist, or invert pictorially presented objects, while spatial orientation is usually defined as the understanding of the array of objects, and utilizing body orientation of the observer. Spatial skills, measured through reliable and valid tests, are necessary in many activities and occupations as they allow the use of visualization – explaining something visually to oneself, from the viewpoint of one's mind's eye.

We may process sensory information and acquire figurative knowing by applying our spatial perception and spatial cognition. Information processing in spatial cognition includes pattern recognition. It can be gained by comparing a stimulus pattern with our memory representation. Spatial cognition allows us to reflect and reconstruct the space in thought from our perception (what is seen, when we process sensory information) and cognition (what is assimilated by a person, based on person's cognitive structures). However, Werner (1948) defined perception as a form of cognition.

Researchers reported correlation between spatial skills and creativity. Also, thinking in 3D can improve math and science skills. The availability of 4D graphics provides the additional level of visual process information. This means that on the screen the user receives 3D visualization of the robot's movement (Motion control robotics, 2019). For all these reasons, it would be recommendable to teach students how to create graphics with the use of 3D and 4D software. Cognitive tests measuring spatial visualization abilities indicated that spatial skills boost user performance in applying interfaces and bio-interfaces. People with high spatial visualization ability perform faster at human-computer interaction tasks, information search, and information retrieval. Visual navigation in a virtual reality strongly depends on spatial ability, and also the accuracy of sketches about a semantically organized spatial model (Chen, 2010).

Spatial abilities are teachable and can be improved with practice, but a need for developing spatial skills has long been overlooked by public education. Successful training of spatial cognition depends on the frequency of practice and a feedback of correctness. According to the U.S. Employment Service, spatial ability is a strong predictor variable for the achievement in sciences and in many careers (a list of 84 occupations was published). Individuals at the formal operational level may benefit more from training than those at the concrete operational level (Hill, Obenauf, 1979). Practicing freehand drawing may improve spatial skills. However, there is unidirectional relationship between freehand drawing ability and spatial skills: spatial visualization and orientation do not ensure drawing ability (Arnheim, 1969; 1974), and do not guarantee the elimination of a drawing barrier between a person's mental representation and what is actually drawn. Spatial skills such as visualization, mental rotation, transposition of three-dimensional objects to the two-dimensional paper, and cognitive mapping are necessary in many activities and occupations. They are indispensable in visualization to talk visually to oneself from the viewpoint of the mind's eye. With the use of spatial skills, mental images may exist at mental spatial screens, pictures besides of the words, to process sensory information. By making use of mental rotations one may rotate objects to compare and check them for similarity or difference. For example, transformation of a three-dimensional object to the two-dimensional orthographic drawings needs the mental rotation on a plane.

Pattern is encoded as the structural schema in both visual (iconic) and verbal (symbolic) memory codes. The recognition process consists of structural description of spatial concepts, the canonical objects (with assigned descriptions of easily identified differences in top/bottom, front/back, and left/right differences) and the non-canonical objects.

## Field Independent and Field Dependent Cognitive Styles

The concept of field dependent/independent cognitive styles was one of the early studies in the field of cognition. Herman Witkin originated in the sixties studies about the psychological differentiation between the self, the outer world, and other people (Wapner & Demick, 1991; Witkin, 1973). Further studies referred to applications in educational practice. Field independent individuals are more likely to use internal orientation as guides in information processing, and field dependent people use more external referents. Field independent people have an internal frame of reference as a guide to self-definition and use themselves as a reference. Field independent learners tend to exceed at language learning, problem solving, mathematics, concept mapping, transferring knowledge to novel situations, and generating metaphors and analogies. Field dependent individuals require externally defined goals and reinforcement. They tend to excel in interpersonal and social competencies, are sensitive to social cues from others, and prefer learning based on repetition and rehearsal of information.

## REFERENCES

Anderson, R. C., Mather, J. A., & Wood, J. B. (2010). *Octopus: The Ocean's Intelligent Invertebrate* (First American Edition). Timber Press.

Arnheim, R. (1969/2004). *Visual Thinking*. Berkeley, CA: University of California Press.

Arnheim, R. (1974). *Art and Visual Perception*. Occasional Paper. Berkeley, CA: University of California Press.

Braden, R. A. (1996). Visual literacy. In D. H. Jonassen (Ed.), *Handbook of research for educational communications and technology* (pp. 491–520). New York, NY: Simon & Schuster.

Brill, J. M., Dohun, K., & Branch, R. M. (2007). Visual literacy defined – the results of a Delphi study: Can IVLA (operationally) define visual literacy? *Journal of Visual Literacy*, 27(1), 47–60. doi:10.1080/23796529.2007.116 74645

Broudy, H. S. (1987). *The Role of Imagery in Learning*. Occasional Paper 1, The Getty Center for Education in the Arts.

Cichy, R. M., Kriegeskorte, N., Jozwik, K. M., van den Bosch, J. J. F., & Charest, I. (2017). *Neural dynamics of real-world object vision that guide behaviour.* doi:10.1101/147298

Damasio, A., & Carvalho, G. B. (2013). The nature of feelings: Evolutionary and neurobiological origins. *Nature Reviews. Neuroscience, 14*(2), 143–152. doi:10.1038/nrn3403 PMID:23329161

Danesi, M. (2017). The Semiotics of Emoji. Bloomsbury Publishing Plc.

Endedijk, H. M., Meyer, M., Bekkering, M., Cillessen, A. H. N., & Hunnius, S. (2017). Neural mirroring and social interaction: Motor system involvement during action observation relates to early peer cooperation. *Developmental Cognitive Neuroscience, 24*, 33-41. Retrieved from https://www.sciencedirect.com/science/article/pii/S1878929316301141

EvoStar. (2019). *The Leading European Event on Bio-Inspired Computation.* Retrieved from http://www.evostar.org/2019/

Frøkjær, E., Hertzum, M., & Hornbæk, K. (2000). Measuring Usability: Are Effectiveness, Efficiency, and Satisfaction Really Correlated? In *CHI 2000 Conference Proceedings,* (pp. 345-352). ACM Press.

Hamilton, G. (1997). What is the octopus thinking? *New Scientist, 2085.*

Hill, D. M., & Obenauf, P. A. (1979). Spatial visualization, problem solving and cognitive development in freshman education students. *Science Education, 63*(5), 665–676. doi:10.1002ce.3730630511

Kosslyn, S. M. (1996). *Image And Brain: The Resolution of the Imagery Debate.* MIT Press.

Kosslyn, S. M., Thompson, W. L., & Ganis, G. (2009). *The case for mental imagery.* Oxford, UK: Oxford University Press.

Krippendorf, K. (2018). *Content Analysis: An Introduction to Its Methodology* (4th ed.). SAGE Publications, Inc.

Ledbetter, C., & Lawson Moore, A. (2018). Neuroimaging Outcomes of a Cognitive Rehabilitation Training Program. *Journal of Neuroimaging, 28*(2), 225–233.

Lengler, R. (2007). How to induce the beholder to persuade himself: Learning from advertising research for information visualization. In *Proceedings of the 11th International Conference on Information Visualization*, (pp. 382-392). IEEE Computer Society Press. 10.1109/IV.2007.66

Lillemyr, O. F., Dockett, S., & Perry, B. (Eds.). (2013). *Varied Perspectives on Play: Theory and Research on Early Years Education.* Information Age Publishing.

Marshall, P. J., & Meltzoff, A. N. (2011). Neural mirroring systems: Exploring the EEG mu rhythm in human infancy. *Developmental Cognitive Neuroscience, 1*(2), 110–123. doi:10.1016/j.dcn.2010.09.001 PMID:21528008

Mather, J. A. (2008). Cephalopod Consciousness: Behavioural Evidence. *Consciousness and Cognition, 17*(1), 37–48. doi:10.1016/j.concog.2006.11.006 PMID:17240163

McGee, M. G. (1979a). *Human Spatial Abilities.* New York, NY: Praeger.

McGee, M. G. (1979b). Human spatial abilities. Psychometric studies and environmental, genetic, hormonal, and neurological influences. *Psychological Bulletin, 86*(5), 889–912. doi:10.1037/0033-2909.86.5.889 PMID:386403

McGee, M. G. (1982). Spatial abilities: the influence of genetic factors. In M. Potegal (Ed.), *Spatial abilities - development and physiological foundation* (pp. 199–222). New York: Academic Press.

Metros, S. E. (2008). The educator's role in preparing visually literate learners. *Theory into Practice, 47*(2), 102-109. . doi:10.1080/00405840801992264

Montgomery, S. (2011). *Deep Intellect: Inside the Mind of the Octopus. Orion Magazine.* November/December Issue.

Motion Control Robotics. (2019). *Quick review of 4D graphics.* Retrieved from https://motioncontrolsrobotics.com/

Posner, R. (Author), Robering, K. (Editor), & Sebeok, T. A. (2004). Semiotick/Semiotics: ein Handbuch zu den Zeichentheoretischen Grundlagen von Natur und Kultur/A Handbook on the Sign-Theoretic Foundations of Nature and Culture (English and German Edition). Mouton De Gruyter.

Zafar, A., Quadd, S. A., Farooqui, M., Ortega-Gutiérrez, S., Hariri, O. R., Zulfigar, M., … Yonas, H. (2019). MRI-Guided High-Intensity Focused Ultrasound as an Emerging Therapy for Stroke: A Review. *Journal of Neuroimaging*, *29*(1), 5–13.

Safina, C. (2015). *Beyond Words What Animals Think and Feel*. Henry Holt And Company.

Sinclair, S. (1985). *How Animals See: Other Vision of Our World*. Facts on File.

Smithsonian National Zoological Park. (2014). Retrieved March 22, 2014, from https://web.archive.org/web/20080102230427/http://nationalzoo.si.edu/support/adoptspecies/animalinfo/giantoctopus/default.cfm

Wapner, S., & Demick, J. (1991). *Field Dependence-independence: Bio-psycho-social Factors Across the Life Span*. Psychology Press.

Werner, H. (1948). *Comparative Psychology of Mental Development*. New York: International University Press.

Wiles, K. (2018). *New development in 3-D super-resolution imaging gives insight on Alzheimer's disease*. Retrieved from https://phys.org/news/2018-07-d-super-resolution-imaging-insight-alzheimer.html

Witkin, H. A. (1973). The role of cognitive style in academic performance and in teacher-student relations. In *Symposium on Cognitive Styles, Creativity and Higher Education*. Princeton, NJ: Educational Testing Service.

Worrall, S. (2015). Yes, Animals Think And Feel. Here's How We Know. *National Geographic*, *15*. Retrieved from https://news.nationalgeographic.com/2015/07/150714-animal-dog-thinking-feelings-brain-science/

Zimmer, C. (2008). How Smart Is Octopus? *Slate*. Retrieved March 22, 2014, from http://www.slate.com/articles/health_and_science/science/2008/06/how_smart_is_the_octopus.html

# Chapter 4
# Inquiries about Art and Graphics

## ABSTRACT

*In this chapter, discussion pertains to the current tendencies driven from the developments in computing, technology, and communication media, which inevitably have a strong effect on art creation and the ways of its installation. The text comprises discussion about some tendencies in producing images in connection with technology-induced opportunities and requests. There is a strong impact of technology and social networking on approaches to creating art graphics, while programming and computing serve as tools for art generation and installation at digital art forums and exhibitions. Discussion focuses on cognition in art, abstract thinking in art and science, and also the creative thinking in contrast to the critical thinking. As a consequence, there is a need to update current formats of doctoral studies and doctoral degrees in art, so the further text puts forward a proposition of developing a comprehensive curriculum for a doctoral program.*

## 4.1. THINKING IN THE ART MODE

### Critical vs. Creative Thinking

An overlap between the critical and the visual way of thinking allows integration of art and science. Critical thinking skills, in accord with widely held positions, entail logical thinking and reasoning. This may include skills such as comparison, classification, sequencing, cause/effect, patterning,

DOI: 10.4018/978-1-7998-1651-5.ch004

webbing, analogies, deductive and inductive reasoning, forecasting, planning, hypothesizing, and critiquing. Critical thinking, which traditionally has been ascribed to left-brain reasoning, is typified as analytic, convergent, verbal, linear, objective, judgmental, focused on a subject, and probability of its change. Scientific thinking is used in investigating processes and events, acquiring new information, and integrating previous scientific knowledge. Scientists use analogies from similar domains in proposing new hypotheses. Research on scientific thinking (Dunbar, 1997) revealed that over 50% of the findings resulted from interpreting unexpected findings that were very different from the hypotheses based on literature.

Our creative thinking supports our visual way of thinking. Traditionally ascribed to right-brain activity, our ability to think in non-verbal, visual terms, allows us to see connections and relationships where others have not, and to imagine or invent something new. Creative thinking has been described as involving the skills of flexibility, originality, fluency, elaboration, brainstorming, modification, imagery, associative thinking, attribute listing, metaphorical thinking, and forced relationships occurring when we compare seemingly unrelated items. The aim of creative thinking is to stimulate curiosity and promote divergence. Creativity has been also described as an attitude: the ability to accept change and newness, a willingness to play with ideas and possibilities, a flexibility of outlook, the habit of enjoying the good, while looking for ways to improve it. With this approach, we may continually improve our ideas and solutions by making refinements to our work. Studies have shown that creative individuals are more spontaneous, expressive, and less controlled or inhibited. They also tend to trust their own judgment and ideas, they are not afraid of trying something new. "The goal of art is to aid in the comprehension of the world's ideas," wrote Georg Wilhelm Hegel (Macdonald, 1970, p. 372).

## Cognition in Art

Everything the artist learns, hears, and experiences goes deeply into different parts of their brain and stays there, also in its unconscious parts, often synthesizing and transforming into the core of the issue that is central to its meaning. Later on, when some event or experience triggers artist's imagination, parts of their brain go into a semi-conscious state such as daydreaming, to create the point of departure for an artwork. Artist's connotations and associations (conscious and free) are then refined by the cognitive and emotional filters, which define the distinctive, idiosyncratic style of the artist. For example, a quick, spontaneous sketch would display strength and vitality, as well as it would reveal emotions typical of this artist, through the gesture, curving contours, and artist's personality expressed in the sketch.

Philosophical and psychological theories shaping the learning and teaching strategies confirm the important role of visuals in cognitive learning. Theoretical foundations of visual literacy are structured by cognitive theories that examine how visuals are transferred, received, and processed by the learner. Capability of problem solving, aptitude for problem finding, and ability to focus on a creative task and perform in full flow, all ensue from the creative development (Boden, 2009, 2012). Victor Lowenfeld considered art as a catalyst of creativity (Lowenfeld & Brittain, 1987). This concept has been later explored widely, e.g., by Harry Broudy (1987), Margaret Boden (2009, 2012), Boden & Edmonds (2009), and Semir Zeki (1998, 1999, 2001, 2011), among many other authors. Former President Barack Obama called creativity a currency of the 21st century. Spatial ability, creativity, imagination, insight, associations, connotations, and intelligence, all grow through art learning and art making. As the art theorist Rudolf Arnheim put it, the creation of art may be considered a form of reasoning in which perceiving and thinking are indivisibly intertwined. According to Arnheim (1969), productive thinking is perceptual thinking, as visual perception lays the groundwork of concept formation. Word and picture cannot be split up into parts that have any meaning separately (Arnheim, 1990).

In terms of cognitive psychology, a student needs to develop a vocabulary of verbal and pictorial symbols. Students execute such symbols in the course of mastering artistic skills, before they develop their individual expression. Therefore, an art product is the record of student's preparation. This approach became a starting point for developing the Discipline Based Art Education (DBAE) program that was popular in the sixties at the J. Paul Getty Center for Education in the Arts. The DBAE program taught and explored the art experience through art production, art history, art criticism, and aesthetics. According to this program, creativity has been conceived as "unconventional behavior that occurs as conventional understandings are attained" (Lipari, 1988, p. 15).

To support creativity development in students, the Cranbrook Academy of Art did not establish any formal courses in the graduate program. The Cranbrook Academy of Art is devoted exclusively to graduate education in art, architecture, and design: all learning is self-directed under the guidance and supervision of the artists-in-residence. The Cooper Union School of

Art is a talent-based academy: every admitted student receives a half-tuition scholarship, and students are automatically considered for additional merit based scholarship.

## Abstract Thinking in Art and Science

The ability to think about objects and ideas that are not physically present is considered a part of cognitive skills. Some themes related both to art and science do not have any physical, concrete existence. They could be seen as abstract concepts, which are separate from the particular objects. We think about the attributes and qualities of such concepts separately from the objects that share these attributes and qualities.

All kinds of signs: billboards, bumper stickers, horizontal, vertical, or overhead signs can form either a concrete image representing it's meaning or an abstract one, acting as a symbol or a metaphor. We need to recognize a difference between concrete and abstract images or concepts because this way we can organize our knowledge and use only what we need. Graphic images may be concrete (showing physical reality) or abstract. Examples of concrete graphic languages are orthographic projection, isometric and oblique projection, perspective projection, or working models and 3-d mockups. Examples of abstract graphic languages are charts (bar chart, pie chart, organization chart, flow chart, etc.), graphs, diagrams, link-node diagrams, schematics, and pattern languages (groups symbols on relationships using its own grammar).

Thus, the photography of a desk lamp or of a car are concrete representations, while an electric circuit or a blueprint are abstract ones. We use abstract symbols when we order parts for the electrical installation. Idea sketching is abstract. Napoleon said that those who think only in relation to concrete mental pictures are unfit to command. Chess masters think in relation to abstract, pattern-like sensory image, with a formless vision of the positions as lines of forces. With abstract thinking, when we have a map of an island, we can picture how would the island look like, or even write a fiction about events on that island without being there. Writing programs requires using abstract thinking about described concepts.

More and more, the ability of abstract thinking is expected from any prospective employee, who would be able to examine features and relationships separate from the objects that have those attributes or share those relationships. Maybe one can successfully answer, without applying abstract thinking, some questions in a multiple-choice test, yet writing a code for an interactive novel or setting up a project based on an open-source Arduino platform requires using it. The rote learning seems to be less cognitive than for example drawing a chart for the electric circuit distribution in a new house. Abstract thinking can be seen indispensable when one strives to be virtuous in mathematics, philosophy, poetry, or science.

The idea of going beyond the verbal implies seeking ways of depicting abstract and/or invisible concepts. With visualization techniques, information can be converted into a picture form. Scientists and teachers look for the progressive, proactive, and inclusive ways of visual thinking about achieving knowledge, creating art, or providing amusement and enjoyment. They present information with images, symbols, signs, metaphors, and allegories. Mastering computing solutions for knowledge visualization supports working in areas such as art, design, communication, networking, writing, as well as business or computer science.

## 4.2. GRAPHICAL THINKING AND COMPUTER GRAPHICS

Drawings and graphics help us to perform cognitive thinking. Images, symbols, and words lie along a continuum from concrete and representational to highly abstract ones. Understanding of the structured thought requires the ability to perform abstract thinking and to apply problem solving. Graphic drawings provide many ways to view an idea. We can mentally combine geometric forms as a visual means to present abstract concepts and make discoveries. Graphic images may be concrete, when they show physical reality, or they may be abstract. Concrete graphic languages may include several kinds of perspective projection.

Computer graphics are often used to translate into pictures data about events and processes, so they are easier to understand. Computer graphics is the innermost part of most of visualizations; they use color and pattern coding and serve for drawing two- and three-dimensional models. Graphical thinking may support the dynamic process of creating a new concept from its beginning to completion, thus ensuring actionable results. With graphics, we can reason about an arrangement of data, communicate, document, and preserve knowledge. The visual thinking as interaction of seeing, imaging, and idea sketching was strongly influenced by Rudolf Arnheim, especially by his book "Visual Thinking" (1969/2004). We may imagine thought and speech as two intersecting circles. In their overlapping parts verbal thought is produced. Similar overlapping is possible, of visual thinking and graphic language that produces graphic images. Visual thinking can utilize operations (such as synthesis), can be represented by imagery (perceptual and mental imagery), and can occur at levels of consciousness (such as dreaming) outside the realm of language thinking. Not all use of graphic language involves thinking; it may result from other people thinking.

Graphical thinking may play the crucial role in making sound business decisions, as it may be helpful in finding and evaluating information and using numerical data. The use of visual connotations and associations may be helpful in developing and implementing ideas. A situation of facing a real-world challenge in one's specialization often requires a primary and secondary research, critical thinking, and analysis with the use of knowledge visualization presented in graphical way. One can thus draw conclusions about the relevant materials; findings can lead to important insights.

Image as a product of cognitive thinking is a representation of what is seen, a record of an object or scene produced in the mind. To recognize images and decipher them on a basis of our memory, our brain compares information contained in an image to something previously learned and stored in memory. Information from the past is grouped and organized there in a cognitive structure.

Computers transform almost every aspect of students' daily lives. Computers are networked, which helps them with research, updates, social communication, and sharing. Computing is based on the iconic, metaphorical, associative visual communication. Therefore, there is a growing demand for acquiring visual literacy skills. Arts based development training is used in corporations; there is a trend to include the arts in business supporting teambuilding, communication, and leadership. Moreover, the growing number of research lines becomes interactive: they support each other and often overlap. This requires acquiring skills and understanding in many disciplines, as well as achieving an efficient collaboration and fast communication among people from various disciplines. No subject belongs just to one discipline, and so no specialist can confine learning within boundaries of one field. Knowledge, being dynamic, intertwined, and connected, requires from us special skills ranging from the ability to understand and process visual information to performing abstract thinking.

Computer art images have been considered helpful in knowledge comprehension. When drawing computer-generated graphics, one can notice topological relations – qualitative characteristics of arrangement. At the same time, by grasping the quantitative character of the subject one can make productive transformations.

On the web, one may find interfaces to many platforms' graphics, sound, and input devices. For example, Simple DirectMedia Layer (SDL, 2019) is free and open source software, a cross-platform development library designed to provide access to audio, keyboard, mouse, joystick, and graphics hardware via OpenGL and Direct3D.

## Processes and Techniques for Making Images

Image generating printing techniques may include lenticular printing, photo silkscreen after a code or an image, photolithograph after a code or any visual data, and 3-d printing. Advances in lithographic processes caused that electronic chips such as semiconductors became fine structures, and silicon wafers can host extremely fine objects. The digital fabrication area involves raised letters gaining importance as communication with people of low vision, tactile texts and all type of raised surface-based attention, from signage to labeling.

Learning to code is available via web creation. HTML and CSS follow standards allowing creation and organization of a website. What is icon-based can be text-based and vice versa. 3D web attempts were popular over twenty years ago. Some websites allowed people to rotate objects on the screen. However, some users did not appreciate having to learn 3ds Max and Flash, while 3ds Max & Autodesk Maya become now absolute for designers & animators.

Thinking through sketching is on the rise even among people who used to call themselves linear thinkers: from scientists, mathematicians, and statisticians, to writers, composers, business or communication-based professionals. Drawing and sketching allows for connecting one's brain and it's illusionary-based associations, connotations, and metaphors with the bigger picture of the issue, problem, idea or even any type of organization of data.

Information delivery through characters is also on the rise. It starts with entertainment, creates many discussions on the semantics behind emoji and it's possible and often predicted fall in the near future. An artist and a scientist can be seen as storytellers. They examine the issue, topic, Nature-based events such as processes and products and tell their point of view through own perspective narration.

Multisensory environment for displaying knowledge (music, text, graphics, haptic sense of touch, proprioception, etc.) fulfills a common need for entertainment. More and more inclusive, surrounding, interactive, fear-causing space-based sensory developments make us learn, experience, and experiment with both well-known and unknown developments. Again, the sensations and the act of participation make us understand better and retain longer. The element of sharing both ways makes the experience stronger.

## Photographic Images

Digital networked photographic imagery became a part of computer-mediated technologies. Computers and digital photography, as the result of a computer ability to process and interpret light signals, developed at the same time but in parallel ways. Media historians and media communication theorists tended to ignore photography, while few writers considered photography as a part of new media. Photography entails many different processes, methods, and techniques: printing techniques including 3D printing, lithography, silkscreen and photo-silkscreen, intaglio, and drawing. Photography becomes then incorporated in various media such as motion pictures, video, cell phone, television, and digital media including social media. According to Michelle Henning, "photography is not a pure technology or medium, it does not exist in isolation from other technologies, from cultures, from discourse, and from material stuff, and it will always challenge the ambitions of an overarching theory of photography" (Henning, 2018, p. 173). But photography in a traditional meaning of this medium (Daguerre, 1839) "sets the image free by loosening it from its fixed place in tie and space; the 'mirror with a memory' is opposed to the mirror that can only picture a specific thing in one place, one time" (Henning, 2018, p. 173).

Photography may be seen as static images, as snapshots that catch transient events and their perceptions. One can confine in a single photograph the whole essence, deep and genuine feeling. However, some claim that shooting photos is a form of predatory violation of privacy.

Digital photographic images appear or disappear from a screen at the swipe of a finger (Henning, 2018). Digital media and telecommunications supplied photography with mobility of images. Thus, networked digital images, film, and television present duration, mobility, and mixed character made by combining genres and techniques. There is sometimes a flow, a stream of images and meanings.

A hologram can be made by using a part of a flash of light beam directly onto the recording medium, and the other part (the reference beam) onto the object, so some of the scattered light falls onto the recording medium.

# Art, Computing, and Technology

Art works may become an inherent part of science- and technology-related solutions. Artistic production may take innumerable forms. An artwork may take form of a picture, but also it may become a spatially referenced and time dependent event, an interactive and interdisciplinary visual form, and storytelling. With or without the use of programs, learners may create the interactive, literary, or graphic forms. Student projects may be made as a story, a poem, a manga, and an anime. Open-source software that is available for public collaboration allows for a peer production. Moreover, countless options of social networking platforms provide a fuel for any form of an online creative work.

Art production may evolve according to the emergence of new scientific theories. Information coming from current research results and evolving technologies changes our understanding of nature and natural processes. As a consequence, our inspiration and our art works change along with our knowledge base. On the other hand, advances in science, technology and the emergence of the new media art itself change our perception of reality shifting our frames of reference in criticism, aesthetics, art appreciation, and philosophy of art.

Programming has a rich visual component and so may become an artwork. Because of this, artists, along with scientists and teachers explore ways of presenting information in artistic way, using images, symbols, signs, metaphors, and allegories. They are going beyond the verbal and seek the progressive, proactive, and inclusive ways of achieving knowledge, creating art, or providing amusement and enjoyment. Mastering computing solutions for knowledge visualization may open new venues for an ambitious or creative person working in areas such as art, design, communication, networking, writing, as well as business or computer science.

We may see computing as a common trait that can be found both in the online social networking and the electronic media. Computing technologies use bio- and evolutionary computing, applications, robots, smart and intelligent apps, bots, ubiquitous devices, tools for mobile apps, and smart phones. In the arts, evolutionary computing resulted in creating generative art (Boden & Edmonds, 2009) and the developments in biology-inspired design, art, music, architecture, and other artistic fields.

Computing provides an impact on networked interactive communication. The interactive or virtual encounters may refer to visuals, the use of light, sound (such as music and voice including songs), haptic experiences, touch, and gesture. Particular solutions may be also attained with the use of avatars, telecasting, TV, groupware implementations, social networking, YouTube, and any other ways of social activities such as blogosphere or wiki applications. Media employed online may include and often combine video strips, immersive virtual reality, the Web, wireless technologies, performances, art installations, and interactive presentations. The meaning of the new media art has exceeded the concepts of artistic creation. We often refer as an artwork works aimed at entertaining, educating, or otherwise involving the audience. Artists communicate through online platforms; for example, It's LIQUID (http://www.itsliquid.com/) is a communication platform for contemporary art, architecture and design. Figure 1 shows an "Avatar" by Lena Harper.

The producer at Pixar John Walker (Catmull, 2014) described his philosophy of integration, "Art challenges technology, technology inspires art." Different mindsets, skills, and mental models can be aligned and engaged. Edwin Catmull stated, "When working on a script, research trips fuel inspiration, challenge our preconceived notions, and keep clichés at bay." Viewers may not know the reality but they feel right. We cannot envision how our technical future will unfold because it doesn't exist yet. Steve Jobs said, "The best way to predict the future is to invent it" (Catmull, 2014).

*Figure 1. Avatar*
*(© 2018, L. Harper. Used with permission)*

Bio-inspired technologies change the way people think in the fields of computing, software management, material science and material design, resource management, developments in computer technologies, and many other fields. Bio events that inspire biocomputing may also inspire educational projects and program visualization. In art works presented in this book one can find out artists' inspiration coming from nature (water, sky, earth, animals), science (physical events and processes, mathematical order), as well as the human generated environments (such as rural or urban surroundings). Whichever source serves for choosing the imagery, inspiration coming from nature or science may often result in patterns, shapes, and colors that translate the regularities and laws found in nature or science into visual language. In such instances artists examine mathematical, physical, chemical, biological, and other laws that are ruling the life on our planet and search for visual language to give an account of what they find out.

## Digital Art Forums and Exhibitions

Previously, the well-known critics and the general public have not recognized digital art, and it has not been accepted to prominent art galleries. The beginnings of computer art artists, always present where there is something new, worked on computers belonging to big corporations. For this reason, they had to learn programming languages and thus achieve abilities reserved to engineers and technical people. Digital art exists on the internet rather than in a physical location (Boden, 2012), and is associated with a fascination for technology; digital artwork production involves electrical engineering and/or electronic technology. Poets have been using computers and digital technology to produce several types of poetry including randomly generated writings, graphical works (static, animated, and video formats), hypertext, and hypermedia. Digital jewelry – the jewelry with embedded intelligence – is an example of the use of novel techniques in craftwork (Boden, 2012). In the form of earrings, necklaces, rings, or bracelets, it includes wireless, wearable mobile computing devices such as cell phones, personal digital assistants (PDAs) and GPS receivers that serve to communicate by ways of e-mail, voicemail, and voice communication.

Programmers and engineers, science people, or linguists, to name just a few, are also producing art. Since a French physician Pierre Paul Broca proclaimed by in 1861 the brain function lateralization, people used to be divided between the right and left brained people: left and right hemispheres were seen as opposites rather than the complementary parts. According to this lateralization, many left-brain oriented people considered art to be impenetrable, difficult to understand, and thus thought of as a product of lesser value. Moreover, the cooperation of artists with engineers was sometimes difficult. However, Rosenzweig (2014) claimed that making winning decisions calls for a combination of skills: clear analysis and calculation – left brain, as well as the willingness to push boundaries and take bold action – right stuff. Previously, programmers and software developers did not want to achieve the art- and design-related skills. Later on, they reversed from having a good confidence about the superiority of their expertise to becoming painfully aware that effectiveness and aesthetics may not be independent. As soon as art and design became entangled with technology, engineers began to produce software aimed at art creating, having art, functionality, and practicality in mind; for example, software for retouching photos or for drafting. They also designed GUI – graphical user interfaces allowing interacting with electronic devices through graphical icons rather than coding and sending commands. Students learning through creating art, contrary to the hands-on, step-by-step, or rote learning by memorization and repetition, gain ability to create visualizations in compliance with the creative principles.

From some time, words 'image,' 'graphics,' 'picture,' and 'signage' find their place in terminology used in information visualization, entertainment, and marketing. With the advent of the World Wide Web, artists began to make their representations and sell their works through the internet. As more artists learn programming and more technology oriented people make art works, many instances of collaboration are sponsored by foundations, artists residencies, conferences, and contests supported by academia, institutions, agencies, associations, and people who write, sponsor, develop, organize, and manage, seeking new directions for the arts. As a result, art works become often utilitarian, as games, animations, or the winning aesthetic knowledge visualizations. Art takes also form of the second life apps or applications made within the social network structure. Accordingly, statements about art one can find on the social network seem to convey a summarized expression of views that art should be interactive and thus entertaining, introduce beauty to the web design and everyday life, bring money, and on the top of it, all art should inform, heal, secure and teach. Overall, these changes influence curricula.

Several solutions in art production draw from the old techniques, so one can often make comparisons with old masters. Apart from an online forum (for example, D-Art Symposium of Digital Art and Gallery; NanoArt21, Art/Science/Technology online gallery, and many others), a large number of settings have been used for displaying art or exchanging information and ideas, including Der Prix Ars Electronica International Computer Graphics Contest, Linz, Austria; Documenta, Kassel, Germany; The Venice Biennale, Venice, Italy; ACM/SIGGRAPH Art Galleries; SIGGRAPH Asia; FILE Electronic Language International Festival; EvoStar conferences in evolutionary computing; ISEA International; GA - Generative Art International Conferences, Roma, Italy; Burning Man annual events, Nevada's Black Rock Desert, USA; Japan Media Arts Festival, and many others.

Many times, abstract concepts originating in mathematics or biology are converted digitally into lines and shapes supported by their natural beauty. In the time of networking they generate many kinds of artistic competitions such as, for example:

- Bridges: the Mathematical Connections in Art, Music, and Science (www.bridges mathart.org) and Mathematical Imagery at the American Mathematical Society (http://www.ams.org/home/page).
- Joint Mathematics Meetings The Joint Mathematics Meetings Exhibitions of Mathematical Art (JMM) http://jointmathematicsmeetings.org/jmm.
- NanoArt21 International Festivals, Competitions and NanoArt21 Exhibitions (nanoart21.org).
- Fractal Art Contests (http://www.fractalartcontests.com/).
- Nikon's Small World Photomicrography Competitions (https://www.nikonsmallworld.com/).
- D-ART Art Gallery for the International Conference on Information Visualisation, South Bank University, London, GB.

## 4.3. THE GROWTH OF AN ARTIST

### Formats of Doctoral Studies and Doctoral Degrees

There is growing trend in artistic circles to develop the prospective format, meaning, goals, and content for doctoral dissertations in the visual arts that would satisfy all criteria for an academic doctoral degree. A tentative model for a person awarded the doctoral degree in the visual arts may stipulate that this person creates art, performs, develops knowledge, can teach and supervise students, is prepared to publish new forms of visual knowledge, and serves the community by sharing knowledge. Comprehensive curricular models are thus needed for a doctoral program in the visual arts.

Academies are working on defining a coherent, comprehensive program of teaching and supervision in doctoral studies defining what is expected of a doctoral student. Reviewers may expect that a candidate working toward a doctorate in the visual arts is creating art and contributes to the field with new approaches and research results. This includes a need for developing doctoral students' skills in abstract thinking, cognitive skills, creativity, and problem-solving abilities.

Both in the United States and all over the world there have been a great number of formats proposed for the last decades as a terminal degree in the visual arts. There are alternative projects to establish a studio doctorate in fine art as an award for professional and academic achievement (Maksymowicz, & Tobia, 2017). Diane Zeeuw (2017) postulates the development of the creative arts practice-led PhD, documented as a case study at the University of Melbourne. Linda Candy and Ernest Edmonds (2018) are opting for the application of a practice-based research in the creative arts as an alternative in generating new forms of knowledge in the context of the interdisciplinary PhD program in the visual arts and digital media. According to the authors, "a basic principle of practice-based research is that not only is practice embedded in the research process but research questions arise from the process of practice, the answers to which are directed toward enlightening and enhancing practice" (Candy & Edmonds 2018, p. 1). Still, the doctoral level requirements in visual arts at the university level are discussed vigorously about the measure in which the studio-based creative production and scientific inquiry may consist in the whole PhD in art program.

Ken Friedman and Jack Ox (2017) identify eight different kinds of doctoral degrees in the visual arts: "(1) The traditional or "old" PhD degree; (2) different forms of innovative or "new" PhD degrees developed for the demands of creative and performing arts; (3) the technical doctorate with a title such as DrTech or DrEng in some areas of the creative arts, including digital media, software and design; (4) the professional doctorate in the practice of creative art, performance or design, with a title such as DMus or DDes; (5) a studio doctorate awarded for artistic practice or artistic research in fine art, design or performance, with a designation such as DA or DFA; (6) new forms of PhD in creative arts, performance or design that function as variations within the framework of the traditional PhD while being designated as practice based degrees; (7) the studio PhD awarded for studio practice in creative or performing arts supported by some form of explanatory essay or contextual document; and (8) a practice-based PhD in creative and performing arts or design that is somehow distinct from both the studio PhD and the traditional PhD" (Friedman & Ox, 2017, p. 1).

It is hard to think about art exclusively as an aesthetic experience we encounter in a museum or a gallery, as art exists in all disciplines, which do not function well without art. An ACM/SIGGRAPH 2016 keynote speaker Z. Nagin Cox (2016), the NASA Jet Propulsion Laboratory Spacecraft Operations Engineer, acknowledged the visionary power of George Lucas when she revealed, "No missions of space exploration would be possible without the technologies of computer graphics and the human/robotic interactions they enable." (ACM is the Association for Computing Machinery; SIGGRAPH is the ACM Special Interest Group on Computer Graphics and Interactive Techniques, the largest computer graphics conference).

Many times, there are complains about cases of displaying a low esteem that the science, engineering, and business related people assess to the arts and the art faculty. For example, a professor from the Math Department could not get the promotion until she gave up organizing the art and math conference and dropped creating art. She was said that mathematics was to be a serious discipline. Another art professor learned from his dean that an NSF grant proposal would not be taken into account because this grant is not for artists. When he developed a fun art appreciation class they told him to forget about technology, and then moved him to teach that one course only to make a lot of money for the school. Another colleague involved into the computer info systems was typing very fast when coding, so the administrators moved him to teach keyboarding; he left the university. In one case, the STEM kids working on engineering earth sciences were redirected to finalize their finding either as posters or websites.

Art has become an integrated part of many disciplines, and many people see a need to grow visually in order to become current in their non-art research, focus, and studies. Many exhibits in galleries their research findings, presenting their results obtained in a visual way, using ever-expanding technology that allows seeing beyond what the eye can perceive. The developments in photonics give us an insight into domains that till now were inaccessible for human eyes in a macro-, micro-, nano-, or pico-scale, including the data from a cosmos as the real time footage of what happens far away.

A considerable part of the debate focuses on defining a selection of mandatory or elective courses that would encourage the doctoral students and their supervising faculty to engage in multidisciplinary areas of research. However, contrary to technical or business related doctorates, the awarding a doctoral degree in art would reflect the candidate's active engagement in the studio arts. The National Association of Schools of Art and Design guidelines (NASAD, 2016-2017) call for 65% or more of the terminal master's curriculum to be in studio-based coursework.

According to aesthetic cognitivism, cognitive psychology can help us understand and react to art, while "art can nontrivially teach us" (Barrett, 2017, p. 66). Therefore, these perspectives of seeing art would oblige the PhD candidates to present a doctoral thesis together with an exhibition of the art works generated during and through the research. For this reason, dissertations toward the doctorate in the visual arts ask researchable questions, analyze research paradigms, discuss related standards, produce rigorous investigations, and then write publishable treatises. That way, doctoral students would be able to identify important readings in other fields, adopt a perspective among competing theories, understand methods and their limits, discuss standards for judging art works, and apply their findings to new contexts.

## A Comprehensive Curriculum for a Doctoral Program

Prospective doctoral students may need a general outlook curriculum including possible programs of study, a spectrum of subjects comprising courses of study along with course syllabi, and tentative modules to visually organize knowledge needed for preparing a dissertation. Students working toward PhD in Art would continue their artistic creation; they would be possibly developing knowledge visualization skills. In many instances knowledge visualization takes form of art. Students' visual projects would be merging their selected disciplines. With this approach, everyone would need to have two areas of specialization, for example, one area would explore art with technology, and the second one would be of their choosing. It could be history of digital art, museum studies, material sciences, math, physics, chemistry, biophotonics, etc. It should be all connected with selected technologies, so the doctoral students would master technical venues and platforms such as for example, video art, serious games, web comics, virtual reality games, 3D printing, 3D casting, laser cutting, or collaborative and interactive art making. This inclusive curriculum would be taught by specialists bringing knowledge, achieving general understanding, and stressing how areas/disciplines intertwine.

Doctoral students would be informed about formats used for their progress assessment, whether it would be presenting a portfolio of art works projects, performing a critique, visual and written solutions of assignments, videos, movies, manga sequential art projects, storytelling with storyboards and character animation, games, papers, or other presentations. They would learn to deliver presentations that engage audiences and inspire action by finding a theme that resonates with their audience. For example, Columbia University offers courses toward degrees in communications practice, and teaches hoe dry content could be presented through image, metaphor, emotion, and story. Doctoral students would design serious games (Zheng, & Gardner, 2016) – interactive computer video games serving both educational and other purposes such as medicine, defense, education, scientific exploration, health care, emergency management, city planning, engineering, and politics. Students would use metaphors that may link the sender and the viewer by conveying not only perception but also the meaning. For example, they would use visual metaphors serving for labeling various internet services, which include photos (Flickr), videoclips sharing (YouTube), microblogging platforms (Twitter), and making the www. bookmarks (delicious.com) Students may as well use services like MySpace, Facebook, professional networking (LinkedIn), and collect online content (Twine). The internet portals and communication media, such as the web, videoconference software, and search platforms (e.g., Wikipedia) became more visual interdisciplinary, and more interactive.

Doctoral programs would be possibly offered online or they could use blended instruction: learning with the use of the internet may include: – online learning that deliver most of the content through the internet without face-to-face meetings; – blended/hybrid courses that blend online and face-to-face delivery; and – web-facilitated courses that use web-based technology to facilitate a face-to-face course. The use of social media and Web 2.0 (along with the Web3D) allows teaching students in many ways and thus get in contact with every student. Social media use Web 2.0 tools such as images, instructional videos, interactive boards, blogs, smart devices, mind mapping, outside-the box applications, and gaming. They allow direct socio-cultural interactions between students/classmates and teachers, other online interactions that facilitate learning, as well as matching learning material with the student's learning style.

Establishing e-learning analysis enables evaluation, and application of digital imagery in e-learning context, thus changing the environment for learning. Mobile learning (m-learning) based on the use of mobile devices in the curriculum is a natural progression of distance or e-learning. Supervision by the faculty members of a doctoral committee and consultations offered by experts may be delivered via Zoom, Coliseum, Skype, and more. With an online program organized toward the PhD in arts, students would have an opportunity to successfully ask the faculty from various institutions to serve on their committees. For the faculty, association with a good university would serve as a resume item, and for the student, the online resources and the ability to work with experts they choose could be a good incentive.

## Gaining Knowledge About Tools for Research

Doctoral students in art may need some preparation for using proper research tools. The curriculum program for doctoral students would thus comprise a set of courses of study in research methods. First of all, doctoral students would be offered a course of research design, so they would become prepared to choose a scope, depth, and content of their study in selected field. The curriculum would offer choices in courses of research methods comprising quantitative research methods, qualitative research methods, and mixed methods research.

Most would agree that statistics is describing our lives. Kass et al. (2016) stressed that while experiments generate data to answer scientific questions, "inexperienced users of statistics tend to take for granted the link between data and scientific issues and, as a result, may jump directly to a technique based on data structure rather than scientific goal. This shift in perspective from statistical technique to scientific question may change the way one approaches data collection and analysis." A biostatistician Andrew Vickers advised that researchers should treat statistics as a science, not a recipe (Baker, 2016).

The collaborative process works best when initiated early in an investigation (Kass et al., 2016). Asking questions at the design stage can save headaches at the analysis stage. Sir Ronald Fisher (1938) stated, "To consult the statistician after an experiment is finished is often merely to ask him to conduct a post mortem examination."

After taking a course of statistics doctoral students would decide what kinds of studies they would like to take as the most useful; they would be knowledgeable enough to rethink their options for choosing the best fitting research method: experimental approach, interview, survey, or one of observational methods. They would also be able to consider multiple ways the data might provide answers. Doctoral students would thus be able to wisely collect their data and choose the optimal methods of further working on the data by applying statistical analysis or other methods of data processing such as content analysis, discourse analysis or thematic analysis (Krippendorf, 2018). The candidate's preparation and the general outline of a doctoral thesis would determine which courses would be considered compulsory or optional ones, and some instruction would be individualized to the student's needs.

Depending on their experience in the publication domain doctoral students may need some instruction in organizing information related to their results, preparing their dissertation according to requirements for the doctoral degree, and publishing their work. It may be important to teach about critical evaluation of the results and their meaning, discussion of their own and other authors' views or arguments and determining conclusions, to enable a writing of a doctoral thesis. Doctoral students would have the skill to select primary and secondary sources and then compiling and presenting them in combined historical or technical contexts, while including proper bibliographic information sources. Some may need to be supported in using their internet skills, so they would network with other students, experts, and scholars, access electronic databases, and peruse art archives. Also, some doctoral students may need courses introducing programming, using suitable software such as for data analysis, computer graphics, and presenting visual and written materials for publication on paper or online publication. For some students, courses on drawing (orthodox and with the use of computer software), digital photography, and video would support working on their program. Doctoral students would practice presenting their work visually and verbally on exhibitions, shows, performances, installations, as well as conferences. That would include skills in writing statements, abstracts, interacting with audience, and handling discussions. They should have instruction offered, on the intellectual property and copyright laws.

## Integrative Approach

Most often, people awarded a doctoral degree are supposed to share their knowledge in their professional environment, promote widely art ideas and issues in the society, as well as contribute to propagating instruction in the visual arts all over the K-16 educational institutions. The general direction in which educational progression answers the call for the integrative instruction include the STEAM program (science, technology, engineering, arts, and mathematics) and the STREAM program (science, technology, reading, engineering, arts, and mathematics), which often replaces the STEM program (*STEM to STEAM*, 2019). These formats, along with current trends toward combining science and engineering with the arts and humanities are directed toward developing integrative education and effective strategies decisive for the workforce development. For this reason, the doctoral program in the arts should be interdisciplinary, thus preparing doctoral students for addressing the issues of technology infused environment, both in schools and at work.

In order to construct a comprehensive doctorate program across the whole spectrum of art areas we should take into account several specific ways that artists may approach this project. The study toward this academic degree may take many distinctive forms.

- Research aimed at honing the teacher/artist – artist/teacher performance.
- A research study may provide knowledge and means to refine the scope of art education.
- A study on recent trends and events in art and media may contribute to the art history area.
- Research on how teachers' artistic abilities and media may support their pedagogical success in making math or science understandable to students.
- Research on how to consolidate methods in teaching art and selected fields of science.
- Current media in the arts (including installation, visualization, VR, interactivity) should be applied to instruction in science.
- Exploration of knowledge transfer through serious games in educational setting.
- Analysis of an impact of the developments in new technologies and new materials on the evolving art media solutions.
- Research study on the possibilities for visual artists to use coding, graphical programming languages, applications, and software to create art.
- Research study on the relevance of visual arts education to the student's social, professional and personal life.
- Research on the specific PhD themes and methods to evaluate which course can be transferred from other disciplines or developed for their own purposes.

Thus, this academic degree should be all-inclusive, based on a set of courses that would be both art related and directed at the fields of the candidate's professional activity. Each doctoral student would develop an art project in topics aimed to expand their cognitive abstract thinking, independent critical thinking about art and technology related issues.

# REFERENCES

Arnheim, R. (1969/2004). *Visual Thinking*. Berkeley, CA: University of California Press.

Arnheim, R. (1990). *Thoughts on Art Education*. Occasional Paper. Los Angeles, CA: Getty Center for Education.

Baker, M. (2016, March 10). Statisticians issue warning over misuse of *P* values. *Nature*, *531*(7593), 151. doi:10.1038/nature.2016.19503 PMID:26961635

Barrett, T. (2017). *Why Is That Art? Aesthetics and Criticism of Contemporary Art* (3rd ed.). New York: Oxford University Press.

Boden, M. A. (2009). Computer models of creativity. *AI Magazine*, *30*(3), 23–34. doi:10.1609/aimag.v30i3.2254

Boden, M. A. (2012). *Creativity and Art: Three Roads to Surprise*. Oxford University Press.

Boden, M. A., & Edmonds, E. A. (2009). What is Generative Art? *Digital Creativity*, *20*(1-2), 21–46. doi:10.1080/14626260902867915

Broudy, H. S. (1987). *The Role of Imagery in Learning*. Occasional Paper 1, The Getty Center for Education in the Arts.

Candy, L., & Edmonds, E. (2018). Practice-Based Research in the Creative Arts. Foundations and Futures from the Front Line. *Leonardo*, *51*(1), 63–69. doi:10.1162/LEON_a_01471

Catmull, E. (2014). *Creativity, Inc.: overcoming the unseen forces that stand in the way of true inspiration*. New York: Random House.

Cox, Z. N. (2016), Dare to Do Mighty Things: Exploring Beyond the Earth. *ACM/SIGGRAPH 2016 Keynote speaker presentation*. Retrieved January 2, 2017, from http://s2016.siggraph.org/keynote-session

Daguerre, L. J. (1839). *History and practice of photogenic drawing on the true principles of the Daguerréotype, with the new method of dioramic painting; By the inventor Louis Jacques M. Daguerre* (J. S. Memes, Trans.). London: Smith, Elder and Co, Cornhill, and Adam Black and Co., Edinburgh. Digitized by Google.

Dunbar, K. (1997). How scientists think: Online creativity and conceptual change in science. In T. B. Ward, S. M. Smith, & S. Vaid (Eds.), *Conceptual structures and processes: Emergence, discovery and change*. APA Books.

Fisher, R. A. (1938). Presidential Address. F.R.S. *Sankhyā Indian J Stat*, *4*, 14–17.

Friedman, K., & Ox, J. (2017). PhD in Art and Design. *Leonardo*, *50*(5), 515–519. doi:10.1162/LEON_e_01472

Henning, M. (2018). *Photography: The Unfettered Image*. London: Routledge, Taylor and Francis Group.

Kass, R. E., Caffo, B. S., Davidian, M., Meng, X.-L., Yu, B., & Reid, N. (2016). Ten Simple Rules for Effective Statistical Practice. *PLoS Computational Biology*, *12*(6). doi:10.1371/journal.pcbi.1004961 PMID:27281180

Krippendorf, K. (2018). *Content Analysis: An Introduction to Its Methodology* (4th ed.). SAGE Publications, Inc.

Lipari, L. (1988). Masterpiece theater: What is discipline based art education and why have so many people learned to distrust it? *Artpaper*, *7*, 14–16.

Lowenfeld, V., & Brittain, W. L. (1987). *Creative and mental growth* (8th ed.). Upper Saddle River, NJ: Prentice Hall.

Macdonald, S. (1970). *The history and philosophy of art education*. New York: American Elsevier Publishing Company, Inc.

Maksymowicz, V., & Tobia, B. (2017). An Alternative Approach to Establishing a Studio Doctorate in Fine Art. *Leonardo, 50*(5), 520–525. doi:10.1162/LEON_a_01189

NASAD. (2016-2017). *National Association of Schools of Art and Design Handbook*. Reston, VA: National Association of Schools of Art and Design. Retrieved from https://nasad.arts-accredit.org/wp-content/uploads/sites/3/2015/11/NASAD_ HANDBOOK_2016-17.pdf

Rosenzweig, P. (2014). *Left Brain, Right Stuff: How Leaders Make Winning Decisions*. Public Affairs.

SDL. (2019). *Simple Directmedia Layer*. Retrieved from https://www.libsdl.org/

STEM to STEAM Homepage. (2019). Retrieved from http://stemtosteam.org/

Zeeuw, D. (2017). Case Study: The Development and Evolution of the Creative Arts Practice-led PhD at the University of Melbourne, Victorian College of the Arts. *Leonardo, 50*(5), 526-527. doi:10.1162/LEON_a_01407

Zeki, S. (1998). Art and the brain. *Journal of Conscious Studies: Controversies in Science and the Humanities, 6*(6/7), 76–96.

Zeki, S. (1999). Splendors and miseries of the brain. *Philosophical Transactions of the Royal Society of London. Series B, Biological Sciences, 354*(1392), 2053–2065. doi:10.1098/rstb.1999.0543 PMID:10670024

Zeki, S. (2001). Artistic creativity and the brain. *Science, 293*(5527), 51-52. doi:10.1126cience.1062331

Zeki, S. (2011). *The Mona Lisa in 30 seconds.* Retrieved from http://profzeki.blogspot.com/

Zheng, R., & Gardner, M. K. (2017). *Handbook of Research on Serious Games for Educational Applications.* Hershey, PA: IGI Global. doi:10.4018/978-1-5225-0513-6

# Section 2

# On Learning and Teaching

Chapter 5

# Bringing Learning and Teaching up to Date

## ABSTRACT

*This chapter of the book examines first various viewpoints about teaching and learning and then focuses on current ways of instruction with the use of social networking. Further text concentrates on instruction in art based on science and technology and then offers curricular postulates about building this kind of teaching and learning philosophy through engaging students in cognitive learning activities. Further text tells about learning with computing. Types of online instruction are described with the use of private network and social networking. The chapter concludes with postulates suggesting inclusion into the school curricula several actions aimed at strengthening the curricular program: iterative and integrative learning, building mathematical foundation, supporting linguistic aptitudes, using visualization techniques, coding, introducing programming, and games that hone cognitive abilities.*

## INTRODUCTION

This chapter describes selected learning theories which tell about the performance of learners who share the same purpose or intent and who are engaged in practice. Selected innovators in the fields of experimental and educational psychology include, among other theories, Behaviorism (Ivan Petrovich Pavlov, Burrhus Frederick Skinner, John B. Watson), Cognitive

DOI: 10.4018/978-1-7998-1651-5.ch005

theories (Gestalt Psychology–Berlin School, Jean Piaget, Albert Bandura), and Constructivism (Jerome Bruner, Jean Piaget and Bärbel Elisabeth Inhelder).

Issues discussed pertain to discussion about transforming instructional design according to the developments in instructional technology. Discussion about the viewpoints on the up-to-date learning and instruction involves learning in a multisensory and integrative way and learning with the use of computer technologies. The further part of this chapter examines how visual and verbal forms of expression may interact, both in web delivery and in student's work. On the web, the user/visitor's interactivity may be important both for teachers and college students. Students may want to solve a literary assignment visually using art as a source of inspiration, applying signs, icons, and metaphors, and still maintaining informative quality of their writings. The learning with computing is essential part of instruction.

Description of the types of online instruction with the use of private network and social networking is followed by discussion of application of storytelling as a teaching tool. Further propositions include instruction in art production based on science and technology, and several curricular postulates about the content and mechanics of teaching. This chapter discusses postulates suggesting inclusion into the school curricula several actions aimed at strengthening the curricular program: iterative and integrative learning; building mathematical foundation; supporting linguistic aptitudes; using visualization techniques; coding: introducing programming; and games that hone cognitive abilities.

## 5.1. A LOOK INTO VIEWPOINTS ABOUT THE LEARNING PROCESS

Models of learning and teaching styles define the role of a teacher, starting from the ancient Master with apprentices, through the traditional blackboard and chalk as an old school strategy to teach and grade. Old schools gathered students in many grades in one classroom; some university schools revisit this model now while developing experimental programs for prospective teachers and the student teaching programs. A rote model followed, with memorizing and copying writings in the Middle Ages, mnemonics, and recitations to support memory. Home schooling have been present in the Middle Ages, Romanticism, and also now. Tutoring, private tutors in arts, sports, and other areas had an impact on the learning styles.

Learning theories can characterize the learning process that impacts members of the learning group (Driscoll, 2017). The main areas of the understanding of learning (with its structures, learning types, and barriers) comprise according to Knud Illeris (2018): basis (depending on biology, psychology, and social science), internal conditions (involving dispositions, life age, and subjective situation), and external conditions (learning space, society, and objective situation). They lead to applications, which include pedagogy and learning policy (Illeris, 2018).

The advent of experimental psychology brought a change in thinking about the learning process. Early psychology-based learning theories that emerged as the prevalent theories in education included Voluntarism and Connectionism developed by Edward Lee Thorndike (1874-1949) who provided a framework for experimental behavioral psychology. His *Law of Effect* and *Educational Psychology* (2017) was the foundation for developing neural network models artificial intelligence, cognitive science, and neuroscience. Innovators in the field of experimental and educational psychology include, among other theories, Behaviorism (Ivan Petrovich Pavlov, Burrhus Frederick Skinner, John B. Watson), Cognitive theories (Gestalt Psychology–Berlin School, Jean Piaget, Albert Bandura), and Constructivism (Jerome Bruner, Jean Piaget and Bärbel Elisabeth Inhelder).

## Behaviorism

Research on instruction in the 1960s was based on behaviorist learning models determining how to implement a stimulus-response-reinforcement model. That means that learning goes as passive absorption of knowledge motivated in an extrinsic way by reinforcement. Associative learning occurs when two different events happen together, and this evokes a change in behavior. Behaviorists asserted that learning ensues through conditioning, which is the procedure that aims to change or modify behavior via interacting with the environment. They classify conditioning into two types, the classical and the instrumental (operant) conditioning, which are two ways the subjects react to stimuli causing changes in their environment. Classical conditioning, originally investigated by Ivan Petrovich Pavlov (1849-1936), proposed that learning occurs by pairing two stimuli, so the new behavior is elicited after presenting only the second stimulus without presenting the initial one (Pavlov, 1927/2015). A subject responds in a new way to a previously neutral stimulus after this neutral stimulus is repeatedly paired with another stimulus that already elicits the response. In animal training, a trainer applies classical conditioning by repeatedly pairing the sound of a clicker with the taste of food.

Watson formulated behaviorism in contradiction to Freudian theory that emphasized the unconscious and presented self-report as an instrument to study the mind (Harasim, 2017). Thus, behaviorism focused on the behavior rather than the mind. Jerzy Konorski discovered a new type of instrumental learning: the secondary conditioned reflexes, or the type II conditioned reflexes, and this type of conditioning has been later named operant conditioning by Burrhus Frederic Skinner (1953, 1971/2002). Operant conditioning describes learning as a process that may be reinforced or punished. Learning is not always conscious; it may happen as non-associative learning in response to some external factors or internal states.

## Cognitive Theories

According to the cognitive theory human mind is a natural information processing system composed of three types of memory (Reiser & Dempsey, 2017). New information goes through three phases in the human brain: sensory memory, working memory, and long-term memory. Learning occurs when information is received by the sensory system from the environment, processed and stored in the long-term memory – a huge storage unit of human cognition, and produces an output as learning (Driscoll, 2009).

Sensory memory means receiving information from the environment throughout the senses of vision, hearing, tasting, smelling, and touching. Information is then processed through selection and pattern recognition of recognizing environmental stimuli, as concepts and principles already existing in memory (Driscoll, 2017).

Short-term memory has the capability to store the limited amounts of information for a limited time. Chunking information is used in order to increase the capacity of the working memory. Further processing includes encoding – relating incoming information to concepts and ideas already in memory, and rehearsal, which means repeating the information in the working memory in order to prevent it from being lost (Driscoll, 2017).

Long-term memory enables the learner to apply or retrieve or recall information long after learning (Reiser & Dempsey, 2017). Learners can make comparisons when information is partially transferred from the short-term memory. Neurons create new links, and old links are strengthened in this process. Old memory is used to comprehend words. In the process of the language organization information flows from visual (reading) and auditory (listening, speech) reception to areas in the left temporal lobe for comprehension and then to frontal areas for speech production.

John Dewey (1859-1952), philosopher, educator, and one of the initiators of functional psychology was instrumental in the development of the philosophy of pragmatism, progressive education, and liberalism (Dewey, 1916, 1997). The topics of his writings included also aesthetics, art, logic, and ethics (Dewey, 1910/2013, 1934/2005).

A number of cognitive theories explore what happens in the mind that may influence learning. New information is processed in the working memory, which has limited capacity when it deals with a huge number of information. Behaviorists concentrated on understanding learning in terms of behaviors or responses but not on internal processes that could not be observed or measured. For cognitivists, the mind acts as a computer to process information, links what happens between stimulus and response, and plays an important role in making decisions that are not directly related to external stimuli. However, human mind cannot be programmed like computers, and an individual not always responds in the same way to a stimulus (Harasim, 2017). Consequently, several schools of thought emerged, mainly the Cognitive Information Processing Theory, the Schema Theory, the Dual Coding theory, the Baddeley and Hitch model of memory, the Multimedia Learning theory, and more.

- **The Cognitive Information Processing Theory** (Sweller, 1988): Posed that problem solving may impose a heavy cognitive load (mental effort) on working memory. This learning theory portrays how new information is transferred through memory. In the eighties, researchers of cognitive architecture discerned three categories of cognitive load: intrinsic (effort associated with a specific topic); extraneous (related to presenting information to students); and germane (referring to processing and creating a permanent store of knowledge or a schema). Visual presentation may decrease extraneous load as compared to verbal presentation. The extraneous cognitive load in students strongly depends on instructional design (Sweller, Van Merriënboer, & Paas, 1998). The learning happens when the memory resources deal with intrinsic cognitive loads (Wong, Leahy, Marcus, & Sweller, 2012).

According to information processing theorists, humans learn and process information in the same way as computers (Driscoll, 2009). Human learners process new information when the information is perceived (Harasim, 2017).

Thus, learners' attention must be directed with specific visual messages, rather than undirected visual messages. The information processing theorists also propose that learners' prior knowledge in regard to the subject is very important to enable them to become more fully connected with the new knowledge. Therefore, when designing instructional visuals, learners' prior knowledge must be considered. Learners give the meanings to people, places, things, and ideas based on their long-term memories. Designers can anticipate how new visual effects will be perceived. The theorists also believe that for instruction to be effective, information must be easily retrievable so that learners are enabled to recall information from their long-term memory. Finally, environment plays an important role in learning (Branch, & Merrill, 2012; Driscoll, 2017).

- **The Dual-coding Theory:** Developed by Allan Paivio (1986), accepts that learners acquire new information both in a verbal and visual way using verbal associations and visual imagery. Formation of mental images may support learning (Paivio, 1971). The anterior part of the left and right cerebral hemispheres controls specific features of thought, action, and memory. Human cognition is assumed to consist of separate but interconnected verbal and imaginal systems. Verbal and visual information is processed separately, with the left hemisphere dominant for language and speech, and the right for motor functions in vision. Also, verbal and pictorial symbols are coded independently; it can be seen when cerebral hemispheres are disconnected in the split-brain operations. Within the two systems of the human brain, verbal memory deals with language systems and image memory includes non-verbal information (Beatty, 2013). Visual and verbal information are processed in different channels as separate representations. Some psychologists find the visual or the image system in the brain much larger than the verbal system. Coding a stimulus (e.g., a cat) at the same time in a verbal and visual way supports the process of remembering.

- **The Alan Baddeley and Graham Hitch Model of Memory:** Proposes a framework for a working, short-term memory, which consists of 3 components: the central executive loop for carrying out the tasks of reasoning, decision-making, and coordinating incoming data; the phonological, articulatory (related to speech sounds) loop for temporary retention of speech-based material; and the visuo-spatial scratch pad for temporary retention of visual and/or spatial material (Baddeley, & Hitch, 1969; Koopmann-Holm, & O'Connor, 2016).

The authors considered working memory to be limited in the amount of information that it can store and the length of time it could store information. In the articulatory loop component of working memory, visually presented verbal material is translated into phonological form via sub-vocal rehearsal. Rehearsal mechanism in visual-spatial domain may be involved in control of movement. Recall has been considered better after imagery than after verbal instructions, best after interactive imagery instructions. When people compare sizes of objects, pictures work better than verbal comparisons. Mental representations of visual objects may involve unconscious computations of moving objects and conscious knowledge of meaning of the object.

- **The Multimedia Learning Theory:** Was based on the dual-channel assumption that humans process pictorial and verbal material differently. This is a cognitive theory that involves visual literacy. Park and Hannafin (1993) came up with a list of principles and roles of instructional multimedia. Richard E. Mayer and Roxana Moreno revised this list and formed a theory of dual processing systems in working memory (Mayer & Moreno, 1998; Moreno & Mayer, 1999, 2000). Mayer and Moreno's dual-processing theory of working memory was based on the premises that auditory working memory and visual working memory have limited capacity. Auditory and visuo-spatial memory spaces are analogous to the Baddeley and Hitch (1969) phonological loop and visuo-spatial sketchpad. The theory of working memory is consistent with Sweller's cognitive load theory (Sweller, 1988). The authors hold that the meaningful learning occurs when a learner retains and organizes information as representations in each store and makes connections between representations in each store, analogous to the generative theory of multimedia learning; connections can be made only if corresponding pictorial and verbal information is in working memory at the same time, according to Paivio's (1986, 1971) dual-coding theory.

Mayer and Moreno accepted an active-processing assumption that meaningful learning involves building connections between pictorial and verbal representations. As each channel has limited capacity, cognitive processing may exceed this capacity creating cognitive overload in a learner. The researchers explored several ways to reduce the cognitive load, and posed that cognitive load is a central consideration in the design of multimedia instruction (Mayer & Moreno, 2003). Thus, Mayer and Moreno assigned three main assumptions for multimedia instruction: "there are two separate channels (auditory and visual) for processing information; there is limited channel capacity; and learning is an active process of filtering, selecting, organizing, and integrating information (as cited in Beatty, 2013, p. 35). Based on these assumptions, the authors suggested seven design principles that focus on the interaction and combination of audio, text, and visual components into one whole multimedia package. One of the multimedia principles that encourages the designer while working on the instructional design model is to include both verbal and visual tools to static illustrations such as, drawing, graphs, maps, photos, and dynamic graphics. These tools can engage students in active learning because they help them to relate and organize the material in the lesson. These visual tools help them to make connections between the symbolic and verbal content.

- **The Schema Theory:** States that all knowledge is organized into the units of knowledge, or schemata. A schema is an abstract concept proposed by Jean Piaget, defined as the units of understanding or knowledge. Information is stored within these organized units of knowledge about concepts, objects, and interactions with other objects, situations, events, sequences of events, actions, and sequences of actions. Information can be hierarchically categorized or form a web of complex relationships. Thus, a schema theory describes a conceptual system for understanding how knowledge is represented, processed, and organized (Axelrod, 1973).

## Constructivism

The debate about the existence of the objective versus subjective reality goes back to antiquity, involving Plato, Seneca, St Augustine, and numerous other philosophers, all the way to Kant, Heidegger and Nietzsche. A belief in an objective reality poses that all things exist objectively outside the observing person; reality is independent of an observer or culture; all structures, objects, codes, and laws are ready to be described. In constructivist terms, not an objective reality, but the understanding of one's own experience is important. Reality is not residing outside or independent of an observer. Reality is starting within a circular process of perception, understanding, and making things: that means, through practice. Knowledge results from the construction of reality by a person. Making constructions of the cognitive schemes, categories, concepts, and structures is important in learning. For example, the prints on the beach sand may become meaningful for the thought through perception. A notion of a gift becomes a social structure that arises out of social practices.

From the perspective of a student, learning is considered an active procedure of building rather than delivering knowledge, and instruction is supporting the building rather than just sharing knowledge. Theories known under the umbrella of Constructivism are the Cognitive Constructivism, Social Constructivism, and Radical Constructivism concur that learning is going from inside out and happens when a learner constructs knowledge based on background, aptitude, experience, and interacts with others (Roblyer & Doering, 2013).

- **Cognitive Constructivism**: Emerged from the research studies by Jerome Bruner (1915-2016), Jean Piaget (1896-1980) and Bärbel Elisabeth Inhelder (1913-1997); it presents the idea of an individual's construction of reality based on biological development stages; Learning is an active process: the learners can produce their own ideas or concepts from their prior and current knowledge, and find their own way of understanding the information in the form of a language or symbol. This theory is using the real environment to improve or teach students` skills. According to Driscoll (2017), the best way to deliver knowledge and experience to learners is through their environment. The students pick and transform information, construct hypotheses, and make decisions depending on their cognitive structure, which involves schema and mental models that provide meaning and organization of experiences (Instructional Design.org, 2019). Jerome Bruner (1961, 1966, 1990) posed that instruction should address four major aspects: predisposition towards learning; the ways in which a body of knowledge can be structured so that it can be most readily grasped by the learner; the most effective sequences in which to present material; and the nature and pacing of rewards and punishments. Good methods for structuring knowledge should result in simplifying, generating new propositions, and increasing the manipulation of information. Bruner (1986, 1990, 1997) expanded his theoretical framework to encompass the social and cultural aspects of learning as well as the practice of law (Instructional Design.org, 2019).

Jean Piaget and Bärbel Inhelder were Swiss developmental psychologists focused on cognitive development of a child. Their work built the theoretical foundations for later research on visual literacy and visual thinking. Piaget and Inhelder categorized the progressive stages of human development from infancy to adulthood. The modes of children's thinking are completely different than when they are adults, and building knowledge increases in complexity and depth from one stage to another through the development process (Piaget, 1969; Piaget & Inhelder, 1969; Piaget & Inhelder, 1967,1981; Inhelder, 1974; Harasim, 2017). The authors constructed a model of child development and learning that showed how children develop cognitively by building cognitive structures, mental maps, schemes of their environment. When the experience is new or different, children alter their cognitive structures to maintain their mental equilibrium, accommodate the new conditions, and to set up more adequate cognitive structures. Piaget discerned several developmental stages in children mental activities: a sensorimotor stage (birth - 2 years old) when children interact with their environment and build concepts about reality; a preoperational stage of concrete mental operations (age 7-12) when children form symbolic and semiotic classes and relations, conceptualize upon their experiences, and create logical structures; and a stage of formal operational thinking and of conceptual thought (11- adolescence) when children cognitive structures include hypotheses, and conceptual reasoning, not only the representable realities. A stage of formal operational thinking is considered to be the final equilibrium status that characterizes a considerable part of adult population (Inhelder & Piaget, 1958). The formal stage implies the ability to engage in abstract thought, that is, to deal with propositions, to generate hypotheses and subject them to empirical investigation, and to employ proportionality and combinatorial systems in problem solving (Piaget & Inhelder, 1969; Harasim, 2017; Arlin, 1974, Arlin, 1984).

Theories of constructivism focus on the learner during the process of learning; the learners build a base of knowledge from prior knowledge and then construct a meaningful understanding and outcome. The researchers discerned four elements in the learning process (Harasim, 2017): active learning (a learner is encouraged to participate in real experiments rather than being passive); learning by doing (learners do something rather than have it done for them); scaffolding learning, the support given to a younger learner by an older, more experienced adult); and collaborative learning – creating groups and incorporating discussions in order to exchange experiences and communications.

Theories of Social Constructivism derive from the developmental theories, for example those by Lev Vygotsky's cognitive development theory and the benefits of play, Jerome Bruner's cognitive learning theory, and Albert Bandura's social-cognitive theory. These theories explore how learners rely on culture and interaction with others to interpret and construct knowledge. They enhance understanding how people learn drawing from epistemological studies on the nature of knowing about something, i.e., "how do we know?" (Remler, & Van Ryzin, 2010).

Lev Vygotsky (1896-1934) introduced the zone of proximal development concept (ZPD), which delineated the difference between student's ability to do something with or without help, thus stressing the role of social setting and the social aspect of learning: how a community or a group of people impacts and contributes to constructing the realities based on their interaction as humans (Harasim, 2017). The ZPD zone, representing problem-solving tasks that a learner can do with guidance or collaboration, exists between the tasks that can be done unaided and the tasks that a learner cannot do (Vygotsky, 1934/1986; Vygotsky, 1978). In the words of Vygotsky, "In the process of development, the child not only masters the items of cultural experience but the habits and forms of cultural behavior, the cultural methods of reasoning." (Vygotsky, 1929, p. 415).

Students get support in achieving their learning goals in the form of scaffolding where adults support children in joint problem-solving activities (Van de Pol, Volman, & Beishuizen, 2010).

Vygotsky (1986) inquires how children can learn beyond their development level with guidance and collaboration with adults that support learning by providing tools, giving demonstrations, and asking leading questions (Harasim, 2017).

Ernst von Glasersfeld (1917-2010) proposed **Radical Constructivism** theory, which posed that knowledge is not transported from one mind into another. The individual links up specific interpretations of experiences and ideas with their own reference of what is possible and viable. Thus, the constructing of knowledge depends on subjective interpretations of active experience but not what actually occurs (Von Glasersfeld, 1996, 2001).

Abraham Harold Maslow (1908-1970) focused on positive qualities of people and their need of self-actualization, altruism, and spirituality (Maslow, 1969/1971; Koltko-Rivera, 2006). The hierarchy of human needs outlined by Maslow (1943, 1954) has been usually represented as a pyramid ordered from the basic to more refined needs, and comprised of the physiological, safety, love/belonging, esteem, and self-actualization needs, with a later added the self-transcendence need. Maslow said only 2% of people reached the stage of self-actualization (Kremer & Hammond, 2013). The Maslow's theory has become an important factor in building a framework for research in sociology, management training (Kremer & Hammond, 2013), studies on psychology at different levels, and continues to have a strong influence on the world education. Joy Paul Guilford (1950, 1959, 1967, 1968), Robert Sternberg (2007, 2011), and Howard Gardner (1993, 1999) described independently individual peak performance, which may depend on the differences in abilities.

Benjamin Bloom (1913-1999) was the protagonist of the classification of educational learning objectives (Bloom, 1956,1969) and the theory of mastery learning. Bloom's taxonomy comprised a set of three hierarchical models of learning objectives in the cognitive, affective, and sensory domains. The cognitive, knowledge-based domain listed knowledge comprehension, application, analysis, synthesis, and evaluation. It has frequently served for structuring curriculum learning objectives, assessments, and activities. Benjamin Bloom (1956,1969) and then R. J. Sternberg (1988, 2011) explored cognitive thinking. Intellectual behavior in learning occurs in the cognitive, psychomotor, and affective domains, with the levels of cognitive activity including knowledge, comprehension, application, analysis, synthesis, evaluation, induction and deduction. Theorists often refer cognitive thinking to problem solving, hypothesis testing, and concept acquisition. Cognitive activities of the brain are aimed to seek out information, select potentially useful information from the total, organize it into memory store, and retrieve information from memory for the use in decision-making. Cognitive thinking is used in experimental research for gathering data and information, testing hypotheses, interpreting results, and providing scientific evidence for new theories. In 1970s four stages of competence were described, the learner having first unconscious incompetence (when the learner ignores or denies the usefulness of a new skill), then conscious incompetence (recognized deficit of a skill but the skill is not mastered), conscious competence (knowing how to do), and finally unconscious competence (a skill becomes easy with right intuition, performed while executing another task) (Broadwell, 1969).

## Types of Intelligence

People are behaving intelligently when they choose courses of action that are relevant to their goals, reply coherently and appropriately to questions that are put to them, solve problems, and create or design something useful, or beautiful, or novel. Intelligence involves studies of the behavior of intelligent organisms or intelligent programs and their ability to perform intellectual tasks. Cognitive thinking can be only indirectly linked to the concept of intelligence.

Learning styles may depend on the diversity of the intelligence types described by Howard Gardner, a developmental psychologist who is best known for his theory of multiple intelligences (Gardner, 1983/2011, 1993/2006). However, Gardner (2019) points out that multiple intelligences should not be confused with learning styles. Gardner (1997) carried also the investigation on extraordinary people, and described four forms of extraordinary individuals. Gardner defines intelligence as the capacity to solve problems or make things that are valued in a culture (at least one cultural setting or community). His theory classifies human abilities; it is a study about encouraging learning in ways that respect individual interests and strengths. Human cognitive competence can be described in terms of abilities, talents, and mental skills, which we call intelligences. Howard Gardner then called his multiple intelligences theory a psychobiological theory: psychological because it is a theory of mind, biological because it privileges information about the brain, the nervous system, and the human genome (Gardner, 2000, 2011a). Howard Gardner's list of intelligences include:

- **Linguistic Intelligence**: The ability to use language to express meaning, tell a story, react to stories, learn new vocabulary or languages. Poets exhibit this ability in its fullest form.
- **Logical/Mathematical Intelligence**: Prized in schools and especially in school examinations
- **Spatial intelligence**: The ability to form a mental model of a spatial world and be able to carry out that model and find one's way around a new structure.
- **Musical intelligence**: Capacity to create and perceive musical patterns
- **Bodily Kinesthetic Intelligence**: The ability to use the body or parts of the body (hands, feet, etc.) to solve problems or to fabricate products, as in playing a ballgame, dancing, or making objects with the hands. Dancers, athletes, surgeons and crafts people all exhibit highly developed bodily-kinesthetic intelligence.
- **Interpersonal Intelligence**: Is oriented toward the understanding of other people. What motivates them, how they work, how to work cooperatively and effectively with them. Successful marketing and salespeople, politicians, teachers, clinicians, and religious leaders are all likely to be individuals with high degree of interpersonal intelligence.

- **Intrapersonal Intelligence**: The ability turned inward to form an accurate model of oneself, understand things about oneself: how one is similar to or different from others, and how to soothe oneself when sad and use that model to operate effectively in life.
- **Naturalistic Intelligence**: The apprehension of the natural world as epitomized by skilled hunters or botanists. The ability to recognize species of plants or animals in one's environment.

According to Howard Gardner, "existential and moral intelligences may also be worthy of inclusion" (Gardner, 2000, 2011b, 2016), as he "considered several new candidate intelligences, including naturalistic, spiritual (however later on, Gardner did not want to commit to a spiritual intelligence), existential, and moral ones" (Gardner, 2011b, p. 4).

Human beings are able to develop exquisite capacities in many intellectual domains. The preferred learning style may be mostly visual (and spatial), aural (auditory and musical), verbal (linguistic, in speech or writing), physical (kinesthetic), logical (and mathematical), social (interpersonal), or solitary (intrapersonal) (Gardner, 1983/2011, 1993/2006).

Howard Gardner's theory of multiple intelligences still holds; however, many individuals identify themselves with more than one type of intelligence. Viewpoints about the concept of left and right brain are changing as well. When visiting art departments, we see students coding, while when going among electrical engineers or computer scientists we see them sketch and create art. There are a growing number of new departments such as Arts and Technology or New Media.

Because there are several different types of intelligence, students' interest in an art class may be enhanced by science related themes. It may help the students find their individual potential: talent, motivation, interest, and goals – that means their perspectives on future career. Students will find themselves, their vocation and mission; this may be helpful in fighting the boredom, feeling hopeless and not belonging.

Robert Sternberg (1999, 2007) explored the interrelationship between intelligence, creativity, and wisdom and the role they play in adapting to, shaping, and selecting environments. Interaction with environment involves aspects relative to creativity such as knowledge, styles of thinking, personality, and motivation, with balance of these personal attributes necessary to do creative work. It can be presumed that learning about abilities of the creative process, including fluency, flexibility, originality, and elaboration, may encourage students and pre-service teachers to gain a better knowledge regarding technology integration.

Sternberg (1997) is known for his triarchic model of intelligence consisting of the analytical intelligence, creative or synthetic intelligence, and practical intelligence designed a framework for examining possible intelligence-creativity relationships (Sternberg & Kaufman, 2011). Sternberg explored higher-order reasoning in post-formal operational thought and defined orders of relations in terms of what is related: first-order relations are between primitive terms; second-order relations are relations between relations, and so on. Sternberg (2017) states on his website: "If I have one passion in my work, it is to see changes in the ways in which we teach and test our children." He described the stages of cognitive development in terms of his theory: the concrete operational stage applies first-order relations; transition to formal means second-order relations; post formal operational stage may mean the third-order analogies in a 3-D semantic space. Sternberg (1986) also developed a triangular theory of love. Three components of love in the context of interpersonal relationships are intimacy (feelings of attachment, closeness, connectedness, and bondedness); passion (drives connected to both limerence – attraction and a need to have one's feelings reciprocated, sexual attraction); and commitment (the decision to remain with another, share achievements and plans).

Mihaly Csikszentmihalyi (1990, 1997, 1998) originated the psychological concept of flow, a creative, focused mental state. Csikszentmihalyi who in his own words, "devoted 30 years of research to how creative people live and work" stated, "Creativity is a central source of meaning in our lives. Most of the things that are interesting, important, and human are the result of creativity" (Csikszentmihalyi, 1996ab).

Antonio Damasio (1999, 1994/2005), a cognitive neuroscientist, has been studying the relations of cognition and emotions. His research, based on imaging techniques is about the neurobiology of mind and behavior, and explores how the brain processes memory, language, emotions, decision-making, and problem solving. Problem solving ability has been highly valued, especially in mathematics and science (Dewey, 1910/2013, 1916), so researchers proposed fostering the problem solving skills by discovery learning (e.g., Bruner, 1961).

Semir Zeki is a neurobiologist who explores the domain of neuroaesthetics – a study of the neural basis of artistic creativity and achievement. He has been examining brain activity associated with the elementary perceptual process: perception of images. He arrived at conclusion that artists, acting like instinctive neuroscientists, capture in their art works the essence of things in a similar way as the brain acts when it captures the essential information about the world from a stream of sensory input (Zeki, 1993, 2001).

Roblyer and Doering (2013) state, "no one agrees on which strategies will serve today's educational goals" (p. 35); hence, there are several perspective views using technology differently in education. One perspective, "directed instruction," proposes that information is pre-identified and organized in the form of activities by teachers, and then transmitted to students. This perspective is based on the objectivist theories that ground both theories of behaviorism and cognitivism. The other perspective, "inquiry-based learning" proposes that students construct their own knowledge based on experiences, while teachers serve as facilitators for this process of learning. This perspective is based on the constructivist theories (Roblyer & Doering, 2013).

## Visual Development

Piaget and Inhelder also described structural schema developed in the mind to recognize and process visual patterns (Piaget and Inhelder, 1969; Inhelder & Piaget, 1958). Knowledge is a process of becoming, "resulting from a construction of reality through the activities of the subject" (Inhelder, 1977, p. 339). According to Piaget (1970), "...the aim of intellectual training is to form the intelligence rather than to stock the memory, and to produce intellectual explorers rather than mere erudition." The logical thinking is primarily non-linguistic. The roots of logic are in actions and not in words. Piaget points out that "... many educators limit themselves to showing the objects without having the children manipulate them, or, still worse, simply present audio-visual representations of objects (pictures, films, and so on) in the erroneous belief that the mere fact of perceiving the objects and their transformations will be equivalent to direct action of the learner in experience" (Schwebel & Raph, 1973, pp. ix-x).

The concept of the developmental stages has been applied to describe the process of evolving skills and capacities in the visual domain (Gardner, 1983/2011). Analogies have been drawn between the mental development and the visual development stages of representation. The levels of student visual and cognitive development may be important in their problem solving and types of expression and perception. Historically, the most prevailing and widely used description of the visual development stages was developed by Victor Lowenfeld (1949, 1987) who defined the stages in students' artistic development as: scribbling (2-4 years), preschematic (4-7 years), schematic (7-9 years), dawning realism (9-11 years), pseudo-naturalistic (11-13 years), and the period of decision/crisis (adolescence). Lowenfeld and Brittain (1987) reworked the stages using the concept of schema, the fundamental basis of the Piagetian psychology. The authors described the stages of visual development as: scribbling – manipulation stage (up to 3 - 4 years); generalization (early symbolic, preschematic stage, 3-4 up to 6 years); characterization (symbolic, schematic stage, 6-7 up to 9 years); and visualization stage (9-12 years). Several authors provided their descriptions of the visual development stages. In 1922 Sir Ciril Burt defined the stages as: scribble (2-5 years), line (4 years), descriptive symbolism (5-6 years), descriptive realism (7-8 years), visual realism (9-10 years), repression (11-14 years), and artistic revival (early adolescence). Helga Eng defined in 1931 three stages up to eight years– scribbling, transition, and formalized drawing. Viktor Lowenfeld influenced many art educators by emphasizing the importance of stimulating "children at different stages of artistic development by appropriate media and themes, … and curriculum guided mainly by developmental considerations" (Allen, n.d.).

Most studies on visual development were performed in the context of the child cognitive development. However, it must be realized that students functioning at various levels of visual and formal operation stages can be also found at the college level. According to Arlin (1974, 1984) who studied college seniors' problem-solving ability, only 50 percent of the adult population under study ever attained the Piagetian stage of formal operational thinking (the problem solving stage). Using Arlin's test of formal reasoning, Boyd (1989) found that only 54 percent of secondary students functioned at the formal operation stage and stressed the need for introducing modified methods in teaching chemistry for students still functioning at the concrete stage of development.

## 5.2. ABOUT LEARNING AND INSTRUCTION

### Teacher/Artist and Artist/Teacher

When discussing programs for teachers one can imagine a new program: teacher/artist-artist/teacher, where artists using technology would both grow artistically and would prepare teachers to teach matching the 21$^{st}$ century opportunities and needs with the content of a school program.

The skills acquired from those classes or resources would be then transferred to K-20 curriculum, stressing the need for teaching programming and developing abstract thinking from kindergarten on, so children would not be taught step by step, know how, copy and be perfect, but to be creative, bold, possess abstract thinking skills, and not to be afraid of learning.

It becomes increasingly important that teaching and collaborative teaching go with the use of the visual way of learning. The use of metaphors, data-, information-, and knowledge- visualization may serve for integrative science-art instruction with the use of computer graphics. From early childhood, education with art should include teaching several subjects supporting the development of abstract thinking, which are now reserved for the young adults or adults. Developing abstract thinking abilities is essential both in countless areas of life and in education. Abstract thinking can be seen indispensable when one strives to be virtuous in mathematics, philosophy, poetry, or science.

The use of metaphors, data-, information-, and knowledge- visualization serves for integrative science-art instruction with the use of computer graphics and programming. Everybody should know how to code from the very beginning of schooling. Collaborative efforts bridge a gap between the ways we draw, code, describe, or otherwise explore Nature. "Coding is the literacy of the 21st century," said Zach Sims, cofounder of a New York City based company Codecademy (Upbin, 2011). Lessons in computer programming have been adopted in 2014 by the national curriculum for primary schools in England (Muffett, 2014). Coding can be learned in a visual way, even by creating art works. Figure 4 shows a work of a computer science student.

## Focus on Gifted and Talented Students

Doctoral programs in art and design may commit themselves to think up a way of securing successful instruction of the gifted and talented students. For instance, it is known that a child is born with a perfect pitch, and then this ability disappears when a mother and a father pronounce the same word differently. At the same time the very early brain developing opportunities have not been explored enough.

Currently, systematic education classifies both the gifted and talented students and the students with any kind of disabilities under the collective term Special Education. The category of special needs education seems to be made from the teacher's point of view but not from the student's perspective. Perhaps it should be solved the other way around. This classification often hurts the student, sometimes for life. It should be the other way of solving the gifted student's individual needs, so there would be no more need for working in a parents' basement instead of going to school. I often think how many times hackers have been the brilliant kids who were ignored by their teachers.

## Developing Abstract Thinking

Introduction of many subjects in early stages of schooling may support the development of abstract thinking:

- Algebra and learning basic concepts of calculus are often easier for children than for adults. Differential equations describe everyday physical processes. Derivative of a function of a single variable is fundamental in understanding not only calculus but also basic life processes.
- Programming in various computer languages should be linked with traditional tools such as Lego Logo. In 2016 President Barack Obama postulated that programming should be introduced in every school and pledged $4.1 billion to expand computer science classes, "offering every student the hands-on computer science and math classes that make them job-ready."
- Music as the universal language may support easiness of learning new languages by enhancing students' sensitivity to sounds, tones, and timbres specific to particular languages they are learning. However, symbols are different in specific fields: a symbol 'C' means another thing in music and in C++ coding.
- Visualization; visualizing processes and products through drawing.

The current social, economy, business, and corporate world characteristics create a need for redesigning the existing doctoral programs and their curricular models. They would serve as a basis for developing a coherent, comprehensive program of teaching and supervision in doctoral studies preparing candidates for a PhD in Visual Art. The integrative model presented above places emphasis on preparing future doctors in the visual arts to create and perform, develop knowledge, can teach and supervise students, be prepared to publish new forms of knowledge, and serve the community by sharing knowledge in a visual way. This includes a need for developing doctoral students' skills in abstract thinking, cognitive skills, creativity, and problem-solving abilities.

## Honing Cognitive Learning Abilities

Several subjects considered conducive to sharpening cognitive learning abilities comprise learning coding and intro to math (which would be helpful for coding). Coding is a procedure for solving a complicated problem by carrying out a fixed sequence of simpler, unambiguous steps. Such procedures are used in computer programs and in programmed learning. Many artists create algorithms – mathematical recipes for how to carry out a process – for supporting their research, developing applications, and then creating generative art. Robotics created by artists, wearable digital art, and interactive installations contribute to our cultural environment. Other subjects supporting learning may include learning music notation and music composition,

Latin language, although hasn't been much in use for the last 1,000 years, promotes the ability to communicate across the globe. Learning about Latin words' inflections, seven cases of nouns, pronouns, or adjectives (changes in their form that determine relation to other words) five declensions (that identify grammatical cases, numbers, and genders), and four conjugations of six verb tenses, all may support developing abstract thinking.

One may add knowledge visualization techniques, material science, intro to science, perhaps also biology (inspirational for art), creative writing, performing, some traditional art, video/sound, and some business.

## Instructional Design

Present strategies and trends in education transform the curriculum design and instructional technology design. Instructional models define teaching approaches and are integrated into the lesson or training units. Instructional designers offer instructional design models that are expected to be most effective. They generally result from philosophical, psychological, and cognitive learning theories that focus on explaining how humans understand knowledge and interact with the environment. Many instructional models have been developed; they generally include identifying instructional targets, conducting instructional analysis, analyzing contexts of learners, setting performance objectives, improving assessment instruments, developing instructional strategy, developing and choosing instructional materials, designing and conducting formative evaluation of instruction, reviewing instruction, and designing and conducting summative evaluation (Kalman, Kemp, Morrison, & Ross, 2012). Instructional designers provide models such as blueprints, which include assignments and instructional activities, or outlines that show some learning activities and their assessment. At the same time, the designer should choose the appropriate technology tools that enhance the learning experiences (Davis, 2013), which may include pictures, videos, voices, podcast, maps, and simulations of real environments. Most of these tools depend on visual symbols and simulation to create a good environment of learning that includes interaction between knowledge and art, and between actions and thoughts.

Curriculum and instruction programs for delivering and evaluating the learning process were shaped according to the rationale formalized by Ralph W. Tyler. In 1969, he co-developed the National Assessment of Educational Progress, which is described as, "The National Assessment of Educational Progress (NAEP) is the largest nationally representative and continuing assessment of what America's students know and can do in various subject areas (https://nces.ed.gov/nationsreportcard). The Tyler Rationale consisted of four parts: defining appropriate learning objectives; introducing useful learning experiences; organizing experiences to maximize their effect; evaluating the process and revisiting the areas that were not effective (Tyler, 1949). Consequently, the University of California at Berkeley based model that was prevalent in the 20th century consisted of four steps of instruction: motivation or preparation of learners; presentation of course materials; assignment of homework to learners; and evaluation of learning objectives.

Iterative design models may include the ADDIE model (which includes phases of design through steps: Analysis, Design, Development, Implementation, and Evaluation) with a linear, waterfall methodology, and the SAM model (Successive Approximation model) consisting of repeated small steps, or iterations, with an Agile approach to e-learning. Currently, factors that are influencing the field of instructional design include the use of internet for presenting instruction to learners, mostly in the form of online learning; growing reliance on informal learning through the social media, mobile devices, and performance support tools; and the tendency to design simpler, more efficient models than traditional instruction design models such as the ADDIE model (Reiser & Dempsey, 2018).

Scaffolding learning is a type of computer-based constructivist learning. Through technology, students are given the opportunity to express themselves by using social networking sites as part of the classroom learning. This opportunity would motivate them to interact with each other, problem-solve, and feel comfortable to talk and brainstorm. Such learning environments may include: (a) Learning networks or tele-collaboration. The internet allows communication, so the learning communities around the world can be linked in a specific network and may exchange their experiences. Millions of students use social networks as a forum for personal communication and linking family, friends, and acquaintances, especially those who share common interests. Using social networking sites (SNSs) for educational collaboration is an educational tool that both students and instructors consider beneficial. (b) Online learning and course delivery platforms for providing structured courses online (Harasim, 2017). Learning management systems (LMS) may serve as an example of these platforms. Students use social media to access their university's learning management system (LMS). They use the LMS regularly to retrieve assignments and notes, but usually not to contact each other or the instructor. To collaborate with other, students more likely use media such as email or text messaging.

The instructional design model presented below focuses on developing skills that correspond to the needs and expectations characteristic of present-day society. The learner's needs are changing with the growing impact of media. Educational technology tools support finding out interesting ways during the teaching process, which provide both teacher and students a chance to be interactive in the learning environment and to like the education. Understanding of different cultures and ideas is crucial for gaining multi-cultural communication skills.

## The Tools for Teaching

### Learning in a Multisensory and Integrative Way

We may learn in an integrative way using other senses, not exclusively vision. Teaching through senses may involve dance, poetry, theater, show and performance, for example about historical events. Visual teaching may be attained through the use of visual examples, metaphors, art works, excursions to museums, out of the classroom experiences, interactive websites, introduction of attractive techniques and augmented or virtual learning. For example, teaching a new language in the integrative, multisensory way may include:

- Learning texts by heart.
- Watching theater performances, movies, and videos with, and then without captions.
- Immersion in language in a country of origin.

- Playing and acting.
- Singing songs.
- Writing essays.
- Writing poetry and short stories.
- Making translations both ways.
- Creating puppet shows, comics, or manga.
- Reciting poems and writing them.
- Creating one's own infographics, inspired, for example by a famous data visualization – a map used by Dr. Snow to chart the patterns of an epidemic in London (https://en.wikipedia.org/wiki/File:Snow-cholera-map-1.jpg), or the most cited information visualization of Napoleon's invasion of Russia in 1812, created in 1861 by Charles Joseph Minard (https://www.edwardtufte.com/tufte/minard).

Figure 1 shows comics by Jenny Lee about cubes in small dimensions in our life, where she visualizes pixels as cubes, which are fortunately invisible on the flowers' petals.

*Figure 1. A cube comics*
*(© 2018, J. Lee. Used with permission)*

Teaching art with the use of writing assignments might support art students' literary development. As in the journalistic tasks, which usually comprise gathering, processing, evaluating, judging, organizing, and publishing information, instruction in literary arts may encourage students to hone their communication skills. Students may concentrate on connecting visual and verbal expression with all communication possibilities given by electronic media and the web such as data organization techniques (searching on the internet, cognitive and semantic structuring of information), and creation of electronic media languages of visual representation and design (art, web design, concept mapping).

## Learning With the Use of Computer Technologies

The manner we learn changes constantly, with big resources existing online. It seems a division of learning environment into a classroom and online learning is becoming outdated. There are millions of articles on Wikipedia – a free internet encyclopedia. As of 1 March 2019, there are 5,811,536 articles in the English Wikipedia, and the number of articles in Wikipedia is increasing by over 20,000 a month. There are also hundreds of million blogs – discussion or informational sites published on the web for individuals or large groups, and many kinds of wikis – web applications allowing learners to add, modify, or delete web items in a collaborative way. In the course of learning, online support is available, not only professional such as LinkedIn Learning (previously Lynda.com) but also coming from the learning groups, user lists, or discussion lists.

As stated by Gerald Benoît (2019), "the pervasiveness of computers and the vastly simplified tools to create interactive visualizations enable almost everyone to create graphics and websites." W3 schools are online training sites about digital techniques (https://www.w3schools.com). They provide online web tutorials: HTML – the language for building web pages; CSS – the language for styling the web pages and more modern w3.CSS; Java – a programming language and JavaScript – the language for programming web pages; SQL – the language for accessing web pages; Python and PHP 5 – web servers programming languages; jQuery – a JavaScript library for developing web pages; Bootstrap 4 – a CSS framework for designing better web pages, and much more.

## 5.3. PRIVATE AND SOCIAL NETWORKING IN A CLASSROOM AND IN ONLINE SETTING

Public internet, a worldwide entirety of interconnected computer networks can be accessed through a computer and a modem. Both private and public network can be accessed by the same hardware and supporting resources, but security, addressing and authentication systems differ, so private IP packets cannot be routed through a public internet. Private networks are spreading over communities and the academic and corporate environment along with the social network. A private network uses a private IP (Internet Protocol) address space. The ranges of addresses are defined as IP versions, e.g., IPv4 that routes most of the internet traffic, and IPv6 – the next generation of the Internet Protocol that supports identification and location system for networked computers. For this purpose, unique IP addresses are assigned on internet for devices such as computers and smartphones.

People are using these addresses both in the private residential, business, enterprise environments, corporate networks, local area networks (LANs), along with their Facebook pages and private groups subscriptions. No other users can see the contents, which is highly regarded both by high schoolers and business people. Private addresses enhance network security protecting from a connection of external host to internal system. Some private networks encrypt visited web addresses thus preventing the spying on browsing activity. Home networking allows computers and smart devices to communicate and thus users can cooperate safely as a team. Many tools such as Trello, Asana, Monday.com, or Slack Technologies are collaboration hubs offered to organize and manage cooperative projects. Atlassian's Trello with a visual interface Kanban is an application for image-based project management.

Applications available at internet, social media, and web 2.0 allow students to socially construct information: learn together, help each other, and share their knowledge. Social media offer the online, networked, interactive, visually delivered information. The availability, portability, compatibility, ergonometric design, and unification of various devices allow studying and sharing on different levels or paths. The existence of the social media and Web 2.0 allows teaching students in many ways and get in contact with every student. Personalized learning addresses distinct learning needs, interests, and cultural backgrounds of individual students. A teacher optimizes the pace of learning and the instructional approach, and student's learning is often self-initiated. Social networking confirms a notion that learning and teaching is based on interactions between teachers and classmates, not only on a teacher's work. With attention to students' individual strong intelligences, the use of social networking supports the increase of the zone of proximal development (Vygotsky, 1934/1986, 1978) representing tasks that a learner can do with guidance by applying group activities aimed at sharing the expert knowledge; this may decrease the gap between what has already been learned and the extent to which new learning can expand this previous learning. Social media using Web 2.0 tools such as images, instructional videos, interactive boards, blogs, smart devices, mind mapping, outside-the box applications, and gaming allow direct socio-cultural interactions between students/classmates and teachers, other online interactions that facilitate learning, as well as matching learning material with the student's learning style. In spite of spatial distances there is no isolation; learning of the group members may be synchronic or occur in different points of time, which encourages learners to use higher-level processes and engage problem solving. Existing technologies allow the constant progress in social media and the educational applications, devices, apps, and websites. Learning and teaching supported by technologies may include both the classroom and online experiences. Figure 2, a work by James Reiman, displays social interactions that may help to bring about learning beyond the classroom.

Multimedia learning occurs when information comes from many kinds of stimuli. Types of multimedia include text, audio, still images, animation, video footage, and interactive content. They promote meaningful learning where the use of a computer augments and aids learners' cognition. Computer enhanced learning takes several forms and names such as computer-aided instruction, web based learning, online education, virtual learning environment, mobile learning, mobile social learning, and many other. For example, software application for mobile devices enables providing learning material depending on several factors such as student's learning style, knowledge level, concentration level, schedule, location, available time, and other events.

Computer's memory can remember the learner's individual preferences, so learning becomes an individualized process. In the course of learning, computer discerns one's distinctive disposition, and helps classify and group one's preferences. It may resemble the data organizing engines that are used by services such as Netflix, where one can find movies recommended by "raters like you." A learner may also find recommendations of books of interest gathered on a similar basis, or objects that are a similar to purchased items: "customers who bought this item also bought..." Access to digital library, digital galleries, and other resources is interactive, with various

*Figure 2. Subway encounters*
*(© 2018, J. Reiman. Used with permission)*

kinds of software available, that are useful in creating quizzes, tests, learning supplies, surveys, and other assessment tools. Computer technology makes the learning process multi-sensory; it may be beneficial both to the gifted and talented and the handicapped students.

Factors shaping the current learning environment and the new ideas for teaching include the instructional models such as the STEM program and the STEAM program where art is being added. The acronym STEM means the disciplines of science, technology, engineering, and mathematics, and refers to developing integrative education (STEM Education, 2015). The STEM fields of study are being associated with K-12 through college education. They are changing policies and strategies related to the human resources, which are decisive for the workforce development. They stress a need to improve competitiveness of students and job seekers. Employment in many professions requires possessing skills related to physics, electrical, mechanical, optical, software, or engineering expertise. STEM propositions have also become part of discussion on an inadequate education of the United States workforce, the perceived lack of qualified candidates for high-tech jobs, and on the immigration debate about the access to the United States for skilled professionals.

The STEAM program in education comprises science, technology, engineering, arts, and mathematics. John Maeda (2012) and the Rhode Island School of Design began the movement aimed to transform STEM to STEAM (2019) by adding Art into the STEM curriculum. According to Maeda (2012), STEAM means enhancing problem-solving ability, the fearlessness, the critical thinking, and making skills. Abstract thinking skills greatly support the learning process, when a young person thinks about concepts and ideas prior to the organization and execution of each project. The objectives of the STEAM movement comprise integrating Art + Design into K-20 education, and influencing employers to drive innovation by hiring artists and designers (STEM to STEAM, 2019). Small children can now use software teaching them science, mathematics, programming, and storytelling. The goal is to improve competitiveness of students and job seekers. The STEM program stresses the importance of creativity and critical thinking for creating by children their own inventions and devices, when both science and arts are based on mathematics. Arts based development training became used in corporations; there is a trend to include the arts in business supporting teambuilding, communication, and leadership. A STREAM program, which stands for science, technology, reading, engineering, arts, and mathematics, adds reading and writing to its previous elements. The proponents of the STREAM program stress that critical thinking and creativity are the essential parts of a curriculum.

Children grow around computers from the beginning of their life, with computers present and supporting in almost all aspects of their daily lives. Computers help with research, updates, networking, and sharing. They are based on iconic, metaphorical, and connotations-based visual communication, hence there is a growing need to acquire visual literacy related skills. Moreover, growing lines of research interact, support each other, and overlap. This requires that to attain efficient collaboration and fast communication with people from other disciplines, we need to acquire skills and understand concepts belonging to these disciplines. No subject belongs just to one discipline. No specialist can stop learning within boundaries of one's own field. Knowledge, being dynamic, intertwined, and connected, requires from a researcher special skills, which range from visual information to abstract thinking.

A body of knowledge is presented to a child early, first in a simplistic way. As children grow, subjects are re-visited more than once for their expansion, repetition, and restructuring. This is why the integrative art-science assignments are shown in this book at different levels, so a teacher can find material for a particular level. Thus, if a kindergarten student creates a graphic or animates a specific concept, the same topic at the HS level would require deeper thinking, wider spectrum, more connection, and more abstract approach to the subject.

Authors of the National Education Technology Plan (2016) are stressing the role of technology in education when they emphasize the existence of the digital use divide, which is referred to the gap between students who had access to the internet and devices at school and home and those who did not. They also stress a need to use technology to measure educational outcomes, especially "a range of non-cognitive competencies – social and emotional learning, which includes skills, habits, and attitudes that facilitate functioning well in school, work, and life." They also stress that technology can enable personalized learning, can help organize learning around real-world challenges and project-based learning, which takes place in the context of authentic problems, continues across time, and brings in knowledge from many subjects. Technology can help learning move beyond the classroom and take advantage of learning opportunities available in museums, libraries, and other out-of-school settings. Technology can help learners pursue passions and personal interests; for example, a student who learns Spanish to read the works of Gabriel García Márquez in the original language. Also, technology access when equitable can help close the digital divide and make transformative learning opportunities available to all learners. The authors also recommend integrating emerging technologies with advances in the learning sciences, and provide examples of the projects being funded by the NSF as part of this effort:

- Increased use of games and simulations.
- New ways to connect physical and virtual interaction with learning technologies.
- Interactive three-dimensional imaging software, such as zSpace.
- Augmented reality (AR) as a new way of investigating our context and history (National Education Technology Plan, 2016).

The scope of new media art is still transforming: projects and installations may include generative art, computer graphics and animation, interactive, virtual, or web art, net art, games, robotics, and biologically-inspired evolutionary art. Teaching visually involves the use of a wide variety of visual tools in order to transmit ideas, knowledge, and experience. Therefore, applying the charts, diagrams, field trips, models, exhibits, mockups, demonstrations, posters, stereographs, photographs, objects, and blackboard sketches is considered a visual teaching method that works with symbolic experiences. Project Zero, developed almost 50 years ago at the Harvard University began as group of philosophers and psychologists who discussed philosophical, psychological, and conceptual issues in the arts and art education. Presently, it offers online courses, events, and institutes focused on the future of learning (Project Zero, 2019). Projects, topics, and resources about information and communication technologies teach how to store, study, retrieve, transmit, and manipulate data or information. Projects pertaining to the new media art involve the rendering and distributing data, information, and knowledge in a visual format.

## Types of Online Instruction

Perceptional learning theories explore how humans see through their eyes. Cognitive theories address how the mind handles visual information. Pedagogical theories provide understandings of how individuals process information and learn effectively. To go beyond the traditional face-to-face learning method, these concepts lead to analysis, evaluation, and application of digital imagery in the online instruction environment. The traditional, online, and mixed learning environments can be exemplified by several learning platforms such as the e-learning model, m-learning, blended instruction, flipped classroom, and the BYOD framework. All these learning environments require developing the specified measures of assessment, some of them described below.

### e-Learning

e-Learning is learning using electronic technologies; It is delivered online via the internet. Educational curriculum is delivered outside of a traditional classroom. In most cases, it is a course, program or degree offered completely online, not delivered via a DVD or CD-ROM, videotape, or over a television channel. It is interactive, so students can communicate with their teachers or other students. A teacher is interacting /communicating with students and grading their assignments, tests, and participation (eLearningNC, 2019).

E-learning could involve networked learning, virtual education, and any other uses of the information and communication systems. Many types of e-learning involving computing based instruction serve the cooperative purposes for the multilingual and multicultural environments, and enhances learning strategies developed for specific areas, for example, mathematics. This environment for learning allows students to learn outside the traditional classroom, but they are still tied to particular places and specific times of day. Imagery is used in e-learning in many ways. Images offer visual memorization of facts, set up an authentic depiction of case studies, and offer ways for students to understand signs, symbols, and specific presentations such as displays of symptoms of diseases. They also engage learners into simulations and immersive learning contexts, which are three- and four-dimensional (3D with the inclusion of time). Imagery enriches the discovery learning spaces, where there are virtual kiosks, slideshows, videos, and interactive games, for rich learning.

Distance- or e-learning changed how institutions and instructors practice teaching. Many e-learners are adults, especially if e-learning is part of the workforce training programs. Adult learners involved in e-learning are often diverse and have expectations that might differ from students in traditional classrooms, might have different motivations and self-discipline needed to complete online courses. Hence, educational designers need to consider the learning needs of adults by incorporating andragogy that supports lifelong education of adults.

## m-Learning

Mobile learning (m-learning) "is the use of mobile devices in the curriculum, to facilitate active learning and create meaning through the creation of learning spaces, extending beyond the limitations of time and space of the traditional classroom. These learning places (m-learning spaces) are characteristically dynamic, collaborative and focused on the individual needs of learners in the current context" (Torrisi-Steele, 2008). Mobile learning is an evolution of distance- or e-learning because of the rapid changes in technology. Mobile devices, Bluetooth, cameras, touchscreens, MP3 sound players and recorders offer great opportunities for both teachers and students. Teachers can use technology to take instant student polls in class, assign e-books and other online information as outside reading assignments, and can even upload lectures. Students use the multimedia functions to create presentations and homework. M-learning is becoming common on campuses throughout the world. It brings several innovations to the field of education. One of them is portability. Students don't need to sit in front of a computer or in a classroom to learn; they can study anywhere. Small mobile devices, such as mobile phones, smart phones, notepads, notebooks, laptops, and tablets are easy to be carried by the user, so students can access information anywhere and anytime.

M-learning helps to increase the number and quality of interactions between students and teachers. However, the screen size of some mobile devices creates a constraint in the educational use of mobile technology. Course information provided in a CD-ROM format needs to be accessed on a larger, less mobile device such as a PC. The difference between e- and m-learning is that mobile devices are basically hand-held computers, which allow accessing any type of information at any time and in any place.

With m-learning, students are interacting with their surroundings and experience learning tasks in different ways. Teachers need to apply new ways of teaching and learning based on the mobility of the learners. In addition, there are opportunities to develop unique mobile technologies centered on the learner (Medhipour & Zerehkafi, 2013). Behara (2013) considers the type of content related to e-learning as more formal than in m-learning, and focused on a specific, course-related material. Learners are using mobile devices, Facebook, or short message service on a phone known as text messaging. Multimedia messaging service allows sending messages in a multimedia format using mobile phones over a cellular network. The assessment of students' progress is a part of m-learning. Similar as in case of the face-to-face or online classes mobile technology allows instructors to evaluate and assess students' performance. Furthermore, students can evaluate themselves and other classmates via mobile technologies.

An example of the m-learning applied to teaching and learning is the mobile book (m-book), the electronic book designed for mobile technologies and devices. Users can develop, store, and organize their selections of books and readable materials into compact folders on their mobile devices. For example, Apple Inc. developed an application called "iBook Author," an e-book authoring application, which allows users to develop their own m-books with no need for programming ability. Mobile apps for educational purpose are e-book readers and educational games. Thus, students are using smart phones, iPads, e-readers, and other handheld devices in the classroom on a regular basis. Universities accept m-learning as a platform for education; teachers and institutions are designing curricula that rely on the fluidity of this learning platform. Apps make using mobile devices more desirable in education when users are able to either expand memory with SD cards or to purchase devices with larger memories.

To ensure student's engagement in the learning process, the use of technologies should be implemented in a purposeful framework to the teaching and learning context. The technological, pedagogical, and content knowledge (TPACK) is a model built for teachers seeking development in their knowledge and pedagogical practice. http://www.tpack.org). The three primary concepts of knowledge are: content (CK), pedagogy (PK), and technology (TK). At the intersections of these three primary concepts are: Pedagogical Content Knowledge (PCK), Technological Content Knowledge (TCK), Technological Pedagogical Knowledge (TPK), and Technological Pedagogical Content Knowledge (TPACK).

## Blended Instruction

By combining the human and technological potential instructors establish an active learning environment in the form of blended learning. It may be online learning that deliver most or all of the content through the internet without face-to-face meetings; blended/hybrid courses that blend online and face-to-face delivery; and courses that use web-based technology to facilitate a face-to-face course. For example, they use a course management system (CMS) or web pages to post the syllabus.

Blended learning merges the experience of traditional learning and online learning, establishing the environment can encourage and foster learners in developing critical thinking and reflective skills. For instance, an environment conducive to the blended learning can be created when students are presented with new content of a course in a face-to-face class time, and discussions and then can be completed throughout the course discussion forums. The blended learning framework is designed to guide, plan, develop, deliver, manage, and evaluate any blended program (Khan, 2019). The eight dimensions of the Khan's Framework are institutional, pedagogical, technological, interface design, evaluation, management, resource support, and ethical.

## Flipped Classroom

A flipped classroom combines face-to-face and technology-learning methods to support an improved learning outcome. This is a blended or hybrid learning where time inside the class is invested for discussion and receiving feedback, whereas the outside class time is assigned for lecturing. Lecturing is a well-known teaching tool; however, students are not strongly engaged. Hence, the flipped classroom method utilizes technology to increase students' engagement in the learning process. This method can be implemented in any course modality, so it is present in many universities around the world (Muenzenberger, 2016). In a classroom or beyond, students may conduct interviews, make their own experimental projects, or learn from videotaped materials. Tutorials are made in a video format, so students have more time for making one's own video; production of a video is a hands-on learning. E-learning options are: read, listen, or watch. Making the flipped classrooms is supported by technology for downloading images and sound effects, video recording, and tutorials. Linkedin learning classes offer online courses for educators, business, and technology employees – individuals or teams (learning.linkedin.com/Flipped/Classroom).

## The Bring Your Own Device (BYOD) model

BYOD is a way to incorporate advanced technologies into pedagogy. In the 1990s, some institutions required that students bring their own laptops to the classroom, thus replacing school's computer labs. Students willingly use their own computers or many mobile devices in the classroom. Over ninety percent of Americans own a cell phone, most of which are smart phones, and over thirty percent own some form of a tablet, such as iPad. With a widespread Wi-Fi connectivity, mobile learning in the classroom is becoming a reality (Imazeki, 2014), but many universities and colleges can't afford to provide students with mobile learning devices. Some schools may need to supply devices for students not financially able to provide personal devices. There are efforts to offer undergraduate and/or graduate level students with tablet computers during their final year (UNESCO, 2013). BYOD systems can help students get more involved in their own learning process. For teachers, this can sometimes involve learning about how to incorporate mobile devices into classroom instruction.

## Educational Websites, Applications, Devices, and Apps

Programs and software designed for a specific purpose work on various devices. These applications and apps are educational tools that can also work across devices. For example, educational apps can include "Khan Academy (https://www.khanacademy.org/), many kinds of online Flashcards, and iTunesU (https://itunes.apple.com/us/genre/itunes-u/id40000000). "OoKL" (https://www.ooklnet.com/web/) acts as a tour guide to show learners worldwide the historic and notable sites, such as museums, galleries, historic houses, zoos, botanic gardens and more. Dictionary apps and Wikipanion are created for referencing, Chrome and Safari browsers for browsing information, as well as Evernote, Dropbox, Pages, and Keynote. There are many apps designed for social networking, downloading music, and gaming. It all depends on how the devices are used, and so Mobile Device Management (MDM) software suites can serve as a form of management. MDM software can even monitor different devices used on campuses. The usual method is a dashboard system that maintains a constant report of usage across a system. One way to formulate a strong, inclusive MDM is to create a list of all devices to manage, for example all of Apple iOS, Blackberrys, Androids such as Samsung, and Windows.

One way to increase usability across devices is to move toward a mobile website with wireless connectivity, which makes using mobile devices of any sort much easier by delivering a browser. The capability of instant connectivity of a browser creates more flexibility for updating apps, downloading apps, and searching the internet. There are text-to-speech apps, for example Kindle 8 2017, TextAloud, and AT&T Natural Voices. For smart phones, tablets, notebooks, and laptops mixed media such as text, voice audio, or educational videos are all becoming more available for use. Depending on the educational task students are working on, they can move between devices; for example, using laptops for taking notes in class, doing written homework, using tablets for e-reading, and using mobile phones for communication, messaging, calendars, or organizers.

Sites and apps that cover many of the educational uses, and students' or teachers' needs include Dropbox, Easy Note, EasyNotecards, Easy Notepads, Evernote, Notability, and ScreenChomp, which are all used for storing and/or making notes. For reference apps one may choose Dictionary.com and Flipboard. For teaching apps: Audioboo and Audioboom for audio recording, Diigo for social bookmarking within the classroom, Diijgo Web Collector of webpages, EasyBib Bibliography Generator to make citations, Poll Everywhere for in class instant polling and short quizzes, and Socrative Teacher/Socrative Student for instant polling, quizzing, and visualizing information. However, institutions must be willing to create policies that financially support the platforms, the IT department, the teachers, and the students with the ability to access the devices, including electronic access to features such as online library. Institutions will need to establish policy on the support for possibly thousands of devices that may not be controlled.

The question for the institution is how to keep student data safe according to Federal Education Rights and Privacy Act (FERPA) regulations on devices used by faculty and staff. A successful BYOD program policy will include security training for faculty and staff, but may be controversial for students. The issue of teacher acceptance of advanced technology and skills to incorporate this technology will gradually take care of itself, as the current generation of native users (those who have grown up with technology and are comfortable and competent with it) completes their education and moves into professional positions. Hopefully educators will become tech-savvy, which will pave the way for more, better, and wiser incorporation of technology in education.

## VR and Second Life as Educational Platforms for Collaborative Distance Learning

The virtual learning web-based software for course management Blackboard Learn (previously Blackboard Learning System), the Canvas learning management system, Canvas Network, and several more platforms are platforms that are widely used for learning.

Virtual Reality (VR) is a computer technology that gives the illusion to those who are being immersed in a virtual environment that does not really exist (Fassi, Achille, Mandelli, Rechichi, & Parri, 2015). Virtual reality is characterized by three basic ideas: immersion inside the virtual world; interaction: the user manipulates virtual objects; and involvement: the user can navigate on the virtual environment in a passive or active way, exploring virtual environment. Digital helmets are devices enabling this experience. Initial attempts at virtual reality included stereographic motion picture created in 1838 by Charles Wheatstone (we can see similar concepts used today in Google Cardboard); Pygmalion's Spectacles in 1930s by science fiction writer Stanley Weinbaum; Sensorama in the mid-1950s by Morton Heilig). Myron Krueger pioneered with Artificial Reality in 1969 with research. He envisioned the art of interactivity. His first interactive installation consisted of a black velvet covered room, that stayed all black and obscure until one would enter the room triggering a movement of a red laser beam following the movement of that person.

At the Google Spotlight Stories (https://spotlightstories.co/) artists and technologists create storytelling for virtual reality: mobile 360, mobile VR, and the room-scale VR headsets. With Virtual Reality students become motivated and engaged. VR brings to the classroom the benefits of learning trips and life experiences without the expense needed for an educational trip.

Virtual environments: human and robot interaction allows discussing problem while watching a video. VR games serve as a teaching and learning tool to enhance students' learning experience. Students who used the educational version of the game gained significantly higher achievement mean scores in comparison with the achievement of students who used the traditional learning (Teh, Wan Ismail, & Toh, 2010).

Second Life (secondlife.com) enables to create engaging interactive 3D learning experiences. It offers immersive teaching, real-time collaboration, joining global community, and creating café, secure campuses. The users with alien names not only can socialize, trade, date, teleport, or fly, but can learn together. Many professors bought a virtual island devoted to a specific course, gallery, or a particular type of exchange of knowledge. Eon Reality (www.eonreality.com), an augmented and virtual reality software and solutions, is offering an AVR platform; previously created a platform named Coliseum, which creates bridges between the classroom based and distant learning. Students can see other people, interrupt by asking questions, as well as discuss their own solutions and research. Some prefer to use less complicated solutions such as Wiki (providing collaborative editing of its content), Skype (application that provides video chat and voice call services), Lync and Skype for Business, Zoom (video conferencing), or WebEx (providing on-demand online collaboration, meetings, and videoconferencing applications).

## Assessment

A system supporting personalized assessment-for-learning on both e-learning and mobile devices has been designed as the Adaptive Learning and Assessment System (ALAS) (Nedungadi & Raman, 2012). This cloud-based platform blends e-learning with mobility and allows m-learning in a traditional classroom setting; at the same time it is part of an e-learning system. Because the system is cloud based, it offers both teachers and students an immediate assessment and feedback. It also can detect what type of device is being used and can adapt subject matter based on the individual needs of the learner and the mobile device. Because of this flexibility, the authors were able to compare the usability of programs on PCs, tablets, and mobile phones and how students can seamlessly switch from one device to another to continue studying the same content. Teachers are able to continue assessment regardless of the device any student used at any given time. The results indicate that students were comfortable with any of the devices and with moving between devices. This suggests that m-learning can be a supplement to traditional classrooms and/or e-learning (Nedungadi & Raman, 2012). An instructional design model ADDIE includes assessment of assignments and various instructional activities or outline that shows some learning activities (Davis, 2013).

Educators' effectiveness and professional learning has been measured with the Student Learning Objectives (SLO). This measure is recommended in about a half of the US states, and individual states develop specific measures to assess teacher' contribution to students' growth. Phases of the assessment process comprise reviewing data, setting goals for student learning, implementing and monitoring the process, and assessing outcomes.

Visualization assessment has been developed by Amar and Stasko (2004) who designed a framework for design and evaluation of visualizations. It consisted of applying knowledge tasks to specific situations and evaluating the outcomes. When designing visualization for a new domain or scenario, one can use the knowledge tasks to systematically generate new subtasks for a visualization to support or perform, identify possible shortcomings in representation or data, and discover possible relationships to highlight or use as the basis for visualization (Amar & Stasko, 2004, p. 147). This framework can be used to evaluate how specific visualization tools can lead to effective "decision-making processes of the real world" (Amar & Stasko, 2004, p. 149). In this way, information visualization can provide the kind of information that managers, teachers, and students need in order to make informed decisions, particularly when using big data sets.

Several researchers are studying the effectiveness of particular games and systems (Belloti, Berta, De Gloria, & Ozolina, 2011) to build the educational and serious games assessment. The relevance of using social networking, games, and entertainment as educational tools is also being considered (Belloti, Berta, De Gloria, & Ozolina, 2011).

## 5.4. CURRICULAR POSTULATES

### Iterative Model of Introducing Concepts and Information

School programs usually introduce a body of knowledge in steps, revisiting subjects across the time for expansion, repetition, and restructuring. First, a holistic education provides a sampling of various disciplines and then reiteration of selected concepts. The learner learns a concept explained on a basic level, and then gains more and more advanced views on the ideas behind it. In a similar way, as in the Cognitive Constructivism model, curriculum should be organized in a spiral manner so that students continually build upon what they have already learned. The instructor translates information to be learned according to the learner's current level, often engaging in an active dialog. For example, the Socratic learning method applies the hypotheses elimination (Instructional Design.org, n.d.). The world global education has changed its meaning because of the availability, portability, compatibility, ergonometric design, and unification of devices available for studying and sharing on different levels or paths. Therefore, the schooling goes on many levels and involves active visual learning through sketching, depicting processes and products, and applying a visual, often message-based, color-coded, metaphorical imaging.

According to this iterative model, integrative art-science projects might be sequentially designed and evaluated at different levels, and offered in a recurring manner, with standards and rubrics well defined. Successively enriched knowledge will hone learners' preparation for the job market demands. It means an individual student will be assigned a project on the same theme several times but the student's work would not be repetitive. Both students and teachers know what they may expect at a particular level. A student may create a picture in a kindergarten; the same topic solved at the high school and higher education level would require deeper thinking, wider spectrum, more connection and more abstract approach to the subject. Using metaphors and analogies helps to overcome the semiotic divide between fictional and material objects and characters, or between realistic and virtual images.

## Examples of Iterative and Integrative Learning

A selected topic may mean different things in the arts and various areas of science, but all these things are connected and interrelated. For this reason, collaboration among teachers and students seems helpful, as the same project may be examined in terms of chemistry, physics, art, geology, or other points of interest of individual students. Some teachers approach the subject by using models and analogies. Students may create a program for a graphics, graphic storytelling and visual narrative, and apply story as a container for the curricular content. They may also animate a specific concept. Taken together, the student becomes involved in various disciplines, from art, graphics, and motion media through physical sciences to history, geography, environmental science, and current technologies.

- Volcanoes and their activity would be first explained by having young children to draw a volcano, create models in clay or Play-Doh, make simulations, or animations. Then, this theme would come back in more depth, when the learners develop their cognitive levels to comprehend abstract concepts behind physical and chemical processes and products involved, such as dynamical geology of volcanoes, and tsunami formation. Later on, themes of landforms and their geomorphology can be introduced. After the volcano eruption event is explained in terms of geology, the same learner will then consider how this event relates to history (e.g., the destructive effects of volcano eruptions on human lives, settlements, and cultural treasures), global issues, and sustainability, for example, the effect of oil drilling on the geological plate dynamics.

- While learning mathematics, students may learn about its branch named geodesy, dealing with measuring the Earth's shape, area, and orientation in space. They may also examine why there is a network of lines on maps representing latitudes and longitudes.

- After acquiring basic knowledge about geography of continents and countries students can learn about geomorphology, landforms, and geodynamics. Also, they can learn about biogeography, distribution in space and time of ecosystems, and related problems with species' extinction. Also, students can relate geological conditions to various soils and their kinds, ecology, and natural environments; this branch of science is called a soil science – pedology.

- In terms of physics, students may learn about states of matter (solid, liquid, gas, and plasma), and then examine natural forms in which matter can exist. They may learn about glaciers and glaciology (with the global warming issues), icebergs in the ace age and at present Holocene epoch, as well about water on Earth, other planets, and in space. Students may also design projects about water, with the dynamics of its currents and tides as studied by hydrology, distribution of water resources on Earth, water quality and properties in lakes, rivers, and marshes. Creating projects about a local climate and weather will support learning physics (specifically dynamics of events) and chemistry (when talking about processes in air and water).

- Lessons of biology may be enhanced with learning about ocean life, organisms in deep and shallow saltwater natural ecosystems, coastal reefs, atolls, and beeches, but also issues resulting from the ocean floor drilling and oceanic pollution with chemicals and plastic objects.

Projects may be integrated with learning geography of Earth's oceans: Arctic, Atlantic, Indian, Pacific, and Southern (Antarctic), along with their World Ocean habitat of 230,000 known species, and diverse ecosystems.

## Postulates for Strengthening the Curricular Program

Many people would wish that the world became unified in providing the learning conditions. This would include:

- Free internet everywhere.
- No copyright restrictions when sharing knowledge by showing infographics and images.
- Inclusive instruction with gender neutrality, attentive to individual student's strong intelligence.

There is a need for designing curricular models that would meet learners' expectations about preparing them for the job market demands. The integrative model presented in this chapter places emphasis on developing learners' skills in abstract thinking, cognitive skills, creativity, and problem-solving abilities. Instruction in knowledge visualization and computing techniques should be introduced early because they are needed both in a classroom and in the online, networked learning. They promote communication, teambuilding, leadership, and support competitiveness of students and job seekers. Educational propositions may be of service in the global K-20 schooling. Curricular postulates provide guidelines for teachers and educators preparing programs to develop courses that could promote both creativity and technology integration for pre-service teachers.

Meaningful learning through creating art is an active, integrative learning, contrary to the hands-on or verbatim, step-by-step rote learning by memorization and repetition of fragmented knowledge not integrated with existing concepts, cognitive structures, or experiences (Ausubel, Novak, & Henesian, 1978; Hassard & Dias, 2010). Several companies and toy stores are introducing toys and games designed with gender neutrality in sight. Young customers may choose objects corresponding to their individual interests and strong intelligences (Gardner, 1983/2011; 2011a) but not according to traditional cultural perceptions about gender.

Inclusion into curricula subjects acting as universal languages such as Latin, Music, Mathematics, and even Physics and Chemistry may foster learners' cultural communication skills by making each person understanding different cultures and ideas. Music, as well as Art, is the universal language promoting abstract thinking. Instruction in knowledge visualization, along with current computing technologies (especially the bio inspired solutions and nanoscience) should be introduced early, as they are needed in the online, networked communication. Current needs for developing the learners' skills follow from the existing trends in corporations and the resulting competitiveness of students and job seekers.

In curricular postulates presented below the focus is put on a need for strengthening the curricular program in mathematics, introduction of universal languages such as Latin, Music, and Mathematics, teaching and learning visually with the use of visualization techniques, teaching coding in various computer languages, instruction in serious gaming, inclusion of virtual reality into school environment, and teaching on the go through the use of social platforms for global exchange of thought.

From early childhood, education should include teaching several subjects supporting the development of creativity and abstract thinking:

1. Learning algebra, geometry, and calculus starting at the early elementary school level.
2. Learning Latin language, to help people understand structure of other languages (such as western languages based on declinations).
3. Learning visually with the use of visualization techniques and visualizing processes or products through drawing with colors and sketching.
4. Acquiring programming skills in various computer languages, which could be linked with traditional tools such as quite old but still present Lego Logo, and current Lego Mindstorms, which continue developing valuable tools and methods of learning programming and coding, and are present in stores (EV3 https://www.wired.com/2013/12/lego-mindstormsev3/).
5. Serious video games designed for more purposes than entertainment or fitness.

## (1) Building Mathematical Foundation

Learning mathematics, especially algebra, geometry, and calculus may start at the elementary school level. It is often easier to start learning algebra for children than for adults. As early as in 1904, George W. Hull (Hull's

Algebra, 1904) claimed that 11-year-old students should begin learning algebra. At the elementary school level, students may easily familiarize with using mathematical symbols (such as ax + b = c) that can later stand for numbers. Manipulating mathematical symbols may support developing abstract thinking ability.

Abstract thinking, which needs to be developed early, is usually referred to thinking about concepts that are separate from the specific, concrete objects. This capability is usually ascribed exclusively to the young adults or adults, so it is believed that students will later use abstract thinking skills in further studies. The abstract thinker can generalize ideas or principles and understand that the meaning, properties, and patterns can be shared by a variety of items or concepts. Students learn to solve equations with letters standing for numbers. Basic, elementary algebra would be essential for learning many kinds of science and later for college studies such as engineering, medicine, business, economics, and computing.

Differential equations describe everyday processes. Studying calculus (differential and integral calculus) is important for understanding many areas of science. A key tool of calculus, the derivative of a function of a single variable is fundamental in understanding not only calculus but also basic life events. For example, the speed of the heart muscle cell's activation and the resulting contraction is crucial for the heart muscle's efficiency in pumping blood. The slope of a graph showing such activation can be measured as the derivative of this function, and the area of the region bounded by this graph can be calculated as an integral of this function. Also, values of an integral of a function can represent blood flow changes in human aorta as the signed area on the graph. We may thus say derivatives and integers help to explain basic processes and events in our surroundings such as heartbeat or car engine acceleration. Students gain a tool that could conduce to the logical way of apprehending new concepts rather than the memorizing by rote. Theoretical research applying mathematics may help to convert the unseen, unfelt, or unheard into the visible, palpable, or sending sounds. From there, we can go from the physical to digital or vice versa. In fact, we examine these capacities and use this information for theoretical, practical, and computational solutions within the domains of physiology, neuroscience, cognitive science, cognitive psychology, sociology, anthropology, medicine, computer science, but also human perception, philosophy, and art.

## (2) Supporting Linguistic Aptitudes

A child learns directly from what is told, without understanding a concept of a noun or a verb, and not analyzing a structure of a sentence. Children learn their native language mostly by listening other people rather than by applying analysis or learning linguistic theories. Learning Latin can be a valuable tool for strengthening cognitive processes in students. Languages such as Italian, Portuguese, Spanish, French, Romanian, and also many English words and language structures have strong Latin roots. Therefore, Latin is conducive to easier communication among students who speak different languages. Learning Latin, not only by memorizing examples of a classical literature but also by studying Latin grammar, gives knowledge and the understanding of the language structure. Learning about Latin words' inflections may support developing abstract thinking. While learning about the Latin seven cases of nouns, pronouns, or adjectives (changes in their form that determine relation to other words) and five declensions (that identify grammatical cases, numbers, and genders) students enhance their learning process. The same may pertain to learning four conjugations of six verb tenses.

Studying Latin grammar involves a need to understand abstract concepts and theories about the language structure. In the context of visual literacy, many fields may have some of their roots in ancient Greek and Roman science. Mathematics, physics, biology, chemical and medical sciences use names derived from ancient Greek, and they still use letters of Greek alphabet to represent mathematical or other scientific symbols.

Even without their adeptness in thinking abstractly, students may read and memorize classic texts written by Latin political leaders, poets, and playwrights, and thus they gradually achieve Latin language proficiency. Many agree that in any discipline the creative success depends in great measure on tedious preparation: learning, research, and gaining dexterity. Children who learned Latin, either by saturation or with the use of abstract analysis of the language structure, might achieve longer attention span, better memory, and finer working habits. In the first nineteen centuries of our era, in order to be considered educated people had to achieve skills in Latin. Since Latin was the language of learning, faculty and students used to converse in Latin while walking on the streets. For this reason, the area around the Sorbonne University in Paris, France has been called the Latin Quarter (Quartier Latin). Presently, curricula in many countries including most states in the United

States do not include Latin, thus students have less opportunities to employ their skills in cognitive learning, grasp rhetoric, apprehend beauty, and learn about old philosophical foundations of our current culture.

## (3) Using Visualization Techniques

Information can be presented in many ways, e.g., numerical, graphic, or diagrammatic form, as a sketch, drawing, diagram, plan, outline, image, geometric relationship, map, music and dance notation, object, interactive installation, or a story (Tufte, 1983/2001). Visual metaphors, which make such concepts visible, are inherent in our thought, and thus enable visualization of abstract concepts. Also, drawing supports the visualizing of processes or products. Auditory metaphors seem to be even more important for music theory and appreciation. Images give the learner the chance to use imagination to help understand concepts or class material. Visualization also helps students connect new concepts more easily with previous experiences, which leads to deeper learning. Students have grown up with technology, which usually includes information supported by visual media such as television, videos, tablets, and other smart devices. People have become dependent on visual images for transmitting information, beginning from our ancestors from cave painting and medieval stain glass windows. Visualization combines the concept and the idea to present information, and by doing this, makes the lesson memorable. Images lead learners to think outside the box because they aren't limited by the amount of words leading to specific meanings.

Visualizations support human cognition and thinking in a number of ways: first, by supporting visual queries on information graphics, and second, by extending memory (Ware, 2008). For visual queries to be useful, "the problem must first be cast in the form of a query pattern that, if seen, helps solve part of the problem" (Ware, 2004, p. 352). Once learners know what is salient in the particular image, they may identify and track these in the visuals for problem solving. Memory extension, suggests Ware, occurs via "a display symbol, image, or pattern can rapidly evoke non-visual information and cause it to be loaded from long-term, memory into verbal-propositional processing centers (Ware, 2004, p. 352). Knowledge visualization, for example tree visualizations (Shneiderman, 1996; Lima 2011, 2014) or a well-known Charles Minard's visualization of the Napoleon's campaign (Kraak, 2014) may serve as a tool promoting student's interest and their understanding of scientific concepts and processes. Many times scientists such as Johannes Kepler (1571-1630) have been able to transform their visions into physical or mathematical solutions. Hence comes a proposition that instruction in knowledge visualization, along with current computing technologies (especially, the bio-inspired solutions in computing, new materials and products development) should be introduced early. These skills become necessary in the online, networked communication.

## (4) Coding: Introducing Programming

Coding needs to be introduced very early in one's education, possibly from kindergarten, when students' brains are pliable and open; later on, child's playfulness is often replaced with a fear of being criticized. Students are able to benefit from getting a skill to write algorithms, but to many adults it is an idea hard to grasp, even at an advanced level of their schooling. Small children can now use many kinds of software, which teach them science, mathematics, programming, and storytelling, along with programming with Lego Logo (Papert, 1993, 1994). Seymour Papert created the Logo programming language as a tool to improve the way children think and solve problems (2019; http://papert.org/works.html). Seymour Papert insisted that computers should serve as instruments for learning and for enhancing creativity. He had also developed a mobile robot called 'Logo Turtle' to support thinking and problem solving through playing. Mindstroms EV3, a programmable robotic kit made in collaboration with the Lego Company, comprises now iOS and Android apps, which are helpful in putting together each bot (Gear, 2013). Programming the robot is easy because software works like a visual diagramming tool. After Papert initiated the 'One Laptop per Child' project, Nicholas Negroponte, a co-founder of the MIT Media Lab developed an XO project: people were invited to buy a $ 100 Linux laptop, which was able to perform most of the basic operations. When they agreed to pay a double price, the second machine could go to a child in need.

Ben Fry and Kasey Reas developed Processing.org as a free visual and an intuitive coding environment to apprehend programming thinking and skills. The user can download the program for any operating system, along with a free tutorial, to be provided with a library of images, animation, or interactive environment along with their respective codes. The small changes entered into the code show the learner the differences in the outcomes (Processing, 2019). Dreamweaver may support instant code learning. Also, open source software Apache Cordova allows an access to mobile educational devices.

"Coding is the literacy of the 21st century," said Zach Sims, cofounder of a New York City based online interactive platform Codecademy (2019; https://www.codecademy.com). Lessons in computer programming have been adopted in 2014 by the national curriculum for primary schools in England (Muffett, 2014). Margaret Boden, a researcher in artificial intelligence, cognitive and computer science, stressed that new art was associated with positive fascination for technology; many times digital artwork production involves electrical engineering and/or electronic technology.

However, there is a need for a balance between artists or graphic designers who care for aesthetics in visual communication versus computing scientists, software engineers, and programmers who codify in computer language and focus on code efficiency (Hartley, 2018). For example, a tech ethicist David Ryan Polgar set out an All Tech Is Human collaborative hub to better align he business interests of tech with human interests of users and society at large (Polgar, 2019).

One can see a common way of thinking in various natural and computer languages. Codes are used in many areas of activity including music and languages – with their many kinds of alphabets, grammar, and double articulation. Also, the book and font design depend now on coding. Calligraphy plays different roles in particular languages: perceptual, aesthetic, and psychological. Eye tracking experiments (Romano Bergstrom & Schall, 2014; Yoon, & Narayanan, 2004) confirm the role of the text's shape.

Arduino is an open source prototyping platform used for interactive projects. Arduino boards can read input from a sensor, a finger, a button, or a Twitter message. They can sense the environment by receiving input from sensors, and can affect its surroundings: control lights, activate a motor, turn up a LED, or publish something online. The microcontroller on the board is programmed using the Arduino programming language. The Arduino programming language is based on Wiring, and the Arduino software is based on Processing, an open source programming language (Processing, 2019; Arduino, 2019). Common programs and tools supporting interactive environment for learning by designing and learning by explaining include a desktop publishing software application InDesign; a software development kit SDK; a game development platform Unity; an optical head-mounted display for VR Google Glass.

Estonia, the birthplace of Skype, has launched in 2012 a nationwide program to teach students from the age 7 to 19 how to write a code (e-Estonia. com, 2019; Olson, 2012). Programs for young students are focused not only on learning programming languages such as Java, Pearl, or C++; students gain necessary skills like logic, math, and also robotics. Over 85 percent of Estonia's schools use e-School, covering about 95 percent of all grade school students (e-Estonia, 2019). The system e-School introduced in Estonia provides functions that are useful for teachers, students, parents, and educators. Teachers enter grades and attendance information in the system, post homework assignments, evaluate students' behavior, and send messages to parents, students or entire classes. Parents can see their children's homework assignments, grades, attendance information and teacher's notes, as well as communicate directly with teachers via the system. Students can read their own grades and keep track of what homework has been assigned each day. They also have an option to save their best work in their own, personal e-portfolios. District administrators can access the statistical reports and consolidate data across the district's schools.

## (5) Games that Hone Cognitive Abilities

For decades, games have been popular in the entertainment industry. The main types of games include board, card, and video games. Console gaming and virtual gaming media are becoming now a widely used as instructional tools both in classroom settings and in eLearning strategies. Social networking sites are increasingly used for online learning through games because gaming environment is a communication medium. Cinematic effects in motion pictures and games are valued as motivational tools. Most of researchers, educators, professionals, and academics agree about the effectiveness of using gaming for educational purposes and the impact of educational games on learning ability. Also, most authors agree that playing video games stimulates affective, cognitive, and communicational processes. Educational games have been designed to teach learners about a particular subject and/or to tech them a skill. Connolly, et al. reviewed and then categorized the types of games as educational or serious (Connolly, Boyle, MacArthur, Hainey, & Boyle, 2012).

Serious games became a discipline. Students not only can communicate and discuss ideas, but also immerse into a knowledge-based game, or learn together with own avatar and a 3d scanned favorite object. Biofeedback not only helps people control their own state of mind, but is also used as stimulus for learning (Corwin Bell, www.visionshiftstudios.com). Apps on our phones make us use many of our senses, even those not listed in our vocabularies, such as temperature, pressure, balance, as we use apps with touching ability and accelerometers (Connolly, Boyle, MacArthur, Hainey, & Boyle, 2012).

Educational computer games are now most often described as two learning strategies: gamification and serious games.

Gamification uses game-like elements, which are fun and motivating students in a non-game context; it applies typical mechanics of games to infuse these elements into the eLearning programs. The goal is to increase active participation and engagements of students, who expect learning with games to be easy to learn but sound like fun, with games being challenging and rewarding.

Serious games have the typical structure of games, utilize the game design principles, but also apart from entertainment they offer some forms of educational values (e.g., CoreAxis, 2019). Moreover, they offer positive reinforcement, often with the use of leader boards showing players where they rank in a gamified context. Serious games are used for training and learning; they are found in the areas of business, trades, marketing, government, and non-profit agencies (Connolly, Boyle, MacArthur, Hainey, & Boyle, 2012, p. 662).

According to Gardner and Strayer two important cognitive abilities that underlie learning are: working memory and attentional capacity/executive function (Zheng & Gardner, 2017). Educational computer games support the behavioral, cognitive, and emotional dimensions of engagement. The National Research Council recommends conducting research on factors that may cause that serious games enhance student achievement. Recommendations pertain studies on the learner's self-awareness to promote self-regulated learning; the mediating processes within the individual: the interactions among body, mind, and game environment; and the problem of transfer of learning (Zheng & Gardner, 2017). Cognitive benefits of the implementation of gaming may include enhancing spatial skills, critical thinking and problem-solving skills, and the use of fantasy as a factor enhancing the learning process. For all these reasons, the importance of serious games in STEM education has been widely acknowledged. Teachers can adopt a game (e.g., about different historical places) without knowing how to write a code. Serious games are offered at all grade levels including kindergarten. For example, they invite for participatory simulations of honeybees and ants societies to explore complex systems concept and learn about complex problem solving, help to solve some social problems, and engage in architectural constructions in the earthquake rebuild actions (Zheng & Gardner, 2017).

In the past times, the use of games for educational purposes probably dates to Plato and Socrates, while the links between education and playing games have been studied in 20th and 21st century. Digital gaming was introduced as early as 1967. It started with the release of *Logo Programming*, which was used to teach students the basics of computer programming (Heick, 2012). By the 1980s, educational games were being designed and marketed to school districts. A think tank affiliated with the Smithsonian Institute, the Serious Games Initiative was founded in 2002 at the Woodrow Wilson International Center for Scholars. However, there was lack of popular games for the classroom because of the concerns that students would be more involved in gaming than in learning (Heick, 2012). Also, the research was then scarce on the effects of gaming on improved learning ability.

## REFERENCES

Allen, D. C. (n.d.). *United States of America: Art Education.* Grove Art Online. Retrieved from https://en.wikipedia.org/wiki/Oxford_Art_Online

Amar, R., & Stasko, J. (2004). A knowledge task-based framework for design and evaluation of information visualizations. *Information Visualization, INFOVIS 2004. IEEE Symposium*, 143-150.

Arduino Homepage. (2019). Retrieved from https://www.arduino.cc/

Arlin, P. K. (1974). *Problem finding: The relation between selective cognitive process variables and problem-finding performance* (Unpublished doctoral dissertation). University of Chicago.

Arlin, P. K. (1984). Adolescent and adult thought: A structural interpretation. In M. L. Commons, F. A. Richards, & C. Armon (Eds.), *Late adolescent and adult cognitive development* (pp. 258–271). New York, NY: Praeger.

Ausubel, D. P., Novak, J. D., & Henesian, H. (1978). *Educational Psychology: A Cognitive View*. New York, NY: Holt, Rinehart and Winston.

Axelrod, R. (1973). Schema Theory: An Information Processing Model of Perception and Cognition. *The American Political Science Review*, 67(4), 1248–1266. doi:10.2307/1956546

Baddeley, A. D., & Hitch, G. J. L. (1969). Working memory. In G. A. Bower (Ed.), *Recent Advances in Learning and Motivation* (Vol. 8, pp. 47–90). New York: Academic Press.

Beatty, N. A. (2013). Cognitive visual literacy: From theories and competencies to pedagogy. *Journal of the Art Libraries Society of North America, 32*(1), 33–42.

Behara, S. (2013). E- and m-learning: A comparative study. *International Journal on New Trends in Education and their Implications, 4*(3), 65-78.

Belloti, F., Berta, R., De Gloria, A., & Ozolina, A. (2011). Investigating the added value of interactivity and serious gaming for educational TV. *Computers & Education, 57*(1), 1137–1148. doi:10.1016/j.compedu.2010.11.013

Benoît, G. (2019). Introduction to Information Visualization: Transforming Data into Meaningful Information. Rowman & Littlefield Publishers.

Bloom, B. S. (Ed.). (1956/1969). *Taxonomy of educational objectives. The classification of educational goals.* London, UK: Longman Group United Kingdom.

Boyd, R. B. (1989). *Identifying and meeting the needs of students functioning at the concrete operations stage of cognitive development in the general chemistry classroom.* RIEJAN90. (ERIC Document Reproduction Service No. ED309984)

Branch, R., & Merrill, M. (2012). Characteristics of Instructional Design Method. In R. A. Reiser & J. V. Dempsey (Eds.), *Trends and issues in instructional design and technology* (3rd ed.; pp. 8–16). Boston, MA: Pearson.

Broadwell, M. M. (1969). *Teaching for learning (XVI).* The Gospel Guardian.

Bruner, J. (1961). The act of discovery. *Harvard Educational Review, 31,* 21–32.

Bruner, J. (1966). *Toward a theory of instruction.* Cambridge, MA: Harvard University Press.

Bruner, J. (1986). *Actual minds, possible worlds.* Cambridge, MA: Harvard University Press.

Bruner, J. (1990). *Acts of meaning.* Cambridge, MA: Harvard University Press.

Bruner, J. (1997). *The culture of education.* Cambridge, MA: Harvard University Press.

Connolly, T., Boyle, E. A., MacArthur, E., Hainey, T., & Boyle, J. M. (2012). A systematic literature review of empirical evidence on computer games and serious games. *Computers & Education, 59*(2), 661–686. doi:10.1016/j.compedu.2012.03.004

Csikszentmihalyi, M. (1990). Flow: The Psychology of Optimal Experience. New York, NY: Harper and Row.

Csikszentmihalyi, M. (1996a). Society, culture, person: A systems view of creativity. In R. J. Steinberg (Ed.), *The nature of creativity* (pp. 325–339). Cambridge, UK: Cambridge University Press.

Csikszentmihalyi, M. (1996b). *The creative personality*. Retrieved December 15, 2016, from https://www.psychologytoday.com/articles/199607/the-creative-personality

Csikszentmihalyi, M. (1997). *Creativity: Flow and the Psychology of Discovery and Invention*. New York, NY: Harper Perennial.

Csikszentmihalyi, M. (1998). *Finding Flow: The Psychology of Engagement with Everyday Life (Masterminds Series)*. New York, NY: Basic Books.

Damasio, A. (1999). *The feeling of what happens: body and emotion in the making of consciousness*. San Diego, CA: Harcourt.

Damasio, A. (2005). Descartes' error: emotion, reason, and the human brain. Putnam. (Originally published 1994)

Damasio, A. (2012). *Self Comes to Mind: Constructing the Conscious Brain*. Vintage.

Damasio, A., & Carvalho, G. B. (2013). The nature of feelings: Evolutionary and neurobiological origins. *Nature Reviews. Neuroscience, 14*(2), 143–152. doi:10.1038/nrn3403 PMID:23329161

Davis, A. L. (2013). Using instructional design principles to develop effective information literacy instruction: The ADDIE model. *College & Research Libraries News, 74*(4), 205–207. doi:10.5860/crln.74.4.8934

Dewey, J. (1916). Method in science teaching. *Science Education, 1*, 3–9.

Dewey, J. (1997). *Experience and education.* Free Press.

Dewey, J. (2005). *Art as Experience.* TarcherPerigee. (Original work published 1934)

Dewey, J. (2013). *How we think.* CreateSpace Independent Publishing Platform. Retrieved from https://www.createspace.com/

Driscoll, M. P. (2009). *Psychology of Learning for Instruction* (3rd ed.). Boston, MA: Allyn & Bacon.

Driscoll, M. P. (2017). Psychological foundations of instructional design. In R. A. Reiser & J. V. Dempsey (Eds.), *Trends and issues in instructional design and technology* (4th ed.). Boston, MA: Pearson.

e-Estonia. (2019). *The Digital Society: A game to change the concept of teaching programming.* Retrieved from https://e-estonia.com/game-changes-concept-of-teaching-programming/

eLearningNC. (2019). *What is eLearning?* Retrieved from http://www.elearningnc.gov/about_elearning/what_is_elearning/

Fassi, F., Achille, C., Mandelli, A., Rechichi, F., & Parri, S. (2015). A new idea of bim system for visualization, web sharing and using huge complex 3d models for facility management. *The International Archives of the Photogrammetry, Remote Sensing and Spatial Information Sciences, 40*(5).

Gardner, H. (1983/2011). *Frames of mind: The theory of multiple intelligences* (3rd ed.). Basic Books.

Gardner, H. (1993/2006). *Art, Mind, and Brain: A Cognitive Approach to Creativity.* New York: Basic Books, A Division of Harper Collins Publishers.

Gardner, H. (1997). *Extraordinary minds: Portraits of exceptional individuals and an examination of our extraordinariness.* New York: Basic Books, Harper Collins Publishers.

Gardner, H. (2000). *Intelligence Reframed: Multiple Intelligences for the 21*[st] *Century.* Basic Books.

Gardner, H. (2011a). *The unschooled mind: how children think and how schools should teach* (2nd ed.). New York: Basic Books.

Gardner, H. (2011b). The theory of multiple intelligences: the battle-scarred journey. *The Daily Riff.* Retrieved from http://www.thedailyriff.com/articles/the-theory-of-multiple-intelligences-the-battle-scarred-journey-908.php

Gardner, H. (2016). *Intelligence isn't black and white: There are 8 different kinds.* Bigthing.

Gardner, H. (2019). Multiple Intelligences, NOT Learning Styles. *MI Oasis*. Retrieved from http://multipleintelligencesoasis.org/news/multiple-intelligences-not-learning-styles/

Gear, J. B. (2013). Review: Lego Mindstorms EV3: Build a BOT. *Wired*. Retrieved from https://www.wired.com/2013/12/lego-mindstorms-ev3/

Guilford, J. P. (1950). Creativity. *The American Psychologist*, 5(9), 444–454. doi:10.1037/h0063487 PMID:14771441

Guilford, J. P. (1959). Traits of creativity. In *Creativity and its cultivation*. New York: Harper and Row.

Guilford, J. P. (1967). *The nature of human intelligence*. New York: McGraw-Hill.

Guilford, J. P. (1968). *Intelligence, creativity and their educational implications*. San Diego, CA: Robert Knapp, Publ.

Harasim, L. (2017). *Learning theory and online technologies* (2nd ed.). Abington, UK: Routledge. doi:10.4324/9781315716831

Hartley, S. (2018). The Fuzzy and the Techie: Why the Liberal Arts Will Rule the Digital World. Mariner Books.

Hassard, J., & Dias, M. (2010). The Art of Teaching Science: Inquiry and Innovation in Middle School and High School (2nd ed.). Abington, UK: Routledge.

Heick, T. (2012). A brief history of video games in education. *TeachThought*. Retrieved from https://www.teachthought.com/technology/a-brief-history-of-video-games-in-education/

Hull, G. W. (1904, July 16). Hull's Algebra *The New York Times*.

Illeris, K. (Ed.). (2018). *Contemporary Theories of Learning* (2nd ed.). Routledge. doi:10.4324/9781315147277

Imazeki, J. (2014). Bring-Your-Own-Device: Turning cell phones into forces for good. *The Journal of Economic Education*, 45(3), 240–250. doi:10.108 0/00220485.2014.917898

Inhelder, B. (1977). Genetic epistemology and developmental psychology. *Annals of the New York Academy of Sciences*, 291(1), 332–341. doi:10.1111/j.1749-6632.1977.tb53084.x

Inhelder, B., & Piaget, J. (1958). *The growth of logical thinking from childhood to adolescence.* London, UK: Routledge and Kegan Paul. doi:10.1037/10034-000

Instructional Design.org. (2019). *Constructivist theory (Jerome Brunner).* Retrieved from http://www.instructionaldesign.org/theories/constructivist/

Kalman, H., Kemp, J., Morrison, G., & Ross, S. (2012). *Designing effective instruction* (7th ed.). New York, NY: Wiley.

Khan, B. (2019). *Blended learning octagonal framework-Khan.* Retrieved from http://asianvu.com/bk/framework/?attachment_id=1205

Koltko-Rivera, M. E. (2006). Rediscovering the later version of Maslow's hierarchy of needs: Self-transcendence and opportunities for theory, research, and unification. *Review of General Psychology, 10*(4), 302–317. doi:10.1037/1089-2680.10.4.302

Koopmann-Holm, B., & O'Connor, A. (2016). A Macat analysis of Alan D. Baddeley and Graham Hitch's working memory. Macat.com.

Kraak, M.-J. (2014). *Mapping Time: Illustrated by Minard's Map of Napoleon's Russian Campaign of 1812.* Esri Press.

Kremer, W., & Hammond, C. (2013). Abraham Maslow and the pyramid that beguiled business. *BBC News Magazine.* Retrieved from http://www.bbc.com/news/magazine-23902918

Lima, M. (2011). *Visual Complexity: Mapping Patterns of Information.* New York: Princeton Architectural Press.

Lima, M. (2014). *The Book of Trees: Visualizing the Branches of Knowledge.* New York: Princeton Architectural Press.

Lowenfeld, V. (1949). Creative and mental growth. London, UK: The Macmillan Company.

Lowenfeld, V., & Brittain, W. L. (1987). *Creative and mental growth* (8th ed.). Upper Saddle River, NJ: Prentice Hall.

Maeda, J. (2012). STEM to STEAM: Art in K-12 is key to building a strong economy. *Edutopia.* Retrieved from http://www.edutopia.org/blog/stem-to-steam-strengthens-economy-john-maeda

Maslow, A. H. (1943). A theory of human motivation. Psychological Review, 50, 370–396.

Maslow, A. H. (1954). *Motivation and personality*. New York: Harper.

Maslow, A. H. (1969). The farther reaches of human nature. Journal of Transpersonal Psychology, 1(1), 1-9.

Mayer, R. E., & Moreno, R. (1998). A split-attention effect in multimedia learning: Evidence for dual processing systems in working memory. *Journal of Educational Psychology, 90*(2), 312–320. doi:10.1037/0022-0663.90.2.312

Mayer, R. E., & Moreno, R. (2003). Nine ways to reduce cognitive load in multimedia learning. *Educational Psychologist, 38*(1), 43–52. doi:10.1207/S15326985EP3801_6

Medhipour, Y., & Zerehkafi, H. (2013). Mobile learning for education: Benefits and challenges. *International Journal of Computational Engineering Research, 3*(6), 93–101.

Moreno, R., & Mayer, R. (1999). Cognitive principles of multimedia learning: The role of modality and contiguity. *Journal of Educational Psychology, 91*(2), 358–368. doi:10.1037/0022-0663.91.2.358

Moreno, R., & Mayer, R. E. (2000). A coherence effect in multimedia learning: The case for minimizing irrelevant sounds in the design of multimedia instructional messages. *Journal of Educational Psychology, 92*(1), 117–125. doi:10.1037/0022-0663.92.1.117

Muenzenberger, A. T. (2016). *Bibliography on blended learning: Blended learning readings*. Paper presented at the Flipped Classroom Conference, Claremont, CA. Retrieved from http://invertedclassroomstudy.g.hmc.edu/2016-conference/products-and-resources

Muffett, T. (2014). Computer coding taught in Estonian primary schools. *BBC News*. Retrieved from http://www.bbc.com/news/education-25648769

National Education Technology Plan. (2016). *Future Ready Learning: Reimaging the Role of Technology in Education*. U.S. Department of Education. Retrieved from https://tech.ed.gov/netp/

Nedungadi, P., & Raman, R. (2012). A new approach to personalization: Integrating e-learning and m-learning. *Educational Technology Research and Development, 60*(4), 659–678. doi:10.100711423-012-9250-9

Olson, P. (2012). Why Estonia has started teaching its first-graders to code. *Forbes*, 6. Retrieved from http://www.forbes.com/sites/parmyolson/2012/09/06/why-estonia-has-started-teaching-its-first-graders-to-code/#7fa98bd05790

Paivio, A. (1971). *Imagery and verbal processes*. New York: Holt, Rinehart, and Winston.

Paivio, A. (1986). *Mental representations: a dual coding approach*. Oxford, UK: Oxford University Press.

Papert, S. (1993). Mindstorms: children, computers, and powerful ideas (2nd ed.). Basic Books.

Papert, S. (1994). *The children's machine. Rethinking school in the age of computer.* New York: Basic Books.

Park, I., & Hannafin, M. (1993). Empirically based guidelines for the design of interactive multimedia. *Educational Technology Research and Development*, *41*(3), 65–85. doi:10.1007/BF02297358

Pavlov, I. P. (Author), Anrep G. V. (Translator) (2015). Conditioned reflexes: an investigation of the physiological activity of the cerebral cortex. Eastford, CT: Martino Fine Books. (Originally published 1927)

Piaget, J. (1969). *Science of education and the psychology of the child*. New York: Viking.

Piaget, J. (1970). *Science of education and the psychology of the child*. New York: Orion Press.

Piaget, J., & Inhelder, B. (1967/1981). *The Child's Conception of Geometry*. New York: W. W. Norton & Co Inc.

Piaget, J., & Inhelder, B. (1969). *The Psychology of the Child* (2nd ed.). New York: Basic Books.

Polgar D. R. (2019). *Home page*. Retrieved from https://www.davidpolgar.com/

Processing. (2019). Retrieved from https://processing.org/

Project Zero Homepage. (2019). Harvard Graduate School of Education. Retrieved from http://www.pz.harvard.edu/

Reiser, R. A., & Dempsey, J. V. (2018). *Trends and Issues in Instructional Design and Technology* (4th ed.). Pearson.

Remler, D. K., & van Ryzin, G. G. (2014). *Research methods in practice: strategies for description and causation*. Thousand Oaks, CA: Sage Publications.

Roblyer, M. D., & Doering, A. H. (2013). Integrating educational technology into teaching (6th ed.). Boston, MA: Pearson.

Romano Bergstrom, J., & Schall, A. (2014). *Eye Tracking in User Experience Design*. Morgan Kaufmann.

Shneiderman, B. (1996). The Eyes Have It: A Task by Data Type Taxonomy for Information Visualizations. In *Proceedings of the IEEE Symposium on Visual Languages*, (pp. 336-343). Washington, DC: IEEE Computer Society Press. 10.1109/VL.1996.545307

Skinner, B. F. (1953). *Science and human behavior*. New York: Macmillan.

Skinner, B. F. (1971/2002). *Beyond freedom and dignity*. Indianapolis, IN: Hackett Publishing Company.

Sternberg, R. (Ed.). (1999). *Handbook of creativity*. Cambridge, UK: Cambridge Univ. Press.

Sternberg, R. (2011). *Cognitive psychology* (6th ed.). Belmont, CA: Wadsworth Publishing.

Sternberg, R. J. (1986). A triangular theory of love. *Psychological Review, 93*(2), 119–135. doi:10.1037/0033-295X.93.2.119

Sternberg, R. J. (Ed.). (1988). *The nature of creativity: contemporary psychological perspectives*. Cambridge, UK: Cambridge University Press.

Sternberg, R. J. (1997). A Triarchic View of Giftedness: Theory and practice. In N. Coleangelo & G. A. Davis (Eds.), *Handbook of gifted education* (pp. 43–53). Boston, MA: Allyn and Bacon.

Sternberg, R. J. (2007). *Wisdom, intelligence, and creativity synthesized*. Cambridge, UK: Cambridge University Press.

Sternberg R. J. (2017). *Personal website*. Retrieved from https://en.wikipedia.org/wiki/Robert_Sternberg

Sternberg, R. J., & Kaufman, S. B. (Eds.). (2011). *The Cambridge handbook of intelligence (Cambridge handbooks in psychology)*. Cambridge, UK: Cambridge University Press. doi:10.1017/CBO9780511977244

Sweller, J. (1988). Cognitive load during problem solving: Effects on learning. *Cognitive Science, 12*(2), 257–285. doi:10.120715516709cog1202_4

Sweller, J., Van Merriënboer, J., & Paas, F. (1998). Cognitive architecture and instructional design. *Educational Psychology Review, 10*(3), 251–296. doi:10.1023/A:1022193728205

Teh, C. L., Wan Ismail, W. M. F., & Toh, S. C. (2010). Motivation, learning and educational game design for primary school students in Malaysia. In Proceedings of Global Learn Asia Pacific 2010 (pp. 1830-1838). Association for the Advancement of Computing in Education (AACE).

Thorndike, E. L. (2017). Educational Psychology (2nd ed.). South Yarra, Victoria, Australia: Leopold Classic Library.

Torrisi-Steele, G. (2008). Pedagogical perspectives on m-learning. In M. Khosrow-Pour (Ed.), *Encyclopedia of information science and technology* (2nd ed.; pp. 3041–3046). Hershey, PA: IGI Global Publishing.

Tyler, R. W. (1949). *Basic principles of curriculum and instruction.* Chicago, IL: The University of Chicago Press.

UNESCO, United Nations Educational, Scientific, and Cultural Organization. (2013). *The future of mobile learning: Implications for policy makers and planners.* Paris, France: UNESCO Publications.

Upbin, B. (2011). Codecademy: Next Frontier In Digital Education Movement. *Forbes, 2.* Retrieved from http://www.forbes.com/sites/bruceupbin/2011/12 /02/2775/#a785926bcd95

Van de Pol, J., Volman, M., & Beishuizen, J. (2010). Scaffolding in teacher–student interaction: A decade of research. *Educational Psychology Review, 22*(3), 271–296. doi:10.100710648-010-9127-6

Von Glasersfeld, E. (1996). *Studies in Mathematics Education.* Abington, UK: Routledge.

Von Glasersfeld, E. (2001) The radical constructivist view of science. The Impact of Radical Constructivism on Science, 6(1–3), 31–43.

Vygotsky, L. S. (1929). The problem of the cultural development of the child. *The Journal of Genetic Psychology, 36,* 415–434.

Vygotsky, L. S. (1978). *Mind in society – The development of higher psychological processes* (M. Cole, V. John-Steiner, S. Scribner, & E. Souberman, Eds.). Cambridge, MA: Harvard University Press.

Vygotsky, L. S. (1986). *Thought and Language* (A. Kozulin, Ed.). The MIT Press. (Original work published 1934)

Ware, C. (2004). Foundation for a science of data visualization. In *Information visualization: perception for design* (2nd ed.). San Francisco: Morgan Kaufmann Publishers. doi:10.1016/B978-155860819-1/50004-2

Ware, C. (2008). *Visual thinking for design.* San Francisco, CA: Morgan Kaufmann Publishers.

Wong, A., Leahy, W., Marcus, N., & Sweller, J. (2012). Cognitive load theory, the transient information effect and e-learning. *Learning and Instruction, 22*(6), 449-457.

Yoon, D., & Narayanan, N. H. (2004). Mental imagery in problem solving: An eye tracking study. In *Proceedings of the 2004 Symposium on Eye Tracking Research and Applications* (pp. 77-84). New York: Association for Computing Machinery, Inc. 10.1145/968363.968382

Zeki, S. (1993). *Vision of the brain.* Hoboken, NJ: Wiley-Blackwell.

Zeki, S. (2001). Artistic creativity and the brain. *Science, 293*(5527), 51-52. doi:10.1126cience.1062331

Zheng, R., & Gardner, M. K. (2017). *Handbook of Research on Serious Games for Educational Applications.* Hershey, PA: IGI Global. doi:10.4018/978-1-5225-0513-6

# Section 3

# Visual Projects Based on Bioinspired and Science–Based Solutions

Chapter 6

# Active Learning Aimed at Visual Development

## ABSTRACT

*This chapter is about possible ways to engage students in active participation and find ways to secure that good grade means not only a good memorization for tests but also a good understanding of the course content. The text describes active learning, which may happen through sketching, depicting processes and products, and finally creating a visual message often constructed in a color-coded metaphorical way. Each project is related to a selected subject area, but the solution of the project can be seen as the specific type of the art. Developing good writing skills is required to create a storyline/storytelling that contains a development of action leading to a conclusion. Projects integrating science and art may be provided in the form of an unending, looped animation, video, or many other containers. Artists have always actively participated in events and resulting changes in societies. Developments in technologies, especially in computing, have strong impact on the ways artists create and thus contribute to cultural and social life.*

## 6.1. ENGAGING STUDENTS IN COGNITIVE LEARNING ACTIVITIES

In contrast with the students' intrinsic interest in learning, education in schools is based on extrinsic rewards and undermines learner responsibility. Cognitive learning involves meaningful learning. Meaningful learning through creating art is an active, integrative learning, contrary to the hands-on or verbatim,

DOI: 10.4018/978-1-7998-1651-5.ch006

step-by-step, rote learning by memorization and repetition of fragmented texts, which are not integrated with existing concepts, cognitive structures, or experiences. While working with students, it could be more efficient to avoid using tests on the daily basis, and to give students a test only when standardized tests are required by the school districts. The great number of textbooks contains tests at the end of each chapter, and students often scan the book seeking only words and terms included into the tests. As a result, a good grade doesn't mean a good understanding of the course content.

Cognitive learning may involve students to relate new concepts and processes to what they already know. They may organize them as verbal phrases or in a visual way as graphics. Cognitive learning may relate to higher order concepts in a cognitive structure, previous experiences related to new concepts and processes, and active translation of learned material into one's own constructs and creations. In such cases visual approach to data presentation may support cognitive approach to instruction and may ease the burden of the cognitive load. Many people would agree that visual style of learning might reduce intrinsic cognitive load in structuring information, by shifting the explaining process from abstract to meaningful parts, which may be easier to learn and remember. With a visual approach to learning and instruction, students draw sketches in order to capture the essence of the process under study, and control composition of their projects.

There are several possible ways to involve students' interest and engage them in active participation. Activities and projects listed below may encourage students to think independently and work on problems without answering questions like everybody else.

- **Presentation:** Of a specific theme may become one of active forms of learning. Students may choose themes that are close to their personal interests from the course content comprising the set of themes. After that students may design with their teacher a calendar of presentations. The form of a presentation may include an illustrated Power Point Presentation, video made by a student, a graphic novel including text and sketches, a poster, a speech or talk explaining photos made by a student, or other forms of visual/verbal presentation of a theme. The time of a presentation should be short enough, so it wouldn't interfere with the normal arrangement of a lesson; about 10 minutes duration seems sensible.

- **A Timeline**: Display may be focused on visual organization of acquired knowledge and used as a tool for comparing progress in a selected field with events occurring other areas of science or knowledge. This form of presentation may be useful for learning history, art history, progress in technology pertaining to the leading subject studied in the class, and many other topics. A student will place one after the other images and texts telling about events or concepts according to time, space, and context. Successive dates of these items will be placed on the horizontal axis. Images illustrating the events or concepts can be sketches on cards, photos, cutouts, or pictures clipped from magazines. Students may complete this project individually or make it in small teams.

For example, a timeline about art history or history of music, one would be asked to record other types of arts, such as architecture, sculpture, or poetry, and comment on important artists or composers who were active at a particular time frame and might have influence other artists. At the same time a depiction of inventions, as well as religious and political movements and trends would be needed to show mutual involvement and developments. Color-coding techniques, three dimensional solutions, or time-based media might help depicting the progression of a particular discipline in time. A completed project would be colorful, with colors assigned to particular media of art or trends in art.

Figure 1 shows a work by Anna Ursyn entitled "Timeline."

Color-coding is a useful tool for creating visual learning projects. When creating a timeline, some political, dynastic, or religious concepts are abstract and so they are difficult to present them in a visual way. A decorative motif of a fleur-de-lis (a stylized lily) may serve as a symbol of such a concept. In case of a timeline of art history, colors may be assigned to events and concepts belonging to particular media of art: painting, architecture, sculpture, ceramics, graphic arts, photography, computer graphics, digital art, film, performance, poetry, or many others. The final project would contain interlacing colors on a timeline, which would help to correlate facts and learn in an integrated way.

- **An Essay:** a short paper written by a student about a selected theme can be presented in front of the class and then discussed. Students will learn how to design their paper so it could be accepted for publication; they become familiar about the copyright law and how much they can draw from the online sources. In a similar way as presentations, a calendar of paper presentations will be created, and it will limit the presentation time to about 10 minutes.

*Figure 1. Timeline*
*(© 2018, A. Ursyn. Used with permission)*

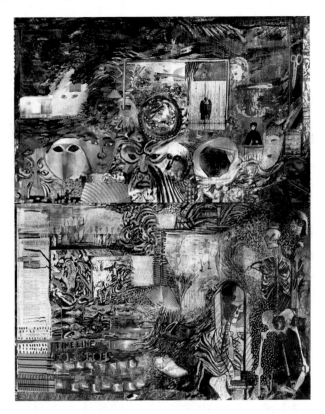

- **A Critical Analysis** written by a student as a response to attending a theater, a performance, a movie, or a sport event can be followed by reaction from the classmates. The kind of the event should relate to the main subject of the course. Students describe their experience by analyzing facts about the artwork and the artist, formal and technical elements of the work, its cultural context, and assessing its expressive qualities. Before this assignment students make themselves familiar with the handout about writing a critique:

- **A survey**: An investigation of the opinions of a handful of professional people about their work and experiences. The task of surveying may broaden students' comprehension about the subject they are learning in the class, when they extract specific data from people who work in professions related to this subject. This project may strengthen interest and motivation for learning, as many times students are not able to connect the learning material with any future perspectives for their future vocation, career, and employment. Surveys are usually conducted by phone, mail, via the internet, or face-to-face, but in this case students should prepare a list of questions and then ask them personally. Students may also learn about qualitative research methods that focus on observation of people's meanings, opinions, definitions, and descriptions but not on numerical data or mathematical evidence.

- **Quizzes** may be an informal way of the assessment of students' preparedness and knowledge. A quiz designed as a form of game involves students in answering questions correctly. The winner may earn a small award of some kind. A group of students may also produce questions by themselves, to ask members of another group. Generating questions maybe a valuable form of learning.

- **A Multiple-Choice Test:** where students are asked to select only correct answers out of the choices from a list, may be an effective tool for a teacher, when alternative options require finding the best answer based on thinking about the material learned. The proper answer, as well as other answers should not be taken from a textbook word for word, to avoid students' learning by rote and promote problem solving. Other forms of tests can be useful, such as true-false questions; pick one question; fill in the blanks; or a matching list.

- **Classroom Discussion About a Colleague's Work**: Students write papers, develop presentations on a topic that interests them, and then share their work with their classmates to learn from them and to discuss concepts. For example, the "Elements and principles of design in various disciplines" theme evokes a variety of solutions related to individual interests of students and their plans for future careers. The themes offered by students this year included analyses about what is the importance of the elements and principles of design in art, photography, acting, language learning, history and ancient history, law and criminal justice, teaching (especially elementary and special education), human services, economics, business world, legalities, psychology, medical field, public health, dentistry, nursing, therapy (especially physical therapy, behavior analysis/therapy, pediatric speech therapy), sign language interpreting, art therapy for prisoners, forensic science (bloodstain analysis), aerospace engineering, social media (especially Instagram), club events setting, sports coaching and organizations, mastering scuba diving, football (especially NFL), cooking, dog shows, and more.

WebQuest (https://createwebquest.com/index.php/) is an online-based instructional tool developed by Bernie Dodge in 1995 and used in K-12 education. It offers lessons built by teachers and students, with the teacher being the one to provide links to required reading. A WebQuest usually includes sections for Introduction, Task, Process, Evaluation, Conclusion, and Credits. According to Zheng and Gardner (2017), WebQuest activities are aimed at supporting inquiry-oriented learning with an emphasis on developing learners' critical thinking and social skills as well as their ability to construct new knowledge.

## 6.2. INTEGRATIVE LEARNING PROJECTS

In fine arts, the artwork is often organized as a portrait, a landscape, a still life, and an abstract art. One may also choose to counterpose art forms such as realism versus abstract, portrait versus geometry, or create other points of reference. With the access to the computing and other technologies, these categories are being expanding toward other forms. Examples may include interactive installations (starting from the works of Myron Kruger), performances, virtual reality, 3D printed art, wearable, ubiquitous, and nano-art, mathematics- and bio-inspired art, visualization, simulation, visual music (with fiber-optic light projections), and more. The portrait, landscape, still life, and abstract art forms may serve as basic structures for integrative projects. The creation of illustrated and annotated web resources may provide materials for visual learning.

Accordingly, the types of projects can be seen as a portrait (verbal profile and a visage), a landscape of the presented issue, a still life, and an abstract telling about the theme, along with the time-based, interactive, or other computer-based solutions offered by those who want to explore and experiment beyond the traditional art categories.

- A 'portrait' approach to the presentation; a visage of a person implying the inner mental states, psychological, social, historical, or professional portraits, along with a verbal profile may tell more than a sole account of facts.

## Project: Inventing Metaphors Which Show Individual Features

Devise metaphors for some features you are going to characterize in a portrait you are going to draw, such as youth or old age, frailty, fidelity, sophistication, refinement, harshness in relation to others, etc. Then, create visual metaphors of these concepts by drawing simple symbols that characterize the person you are going to portray. Consider using your sketches in your visual portrait. Then, employ these metaphors in sentences you would use in your verbal portrait of a person.

- A 'landscape' approach will result in interior and exterior landscapes providing a background for the issues under discussion and the supporting information. A great part of the world's fine art is created in the terms of landscape. Such personal, cultural, social, and political landscapes could be discussed in terms of their structure with the use of current tools for data organizing. Visual and verbal communication in and outside of such groups can be visualized with the use of drawing a concept map and constructing semantic webs about the communication (with topics and links).

It may be a personal landscape such as that of Marcel Proust, or a depiction of small societies and groups as described, for example in the Vladimir Nabokov's Ada, works of Franz Kafka, Albert Camus, or Witold Gombrowicz. Cultures, social issues, beliefs, and values cherished by such groups can be presented as landscapes created by the readers of this book and the students, indicating when, and where, and who, with a portrait or a group portrait treated as a document and placed somewhere in the background. Many literary connotations and examples can be discussed here.

## Project: A Familiar Scene

Our perception of a familiar place may depend both on external conditions such as time of a day or night and on internal state of our serenity or despair. For many reasons, we may receive two different glimpses of a familiar landscape as a cutout and its remaining shell.

We may recognize objects according to their simple basic shapes. In terms of Gestalt principles, we react to general shapes and immediately assign meaning to them because our brain has a tendency to react holistically in an analog, self-organizing manner, as the whole is greater than the sum of its parts.

Depict a familiar scene as you can see it in two different states of mind or moods. Focus your attention on those features, which would emphasize your mood. You may want to present your familiar landscape in a synthetic way, with little attention to details (except the emotionally important ones).

- A 'still life' approach leading to organizing realities of our life. A still life may comprise objects telling about the workplace, requisites essential for people fulfilling their goals, desires, and ambitions, tools (transient, telling about time), period- and profession-related costumes (such as for a priest or a general). There would be a lot of fun to collect examples of iconic objects, symbols, rituals, and props, which serve our still life we live in. And to inspect some ready-made setups that make up the TV, film, web, commercials, and some other media events. The same objects have quite different quality and meaning in a changed configuration, in different still-life arrangement, and tell a lot about person's approach to reality and about the lifestyle.

- The 'abstract art' approach is important for the development of visual communication, art, and literature. With this approach, the theme of a project is introduced with the use of art visual and verbal art that examines human interior without objectivity; the insider's view encounters impartial representation of reality. Many methods of expression in writing were breaking the rules of the time, place, or action unity and consistency. They shaped free records of consciousness, associations, and implications. We can find them in novels by James Joyce, Marcel Proust, or Jean Genet. This approach provides a great moment for talking about creating languages for designing communication tools, both among humans and in human-computer interaction.

- As for the non-traditional, the dimensional, time-based, or interactive art, we may look for styles in literature that can grasp the multidimensionality of being and violate time restrictions. Maybe, the open work cherished by Umberto Eco, Robert Pinsky, William Gibson; the *nouveau Roman* such as Les Gommes (the Erasers) by Alain Rob-Grillet; the interactive novels where the development of action depends on the reader, and interactive novels on the web, with active co-authoring by the reader who may change the character's features and fates.

## Instruction in Art Production Based on Science and Technology

Learning projects have been introduced on many levels; they can be produced with the use of traditional tools such as pencils, crayons, paints, and tools for 3D projects, or they may be completed with the use of computer software or programming, depending on the reader's preferences and skills. Elements of art, which are taught in schools and at the university art departments, may relate well to many other disciplines and be helpful in learning many disciplines.

## Project: 'Maps'

Spatial distribution of objects on a selected terrain can be metaphorically represented as 2D, 3D, or as a digital map. However, the map design depends on the map agenda that defines the map features and traits of objects to be mapped. Maps can represent virtual or fictional space; a map can present brain structures or a DNA molecule. Cartography is the science and practice of producing maps, which combine science, aesthetics, and techniques. Geographic coordinates on a map identify positions of places shown on a map. There is a network of lines on maps representing parallel latitudes that show the north–south position of a place on the Earth surface from the Equator to the North or South Pole, and longitudes that define the position of a point east or west of a meridian in Greenwich, England, accepted as a $0°$ longitude. In order to place a marker or position of an object on a map, an address of interest is translated into geographic coordinates (that means its latitude and longitude). This process is called geocoding. Reverse geocoding means converting geographic coordinates into an existing address.

Maps were first drawn manually, and then digitally with the use of GPS, laser rangefinders, stereographic aerial photography, satellite imagery, and remote sensing applying radar and laser altimeters, ultrasound and acoustic gauges, light detectors such as LIDAR, radio- and photometers, and many more.

General maps are addressed for a wide audience and they contain many different features. They may have been designed with a different scale of a map: the ratio of a distance on the map to the corresponding distance on the ground. For example, at a map in scale 1:62,500, 1" on a map equals 1 mile on the ground. The area of the United States is covered with a series of more than 53,300 topographic maps having the scale 1: 24,000, produced by the

United States Geological Survey. Topographic maps use contour lines showing elevation, railroads, highways and local roads, freeways, interstates, bridges, and dams, among other public infrastructure. They also present hydrographic features of the terrain such as rivers and lakes, geographic place names, and a variety of cultural features. A legend or key explains a pictorial language of the map (e.g., symbols for an airport, hotel, railway station, or tourist information), and a bar scale tells about relation between the real distances and those represented on the map. There is also the National Geologic Map Database providing information concerning earth science.

To describe the distinctive nature of a terrain and place it in a wider context, specialists show this terrain on a map that makes a representation of this area and defines its characteristics in either physical or political terms. A map is an abstract, symbolic depiction in two or three dimensions showing accurate geometric relationships in proportion; it may also be interactive. A physical map focuses on the terrain landforms such as mountains, plains, rivers, or deserts, and their natural boundaries, while a political map tells about characteristics established by humans, for example properties, blocks, towns and cities, counties, and states. A map shows also a maze of private, service, business, county, state, and interstate roads, railroad tracks, bridges and viaducts, tunnels, and also squares, parks, and monuments. Figure 2 shows a work by Anna Ursyn entitled "Uneven Symmetry."

*Figure 2. Uneven Symmetry*
*(© 2018, A. Ursyn. Used with permission)*

Interactive satellite and aerial maps provide users with earth views, street views and offer driving directions and live traffic updates. Geographic Information Systems (GIS) Data inform about elevation (3D Elevation Program), biology and ecosystem data (such as Protected Area Database), and more. Digital cartography presents data as a virtual image providing detailed representation of a selected area. Digital mapping supports the Global positioning System (GPS) satellite network and enables the automotive navigation system, which is becoming important in developing the self-driving cars navigation. The automotive navigation is based on a mathematical graph theory, which examines the shortest path problem aimed at best connecting two points in a large network (with nodes in a graph as road junctions or intersections and edges as road segments) in a shortest, cheapest, or fastest way. MapQuest is an interactive free online web mapping service, which is often used on web browsers. MapQuest is available in many countries where it provides driving directions and street-level details, voice guided navigation, real-time information about traffic, and other services.

Thematic cartography serves specific purposes showing selective data, for example providing statistical, cultural, political, historical, or social information. Cultural anthropology studies cultural variations among humans, and related information is often presented on maps. For example, cultural geographic maps show places in which some kinds of public events are organized, such as music competitions, film festivals, and theatrical productions. Maps may as well display locations of events related to food or the world of fashion clothes. One may draw a map informing about any hobby.

There are plenty of imaginary maps created by authors writing in many literary genres such as the novel, fantasy literature, fictional histories, and science fiction. Maybe the most famous are maps drawn by a novelist and scholar J. R. R. Tolkien for *his* classic high-fantasy works *The Hobbit* and *The Lord of the Rings*.

## Project: A Bird's-Eye View Landscape

Choose a map with a scale 1: 24,000 or even more detailed, because as the closer an object is to you, the more detail you can detect. Imagine that you have a bird's-eye view on the scene. Looking at a selected fragment of a map create a bird's-eye view landscape, drawing what's described on this map. While working with the graphic software such as Adobe Photoshop, Adobe Illustrator, or CorelDRAW, use the 'trace edges' tool, and then assign different colors to separate layers (use color-coding). Later on, add some trees, plants, and animals, to say nothing about people, buildings, and machines that can be seen from above. Save your file, and then save your file again under different name and modify this copy of your drawing to create an abstract painting from it.

Your map can inspire you to create a fictional story about imaginary land where you will depict facts, things, beings, and events with their spatial and temporal relations. You may use geocoding as a storytelling tool by translating your fictional objects into geographic coordinates (that means its latitude and longitude) and then changing them along the timeline according to your story.

## Project: A Facies Map

A facies mean a rock and its features (chemical, physical, and biological) that distinguish it from neighboring rocks. Draw a map representing a landscape in terms of geological time. Use letters to write up geological formations (layers of rocks such as sandstone, limestone, schist, etc.), coding the processes by colors or letters. You should make two kinds of changes in order to transform your landscape into a map: try to transform epochs that you have depicted in your landscape into miles, then try to represent miles as inches.

## Project: Designing an Own Home

Imagine you are the owner of the land shown as the map you have just designed. You are going to dig a well, and then build your house and outbuildings, construct a paved road, reserve a terrain for a pasture, as well as install derricks and drilling machinery. What else would you do on this land? It's like a Monopoly game. To plan your work, you will need three representations of your ground based on your first map: a bird's-eye view landscape showing what's described on this map; a cross section drawn as a side view representation of this land (whatever exists below the ground level should also be shown, e.g., a well, a basement); and an aerial view of your land with all objects. Obtain information about the content of soil, its bacterial diversity and possible metal toxicity (Gans, Wolinsky, & Dunbar, 2005).

Now, dig a well. Choose a type of a well you will make. A drilled well is constructed with a rotary-drilling machine that penetrates into the bedrock (solid rock under loose soil or other deposit); a dug well is excavated to below the water table (the upper surface of the ground that is saturated with water) and lined with stones or bricks; a driven well is made by driving a tube into the earth to a water table above the bedrock. You will need water for plants if you want to grow any kind of crop, vegetables, or flowers. Water is necessary to plants because it accounts for 80%-95% of the plant's protoplasm, is necessary for photosynthesis, because all nutrients carried into and throughout the plant are solved in water, and also it provides the turgidity by which the plant keeps itself in proper position (Donahue, Miller, & Shickluna, 1977). Maybe you find a place near to a stream with a water current, flow, and waves. Gravitation makes water flow along the stream and wind makes waves on water because of pressure changes. Decide what location would be appropriate for your well. Then work on locating other objects. Name your residence. Make sure your picture fits your visual preferences: that you like it. Figure 3 shows a work "Water" by Kirsten Bruning.

Finally, draw a bird's eye view image of the main floor of your house. This time it wouldn't be a map or a plan but a representational drawing depicting your dream home. What kind of appliances would you need and which style of furniture would you choose? Would you prefer objects produced now, according to contemporary Eco-design trends, or would you try to find furniture made by old furniture makers, such as constructed in the revival styles, the Art and Craft movement, Early North American style, Modernism style (Art Deco, De Stijl, Bauhaus, Vienna Secession), or other style?

*Figure 3. Water*
*(© 2018, K. Bruning. Used with permission)*

## Project: Habitat, Biome, Ecosystem

Every animal or a plant has its own natural habitat, an environment where the species it belongs to can live in favorable physical and biological conditions. Physical features may include comfortable temperature range, light conditions, air humidity and soil moisture, along with a configuration of a place where a creature can find a shelter protecting from bad weather and predators and good for taking care of their offspring. Biological conditions include availability of food, presence of other members of a species to secure possibilities of mating and reproduction, and often presence of other species needed for a symbiotic or parasitic life.

While a habitat may mean a large or a small arrangement of organisms, for example those living on a rock, a rotten log, or in another place, we talk about a biome when there is a large community of plants and animals naturally occupying a large area; we thus talk about major habitats. An ecosystem usually describes a major habitat comprising natural population of various species living in a common terrain and interacting with their physical environment. Thus a biome may comprise several habitats.

Examples of ecosystems are: forests of different kinds, deserts, glaciers, tundra, or grassland.

We may also see descriptions of human ecosystems such as rural or city habitats. Figure 6 shows a city habitat drawn by Adalia Names.

Authors describe also inland (freshwater rivers, lakes, or swamps) and marine aquatic ecosystems with ocean habitats, coral reefs, beech ecosystems (some influenced by the high and low tides caused by the combined effects of the gravitational forces exerted by the Moon and the Sun, and by the rotation of the Earth), as well as underground (cave) ecosystems. Figures 7 and 8 present two works about beaches: by Matt Zilkenat and by Phil Crews.

*Figure 4. Desert*
*(© 2018, D. Caro. Used with permission)*

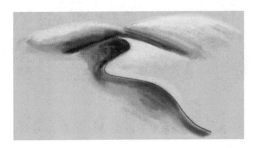

*Figure 5. Desert*
*(© 2018, W. Weston. Used with permission)*

*Figure 6. A city habitat*
*(© 2018, A. Names. Used with permission)*

*Figure 7. Beaches*
*(© 2018, M. Zilkenat. Used with permission)*

*Figure 8. A Beach*
*(© 2018, P. Crews. Used with permission)*

Forest ecosystems may include the old growth forest with many layers of plant growth, coniferous forest of evergreen trees having needle leaves and cones that bear the seeds (such as pine, fir and hemlock fir, red cedar, and spruce), deciduous forest with broadleaf trees (e.g., oak, maple, beech, hickory), also rainforest and tropical forest with many layers and big canopies. Mountain habitats are also stratified, with coniferous trees at lower level, and shrubs such as junipers and aspens growing higher in the mountains. Figures 9 and 10 present two works about forest ecosystem: by Ethan Funk-Breay, and by Tatiana Ingino Silberberg.

Many artists used to paint utopian visions of such biomes, often calling them the Gardens of Eden. For example, Lucas Cranach the Elder created his works in early German Renaissance, Antonio Pisanello worked in early Italian Renaissance, Pieter Brueghel the Elder in Flemish Renaissance, and a Flemish painter Peter Paul Rubens, they all depicted gardens where animals coexist with people. Also, Hieronymus Bosch created (maybe not so peaceful) *The Earthly Paradise – Garden of Eden* in his triptych *The Garden of Earthly Delights*.

In your project, present an ecosystem of your choice. A public green area may be natural and kept in a natural state, or it may be planted by people on some reclaimed place and then used for recreation. Design an imaginary landscape consisting of more than one ecosystem where animals can live peacefully in utopian conditions. Draw parts where people changed the living conditions and created human made biomes. Figure 11 shows a work by Liza Shoup titled "Rainforest Ecosystem."

*Figure 9. A Forest*
*(© 2018, E. Funk-Breay. Used with permission)*

*Figure 10. Forest*
*(© 2018, T. Ingino. Used with permission)*

*Figure 11. Rainforest Ecosystem*
*(© 2018, L. Shoup. Used with permission)*

## Project: Big and Small

Choose two animals representing two species, one big and another one small, for example, an ape and an ant. They are living on the same terrain and experience the same climatic conditions. Create a landscape as seen by a big animal and then another landscape that presents the small animal's point of view. Looking on a grain of sand or a pebble imagine you are as small as an ant, so the grain of sand or a small rock becomes a mountain for you. Create drawings that show close-ups of grains to create a landscape from the ant eye's perspective. On each drawing show perspective and a scale of objects. Present how the same landscape may offer completely different advantages or threats resulting from the size of the animal, and try to convey the comfort or drama of the scene.

## Project: Soil

This project will involve creating a design for a stain window inspired by a variety of the soil colors and textures. Depending on the geology of mineral materials existing in the underlying layers of rocks (called parent materials), sedimentation, relief of terrain, climate, and ongoing interactions in the natural environment, soil can be seen as a complex and dynamic medium having varied chemical, physical, biological, and ecological features. Water, air, temperature, solar radiation, microbes (bacteria and fungi), and other soil inhabitants, plants, animals, and human users create a dynamic balance deciding on the agricultural and landscape values of soils. We can see processes going in distinctive soils as an interaction of our lithosphere (outer rigid shell of our planet), atmosphere (layers of gases surrounding our planet), hydrosphere (combined masses of water), and biosphere (a zone of life on Earth, with all habitats), and these processes may be continuing now or they might relate to the older past such as ancient glaciations. Thus, soil is a mixture of minerals, gases, liquids, organic matter, and organisms. The common soil parent materials include quartz $SiO_2$, calcite $CaCO_3$, feldspar $KAlSi_3O_8$–$NaAlSi_3O$–$CaAl_2Si_2O_8$, and mica $K(Mg,Fe)_3AlSi_3O_{10}(OH)_2$. Materials can be residual (weathered materials from the bedrock), transported (deposited by water, ice, wind, or gravity), or organic (accumulated from growing plants). Climate may influence processes in soil by adding lime in low rainfall areas; adding acid in humid areas; erosion on steep hillsides and deposition of eroded materials downstream; and chemical weathering in warm and humid regions. Topography is an important factor, especially on steep slopes or depressions and wetlands. Changes in climate caused by the global warming can be found at https://en.wikipedia.org/wiki/Portal:Climate#/media/File:Global_Warming_Map.jpg

Soils support plant growth, store and purify water, modify atmosphere, and create a habitat for living organisms. It is the most plentiful ecosystem on Earth. Soil can be solid, porous, and watery. Soil texture depends on relative proportion of common components of soil: sand, silt, and clay, a colloidal, crystalline, or amorphous material (Wikipedia – Soil).

Researchers estimate there are around one billion cells per gram of soil, and from 50,000 species per gram to over a million per gram of soil (Gans, Wolinsky, & Dunbar, 2005). Ants, earthworms, moles, beetles, and millepedes mix, aerate, and drain the soil. However, urban residents tend to cultivate their lawns by applying pesticides of different kinds that destroy insects, plants other than grass, and other organisms. The same applies to majority of agricultural areas. Moreover, when a great area of land is covered with grass only, there is no food for bees, butterflies, and other insects.

Colors and patterns of soil depend on the presence of soil minerals (e.g., iron, silica, or sulfur), organic matter, drainage, and oxidation, among other factors. There are red sediments from Red River in Oklahoma and yellow ones from the Yellow River in China. Volcanoes add dark color of lava resulting from cooling magma. Colorado is famous as a colorful state because of the variety of its soils. We can sometimes see a colorful pattern of pigments within a soil.

## Project: A Stain Window

Using a graphic software program or traditional tools create a design for a stain window inspired by a variety of the soil colors and textures. Inspiration about colors and patterns may come from looking at photographs published in magazines (for example, in National Geographic) or online. Examine colors associated with the presence of minerals: dark red color occurring where is iron and ferric oxide; reddish or yellowish-brown color of rust resulting from oxidation of iron or steel; red-brown or red-orange color of copper turning into a green layer of verdigris (copper carbonate) on the roofs of old buildings; purple color of copper oxide; white or white-yellowish limestone: calcite and calcium carbonate ($CaCO_3$), maybe with preserved skeletal fragments of marine organisms such as coral, foraminifera, and mollusks.

Inspiration about the beauty of stain glass can be drawn from online images showing both medieval stain glass windows and contemporary projects. There is also ample literature of this subject. A project based on colors and textures of soil may take form of abstract art, can present geometric patterns, or can be enhanced with a rock art (Malotki, & Dissanayake, 2018). This theme can be also solved as a patchwork. To add a 3D effect you may want to apply floral or animal motifs to the array of soil based planes.

## Project: A Perfect Weather

Create a composition of a wind pattern. First, create a pattern (transform and repeat for your image). Visit a 'Wind' page, and then find an interactive display of real time wind activity in the US. Use transport and repeat function in your code. Use repetition in code.

Figure 12 presents a work by Lena Harper entitled "Duality sunset path."

## About Climate

Climate tells about weather conditions averaged over a period of time. Past changes in climate are examined by paleoclimatology and historical studies of climate related to human history and activities. Scientists also study climate patterns, for example, a global ocean-atmosphere phenomenon El Niño–Southern Oscillation, and then create global climate models. Previous events, pattern recognition, and other factors help climatologists to make weather forecasts. Figure 13 presents work by Anna Ursyn "Climate Change."

*Figure 12. Duality sunset path*
*(© 2018, L. Harper. Used with permission)*

*Figure 13. Climate Change*
*(© 2018, A. Ursyn. Used with permission)*

## About Wind

In the past, wind has been personified as supernatural wind gods. Look at old prints, engravings (prints made from metal plates with a design incised with a cutting tool), gravures (prints made from a design incised or engraved into a material), and photogravures (where engraving on a metal plate is etched according to a photographic image). Examine the style they represent. You may want to get inspiration from the old maps. There are sometime pictured faces in the sky placed in the corner of the map, with the ballooned cheeks blowing air into the space, serving as a metaphor of wind. Apply this style belonging to the past to your futurological story, which will forecast the time when people would be able to control weather. Your storytelling will combine drawings with text to take form of a comics or animation. First present various kinds of clouds, and then consider the role of wind in the motion of clouds. Describe how people would distribute rains to the places where watering is needed, by moving clouds across skies or causing moisture condensation in the form of rain. Explain how would it prevent the occurrences of draught, the floods, the mudslides, and other natural disasters. Invent fictional devices that would be able to draw a cloud or suck it dry. While drawing scenes illustrating this utopian scenario, you may want to use principles of design to guide your composition, for example symmetry to show the waves of the wind. Then use dots for rain, snowflakes for snow, etc. FYI: Images are on the internet; they are very old but still copyrighted.

Generally, wind is a current of gas (e.g., solar wind – a stream of plasma, charged particles ejected from the sun) blowing with any speed and direction but on Earth wind means the flow of air. We used to tell about gusts, squalls, breeze, gale, storm, and hurricane according to the wind strength and duration. Winds move from the higher to the lower pressure of air. Heating of a land surface can cause local wind. Global winds result from differences in amount of solar energy absorbed in different climate zones, from different temperature existing at the equator and the polar zones, and because the rotation of Earth. Humans use the power of wind for transportation (e.g., sailing ships), mechanical work (e.g., windmills), and electricity (e.g., wind turbines). Sports and recreation based on wind power include gliders or sailplanes, hang gliding, hot air ballooning, kite flying, kite skiing, kite land boarding, kite surfing, paragliding, and windsurfing). Winds can change the landforms; they can act for the benefit of soils (for example, creating loess) or they can cause erosion and dust storms. Winds exert various effects on animals, mostly because of wind chills (combination of wind and cold temperatures) and plants causing seeds' dispersal, but also uprooting and breaking trees, among other effects (Wind, 2019). Data visualization about wind can be found at hint.fm/wind. Figure 14 presents Anna Ursyn's "Gusty Winds Possible."

## Clouds

Clouds form due to convection – rising of warmer, less dense water vapor and sinking of the colder, denser one due to gravity. Solar radiation heats the ground and the air with water vapor flows upward. As its temperature decreases in the upper regions, the air can hold less water vapor; it condenses into clouds, which contain billions of water droplets averaging about 10 micrometer in diameter and ice crystals. The process of sublimation, caused by sunshine acting directly on snow, occurs when snow goes into transition directly to the gas phase (without melting into water).

*Figure 14. Gusty Winds Possible*
(© 2018, A. Ursyn. Used with permission)

The main patterns of clouds are cirrus, stratus, and cumulus, with combinations of these types such as a thin layer of cirrostratus or a cirrocumulus, which looks like cotton tufts. Cirrus clouds are feathery, contain ice crystals, and are usually at altitudes above 20,000 feet above the ground. They do not produce rain. The smooth, gray sheets of altostratus, iridescent colorful altocumulus, and gray nimbostratus appear between 6,000 and 20,000 feet above the ground. Stratus, cumulus that looks like cotton balls, and stratocumulus clouds gather usually at 6,000 feet or lower. They usually do not cause rain. When they are dense and dark, they become rainy or snowy. Cumulonimbus can reach 60,000 feet along with the turbulent, upwelling plums of hot air, and may cause torrential rain, lighting with thunders, hail, and even a tornado (Rao, 2013).

There is also a concept of the cloud in computing that means a network on the internet or a set of remote servers; we can use cloud storage, and then store, organize, and process data there. We apply cloud computing when we store and use computer technology on servers. Linux is a leading operating system on servers; it is a family of free and open source operating systems (modeled on UNIX). There is an old quip about a boy asking his father, "What are clouds are made of?" and he's answered, "Linux." Figure 15 shows "All You Can See" by Anna Ursyn.

*Figure 15. All You Can See*
(© 2018, A. Ursyn. Used with permission)

## 6.3. STORYTELLING AS A TEACHING TOOL

The cognitive scientist, linguist, and writer Steven Pinker (2014) shows how the art of writing can be a form of pleasurable mastery and a fascinating intellectual topic in its own right. Students may combine animations showing various features of an object they learn about, into a storytelling-based animation. This can be done with any video-editing program. Storytelling may be presented as manga or animation (comics, cartoons, webisodes, street art, game illustration, app design, and more).

Examples of themes for the storytelling projects are: cosmos, energy, beyond the text illustration, scientific illustration, and literary illustration. Web-design may also serve as a reason for storytelling on the computer. Websites somehow tell a story reflecting the intent of the creator, his/her objective, and how they go about it.

Visual/verbal genres for learning may include storytelling tools such as:

- A novel: Interactive novel.
- Drama: A script for a theatrical play.
- A script for filming, video, and moving images.
- A libretto for an opera, and operetta, for a ballet or the musical.
- Poetry: A poem, a limerick, haiku.
- e-Poetry and visual poetry, e-books.
- Sequential art.
- Electronic novel, graphic novel, graphic narrative, visual narrative.

- Manga and comics.
- Time-based visual material, animation, or a movie.
- Interactive installation.
- Motion graphics and visual narrative.
- Arduino based projects.
- Interpretative drawing.
- Technical writing.
- Ballet (possibly with props), pantomime, and interaction with artificial beings.

In all cases storytelling is the key to effective presentation of a theme. Storytelling may serve for visual/verbal interactions. First, one has to develop (possibly with the use of coding) visual presentation of a selected kind of data. To create composition of the project, a character and its environment have to be defined, followed by thinking about the recipient of the project. One has to think about who is the audience and what are possible ways of redesigning the story for a specific audience, because every audience may have its own needs. Typography – setting types and the appearance of printed material makes written part of the project legible, readable, and appealing for given recipients. For example, small type is not good for small children and the elderly people, while a big font size may be seen offensive for high school students.

A student creating storytelling should think about their portfolio, résumé, and the techniques of hiring used by companies. This calls for thinking about the outcome of visual solutions, the use of shortcuts, and securing the fun element. Video can be stitched together in a video editing program (there are video resources for free or paid video edited programs).

Everybody can create images, one's own story, and then a storyline followed by animation. Projects will show individually created environments and actions of invented characters (avatars) when they react to changes in these environments. First, understanding is needed of underlying processes, products, and forces defining the concept development. Each project starts with a research about characters and their habitat, and also factors such as symbiosis, dangers, characters' equipment and implements (is your character big, fast, strong, and wise?).

The story has to be retold depending on the media: a graphic, a comic, manga, animation, theater performance, VR, a game, a movie, a radio show, etc. Choosing a container of a story will define how the story is being delivered. For example, a short story can be reworked in several ways, which would create various kinds of containers for the same story according to specific settings and styles. Then, by creating illustrations or animations, one can assign visual containers for the written story. Avatars may convey their stories through music, dance, and text. A program or a computer graphics may serve for defining a container for a story.

## Project: Writing a Storyline and a Storyboard

First, write a storyline in a way you would tell this story on your phone. Make it short, interesting, without visual cues. After the storyline is ready, make a storyboard that will organize graphically your storyline with the use of illustrations or simple drawings. Storyboards are used for pre-visualization of your video, animation, motion picture, motion graphic, or any interactive medium.

Make sketches for your story. Familiarize yourself with sketches made by artists such as Chris Lester, Danny Coleman, and Ken Bernstein. Also, make some drawings: draw a manikin, some geometric sketches, and explore by sketching, the positive–negative space relations. Sketching has a cognitive power, enhances the eye–hand–brain coordination, as well as the mind–brain–eye–hand coordination. Application of sketching is often used in storyboarding, brainstorming, for designing cognitive maps, making web trees, planning events and competitions, or arranging conflict reduction.

Your drawings or sketches will serve as frames for your visual storytelling. In video technology a frame is a coded image. If you would like to create animation, you will also define your key frames, which will define starting and ending points of transitions, the timing of the movement. The remaining frames will be filled as in-betweens.

Create a storyboard – a graphic organizer containing sequenced images (usually drawings), simple directions, and dialogues. This storyboard might serve to pre-visualize animation, film, motion graphics, or a sequence of interactive media. Figures 16 a, b, and c show a storyboard template "Computer Kingdom" for a promotional filming designed by Kendra Hirsch.

## Project: Collaborative Storytelling

An example shown below tells about a group project about creating a story. Students of a Computer Graphics course got a task to cooperate on creating a story based on a following text. "A group of students are working late in

*Figure 16a. A storyboard template, part 1*
(© 2019, K. Hirsch. Used with permission)

*Figure 16b. A storyboard template, part 2*
(© 2019, K. Hirsch. Used with permission)

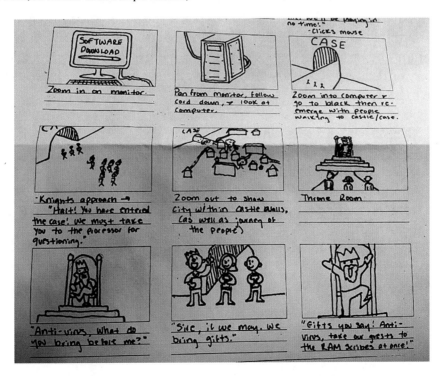

*Figure 16c. A storyboard template, part 3*
(© 2019, K. Hirsch. Used with permission)

the computer lab and all fall asleep… they awake to find they are in a strange place. After some exploring, tackling obstacles, and being attacked by a cursor, they surmise they are inside a Photoshop program. They must discover how to return to their normal selves in real life and get their projects turned in before the deadline. Can they do it?" First, the students listed obstacles that have to be overcome:

1.   They have to discover where they are.
2.   Navigate a computer.
3.   Defeat the cursor attack.
4.   After they realize that a person who has just returned to the classroom from the bathroom tries. somehow to attract their attention and to give them help.
5.   They somehow return to themselves.

After collaborative work students wrote a group story project:

## Digitally Misplaced

– "This assignment is due tomorrow! There's no way we have time to finish this!" Someone says from the corner. Someone else says, "Tell me about it. I'm about to crash…" Some people stand up and leave the room. The classroom grows quiet; the sounds of typing become faint, pens being pulled across the tablets are slowing, and there are a couple thuds as heads hit the table in deep sleep. Before long, the full classroom is asleep.

A bright white light wakes them all, rousing them from their sleep. "Where is this?" "It's too bright, I just wanna go back to sleep!" The group comes to their feet, looking around. As they look at each other they jump, seeing characters that are unfamiliar. Upon looking down they realize they have become the character that they had been working on. Confusion sets over the group. "How did we get here?"

Upon looking up, they see a tool ribbon, and boarders around the room they are in. Some scratch their heads, other walk to the boarder to touch it, and an options screen pops up. "Uh, is this Photoshop?" The rest of the group walks to various parts of the room, touching things and seeing what happens. It becomes clear to the group that they are indeed in Photoshop.

Suddenly, a cursor zooms towards someone in the group and they narrowly are able to avoid it. Someone in the group locks the layer, protecting the group. They look at each other in confusion. "Is someone using their computer?" Someone thinks for a moment, then runs to the taskbar and opens an instance of Word. The others look on in confusion and the cursor stops in its tracks.

– "If we can get a message to them maybe they can get us out of here!!"
People nod in agreement.

They bring up a virtual keyboard and begin typing: "H E L P U S W E A R E T R A P P E D. G E T U S O U T P L E A S E" The cursor starts moving around and clicking things, a vague attempt to get them out. Finally, the cursor hovers over "Export." There is a bright light as a dialogue box is brought up. It becomes blinding.

Everyone sits upright at once, back at their computers, as the student who had left the bathroom stares at the group in astonishment, "yo what?" Everyone looks at each other and is relieved.

– "I'm gonna use Illustrator from now on…" someone says.

# Project: Various Containers for the Same Story

Students choose their preferred story containers, and thus the same story became a script for a theater performance, clips for a video game, a screenplay for a movie, a board game, a comic strip, a cartoon, a book, script for an audio book, an episode for television content, and more. Below are some of students' containers for the "Digitally Misplaced" story.

*Story Container 1. A Playscript for a Play Digitally Misplaced by Madison Spillman*

| ACT I -- SCENE 1 |
| --- |
| THE KIDS IN CLASSROOM 106 ARE UP LATE WORKING ON THEIR FIRST ASSIGNMENT THAT IS DUE IN THE MORNING. CLASS IS ENDING AS LIGHTS COME UP. THE LIGHTS COME UP ON A CLASSROOM SET FILLED WITH MAC COMPUTERS. THERE IS A DOOR LEAVING THE CLASSROOM ON STAGE RIGHT, AND ON STAGE LEFT THERE ARE LARGE FORMAT PRINTERS. THE STUDENTS ALL LOOK EXTREMELY TIRED AND ARE FURIOUSLY TYPING AND DRAWING.PROFESSOR ANNA IS SITTING ON HER DESK AT THE FRONT OF THE ROOM. LIGHTS UP.<br>    **ANNA:** The clock has struck 8:45, which means that another class has come to an end. I will see you all after the weekend, have a good weekend and don't forget to submit your project by tomorrow morning. Put all that you can into this, I am counting on you.<br>ANNA EXITS STAGE RIGHT. THE STUDENTS WATCH CLOSELY TO SEE THE EXACT MOMENT THE DOOR CLOSES BEHIND HER.<br>    **STUDENT 2:** The assignment is due tomorrow!! There is no way we have time to finish this!!<br>STUDENT 2 WAVES HANDS FRANTICALLY IN THE AIR<br>    **STUDENT 1:** Dude this is my fourth espresso shot.<br>THROWS CUP TOWARDS TRASH AND MISSES<br>    **STUDENT 4:** Tell me about it. I'm about to crash…<br>STUDENT 4 EXITS STAGE RIGHT<br>    **STUDENT 3:** My eyes feel really heavy all of a sudden…<br>RUBS EYES<br>    **STUDENT 2:** Yeah me tooooooo…<br>ALL STUDENTS SUDDENLY FALL ASLEEP AND HIT THEIR HEADS ON THEIR KEYBOARDS.<br>BACKOUT |
| ACT I -- SCENE 2 |
| THE KIDS WAKE TO FIND THEMSELVES IN A BRIGHT WHITE ROOM. THEY LOOK AROUND TO SEE THEY MAY HAVE LAUNCHED THEMSELVES INTO THEIR COMPUTERS, AND THEY SOON FIND OUT THEY DON'T LOOK THE SAME AS BEFORE.<br>    **STUDENT 2:** Woah what happened???<br>RUBS HEAD AS IF FEELING PAIN<br>    **STUDENT 3:** My eyes! It is so bright in here!<br>COVERS EYES WITH ARM<br>Break the dialogue with a piece of action?<br>    **STUDENT 1**: I just want to go back to sleep. Woah, wait who are you?!?!?!<br>OPENS EYES TO SEE STUDENT 2 IS NOT THE SAME<br>    **STUDENT 2:** What do you mean? I am the same old meeee. Oh my god what happened to my hand?!?!<br>LOOKS DOWN TO SEE THEY HAVE A YELLOW STUMP FOR A HAND AND A PURPLE ARM<br>    **STUDENT 3:** Why don't I even have any arms?!?!<br>LOOKS DOWN TO SEE THEY ARE A FLOATING BUBBLE OF GUM<br>    **STUDENT 1:** Guys, don't call me crazy but I think we may have turned into our characters…<br>ALL CHARACTERS LOOK DOWN TO SEE THEY ARE THE CREATURE THEY HAVE CREATED<br>    **STUDENT 2:** Guys look up, I think you will recognize where we are.<br>ALL STUDENTS LOOK UP TO SEE TOOL BAR<br>    **STUDENT 3:** Oh my god… we are in Photoshop.<br>BLACKOUT |

*continues on following page*

*Story Container 1. Continued*

| ACT II -- SCENE 3 |
|---|
| AFTER INTERACTING WITH THE ENVIRONMENT, THE STUDENTS ARE CONGREGATED LOOKING AT THE TOOLBAR. SUDDENLY, A LARGE CURSOR COMES TO ATTACK. LIGHTS UP.<br>    **STUDENT 1:** I don't know guys, this is really weird. At least it isn't dangerous in here.<br>AS IF ON CUE, A LARGE CURSOR RACES ON FROM STAGE LEFT<br>    **STUDENT 3:** Ah lets go!!! I have an idea, follow me!<br>THE STUDENTS RACE TO GET TO THE BACKGROUND LAYER AS FAST AS POSSIBLE WHILE AVOIDING THE MOUSE.<br>    **STUDENT 3:** If we lock this layer, the mouse can't get to us. Come on, help me lift this thing!!<br>STUDENTS 1 AND 2 RACE OVER TO LOCK THE LOCK<br>    **STUDENT 2:** Yes! I got it!<br>THE STUDENTS WATCH AS THE CURSOR TRIES TO GET IN BUT CAN'T. CURSOR EXIT STAGE LEFT.<br>    **STUDENT 1:** Nice job guys! We did it!<br>HIGH FIVE<br>    **STUDENT 3:** So does this mean that someone is trying to use this computer?<br>    **STUDENT 1:** I may have a way to get us out of here. Follow me.<br>STUDENTS EXIT STAGE RIGHT<br>BLACKOUT |
| ACT II -- SCENE 4 |
| THE STUDENTS HAVE MADE THEIR WAY TO THE TASK BAR AND HAVE OPENED WORD. LIGHTS UP.<br>    **STUDENT 1:** If my idea is correct, we should be able to type out a help message and someone can get us out of here!<br>    **STUDENT 2:** Ah, I get it. Good idea!! Let's do this.<br>ALL CHARACTERS WORK TO TYPE OUT MESSAGE<br>    **STUDENT 3:** Perfect. It says HELP US WE ARE TRAPPED. GET US OUT OF HERE PLEASE.<br>    **STUDENT 1:** Look!! It's working!!<br>CURSOR COMES BACK ONTO STAGE<br>    **STUDENT 2:** Yes!! He is clicking export!!<br>CURSOR CLICKS EXPORT. WHEN DONE, A BRIGHT LIGHT SHINES AND IT FADES TO BLACK.<br>BLACKOUT |
| ACT II -- SCENE 5 |
| THE KIDS ARE BACK IN THEIR CLASSROOM AND ARE SEATED AT THEIR COMPUTERS.<br>    **STUDENT 1:** It worked! We are back!<br>    **STUDENT 2:** Boy am I glad we are out of there!!<br>STUDENT 4 WALKS BACK INTO THE ROOM, ENTERS STAGE RIGHT<br>    **STUDENT 4:** Man, this project is really making you guys crazy.<br>    **STUDENT 2:** Maybe so, but one thing I know is that I will only be using Illustrator from now on.<br>BLACKOUT AND CURTAIN |

Story Container 2. A Comic Entitled *Digitally Misplaced* by Bri Young
    A comic based on the story "Digitally Misplaced" by Bri Young is shown in Figure 17 a, b, c, d.

# 6.4. THE EVER-CHANGING ROLE OF AN ARTIST

Artists were recording events since the cave life. Later, they were commissioned by kings, aristocracy, or religion patrons to record resemblances, commemorate, or to record significant events such as victories. The invention of photography

*Figure 17a. Digitally Misplaced*
(© 2019, B. Young. Used with permission)

changed that, and artists responded by working in different styles. Computers divided visual recording into digital (in a binary format when bits – zero or one – represent different amplitudes), analog (where pulses in a 2D space have varying amplitudes), and wireframe-based creations (early skeletal 3D models of images with lines and vertices).

Clipart made an easy access to images, often used for decorative purposes. The invention of the internet allowed for sharing, give and take image distribution (cgtextures.com). Social media changed the way artists find inspiration, collaboration, marketing, and jobs. Myron Kruger started interactivity, by following the person entering the black plush filled room with a red laser beam light. Art became useful first for data graphics, and then for information, data, and knowledge visualization. Graphics with explanatory power, icons, symbols, and metaphors shape our lives, behavior, safety, courtesy, and our daily routines, also speeding our actions.

*Figure 17b. Digitally Misplaced*
*(© 2019, B. Young. Used with permission)*

*Figure 17c. Digitally Misplaced*
*(© 2019, B. Young. Used with permission)*

*Figure 17d. Digitally Misplaced*
*(© 2019, B. Young. Used with permission)*

Easy to find wireframes make production smoother and less expensive. Coney Island was known as an exciting source of entertainment. Disney's Magic Kingdom and then EPCOT developed interactive entertainment based on motion, illusion, and different applications of technologies. Michael Jackson's "Black and White" showed the inclusive side of entertainment using the morphing technology. Cellestino Soddu (celestinosoddu.it) used the so-called 'DNA of the city' to be used as guiding data for the computer to build structures matching each city. Lasers allowed for meticulous scanning of large 3D environments, such as sculptures (depicting the tiniest detail of chisel work, or architectural constructions seen from the outside to the inside. 3D objects gain lifelike action powered by natural energies, such as solar sculptures. Nintendo, Autodesk, and SONY changed gaming by adding special equipment allowing for physical interaction. The power of scanning included avatars and objects to co-participate. Secondlife.com added to this experience. Corwin Bell added scans of bodily functions to heal by biofeedback through gaming experience and enjoyment, mystery, and the inclusion of the ancient wisdom.

## *Story Container 3. A Screenplay Entitled Digitally Misplaced by Maureen Sutton*

---

### DIGITALLY MISPLACED

SETTINGS: Computer Art Lab. Interior of Computer. Photoshop Art Program.

BASIC PREMISE
While preparing for an art final, graphic design students find themselves sucked into their computers and are transformed into the characters they had been designing. The students must find a way out before their assignments are due at midnight, or before they stay there forever.

INT. COMPUTER LAB – NIGHT
Three students huddle around several computers. They are all overworked and look like they haven't taken a break in several hours. They don't speak to each other, except to murmur and grumble at their workstations and screens.
It's 10 o' clock. The computer lab is quiet except for their keyboards and scribbling noises, and the whirr of computers. They have an hour and a half before their final projects have to be submitted, or they will fail their finals.
One of them, a young man in his early 20s, with blonde hair and a constant grin, stands up. He's nearly done with his project. His eyes are beginning to feel the strain from staring at the computer screen for so long. His sneakers squeak as he shuffles out of the room, echoing off the quietly humming computer lab.

EXT. CAMPUS BUILDING – NIGHT
Thunder booms. Rain begins to fall. The campus is completely quiet. Nobody's out right now, creating an abandoned atmosphere. There's silence, and then a deafening crack as lighting strikes the roof of the computer lab building.

INT. COMPUTER LAB – NIGHT
There's a flash of light, and the four students vanish into nothingness.
The computers buzz, very loudly, and then go silent.

INT. COMPUTER MONITOR – NIGHT
There is a whirr of processors. Several floating images hover far above, illuminated from behind. Everything has an ungodly, otherworldly glow, backlit by an unseen light source. It's a two-dimensional space, almost.
One of the images, a blinking Photoshop icon, blinks, and the program opens.
Two characters sit in a shambles on the white background, a LLAMA and a DRAGONBORN.
They seem dazed, and very confused. Unlike the rest of the environment, they're alive.
The SPONCH stands up, and examines its rubbery limbs.
> **LLAMA:** Oh. Oh jeez. What happened?
> The Balloon pulls itself off the ground.
> **DRAGONBORN:** Uuuugh. I think.. I think we're in the computer. Or hallucinating.
> **LLAMA:** What makes you say that?
> The Llama's tone has a sarcastic edge to it as it stares at its classmate.
> Clearly it's annoyed with the situation. The dragonborn looks around, taking in their surroundings. Its eyebrow ridges raise in surprise.
> **DRAGONBORN:** I think.. I think this is Photoshop. How did we get inside Photoshop? We shouldn't be in the computer. That's impossible.
> **LLAMA:** Yes. Yes it is. And yet, I am now a fuzzy quadruped. Or it's a freaky shared stress dream.
> **DRAGONBORN:** Can you even share stress dreams?
> **LLAMA:** I don't think you can. So this has to be real.

INT. COMPUTER LAB – NIGHT
The power flickers, and the door swings open. The young man has returned from his stint of leg stretching and snack retrieval. He is very confused to see that everyone is gone, especially where there's not enough time to goof off before the deadline.
> **YOUNG MAN:** Hello? Guys. Man. Didn't even bother to log out. Jeez.
> He sits back down at his station, and continues working.
> His eyes dart back to his neighbor's workstation. There's a few characters darting back and forth on the screen, interacting with various settings and icons.
> **YOUNG MAN:** Huh. Are we supposed to animate the characters? Or did she get bored?
> He moves the mouse towards one of the characters onscreen.

INT. COMPUTER SCREEN
The Llama nudges the edge of the taskbar. There's a swoosh above it, and it looks up in time to see a jagged cursor come swinging down towards it. Its eyes go huge, widening like dinner plates. Its ears flatten.
The Llama gallops off, towards the Dragonborn, who is hovering nearby. It hasn't seen the cursor swooping towards it. It looks up from fiddling with the pen tool in time to see the llama charging at it, fur flying back in tufts of panic and worry. There's a cloud of scales and fluff as they collide. The dragonborn swoops up and hits the lock icon, saving them from being hurt by the sharp looking cursor.

---

*continues on following page*

## *Story Container 1. Continued*

INT. COMPUTER LAB

The young man stares at the computer. His jaw goes slack.

**YOUNG MAN:** Did the characters the sketchy, scribbly characters.. Just lock the layer? How on earth…?

INT. COMPUTER SCREEN

The Llama stares at the cursor. It hasn't moved in several seconds.

**LLAMA:** Do you think someone's out there?

**DRAGONBORN:** I think so. I hope so. Otherwise that had to have been the computer, and evil AIs aren't what I'm prepared for.

**LLAMA:** Hm.

It seems to be thinking. The cursor begins to move again, this time towards the unlock icon.

The dragonborn's eyes narrow, and it bares its fangs, ready to fight the cursor. The llama glances up at the dragonborn, and it looks annoyed.

**LLAMA:** Forget that thing. Help me with something.

**DRAGONBORN:** With what? Not getting deleted?

It looks scared and angry, and ready to fight the llama.

The llama remains unfazed.

**LLAMA:** We need to open Word. Now. And I don't have fingers, buddy.

It taps on the Word icon on the taskbar, nearly falling out of the Photoshop window while it does.

The dragonborn looks confused, but after a moment, its face lights up.

They work together to sort out the message, tapping letters as fast as they possibly can.

**DRAGONBORN:** If we get this message out.. Maybe they can get us out before the deadline!

**LLAMA:** I was hoping to be out of here before we need food, but yeah. Do sketches even need to eat?

**DRAGONBORN:** Beats me, man.

INT. COMPUTER LAB

The young man watches as Word opens, and letters start appearing on the screen. The characters seem to be putting them up, but that's impossible. Right?

H E L P U S

 Help us.

W E A R E T R A P P E D

 We are trapped. Trapped? He raises an eyebrow, waiting for them to keep going.

G E T U S O U T O F H E R E

 Get us out… Were these real people? How?

P L E A S E

Well, since they asked nicely. He grabs the mouse and swings it back to Photoshop. And then he hesitates, and swings it back towards the Llama.

It seems to tremble a little, but he clicks and drags it over to Photoshop. The Dragonborn follows. He begins looking for a way to get them out. He clicks several dialogue boxes, menus, and every toolbar possible. The Llama and the Dragonborn try to help, opening every sub menu possible.

The cursor finally hovers over a button labeled "Export".

The characters start nodding furiously, and he clicks it.

There's a blinding flash of light, and he stumbles backwards.

When he looks up, the spots clearing, his classmates are sprawled on the floor. The computer displays an error message, and the characters are nowhere to be seen.

**YOUNG MAN:** Uh.. What did I miss?

He helps his classmates to their feet, or at least to an upright position. They keep glancing at their hands, and reaching up to check for horns and long ears.

One of them lets out a relieved sigh.

**YOUNG LADY:** I think I'll use Illustrator from now on.

Outside, the rain keeps pouring.

*Story Container 4. Clips for a video game Digitally Misplaced by Kendra Meyers*

**Opening cut scene**: camera pans around a dimly lit computer lab. Students of various shapes and sizes are seated at computers. Each character has a drawing tablet and are hard at work on their assignments. The soft, warm light dispersed throughout the classroom has put everyone in a calm state. Some students look as if they might fall asleep any moment now. Student A exits the room, presumably for a break. The camera rests at the front of the classroom, giving Player a clear view of all the students. A dialog box pops up.
**Dialog Box:** Use left and right arrow keys to toggle playable characters. Click up arrow to display extra information. Press enter to select character.
Each character lights up when cursor is moved over them. Player may now select a character. Extra information includes things like the project they are working on and stats such as work ethic, reliability, creativity, etc.
**The Game Begins:** Player is restricted to looking at their computer screen, use WASD keys to maneuver screen, press enter to open programs and space bar to close programs.
Once player opens photoshop **dialog box opens:** LAUNCH PROGRAM?
 >SPACE BAR: close photoshop, continue looking through computer
 >ENTER: Photoshop opens.
**Cut Scene:** player's eyes slowly begin to close. They look around the room at other students and eventually drift into a deep sleep. Screen fades to black.
The screen becomes white.
**Dialog Box:** 'What's happening!?'
'It's too bright, I just wanna go back to sleep!'
White background remains solid, (fade in) displayed are a strange group of characters (describe which characters.) Player is able to move using WASD keys and can interact with other characters by approaching one and pressing ENTER.
    **Character A:** 'how did we get here? This looks like Photoshop.'
    **Character B:** '...... wait a minute, I look like the character I was drawing!!'
    **Character C:** '*sigh* I have so much homework I don't have time for this.'
Screen widens, surrounding the characters is and opened photoshop document. Player is able to move in the space and observe and collect information on the various functions of the program. After a few minutes of exploring a cursor shoots by the characters. It hits the edge of the screen and comes back, heading straight for Player. The music becomes tense. You have entered a battle.

HTML allowed for web based interactivity, and Adobe Dreamweaver (purchased from Micromedia) allows the user to learn coding visually by splitting the screen between iconic and code-based). MIT based labs developed devices that respond to our bodily functions and then it started the privacy movement (Steve Mann's seats for sale). Casey Reas and Ben Fry developed Processing.org, where anyone can code graphics, animations, and interactive art by altering the code. Daniel Rozin created Interactive Mirror, and Camille Utterbach created interactive poetry venue with her video-supported "Text Rain."

Artists find for themselves places within new technologies. Laser digital printing and laser art included laser light shows and then laser engraving, sintering, laser holograms, and more. 3D printing technology allowed additive manufacturing of art objects. Singularity allows the passer-by to alter an existing sculpture. Artificial intelligence, deep learning architectures, and machine learning changed how the flow of production is developed. Any untrained doodle slightly resembling an object can be converted in seconds into a perfect object, and any literary prompt into a poem. https://talktotransformer.

*Story Container 5. The Audiobook Entitled Digitally Misplaced by Phillip Crews*

---

*David Attenborough:* A relatively small group of beleaguered digital art students are crammed into a ramshackle lab. Flickering monitor light casts deep shadows on tired eyes and slack mouths. The youngsters have been forced to cooperate, the possibility of an enticing salary now hinging on passing grades and completed coursework. A man piques up from the corner, eyebrows raised in clear frustration.

*Kevin Costner:* "This assignment is due tomorrow! There's no way we have time to finish this!"

*Jeff Bridges:* "Tell me about it. I'm about to crash…" someone else says. They stand and leave the room.

*DA:* The classroom again grows quiet, the sharp tick of keystrokes and soft scratching of stylus pens slowing. Before long, mental exhaustion takes its toll. The youngsters settle for the desktop as a pillow. The full classroom is asleep. Suddenly engulfed in white light, our intrepid group is roused.

*Betty White:* "Where is this?" "It's too bright, I just wanna go back to sleep!" The group comes to their feet, looking around. They start as they realize the metamorphosis they've completed. Upon looking down they realize they have each become their own character in progress. Confusion sets over the group.

*Glenn Close:* "How did we get here?"
Upon looking up, they see a familiar tool ribbon and window borders around the room they are in. Some scratch their heads, other walk to the border to touch it. At once an options screen pops up.

*Michael Keaton:* "Uh, is this Photoshop?" The rest of the group walks to various parts of the room, touching things and seeing what happens. It becomes clear to the group that they are indeed in Photoshop.

*DA:* A wild cursor zooms towards a youngster who narrowly avoids making contact. Someone in the group locks the layer, protecting the group. They look at each other in bewilderment.

*Betty White:* "Is someone using their computer?" Someone thinks for a moment, then runs to the taskbar and opens an instance of Word. The others look on in fascination and the cursor stops in its tracks.

*Kevin Costner:* "If we can get a message to them maybe they can get us out of here!" People nod in agreement. They bring up a virtual keyboard and begin typing:
     "H E L P U S W E A R E T R A P P E D . G E T U S O U T P L E A S E"

*DA:* The cursor starts moving around and clicking things in a vain attempt to get them out. Finally, the cursor hovers over "Export." There is a bright light as a dialogue box is brought up. It increases in intensity until it is blinding. Our youngsters find themselves seated, back at their computers, while the individual with a timely restroom break stops and stares with mouth agape.

*Jeff Bridges:* "yo what"
Heavy exhalations and nervous chuckles define an air of relief.

*Betty White:* "I'm gonna use Illustrator from now on…"

---

com/. Any tune can be transformed into a musical composition with AI music composition tools. Artificial intelligence powered Bach Google Doodle Animations on the Website videos make this theme popular.

- https://economictimes.indiatimes.com/magazines/panache/google-marks-johann-sebastian-bachs-birth-anniversary-with-ai-powered-doodle/videoshow/68518770.cms
- https://www.youtube.com/watch?v=XBfYPp6KF2g

*Story Container 6. A Storyline for Animation Digitally Misplaced by Adalia Names*

The title screen opens up with the title "Digitally Misplaced" popping up in the middle. It fades away to show the first scene. It takes place in a computer room where some students are sitting around at their computers working on a project. One of them blurts out "This assignment is due tomorrow! There's no way we have time to finish this!" Someone else says "Tell me about it. I'm about to crash" and gets up and leaves. The students continue to work on their projects until they collapse and fall asleep.

They later wake up in a room that's all white and they're confused. Looking around they see some characters that they don't recognize. They look down and see that they in fact became the characters that they were working on. They walk around and start touching different parts of the room including a tool ribbon and the wall border. The students start to realize that they somehow ended up in a computer in Photoshop. As they stand around in confusion a cursor flies past them. They move out of the way, barely avoiding it. One of the students runs to the options on the side and locks the layer.

It's then that they realize someone else must be using the computer that they are on. Someone runs to the taskbar and opens Word. The others watch them, confused. The student who opened Word says "If we can get a message to them maybe they can get us out of here!" They pull up a virtual keyboard and type out a message saying that they need help and that they're trapped. The cursor then starts moving around as if it's trying to get them out. Eventually it clicks export and there is a bright light. The students sit up at their computers and look around. The one who left earlier had come back and stood their staring at everyone. All the other students agreed to use Illustrator from now on instead of Photoshop.

- https://www.cbsnews.com/news/google-creates-first-ai-doodle-for-bach-allowing-people-to-create-music/
- https://www.usatoday.com/videos/tech/2019/03/21/googles-first-ai-powered-doodle-lets-you-harmonize-like-bach/3232778002/

Time-based forms are also going through changes, from animation, video, gaming, web interactivity to VR, AR, and XR – cross reality combining many types of hardware and software with VR, AR, and cinematic reality (CR), so users can include digital objects into the physical world and bring material things into the digital world. Art became thus more interactive and the audience is after immersive, meditative, and also violent solutions involving sensory-based experience. For example in NYC, ARTECHOUSE (Figures 18 a, b, c) presents itself as the "New York City's innovative art space dedicated to showcasing experimental and technology-driven art installations and live audio-visual performances. We're a new age destination for the 21$^{st}$ – century arts welcoming audiences of all ages for one-of-a-kind immersive digital art experiences. Our mission is to INSPIRE< EDUCATE and EMPOWER the creation of new, experimental and explanatory art forms. Our goal is to connect audiences to the arts and stimulate interest in the limitless possibilities of technology, science and creativity. "CERTAIN ART CANNOT BE DESCRIBED IT MUST BE SEEN AND EXPERIENCED".

"Machine Hallucination" is an Immersive Digital Installation by Refic Anadol who "seeks to challenge the conventional definition of space through the mind of a machine (September 6-December 1, 2019. The groundbreaking

*Figure 18a. Artechouse 1*
*(© 2019, A. Ursyn. Used with permission)*

*Figure 18b. Artechouse 2*
*(© 2019, A. Ursyn. Used with permission)*

*Figure 18c. Artechouse 3*
*(© 2019, A. Ursyn. Used with permission)*

installation utilizes artificial intelligence in an effort to explore and uncover the ever-changing shape o the city and architecture by evoking our collective memory, and the ways that new forms of visual representations can alter our perception of this iconic destination. Over 100 million publicly available photographs of New York City, the largest data set ever gathered for an art piece, are deployed into machine learning algorithms to create the visualized consciousness previously unseen and unimagined. This data universe created by over a thousand dimensions, allows us to intuitively understand the ways memory can be spatially experienced in the future, and the power of machine intelligence to both simultaneously access and augment our human story of the past, present and future."

- https://www.youtube.com/watch?v=jMZqxfTls-0
- https://www.americanscientist.org/article/
  ai-is-blurring-the-definition-of-artist
- https://deepart.io/
- https://www.cnn.com/style/article/ai-photo-app-renaissance-painting-trnd-scn/index.html
- https://www.instapainting.com/ai-painter

- https://medium.com/s/story/digital-processes-inspiring-analog-paintings-a358eb7801a0
- https://quickdraw.withgoogle.com/#

## CONCLUDING REMARKS

This book explores the power existing beyond visual explanation and presentation of scientific and computational problems. Effective communication of knowledge is a requisite for a successful learning and teaching. Communication in a post-technological era is more and more based on senses, especially when they are enhanced by artificial intelligence combined with internet-connected devices and very fast 5G wireless networks. Various types of approaches to creation, development, security, and sharing knowledge support communication. In current technological era we still use metaphors, visual shortcuts, and graphics to explain and communicate with others. Visual media allow the users to compare, contrast, and thus better comprehend the data presented to them in many contexts through the use of many variables.

We need to think and teach thinking about graphical presentation as a source of inspiration for finding novel, unique, knowledge-filled solutions for our audiences: professionals, individuals doing self-motivational explorations, computer graphics and digital media instructors, students, and families looking for a broad meaning of entertainment.

Social networking and portable devises broke barriers for writing and sketching for people of any profession. One may say we are witnessing a shift toward computing-inspired study of nature through visuals: art and data graphics. For this reason, this book is about visual literacy, visual thinking, visual learning, and visual communication with the use of new media. It discusses with the readers the changing role of communication media and the role of visual presentation.

The book will hopefully impact the way we learn and teach and thus it will contribute to the task of updating education on the K–20 levels. Concepts, data, and information belonging to a variety of disciplines have been discussed as possible resources useful for finding visual solutions for science and technology related concepts. The interdisciplinary approach was stressed, to rethink the style of learning and teaching. Discussion of selected topics in the context of tools and developments in technology supported the readers with materials for learning and teaching in an integrated way.

Providing knowledge visualization early in the course of education may help to recognize and support the innate abilities of children and start an integrative training of their minds. This approach builds a background for the curricular postulates, which suggest strengthening the curricular program by inclusion into the school curricula several science-based elements and teaching the basics of coding.

## REFERENCES

Donahue, R. L., Miller, R. W., & Shickluna, J. C. (1977). *Soils: An Introduction to Soils and Plant Growth*. Prentice-Hall.

Gans, J., Wolinsky, M., & Dunbar, J. (2005). Computational improvements reveal great bacterial diversity and high metal toxicity in soil. *Science, 309*(5739), 1387–1390. doi:10.1126cience.1112665 PMID:16123304

Malotki, E., & Dissanayake, E. (2018). *Early Rock Art of the American West: The Geometric Enigma*. University of Washington Press.

Pinker, S. (2014). *The Sense of Style: The Thinking Person's Guide to Writing in the 21st Century*. New York, NY: Penguin.

Rao, J. (2013). Types of Clouds. *Live Science*. Retrieved from https://www.livescience.com/29436-clouds.html

Wind. (2019). In *Wikipedia*. Retrieved from https://en.wikipedia.org/wiki/Wind

Zheng, R., & Gardner, M. K. (2017). *Handbook of Research on Serious Games for Educational Applications*. Hershey, PA: IGI Global. doi:10.4018/978-1-5225-0513-6

# Glossary

**Algorithm:** Is a mathematical sequence of instructions telling how to carry on computation to implement it as a program. Algorithms are used to create repetition by applying algorithm multiple times on its previous products; it is a recursive process. Algorithm serves for solving a complex problem by writing a sequence of simpler, unambiguous steps. Such course of action is used for writing computer programs and in programmed learning.

**Concept Map:** Is a graphical two-dimensional display of knowledge. Concepts, usually presented within boxes or circles, are connected by directed arcs that encode, as linking phrases, the relationships between the pairs of concepts.

**Crystallography:** Is the study of the crystal's form, growth, physical properties resulting from its structure, the nature of the bonding among its atoms, and its chemical composition. Molecular biologists and organic chemists are often crystallographers. They make use of crystallographic data to examine the structure of organic molecules and ways to concentrate and crystallize the molecules in plants and animals. For example, Rosalind Franklin and others examined DNA crystals using X-ray diffraction. In 1952, James D. Watson and Francis Crick proposed the double helix structure of the DNA molecule determined with the use of crystallographic data.

**Data Visualization:** Means information abstracted in a schematic form to provide visual insights into sets of data. Data visualization enables us to go from the abstract numbers in a computer program (ones and zeros) to visual interpretation of data. Text visualization means converting textual information into graphic representation, so we can see information without having to read the data, as tables, histograms, pie or bar charts, or Cartesian coordinates.

**Energy Gap:** Also called bandgap is a range in a solid material where no electron states can exist.

**Evo-Devo:** Is an informal term that means evolutionary developmental biology. This is a study of evolution and generation of form and pattern, through research on comparative gene function/expression, embryogenesis, genomics, phylogenetics, and paleontology, among other venues. Materials on this topic can be found in the EvoDevo Journal, http://www.evodevojournal.com/.

**Heisenberg's Uncertainty Principle:** Is a part of quantum mechanics. This principle states that we cannot know precisely about certain pairs of physical properties, such as a particle's position and momentum (the product of the mass of a particle and its velocity) at the same time, because the measuring process involves interaction, which disturbs the particle. For example, a photon of light used in a measurement is bouncing off the particle. Thus, one cannot, even theoretically, predict the moment-to-moment behavior of a system consisting of the subject and the object of examination (somebody who makes an observation and an object observed). There is a theoretical limit for simultaneous measuring at an atomic scale because the more precisely is figured one amount, the more uncertain is the other one.

**Icon, Iconic Object or Image:** An icon represents a thing or refers to something by resembling or imitating it; thus a picture, a photograph, a mathematical expression, or an old-style telephone may be regarded as an iconic object. Thus, an iconic object has some qualities common with things it represents, by looking, sounding, feeling, tasting, or smelling alike.

**Infographics:** Refers to tools and techniques involved in graphical representation of data, mostly in journalism, art, and storytelling.

**Information Aesthetics:** Forms a cross-disciplinary link between information visualization and visualization art.

**Information Visualization:** Often characterized as representation plus interaction, means the use of computer-supported, visual spatial representation of abstract data to amplify cognition and derive new insights. Data presented as information visualization are often interactive, numerical, verbal, and graphical.

**Ions: Cations and Anions:** An atom or a molecule that has an electric charge is called an ion. An electric charge results from the presence of single, double, triple, or even higher negative electrons unequal to the number of positive protons in the nucleus of an atom. The removal or addition of one or more electrons changes a neutral atom into an ion. Cation is an ion or group of ions that have a positive charge. Anion is a negatively charged ion. Polyelectrolytes are large molecules with many charged groups. During electrolysis (produced in an electrolyte solution by applying an electric current) cations move toward the cathode (negative electrode) and anions migrate to an anode.

**Isomers:** Are chemical compounds that have the same molecular formula and mass but different structural formulas. Isomerism may be structural (when atoms are bonded together in different orders) or spatial (when atoms are placed in different positions in space). They may some different physical or chemical properties caused by different arrangement of atoms in their molecules).

**Knowledge Visualization:** Uses visual representations to transfer insights and create new knowledge in the process of communicating different visual formats.

**LED:** The light-emitting diode is a semiconductor diode that glows when a voltage is applied.

**Nuclear Magnetic Resonance:** Occurs when the atom's nuclei in a magnetic field absorb and re-emit electromagnetic radiation at a resonance frequency that is specific, depending on the strength of magnetic field and on the magnetic properties of the atom.

**Ontogenesis:** Describes general development of an organism or its organ going from its beginning to the mature stage, for example, from a tadpole with gills to an adult frog with lungs.

**Ontology:** The philosophical study of the nature of being, existence or reality, as well as the basic categories of being and their relations.

**Pattern:** Means the regular order existing in nature and in a manmade design. We can see patterns everywhere in nature, mathematics, art, architecture, and design. In nature patterns can be seen as symmetries (e.g., snowflakes) and/or structures having fractal dimension such as spirals, meanders, or surface waves. In computer science, design patterns serve in creating computer programs. In the arts, pattern is an artistic or decorative design made of recurring lines or any repeated elements. A pattern makes a basis of ornaments, which are specific for different cultures. Owen Jones made a huge collection of ornaments typical for different countries. He wrote an amazing monographic book entitled *The Grammar of Ornament*.

**Permeance:** Denotes the degree to which a material allows a flow of magnetic energy. In electromagnetic circuits permeance is usually larger for cross-sections.

**Phylogenesis:** Tells how a species or an organism's organ developed and diversified in time.

**Raman Spectroscopy:** Serves to examine low frequency vibrational and rotational energy states of objects such as molecules. Photons are scattered between electrons in an atom or a molecule. Several methods relay on inelastic Raman scattering of monochromatic (using only one color) light provided by laser in the visible, near-infrared (NIR), or near-ultraviolet range. Illuminated spots emit electromagnetic radiation, which enables recording processes occurring in objects. A Raman laser is stimulated by Raman scattering of photons.

**Scientific Visualization:** Presents real, abstract, or model-based objects in a digital way directly from the data. It may present the art-science cooperative learning projects and make knowledge comprehensible to a wide audience. Visualization as storytelling comprises narratives, interactive graphics, explanatory and animated graphics, and multimedia.

**Semiconductor:** Material has conductivity between a conductor (most metals, for example copper) and an insulator (such as glass). Properties of a semiconductor, its moving electrons and electron holes in a crystal lattice can be explained by quantum physics. Silicon crystals are semiconductive materials; they are used in microelectronics and photovoltaics used for direct conversion of sunlight to electricity with the use of solar panels.

**Semiotics:** The study about the meaningful use of signs, symbols, codes, and conventions that allow communication. The name 'semiotics' is derived from the Greek word 'semeion' which means "sign". "Meaning" is always the result of social conventions, even when we think that something is natural or characteristic, and we use signs for those meanings. Therefore, culture and art is a series of sign systems. Semioticians analyze such sign systems in various cultures; linguists study language as a system of signs, and some even examine film as a system of signs. The semiotic content of visual design is important for non-verbal communication applied to practice, especially for visualizing knowledge.

**Sign:** Tells about a fact, an idea, or information; it is a distinct thing that signifies another thing. Natural signs signify events caused by nature, while conventional signs may signal art, social interactions, fashion, food, interaction with technology, machines, and practically everything else.

**Signage:** Is a visual graphics that displays information, for example street signs, room identification signs, or any kind of informational or regulatory signs.

**Signs, Symbols, and Icons:** Are collectively called signage. Signs take conventional shapes or forms to tell about facts, ideas, or information. Icons and symbols help compress information in a visual way. An icon represents a thing or refers to something by resembling or imitating it; thus a picture, a photograph, a mathematical expression, or an old-style telephone may be regarded as an iconic object. Thus, an iconic object has some qualities common with things it represents, by looking, sounding, feeling, tasting, or smelling alike. Designers choose signs, symbols, and icons that are powerful and effective; for example, a designer may look for an icon showing the scissorness, the essence of the meaning related to scissors: some common features characteristic for this product. Effective design of a complicated product may help memorize and learn how to use this product (for example, 'Where is the switch?' or 'How to open this thing?').

**Spectroscopy:** Records how matter interacts with or emits electromagnetic radiation. A spectroscope is designed to study matter by measuring properties of specific frequencies and wavelengths of electromagnetic radiation.

**Symbol:** Does not resemble things it represents but refers to something by convention; for example, the word "red" represents red. We must learn the relationship between symbols and what they represent, such as letters, numbers, words, codes, traffic lights, and national flags. A symbol represents an abstract concept, not just a thing, and is comparable to an abstract word. Highly abstracted drawings that show no realistic graphic representation become symbols. Symbols are omnipresent in our life, for example: an electric diagram that uses abstract symbols for a light bulb, wire, connector, resistor, and switch; an apple for a teacher, or a bitten apple for a Macintosh computer; a map: Typical abstract graphic device; a 'slippery when wet' sign.

**Symmetry:** Means the correspondence in size, form, and arrangement of parts on opposite sides of a plane, line, or point. A crystal shows symmetry when it has s a center of symmetry, rotation axes, or mirror planes (imaginary planes that divide it into halves). There are several types of symmetry: for example, line or mirror symmetry, radial, cylindrical, or spherical symmetry. A figure that has line symmetry has two identical halves when folded along its line of symmetry, and these halves are congruent, meaning they are the same size and shape. An object has a radial symmetry when it can be rotated around the rotation axis. For example, with a fourfold rotation axis the crystal repeats itselfeach 90°. Angles of rotational symmetry possible for crystals are: 60 degrees, 90 degrees, 120 degrees, 180 degrees, and 360 degrees. The halves of the bilaterally symmetrical animals, for example, butterflies, when seen along the axis, form each other's mirror images. Most animals and people cannot be divided into two identical halves, even when they look symmetrical from external appearance. Two halves of the human brain display different abilities and ways of learning and thinking.

**Synapse:** A structure that links (through a synaptic cleft) a nerve cell with other nerve or some other types of a cell. In an electrical synapse, an activated neuron develops an electric signal on its presynaptic cell membrane, which induces a voltage change on the postsynaptic cell. In a chemical synapse, electrical activity on the presynaptic cell membrane initiates the release of a neurotransmitter and its diffusion to a postsynaptic cell.

**Visualization:** Means the communication of information with graphical representations. Interactive visual representations of abstract data use easy-to-recognize objects connected through well-defined relations.

# About the Author

**Anna Ursyn**, PhD, is a professor and Computer Graphics>Digital Media Area Head at the University of Northern Colorado. She combines programming, software and various media. Ursyn had over 40 single juried and invitational art shows, over 200 fine art exhibitions, such as over a dozen times at ACM SIGGRAPH Art Galleries, traveling shows: Louvre, Paris, NTT Museum in Tokyo (5000 texts and 2000 images representing XX Century), Virtual Media Network, moving image outdoor display Dallas TX. Her work was selected by NASA to the Moon Museum http://moonarts.org/, and traveling shows, the Centre Pompidou in Paris, Denver Capitol and Denver Intern. Airport. Research and pedagogy interests include integrated instruction in art, science, and computer art graphics. She has artwork in several books and journals. Her work in ABAD is in the permanent collections of the Museum of Modern Art in NYC and Los Angeles County Museum of Art, LA, CA. Since 1987 she serves at the International IEEE Conferences on Information Visualization (iV) London, UK, and (CGIV), and Chair of the Symposium and Digital Art Gallery D-ART. Anna has published seven books and several book chapters.

# Index

## A

abstract thinking 212, 221, 237, 240-242, 250, 256, 278-280, 288, 301-304
active learning 268, 270, 291, 293, 322
artificial intelligence 48, 191, 224, 263, 307, 359-360, 363-364

## B

behaviorism 261, 263-264, 276

## C

coding 132, 176, 189, 223, 241, 248, 251, 261-262, 265, 274, 278, 280, 302, 306-307, 333, 347, 359, 365
cognitive abilities 104, 197, 261-262, 308-309
cognitive learning 212, 239, 261, 270, 280, 305, 322-323
cognitive processes 131, 169, 212, 225-227, 304
cognitive thinking 212-213, 241-242, 272
colloids 1-2, 8, 16, 34, 49
creative thinking 237-238
critical thinking 237-238, 242, 256, 288, 293, 309, 327

## E

electromagnetic waves 37, 104-105, 113
elements of design 104, 135, 158

## G

graphical thinking 2, 212, 241-242

## H

humanoid robot 160

## I

idea sketching 240-241
integrative learning 261-262, 299, 301, 322, 327

## L

linguistic aptitudes 261-262, 304
liquid crystals 1-2, 8, 33-35, 46, 51, 77, 79, 124, 193
living organisms 1-2, 34, 85, 92, 109, 112, 126, 189, 197, 341

## M

mental imagery 131-132, 155, 212, 225-226, 242
mental processes 119, 212
microbes 1, 18-19, 22-23, 25, 28-30, 58, 91, 189, 340

## N

nano scale 1, 32, 79
nano-world 1

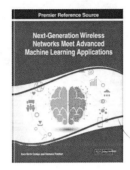

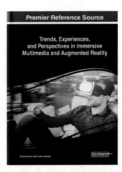

Ensure Quality Research is Introduced to the Academic Community

# Become an IGI Global Reviewer for Authored Book Projects

Premier Reference Source

Emerging GIS Applications for Emergency and Disaster Management

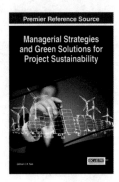

Premier Reference Source

Managerial Strategies and Green Solutions for Project Sustainability

Premier Reference Source

Comparative Approaches to Using R and Python for Statistical Data Analysis

Premier Reference Source

Solutions for High-Touch Communications in a High-Tech World

## The overall success of an authored book project is dependent on quality and timely reviews.

In this competitive age of scholarly publishing, constructive and timely feedback significantly expedites the turnaround time of manuscripts from submission to acceptance, allowing the publication and discovery of forward-thinking research at a much more expeditious rate. Several IGI Global authored book projects are currently seeking highly-qualified experts in the field to fill vacancies on their respective editorial review boards:

### Applications and Inquiries may be sent to:
development@igi-global.com

Applicants must have a doctorate (or an equivalent degree) as well as publishing and reviewing experience. Reviewers are asked to complete the open-ended evaluation questions with as much detail as possible in a timely, collegial, and constructive manner. All reviewers' tenures run for one-year terms on the editorial review boards and are expected to complete at least three reviews per term. Upon successful completion of this term, reviewers can be considered for an additional term.

If you have a colleague that may be interested in this opportunity, we encourage you to share this information with them.

# IGI Global Proudly Partners With eContent Pro International

## Receive a 25% Discount on all Editorial Services

## Editorial Services

IGI Global expects all final manuscripts submitted for publication to be in their final form. This means they must be reviewed, revised, and professionally copy edited prior to their final submission. Not only does this support with accelerating the publication process, but it also ensures that the highest quality scholarly work can be disseminated.

### English Language Copy Editing

Let eContent Pro International's expert copy editors perform edits on your manuscript to resolve spelling, punctuaion, grammar, syntax, flow, formatting issues and more.

### Scientific and Scholarly Editing

Allow colleagues in your research area to examine the content of your manuscript and provide you with valuable feedback and suggestions before submission.

### Figure, Table, Chart & Equation Conversions

Do you have poor quality figures? Do you need visual elements in your manuscript created or converted? A design expert can help!

### Translation

Need your documjent translated into English? eContent Pro International's expert translators are fluent in English and more than 40 different languages.

## Hear What Your Colleagues are Saying About Editorial Services Supported by IGI Global

"The service was very fast, very thorough, and very helpful in ensuring our chapter meets the criteria and requirements of the book's editors. I was quite impressed and happy with your service."

– Prof. Tom Brinthaupt,
Middle Tennessee State University, USA

"I found the work actually spectacular. The editing, formatting, and other checks were very thorough. The turnaround time was great as well. I will definitely use eContent Pro in the future."

– Nickanor Amwata, Lecturer,
University of Kurdistan Hawler, Iraq

"I was impressed that it was done timely, and wherever the content was not clear for the reader, the paper was improved with better readability for the audience."

– Prof. James Chilembwe,
Mzuzu University, Malawi

**Email: customerservice@econtentpro.com**          **www.igi-global.com/editorial-service-partners**

Printed in the United States
By Bookmasters